A POTTERIES PAST

CYRIL KENT

WITAN BOOKS

For Mother and Dad

Witan Creations
2010 Main Catalogue

WTN 001: *Butcher's Tale/Annie, With The Dancing Eyes* – Jeff Kent & The Witan (animal rights protest single), 1981 - £2.50, including p & p.

WTN 027: *The Mercia Manifesto: A Blueprint For The Future Inspired By The Past* – The Mercia Movement (128-page radical political manifesto), 1997 - £8.25, including p & p.

WTN 030: *Only One World* – Jeff Kent (13-track environmental concept CD), 2000 - £11.15, including p & p.

WTN 032: *A Draft Constitution For Mercia* – The Mercia Movement (20-page draft constitution for an independent Midlands), 2001 - £2.20, including p & p.

WTN 033: *The Mysterious Double Sunset* – Jeff Kent (203-page study of the extraordinary phenomenon), 2001 - £14.55, including p & p.

WTN 038: *The Constitution Of Mercia* – The Mercian Constitutional Convention (22-page constitution of independent Mercia), 2003 - £2.20, including p & p.

(All other publications and releases by Witan Creations are now out of print or unavailable from the catalogue.)

A POTTERIES PAST

First published in November 2010 by Witan Books, Cherry Tree House, 8 Nelson Crescent, Cotes Heath, via Stafford, ST21 6ST, England.
Telephone: (01782) 791673.
E-mail: witan@mail.com
Website: www.witancreations.com

WTN 059

ISBN 9780 9529152 7 0

A Cataloguing in Publication record for this book is available from the British Library.

Design and cover concept: Jeff Kent.
Cover artwork: Gary Devreede.
Editor: Jeff Kent.
Editorial advisers: Sue Bell, Gill Evans and Hazel Statham.
Main research: Jeff Kent and Cyril Kent.
Printed and bound by: Hanley Print Services, Units 90 & 79, Shelton Enterprise Centre, Bedford Street, Shelton, Stoke-on-Trent, ST1 4PZ. Tel. (01782) 280028; E-mail: gstock1@btinternet.com.

Front cover photo: Cyril at work as a china turner at Mintons Ltd., in London Road, Stoke, about 1950.
Back cover photo: Cyril in army service dress in Dundee or Perth in 1944.

v

ACKNOWLEDGEMENTS

The author and publisher would like to express their thanks to the following people and organisations for their invaluable assistance, not credited elsewhere, in the production of this book:
Aberdeenshire Library and Information Service, Alsager Dental Practice, Army Museums Ogilby Trust, Army Personnel Centre, Mavis Asher, Ian Bailey, Joan Ball, Ballater Library, Ballater Tourist Information Centre, Beauly Library, Peter Beckett, Eva Beech, John Bennison, Jim Bentley, Steve Billington, John Birchall, Birmingham Central Library, Dave Birtles, Blackpool Central Library, Blackpool Council, Blacks, Barry Blaize, Jill Bloor, The British Library, Campbell Dental Practice, Jean Cattell, Terry Chell, Colinton Library, the Communication Workers Union, Steve Cooke, Coventry History Centre, Louise Cross, Pam Edwards, Flintshire Record Office, Wayne Griffiths, Lynn Halliburton, Eddie Hampton, Harley Street Medical Centre, Hertfordshire Archives & Local Studies, Fred Hobbs, Graham Hulse, Derek Hurst, Grahame Jeffries, Basil Jeuda, Ray Johnson, Trefor Jones, Mark Kennerley, Paul Kennerley, Dorothy Kent, Leek Library, Anthony Lynn, V. Maddocks, Garry Marsh, Marske Library, John Middleton, Jean Mitchell, Mandy Morrey, Asher Mupasi, The National Archives, National War Museum of Scotland, Newcastle-under-Lyme Library, Bill Norman, North Staffordshire Primary Care Trust, Stan Palin, Mick Pender, Shaun Pender, Harry Poole, Scott Poole, Prestatyn Library, David Rayner, Redcar Central Library, Terry Robinson, Evelyn Royle, Saltburn Library, Sandwell Community History & Archives Centre, Helen Sargent, Beth Savery, Russ Scott, *The Sentinel*, Phil Sherwin, Vic Shotton, Ray Skerratt, Bob Smith, Betty Smithson, Stafford Library, Staffordshire Record Office, Colin Stanyer, Allan Staples, Gary Stockton, Stockton Brook Post Office, Stoke on Trent City Archives, Stoke-on-Trent City Central Library, Stoke-on-Trent City Council, Pete Stonier, Jean Stringer, Harry Thomas, Andrew Thompson, Martin Tideswell, Torquay Library, Unity, Vera Dry Cleaners, Veterans UK, Wakefield Learning and Local Studies Library, Maureen Wallett, Walsall Local History Centre, Watford Museum, Miriam Werner, Pete Wyatt and York Explore Library.

ILLUSTRATION CREDITS

Illustrations were kindly supplied by the following:
Sue Bell – 71; John Booth – 12, 13, 15, 69; Chris Doorbar – 70; Lynn Halliburton – 53; Cyril Kent – front cover, back cover, 1-5, 7, 8, 10, 14, 16, 17, 22-29; 32-34; 36-50, 54-64; 66-68; 72-76; Dorothy Kent – 35; Jeff Kent – 9; Harry Poole – 30, 31, 65; Evelyn Royle – 6; *The Sentinel* – 11, 18-21, 51, 52, 77.

Contents

Preface

For most of my life, I never thought that I'd write a book, let alone have one published! I always liked reading, but I wondered how writers managed to put their stories together and write books full of them. I suppose I thought they were different than me and cleverer, with talents that I hadn't got. All they seemed to do was to dream up stories, but they had to be pretty intelligent to do that. I thought they were in a higher class than me and lived in posh places. I didn't imagine them coming from or living in Stoke-on-Trent. For a long time, the only writer I'd heard of who'd been born in the Potteries was Arnold Bennett and I didn't know much about him.

My son, Jeff, had always taken a great deal of interest in my life and, from about the mid-1980s, he kept suggesting that I should write down things that had happened to me. I resisted because there didn't seem much to write about. Then I thought about my own dad. What did I know about him? I realized I knew very little and wished I'd asked him questions about his life. Of course, by then it was much too late because he'd been dead for over forty years.

So, around Christmas 1987, I decided to put down in a notebook things that I could remember. Nothing much had happened to me, so I thought I wouldn't be very long on the job and then I'd be able to get back into my usual routine. I started writing and at once ran into snags. I was uncertain about dates and details, but I looked into them and sorted out most of the problems. I kept on writing and it was remarkable how I remembered lots of happenings and what life had been like in the past. Then later, I thought of other events and had to go back in my book and fit them in.

It was marvellous how my stories seemed to come out of nothing onto paper, but I was amazed at the amount of work that had to go into writing them and looking things up before my book was finished. There seemed no end to it and it was November 1990 before I got up to date, having filled almost seven notebooks by then! Jeff regularly read what I'd written and he was very pleased with what I'd done.

I thought I'd finally finished the job, but Jeff kept asking me questions about what I'd written. So I had to find the answers and that often meant me having to delve into the records at Hanley Library, which by then had been given the fancy title of Stoke-on-Trent City Central Library!

Jeff thought there were plenty of stories in my book that would appeal to the general public, so he became keen to publish it. However, I was uncertain what my wife, Helen, would think about information from our private lives being read by outsiders and so I decided to leave it for the time being.

The book gathered dust for years, but, in about 2002, Jeff again came up with the idea of publishing it. I still felt more or less the same about that, but I told him that the book was his, for him to do with what he wanted. He reread it and came up with more questions for me to look into, so I was back at the library regularly again! It took a long time to get the information required and I didn't always feel like bothering to find it, but finally I got all the answers I could.

On 20 August 2005, Jeff got me a computer and I thought I'd type my book up, but it took me so long to do a few pages full of mistakes that I realized I'd probably never achieve it. So I gave up and Jeff took on the job instead.

By that time, nearly fifteen years had passed since I'd originally written the book and obviously many more things had happened to me in the meantime. Jeff thought it was important to get it up to date and was keen for me to write up the new stories. Unfortunately, I was having to spend a lot of time looking after Helen by then, which was very tiring, and I didn't have the inclination to write any more. So I asked Jeff if I could tell him the stories and he could write them down, which is what we did. We started on 18 August 2007 and are still continuing to put things down even now, as they happen!

Eventually, we'd produced so much detail that there was too much for a single book, so A Potteries Past is the first part of the story of my life and times and it's intended that the second part will follow, hopefully next year. This book has been a long time in coming out and I don't suppose many authors have had their first book published at the age of 94, but I hope the readers will think it's been worth all the effort!

I've wondered what will happen when my book comes out, but I'm resigned to the fact that it isn't a patch on what the established writers do. I think that a lot of people could do as well as me, if not better, but it helps if you've got the kind of backing, the dedication, that I've had from Jeff. But not everybody can write a book because some people would get disheartened when they got bogged down and would give up. You've got to have a lot of patience and determination. So I think it's an achievement for me, as an ordinary working-class man, to have written a book and I hope that you will enjoy reading my stories from a bygone age.

Cyril Kent,
Shelton,
Stoke-on-Trent,
November 2010.

1 Cobridge Community

In 1915, the Great War was raging, but neither side appeared to be the stronger and fighting had become bogged down on the Western Front, with trenches hundreds of miles long manned by the opposing Forces. To try to end the deadlock, the Allies attempted to break through the Dardanelles and capture Constantinople, but they suffered big losses at Gallipoli and were forced to withdraw. Amongst the soldiers involved was my Uncle Bill. On 14 December, as they were planning to pull out, I was born in the middle of a row of terraced houses at 56 Derwent Street, Cobridge, in Stoke-on-Trent.

My parents, William Henry and Lily Kent, both worked at James Macintyre & Co. Limited, the electrical porcelain company, in Waterloo Road, Burslem. I presume that they met there. Dad was a potter's turner and my mother was, I suppose, just an assistant of some kind. Dad didn't have to join the armed services in the war, but was exempted because he was in a war-work occupation and had a badge saying so. Feelings began to run high with the heavy casualties in the war and some people thought all men should be in uniform. One day, a girl presented Dad with a white feather, which meant she thought he was a coward. He must have been deeply hurt, but he didn't say anything in reply.

Dad was of medium height and always wore shirts with a soft collar, a tie, a pullover under his jacket and a flat cap. He walked with a slight stoop. He was a mild fellow and I never saw him lose his temper. He smoked fairly heavily, but was a teetotaller. He was a good workman and very skilled. He looked after his money, didn't go boozing and always made sure there was food on the table at home. He was also a keen Stoke supporter.

My mother was about the same height as Dad, but was heavier. She wore pince-nez glasses and was also mild in temperament.

My mother's parents, George and Ann Wallett, did a lot of "flitting", but, when I was born, they lived in the next road, Windermere Street, at number 19. Grandad had been born in Ironville, in Derbyshire, in 1861, and played the squeeze-box. He was a coal miner and had moved to Burslem to work. He was a small man, with grey hair, who was mild-mannered and didn't say much.

The Walletts were probably Welsh and came from the Shifnal/Ironbridge area. In the seventeenth century, their name was Cadwallader, which became shortened to Dwalled and then changed to Wallett. They were miners and dug the coal that was used to start the Industrial Revolution in Coalbrookdale and Ironbridge. But the forges closed in the late 1790s and 3,000 miners were thrown out of work. The Walletts then moved to Wolverhampton, Bilston and Ironville before finally arriving in Burslem.

Grandmother Wallett had been born in Burslem in 1864 and was a little, grey-haired lady, but was more forceful than Grandad and used to be bossy with him. They didn't have many clothes to wear and I don't think they ever had a holiday. They had nine children, which must have been hard work!

The earliest known Kent in my family was named Josiah and his son, Charles, was baptized in the Staffordshire village of Ellastone in 1724. The Kents lived there for the next hundred years or so, but my great-grandfather, John, became a boot maker in Stoke. My grandfather, Edmund, was born in the same town in

1860. He married Mary Grainger, who'd been born in Coseley in 1864 and was the daughter of William Grainger, a forge manager at an ironworks, probably Shelton Iron and Steel Co. Ltd. Grainger lived at 2 Cobridge Road, which was right at the bottom of the hill, adjoining Etruria Road, and next door was the Furnace Inn, which was no doubt popular with the forge workers, who had a big thirst after working all day around the furnaces.

My father was born at 110 Etruria Vale (which later became Etruria Vale Road) on 29 October 1889 and his family later moved to number 344, where he was living when he married my mother. She'd been born on 24 August 1891 at 69 Bold Street, in Northwood, and appears to have been pregnant with me at the time of their wedding on 28 June 1915. They then set up home in a rented house in Derwent Street, which is where I was born.

I was baptized at the United Methodist Chapel in Portland Street, Boothen, on 5 January 1916, but cried a lot virtually every night as a baby, so that my parents soon became exhausted. However, on the night of 27-28 November, I slept right through and so did my parents. The following day, the neighbours asked them what they thought about the German zeppelin, which had flown over during the night. It had dropped bombs on slag heaps near to Goldendale Iron Works, a spoil bank by Birchenwood Colliery and the back yard of 6 Sun Street (now St. Aidan's Street), Tunstall, making a six-feet deep crater. My parents had to confess that they hadn't heard or seen a thing!

After a year or two, we moved to 27 Windermere Street, another typical terraced house that we rented, four doors away from my grandparents. This was perhaps fortunate because some years later there was a gas explosion at 56 Derwent Street, although I don't think anybody was injured. The road in Windermere Street was still a rough track and the pavement was made of blue bricks. A poor job had been made in laying them and some of them were missing. But everybody in the street knew everybody else and it was a pretty friendly place to live. Our landlady, Sarah Grant, lived nearby, at 362 Cobridge Road, the last house before the crossroads.

Our new house had a parlour at the front, which we rarely used, except at Christmas, when Dad would light a fire of coal to keep me warm while I played with my presents that Santa had brought the previous night. Between the parlour and the living room, underneath the stairs, was the pantry, which was used to store our food.

Behind the pantry was the living room or kitchen, where most of our time was spent. It was heated by a coal-fired grate, which was about twelve to eighteen inches high, with the actual fireplace being around eight inches wide. Most of the fire grate was made of cast iron and Mother applied black lead to clean it and polished this up with a black lead brush. It was a dirty job for her.

On one side of the fire was an oven and on the other side a boiler, which had a tap to run hot water off. I can't remember us actually using this boiler, but there was always a kettle full of water on the boil on the fire. The fire had to be kept going, even in the summer, to cook our meals in the oven or in a frying pan on the fire. It was also used for toast, which was done by sticking a big wire fork (a toasting fork) into a slice of bread and holding it in front of the fire till it was brown and then turning it over to the other side. The fire was also used to heat up a smoothing iron to iron out clothes. The all-metal iron was put on the fire till hot enough and then the smoothing surface had to be wiped clean with a cloth. Of course, the iron soon cooled and the heating process had to be repeated.

Hanging from the ceiling was a rack, with three or four rails on for airing clothes. The rack was lifted up or lowered down by means of ropes and pulleys and the idea was to hoist the clothes up to the ceiling where the warm air would dry them off after washing. To lift the rack up, you had to pull on both of the ropes, but, to lower it, you had to untie the ropes from the wall, so it would come down under its own weight. It was marvellous, but it was unsightly and the clothes could get smutty from soot from the fire.

In the back kitchen, there was a brown pottery sink, with just a single cold water tap. There was no stop tap and when Dad had to replace a worn washer in the tap, he had quite a job on. First, he would turn on the tap and then place a thick cloth over the whole of it. He would next unscrew the top half, while holding on to the cloth, to prevent the force of the water shooting up to the ceiling. Dad would then remove the old washer and put a new one on. Finally would come the trickiest bit, where he had to hold the cloth down over the strong force of water while he tried to screw the top half of the tap back into place. What a mess there would be, with the back kitchen soaked!

Mother did the washing in a zinc dolly tub, though I can't remember how the water was heated up. I know that some people had a brick-built boiler fired by coal under a metal bowl. The water would be poured into the tub by bucket and, when the tub was half full, the soiled clothes would be put in and the contents agitated with a dolly peg in a twisting motion. After about ten minutes of agitating, which was a very tiring job, the hot clothes would be lifted out with a stick and run through a mangle. Mother later replaced the clothes stick with a pair of tongs, which made the clothes easier to pick up. I've still got the tongs and have used them in recent years to reach and open and close a window in my kitchen!

The mangle was a cast-iron monstrosity, about five feet high, which must have weighed nearly a couple of hundredweight. The clothes would be squeezed between two wooden rollers by turning a big cast-iron wheel. After the clothes had been mangled, they would be rinsed in clean water and then mangled again. The women in those days must have been strong to keep turning the mangle wheel. Finally, if the water in the tub was still hot, it would be emptied with a scoop because it would have been awkward and dangerous to have dipped a bucket into the hot water.

The coal house was down the back yard, but was built on to the end of the back kitchen, and then there was the outside toilet. It was in a brick building, about seven feet tall, which had just enough room to get in! The toilet had no tap and sink, but only a closet, which was flushed from a rusty cast-iron tank by pulling a chain. It was perishing going out in the winter and you'd have to put your coat on. We had good bladder and bowel control to avoid going out there whenever possible! We couldn't afford toilet paper, so, like everybody else, we cut up newspapers into smaller pieces and piled them about two inches thick. A hole was bored into one corner, through which was threaded a piece of string. We then tied the two ends of the string together and hung the lot on a nail on the inside toilet wall ready for use. Unfortunately, your bum would get newsprint on it and this problem was shared by all the working class!

Beyond the toilet was a small garden. This was like a playground because

Mother and Dad weren't interested in gardening.

The ash bin was set into the back wall and had pivots on either side, so that when the bin men came along the back entry, they just tipped the contents into their container. The trouble was that lads so inclined could tip our rubbish out on the ground, which they did from time to time, so that we'd have to gather it up again!

Upstairs, there were just two bedrooms, each off the staircase and with one window at the far end. I slept in the back bedroom and it was cold in the winter because we didn't have a fire on.

We had no bathroom, but used a portable zinc bath, which was placed in front of the living room coal fire. Mother heated the water in a coal-fired boiler we had in the back kitchen and then carried it in in a bucket, to pour into the bath. It was lovely and warm!

There were no carpets in the house. Like everybody else, we made our own rugs by cutting up old clothes into strips and threading them through the holes in pieces of old sacking. We'd carry on with this laborious job until all the holes were filled up. It could be worked to any size and, being closely knit, gave quite a nice rug. I tried doing a bit once or twice when I was old enough, but the rugs were mainly done by Mother. We only had them in front of the fireplaces and elsewhere downstairs the floors were bare tiles, while upstairs there were uncovered floorboards.

The very first thing I can remember is walking home with Mother and Dad from Hanley when I was about three. When we got to the top of Hope Street, I became tired, so Dad picked me up. I put my head on his shoulder and went fast asleep, not waking till we got home. It may be silly, but I have always treasured moments like that.

From when I was perhaps about two, Mother and Dad started to hang a stocking on my bed on Christmas Eve. There was no nylon then and ordinary woollen stockings came up to the knees, whereas socks only went up to the ankles. When I'd gone to bed, they'd say that Santa would come and fill the stocking up before the morning. It was exciting! They'd put in an apple, sweets and toys and maybe a banana, but they'd leave bigger items on the side of my bed. They didn't use wrapping paper then because it was too expensive. As I got older, the stocking was replaced by a pillowcase, which fitted bigger presents in.

I was so excited that a time or two I woke before they'd put anything out and other times I got things out of the stocking and shouted them to come up and have a look at what I'd got. When I got older, I'd often be given a book and this would keep me quiet for quite a while because I did a lot of reading.

When I got up, it would be nice and warm in the parlour, where I'd go with my toys. Mother and Dad would have put up their own decorations they'd made from sheets of coloured paper, which they'd cut into strips and linked into chains. We'd have chicken or a bit of meat with Brussels sprouts for Christmas dinner. We didn't have turkey then.

I'd play with my toys on Christmas afternoon and then we'd have cake, jelly, custard and pop for tea and it was really good! Afterwards, I'd carry on playing with my toys. I can't remember seeing my grandparents at Christmas and we didn't go to see them then either, which is funny.

Some time after the war, Dad went to work at Taylor Tunnicliff & Co. Ltd., in

Hampton Street, Eastwood, as a turner. Dad wanted Mother to stop working and stay at home, which she did after a while. That may have been for health reasons because she wasn't very well for years, but I don't know what the matter with her was.

When I was five, I started to go to Granville Council Mixed School, which was across Waterloo Road, in Granville Street. It had been opened in 1854 by the 2nd Earl Granville, the owner of Shelton Coal & Iron Works, and was named after him. The school entrances were divided into two. On the left side of the building were the infants' and junior girls' entrance and playgrounds and on the right, the junior boys' entrance and playgrounds. They were separate to protect the girls and small children from the rough older boys.

At the far end of the playgrounds, over the wall, was a deep cutting, at the bottom of which ran the double-track North Staffordshire Railway Loop Line, which carried the trains from and to Waterloo Road Station. Further along the line to the left, the track entered a tunnel, which went under Myott, Son & Co.'s Alexander Pottery and several streets to emerge near to Cobridge Station.

The classrooms were heated by big coal fires, but the far corners of the rooms were a little chilly. The toilets were at the far end of the playgrounds. All of the infants' teachers were ladies and one of them I remember wore an ankle-length dark skirt, in the pre-Great War fashion, along with a dark blouse, with a high collar. At play time, we played a bit of kick-about football and I was in goal once when I made a fantastic save – or so it seemed!

Most of the time in the infants' school, we played with toys and we used black slates for what bit of class work we did. They had a wooden border round them, perhaps to stop the slates from breaking. They were owned by the school and there was one for each desk. We were given a pencil-shaped thing, which was perhaps a piece of slate, to write with. It made a mark and we used a damp cloth to rub the slates clean. There was also a sink for us to wash our hands. The teachers had more modern equipment than us, so they wrote in chalk on blackboards!

For a while, I was taken home after school by my cousin, Prudence Wallett, but one day I came out on my own and ran past the Granville Inn onto Waterloo Road, where I was knocked down by a motor van or a truck. I was very unlucky because there weren't many motor vehicles about at that time. I was unconscious, but not badly hurt and came to in Dr Sworn's surgery at 448 Waterloo Road.

Not long after, Prudence emigrated to Canada with her parents, my Uncle Fred and Aunt Maud. That was under a scheme to colonize huge empty tracts of land with ex-servicemen and the land was given free. First of all, they had to have somewhere to live, so they borrowed tools from farmers living in the area and built themselves a log cabin. The farmers also supplied the know-how and some labour. The family's parcel of land had to be cleared of trees and scrub, and then ploughed and seeded, with nothing to show for the effort until the crop was sold. It was back breaking and they worked long hours. Also, they had to cut a big stock of logs for the fire before the winter set in. The winters were very hard and the family was isolated for weeks, with the snow getting up to the roof. I was told that the snow there was dry, so it was difficult to make snowballs. Uncle Fred and his family didn't stay in Canada very long before they came back home.

Later, they had a shop in Waterloo Road, Burslem, on the Cobridge side of the town centre. There didn't seem much for sale, but they took in actors as guests, who performed at the Hippodrome theatre in Wedgwood Place. I think Aunt Maud was on the stage in a small way and she was good at dancing the Charleston, which became a craze in the 1920s.

Our street lamps were lit by gas and every night a lamplighter came along and switched on the lights. He carried a six- or seven-feet-long pole on his shoulder and pushed the end of it through a hole in the bottom of the glass and turned a switch to turn on the gas. There was a small light at the end of the pole, which then ignited the gas. To make the gas burn brighter, a delicate gas mantle was attached to the flame. Once, one of the local lads climbed up a lamppost with a stick to turn off the gas and he almost broke the mantle.

Our houses were also lit by gas and had the same type of gas mantle, which was attached to a pipe coming down from the ceiling. The mantle was made of a kind of cloth and, when ignited, it turned into a dry, delicate material. The mantle was just above head height and when a man came into the house wearing a trilby, he'd sometimes knock the mantle off. That would make a big difference in the brightness of the light, so a new mantle would have to be bought from the corner shop. Often, there would be no money left in the purse, so the household would have to manage with a feeble, flickering light, which covered the black looks that would be given to the culprit.

When I went to bed, I was allowed a small light in the bedroom, which was a gaslight without the mantle. The low light flickered and cast dancing shadows on the wall and that frightened me. Also, I don't think I had a curtain over the window and I used to imagine bogeymen were looking at me from outside. When I grew older, I plucked up the courage to get out of bed and looked through the window. To my great relief, I saw nothing unusual and so I got over my fear of the dark.

On another occasion, near Christmas one year, I was sitting in the living room with Mother and Dad when the stairs door opened and there was Santa Claus, dressed in red. Well, I was petrified! I assume a relation or member of the family had dressed up in the costume, but I never did find out who it was!

Dad used to take me to see Grandmother and Grandad Kent on a Sunday morning. They still lived at 344 Etruria Vale, opposite Etruria Park. Living with them were Uncle Ted and Aunt Florrie and their children, Sam and Annie. Later, Uncle Ted and Aunt Florrie had another son, Bernard.

Grandad was a smallish man, with a bald head and a long grey moustache. He was a tailor and, in those days, I believe suits were hand made. While sewing, he sat cross-legged on a raised platform and once or twice demonstrated his ability to place both his feet behind his head!

Grandmother was rough and ready and more belligerent than any of my other grandparents. When she saw me arriving, she'd say to Sam, 'Hey up, Cyril's coming!' Then he'd try to put all his toys away so that I couldn't play with them! He had a lot of lead soldiers and cowboys and Indians – the danger of lead poisoning wasn't then realized. He called one of the Indians "Big Chief Sitting Bull", which I thought was a silly name, not knowing that there had been such a real person!

Grandmother had a lovely round table in her parlour and on it were some pieces of Wedgwood black basalt. Uncle Ted worked for the company and was able to purchase them as seconds. Also in the parlour were an organ and a harmonium, which I think likewise belonged to Uncle Ted.

The back entry, at the rear of their house, finished at one end with a fence and behind it was a cutting in which the Loop Line ran. Their toilet was by the entry, at the bottom of their yard (as was common at that time), and was the old type, which consisted of a couple of buckets, with a seat on top. The night soil men came around at intervals and emptied these buckets into a horse-drawn contraption. They worked during the night when people didn't notice the smell unless they slept with their windows open. But everybody would be woken by dogs barking all around the area after hearing the noise! What a terrible job it was, though some people claimed the smell was healthy!

After a while, Grandmother's toilet was replaced by a modern flush type. Sam told me that the water in it was pure and clean and proceeded to scoop some out of the pan with his hands and drink it! I wasn't very convinced! I suppose he'd got things mixed up, having been told that clean water came in from the mains to flush the toilet out.

My Aunt Pru lived with her husband, Bill Banner, at 19 Garden Row, which ran at right angles to Windermere Street and was later renamed Bowness Street. Uncle Bill came from the top of Bucknall New Road, in Hanley, and his father, Dick, was a local tough guy, who helped the police at times, when they had to deal with hard characters from the "Rocks", which was a particularly rough area just off Bucknall New Road.

Uncle Bill was a boxer and I gather he did a bit of sparring with Tommy Harrison, a local lad, who became the European bantamweight champion. Uncle Bill worked as a bus conductor and once a drunk tried to tip up his money pouch, but Uncle soon stopped him, with a punch!

Uncle had fought in the army at Gallipoli in the Great War against the Turks. He told me that for a period the situation was so desperate that the private soldiers were rationed to a pint of water a day for all purposes, including drinking and shaving. He said that they'd shave and then filter the water through a handkerchief before drinking it. I wondered why it was necessary for the men to shave when water was so scarce, but I've realized since that the army loves to have the troops looking nice regardless of the conditions! Uncle also said that the officers continued to have baths while water was being rationed to the men.

During this campaign, Uncle was charged with dumb insolence for allowing his face to make some kind of expression when talking to an officer. He was duly punished, but he didn't say how. He could have been tied to a gun wheel for a period or maybe he was drilled at the double (at two or three times the normal speed), wearing a full pack, till he dropped.

After Gallipoli, Uncle must have been drafted to the Western Front because he mentioned the primitive equipment, which amounted to a piece of cloth, that he'd had to use during the gas attacks! He also said that he'd been shot through the mouth with a bullet!

One of Mother's brothers was named Bramwell. He'd been a soldier in the war and I think he then joined the Black and Tans, which was a military organization sent to Ireland to quell any trouble. They had a bad reputation and there was some talk about Uncle deserting. I believe he'd been a miner when he was young, but he finished up a "gentleman of the road", in other words a tramp.

I didn't see him many times, but, when he did call in to see Grandmother and Grandad Wallett, they were ashamed because the neighbours would be talking about them. My grandparents were so upset by his visits that they quarrelled with each other and were glad when he finally moved on. Uncle Bram was always pretty tidy and not at all like how cartoonists depicted tramps. The first things he asked for were brushes and blacking to clean his shoes with. He was a pleasant fellow and wouldn't retaliate when his parents stormed at him for his way of life. He showed me how to arm wrestle and then asked me what the lesson was worth, even though I was only a schoolboy! He was trying to get a penny or two from me, but he didn't succeed.

When I was about six, I had a wooden spinning top, with a piece of string wrapped round it and tied to a stick. The idea was to throw the top on the ground with one hand and pull the string with the other hand, so that the top would go spinning round.

Around the same time, I had a three-wheeled bike, which I used to peddle, mainly along Windermere Street, around the corner into Garden Row and then into Mulgrave Street, stopping at the far end where the pavement ran out. Billy Gritton, of 16 Mulgrave Street, was the only other little lad who had a bike and he used to race with me. We had no brakes and it was hair-raising going around the corners!

The other lads I played with were Billy's brother, Wilf; Billy and Teddy Anetts, who lived next door, at number 25; "Monty" Royle, of 5 Windermere Street; Norman Ball, of 24 Mulgrave Street, and Lenny Skerratt, of number 32. They all called me "Sid", which they thought was short for Cyril. The only girl I can remember at that time was Lenny's sister, Evelyn. Their father walked with a stoop, but their mother was elegant and had a ladylike manner. The Skerratts were a very poor family, but Lenny and four of his five brothers, who were all tall, later joined the Grenadier Guards.

Grandad Kent died on 12 December 1922 in the North Staffordshire Infirmary. In those days, when people died, they used to be displayed in their coffin in their own parlour and any relative or friend could go and have a look at them. Grandad was the first dead person I saw. I was told he was dead, but, of course, I didn't know what that meant. I wandered in to the parlour and was startled to see him waxen-faced, lying in a box!

The local lads and I used to play football with a pig's bladder, but I can't remember owning one. Every now and again, somebody had one, which I think would have been bought from the local butcher, Mr Travis. The bladders were like balloons and about as thin as them. They were skin-coloured, but slightly pink, and blown up and tied at the neck. They were very light, so they kept going in the air and sinking slowly, but they didn't last long before they burst. We kicked them about in the streets and never gave it a thought that they'd come from pigs and had had urine in them!

Although I wrote left-handed, I was right-footed at football. In cricket, though, I batted right-handed and bowled left-handed. That was just what I did naturally.

Opposite our house was some rough ground. One day, I was running down a gulley when I fell and gashed my left knee. What a mess it was – there was a gap as wide as a finger! The wound needed four or five stitches, but I wasn't taken to a doctor, perhaps because I was afraid of being stitched up. Mother and Dad cleaned the wound, bandaged up my knee and then put a splint on my leg. I was off school for weeks, hobbling around with a straight leg, and I still have a scar below my kneecap to this day.

When I was seven, I think, I moved into the big school in the main building and it was a shock because there was no more playing with toys. It was hard work from then on!

At the start of the school day, we'd have to get into lines in the playground and file through the doorway into the hall, where the headmaster, Mr Thorley, was sitting at a desk on an elevated platform. We had to march past him and then disperse to our classes. He didn't seem to be watching us, but perhaps he was keeping an eye on us. He was smallish, with a big walrus moustache, and seemed to be mild-mannered.

We moved on from slates to nibbed pens, which we dipped in ink in the inkwells that fitted in holes cut into our desks. Writing was a messy job and there was ink all over the place. The desks and floors were stained with it and it got on the kids' clothing. Also, splodges would appear in our writing books, which we'd mop up with blotting paper.

I think all the teachers in the big school had a cane. It was hanging up on show near the blackboard where our eyes were concentrating. I didn't fancy having my hands whipped, but I didn't get into any trouble at school and so I didn't have the cane. It was only used on odd occasions for whatever the teachers deemed criminal.

One of the teachers I remember was Mr Hancock. When he was mad with us, he used to hold his cane clasped in both hands and shake them up and down and stick his tongue out at the same time!

Another teacher, Miss Michael, tried to make me write with my right hand. It was difficult and terrible and I was upset. It was almost a sin to be left-handed in those days, but, after a while, I was allowed to revert to my natural hand. There was also Miss Wren, who was young, small and slim and always seemed to be scratching her genitals.

All but one of the women teachers in the main school wore colourful blouses and the smarter shorter skirts which had come into fashion in the war because they were more practical in the jobs that they'd taken over from the men in the Forces. The exception was Annie Lander, who wore dark clothes. The male teachers always dressed soberly and very smartly and wore a suit, tie and waistcoat, with shirts with white starched stiff collars.

The lads nearly all wore woollen jerseys with high necks, so that our shirts were covered, which saved having to buy ties. We all wore short trousers, some of which had formerly been long ones, belonging to older brothers, and had had part of their legs cut off. I was lucky because my trousers had belonged to no-one else. We also wore long wool stockings, which came up to our knees, and black boots, never any other colour. No lad wore shoes because they were considered to be cissified! Our boots had hobnails knocked into them and most had steel toe tips and heels to help save the leather soles. Also, wearing a cap was most essential, even outside school. I seem to remember the girls wearing pinafores.

Next door to us, at number 29, lived Emma Gilbert, who was rather aggressive. One day, she started going on at Mother across the back wall and kept on until Mother could stand it no longer. Then she came out of her shell and really told

Mrs Gilbert off. Dad was sitting on the toilet, down the back yard, at the time and, when he got back in the house, Mother was very upset. She asked him why he hadn't come to help and he said, 'You seemed to be doing alright, so I left you to get on with it.' I suppose he'd have been too embarrassed to have come out of the toilet for a row or maybe he was shirking it!

When I was eight, I started to attend Sunday school at Cobridge Gospel Mission and used to go in the morning and the afternoon until I was about thirteen or fourteen. At first, the mission was in Elder Road, on the left, going towards Leek. Later, a new wooden structure was built in Derwent Street, on the right-hand side, going from Windermere Street. The main people running the mission were Mr Gough, his wife and his mother. Mr Gough was a very nice gentleman, who worked in the office at Shelton Bar (the iron and steel works), but his mother was very stern and the children used to be afraid of her. I was a pretty good attender and my star card was nearly always full, so I usually had a good prize book for my efforts. Also, when I was about twelve, I was awarded a silver-plated pencil for collecting the biggest amount of money, over a few weeks, for the mission.

There were quite a number of cinemas about when I was a lad, but the one I patronized, from when I was about eight, was Cobridge Picture Hall, which was on Waterloo Road, on the corner of Grange Street and next to St. Peter's Catholic Church. We called it the "Bug Hut", but that was the description given to most of the cinemas in Stoke-on-Trent. It was run by the Grant family and there was a special show for kids on Saturday mornings. The admission price to sit on long, hard, wooden forms was a penny, but the four or five rows at the back had plush tip-up seats priced at three ha'pence and I sometimes used to pay the extra to avoid sitting with some of the rougher types.

There was bedlam, with kids of all ages throwing orange peel around, making noises and stamping their feet because they were so excited, but, when the lights went out, the bedlam subsided, even though all the films were silent. Cowboy and Indian films were the favourite, especially if the hero was Tom Mix. He shot no end of men and beat up a lot more. What a man! He was always the hero and wore a Stetson hat.

I went with Dad sometimes and, on one occasion, when Tom Mix was particularly bloodthirsty, a man sitting behind got up and said to me, 'Has he killed enough for you yet, son?' He then went out. I couldn't understand what he was on about because I thought it was great stuff! Once, Tom was fighting about twenty guys at the top of a six-storey wooden building, which collapsed. Of course, all the bad guys were killed, but Tom walked out unscathed! I did think that was a bit far-fetched, even though I believed the film was of a real incident.

Some of the films were put on as serials and always finished in an impossible situation for the hero or heroine, but in the next episode they always came through unharmed. One of these serials was about a Dr Fu Manchu, a Chinese villain, who was the leader of a gang and very scary. He wore a gown and had a long, thin moustache, which hung down each side of his jaw. He was always doing fiendish things and then the film would cut off and say, 'More next week'!

Felix the Cat was a cartoon character who was on regularly. He was humanized and walked on his back legs. He had all kinds of crazy adventures and got into disastrous situations, but kept surviving! There was a catchy popular song about him and I can still remember and sing some of the words from it.

One day, when I was about eight, some of the older lads were chasing some of the girls around the corner of Mulgrave Street, which got me excited. So I threw a stone after them, but, with not being very old, my aim was poor and the stone went through Skerratts' back window! I said nothing to my parents, hoping nothing would happen, but they found out and Mother really shouted at me and gave me a light clip round the back of my head, which was the only time that either of my parents ever hit me. She also made me pay for the damage, which came to a shilling. That was a tidy sum for a little lad and it came out of my pocket money for weeks!

I had some "stonies", or marbles, which were like little ball bearings, but made of glass or pottery. Some of them were coloured and had really nice designs. They were worth more than the plain ones, although I can't ever remember buying any. My friends and I would make up our own games with them and shoot our stonies at our opponents', trying to knock them out of the way.

I used to have some pretty good toys compared with most of the other lads. One was a scooter, which must have cost a lot of money. It had a platform between two wheels and I'd push it along with one foot until I'd attained a good speed and then I'd lift my pushing foot onto the platform as well. Sam also had a scooter, but his had a pedal attached to the rear wheel, which, when pressed, would propel the scooter along.

About that time, someone bought me a cheap case ball and, while I was kicking it, a gang of big lads came past, took it off me and went kicking it pretty hard down Mulgrave Street. When I finally retrieved it, it was in a state because it was only made from wash-leather and the stitching had come undone, letting the bladder through the joints. It was ruined and I can't remember playing with it again.

We played a variety of games in addition to football, cricket, tick and leapfrog:

Big-fish-in-water was played by pretending a road was the river and the pavements were river banks. The big fish tried to catch whoever crossed to the other side and, if caught, that person then became the big fish.

In badger-off-again, one side would bend down and catch hold of the person's hips in front, with the first person putting his hands against a wall to stop his head getting damaged. The other side had to run and jump on to the backs of those bending down and keep their feet off the floor. When they were all mounted, they had to shout as quickly as they could, before they fell off or touched the ground, 'Two, four, six, eight, badger off again,' and so win the game. If the side bending down collapsed, they lost the game.

Tip-it was played by putting two bricks about four to six inches apart and then placing a short stick across them. A quick flick of the wrist would send it upwards, to be hit by a longer stick from underneath and whoever knocked it the furthest was the winner. An alternative was to put the short stick overhanging one brick and knock the end of it so that it spun upwards, then hit it away with the longer stick.

In Jack-shine-a-light, a person with a flashlight would hide in one of the back yards. The seekers would shout, 'Jack shine a light,' and the hider was supposed to flash a light to give the seekers a chance to find him. But, of course, the hider would put his hands over it, so that the seekers had a job to find the hiding place!

Some kids' parents worked for tile makers and would "acquire" bits of mosaic tiles of different shapes. A lad would put half a dozen or so of the pieces on the palm of one of his hands, then throw the bits up and try to catch them on the back of the same hand. Then the other kids would have a go and the idea was to do better than the others. I joined in with this game and it was called Jacks.

We used to have hoops, which we pushed along with a stick as quickly or slowly as we wished. The hoop was called a "bowler", was made of round steel wire and was about two feet across. One day, I saw a lad with one which had a short length of wire fastened around it, so that a stick wasn't needed. Just by pushing this wire, the bowler turned and rolled forward. I asked the boy where he'd had it from and he said, 'From the blacksmith's.'

The forge was in Sneyd Street, near the Elder Road end, on the left-hand side, near to where the Loop Line emerged from the tunnel. I walked over there and watched the blacksmith at work making horseshoes. He got a length of iron and pushed it into the open furnace. Then he worked the bellows to blow air into the fire to make it very hot. Next, he pulled the red-hot iron out of the fire with a long pair of pliers, put it on the anvil and hammered it into a "U" shape. He then heated the length of iron up again, removed it and hammered it flat. The shoe was heated once more and then holes were knocked into it for the nails to go through when they were hammered into a horse's hoof.

While this was going on, the blacksmith asked me what I wanted, which I explained. He knew exactly what it was because he already had several bowlers hanging on a nail. He lifted one down and gave it to me. It cost either a penny or tuppence.

Our meals were fairly basic. For dinner, at lunch time, Mother would cook some meat, potatoes and veg and we'd have slices of bread and butter or margarine with jam at tea time. Sometimes, we'd have fruit salad out of a tin, with some bread. Perhaps once a week, I'd be sent to Louie's fish and chip shop at 416 Waterloo Road. She had a cooker made up of two or three frying bowls in a kind of cabinet over a coal fire. It had tiles on top to make it decorative. She fried chips and fish in different bowls and worked on her own most of the time. We had chips and mushy peas from her, but I can't remember having any fish. She also used to sell bits that had dropped off the fried fish and chips, but these were full of fat and we didn't have any of them.

Some children never had fruit, except perhaps an orange in their Christmas stocking. For the poorer kids, even an orange was a luxury. I didn't have fruit very often myself, but, sometimes, when I was finishing an apple and ready to throw the core away, a lad would say to me, 'Giz thee core,' meaning he wanted me to give him the apple core to eat.

One lad's family was so poor that he had to wear his sister's old black stockings, which went up under his shorts. At the time, I was about eight or so and thought he looked great, so I asked my mother if I could have the same kind of stockings! She tried to explain why the lad was dressed like that, but I wasn't entirely convinced.

When I was about eight or nine, I started having piano lessons from a young lady from 45 Derwent Street, named Miss Trigg. We didn't have a piano at that time, so I practised on Grandmother and Grandad Wallett's instrument, which was old-fashioned because it had swivelling candle holders on each side to enable the pianist to play by candlelight when it was dark! I couldn't understand how they could have afforded to buy the instrument because they were very poor. Eventually, Mother and Dad bought me a piano, a Tennyson, from Davis Bros, 8 Waterloo Road, Burslem, which I still have. I believe it cost £60, which would have been about ten months' wages at that time, and I carried on having lessons for quite a few years.

Once, Tilly Anetts, who lived next door and was eight or nine years older than me, asked me to accompany her on the piano while she sang at Cobridge Gospel Mission. At the appointed time, we were announced and got on the stage. I was nervous, not having played in public before, and finished first, having left Tilly a little behind! There was some clapping, so maybe it wasn't too bad, but I was never again asked to play with anyone!

I used to play one piece of music where I had to cross my hands and Grandmother Wallett loved it, being mesmerized by my intricate manoeuvres! She used to come to our house to keep an eye on me while Mother was at work. Sometimes, I'd be practising on the piano when she knocked on the door, but, if I was in the middle of a piece of music, I wouldn't open it until I'd finished!

When I was about nine, I had a peashooter, which consisted of a tube, about eight inches long, and a mouthpiece and was made of tin. I used to blow a dried pea out of it to shoot at somebody. It wasn't very accurate and the pea would only go about twenty yards, say. Peashooters were quite common and only cost a ha'penny or a penny from shops round and about. I didn't use it much and I can't remember hitting anybody with a pea, nor being struck with one myself, but I think being hit on the head would have hurt.

About the same time, I had a potato gun, which was a metal tube, maybe a foot long and open at each end. I'd dig one end into a potato and pull it out and then I'd do the same with the other end. There was a rod with it, which I'd push into one end of the tube and compress the air until the pressure built up inside and fired the further piece of potato out, like with a peashooter. I remember having a potato full of holes, but I can't recall ever hitting anybody with the gun.

I also had a cap gun, which was rather crude. The caps were on a roll, with a bit of gunpowder every inch or so. I'd put the roll in the imitation pistol and, when I pulled the trigger, a little hammer would come down and hit the pocket of gunpowder, as it did in a rifle. The powder would explode and make a cracking noise, like gunfire. The powder wasn't placed very accurately, so sometimes the hammer missed. Other kids who could afford them also had these guns and the local lads and I more or less played cowboys and Indians, but nobody wanted to be the Indians because they were the underdogs and the cowboys always won in the films. We played in the street and round about and would jump out from behind corners, firing our guns. We also played cops and robbers in very much the same way.

Dad dabbled in wireless, which was pretty new at that time and there were very few people around who had a receiver. He started off with a crystal set, which was very elementary and consisted of a crystal and a fine contact wire, called the cat's whisker. The end of the wire was touched on the crystal and, if you got it on the correct place, you might hear something in your earphones, but you would have to tell the other people in the room to be quiet! The reception was very poor, but, of course, everything was in an experimental stage.

We had a local broadcasting station, Stoke Wireless Broadcasting, which had come into being on 21 October 1924 and had perhaps inspired Dad's interest. Its first studio was at the back of the Majestic Buildings, in South Wolfe Street in Stoke, and was about as big as a kitchen. The broadcasters had to be a certain height because the microphones were not adjustable! Its official title was 6 S.T. and it operated on 306 metres. They used to start off with, 'This is 6 S.T. Stoke-on-Trent calling.'

Later, as design improved, Dad built his own set from plans and parts, which he fitted together. Then, instead of earphones, he was able to purchase a loudspeaker, which was separate and shaped like a bent horn. To get better reception, Dad bought a very long pole, which was something like a telegraph pole and was laid in the back yard while a hole was dug by the back entry wall. Before the pole was erected, an aerial wire was fixed to the top and run to the back bedroom window, then down to the kitchen window and through it to the wireless set. Then, helped by two or three people, Dad got the bottom of the pole in the hole, which was filled in. No-one else in Windermere Street or Mulgrave Street had got one of these poles at that time. There was no mains electricity, so we had an accumulator to give the power to run the wireless. It was something like a small car battery and had to be recharged every so often at a local shop or garage. As technology improved, Dad put in an indoor aerial, which was a wire that he ran upstairs and maybe into the roof space.

One programme we had on was scary. *The Radio Times* previewed a story about some white men being trapped in a hut in the middle of the jungle, surrounded by natives, who were very hostile, and we were told to listen with the gas light turned off. When the time came, our house was in darkness and the wireless was switched on and tuned in.

The white men were in the hut and the tom-toms began to beat. The men debated how far away the natives were and what the drums were saying. The drums became silent and then started again, only this time they were nearer. One of the trapped men became hysterical, but calmed down after a while, becoming as stiff upper lipped as the others. The drums stopped playing every now and then and the men listened for sounds that would indicate that the natives were near and ready to attack. The only light in the hut was from a single oil lamp and somebody shouted, 'Put that light out!' One of the men lifted the glass cover and blew out the light, leaving total blackness. There was an occasional whisper and a long silence and then all hell broke loose, with shouts, shots and screams. After a short while, the gunfire ceased as the white men were killed. Then there was a bit of native chatter and, finally, silence.

The programme had finished, so Dad struck a match and lit the gas light. It hadn't been as terrifying as I'd thought it might have been, but, as time went on, the programmes got better.

When I was about nine, the Gilberts moved to 8 Windermere Street, a house on the other side of the road, and were replaced by John and Ellen Thomas, who opened a shop, selling, I think, sweets, biscuits and things like that. One day, they asked me if I could look after the shop for an hour or two because they had something urgent on. I agreed with some trepidation, but, fortunately, I only had one customer the whole time!

Mr Thomas was a van driver, I think for W. S. Brown & Sons, the butchers, who at that time had a shop at 75 Stafford Street, Hanley. One day, he asked if I'd like a ride in his van because he was making a trip to Market Drayton. I said I would, so off we set, but the road was narrow and twisty and I noticed from the speedometer that at times he was touching fifty miles per hour, which seemed hair-raising, although there were few motor vehicles about to trouble us!

I think I was Grandad Wallett's favourite grandchild. One day, he whispered to me to go with him down to the lavatory, which was at the bottom of the yard. There he gave me a shilling, which was probably all he had. He kept it quiet because he didn't want Grandmother to know because she would have shouted at him.

Grandad and Grandmother had been very poorly educated. Grandad told me his education had been part-time, going to school half the day and to work, which I suppose was down the pit, the other half. He wrote his signature for me and it took him ages because he really had to think about what he was doing when he was joining his letters together! Once, he and Grandmother were talking to me about using an awl, but they called it a 'nawl'. I corrected them, but they were offended and would have none of it!

When I was about ten, I was given a dartboard as a present and it was hung on the living room door. I used to play with Dad and, during one game, an arrow hit one of the wires and bounced back, sticking in my forehead. No harm was done, except I seem to remember there being a small hole in my skin for a few years, but it covered over.

Between Portland Street, Rutland Street and the Hanley Deep Pit railway was a huge coal waste tip, as high as a house. The lads from the area around Portland Street would stand on top of it and throw stones at us lads from Windermere Street and Mulgrave Street. Then someone from our lot would shout, 'Charge!' and we'd rush and try to chase the enemy off. We'd get partway up, but then we'd be chased back again. We had a similar rivalry with the Granville Street area lads and we'd charge across Waterloo Road after them, but I can never remember anyone getting hurt.

About that time, Dad took me to see Stoke City play a time or two and we stood on the Stoke End, which was like a sloping dirt tip. But I got bored with it and wandered off to explore the ground. I don't think I really understood then what the game was all about.

In 1926, during the coal strike, I was going to the picture palace in Cobridge when I heard the sound of marching feet and there, coming towards me, along Waterloo Road, from Burslem, was a squad of miners, all in formation, like soldiers, as some of them must have been a few years previously. I suppose they were going to a meeting and that was the best way of doing it, rather than wandering along in a mob, which may have frightened people.

Some of the miners started to dig for coal themselves on spare ground. There were several shafts sunk behind our school and quite an amazing amount of coal was sold. This mining was a risky business because the shafts didn't seem to be supported enough against the soil collapsing and the men could have been buried alive. I went to the edge of one shaft and it looked to be about twenty feet down, so I soon backed away. It was hard work for the miners hauling up buckets of coal at the end of a rope.

The timing of the strike was bad because it happened late that spring, at a time when less coal was needed than in the winter and Taylor Tunnicliff converted their kilns to being powered by burning oil. The miners were eventually forced back to work because the country managed to struggle along without them. After the strike, the shafts were filled in, but, when I went past in about 1975, I could just see the hollows where the holes had been.

Around 1926, we started going on holiday for the August bank holiday week, which at that time started on the first Monday of the month. We always went to the seaside because that was the thing to do then. The places we visited were New Brighton, Rhyl, Blackpool, Southport and Morecambe. It was exciting going down to Waterloo Road Station to wait for a connection to Stoke.

When we went to New Brighton, we'd get off the train at Lime Street Station in Liverpool, take a tram to the landing stage and then cross the Mersey on a ferry to our destination. One year, we went with Aunt Pru and Uncle Bill. The railways in our area were owned by LMS (the London, Midland and Scottish Railway) and, when our connection was late, Uncle remarked: 'LMS. They are hell of a mess!'

We spent some time on deck chairs on the beach and one day, while sitting on one, Uncle put his fingers in the sand and was nipped by a crab. He lifted his hand up quickly and the crab still had hold of one of his fingers! He then searched about in the sand and found two more of the beasts.

The deck chair owners had a dud, which they mixed up with the others for a bit of fun. Whoever hired the dud chair out tried to put it up, which was impossible, but he'd persist with it. Then the people near to would go over to show him their skills because they thought they could fix it up in about ten seconds, but, of course, their efforts also were to no avail. It was really funny seeing half a dozen men wrestling with this chair and hearing the women calling them a dozy lot! After about half an hour, they'd all give up, leaving the victim eventually to return the dud and get a good chair in its place.

Partway into the River Mersey was a fort, which was surrounded by water at high tide. It was equipped with heavy guns ready for use against any approaching German vessels during the Great War.

It was on one of our visits to New Brighton that I saw something that shocked me. Coming towards me appeared to be a small child, who was not walking, but moving in an unusual way. It turned out to be a man with no legs. He moved by putting his hands on the ground before him and swinging his body forward. Under the bottom of his body was a piece of tarpaulin to take the wear and tear!

We stayed in boarding houses, which were pretty strict, and none of them had washbasins. Instead, we were supplied with a big jug of water (which was usually cold), a bowl to wash in and a bucket to empty the dirty water into! No baths were allowed and there was one toilet for about ten rooms, so it was terrible first thing in the morning queuing up to use it. There was no stopping out after ten o'clock, except by special permission, and there was an extra charge for cruet, which was salt, pepper and mustard. A cheaper type of accommodation was also available. This was "apartments" and was where you bought your own food and the landlady cooked it for you.

When we went to Blackpool, we detrained at North Station because we always had digs in the posher north of the town. I was allowed to wander off on my own and usually I walked all the way along the Promenade to South Shore Pleasure Beach, which was about 2½ miles. I didn't go on many things because I didn't have a lot of money to spend, but I did like the Dodgems.

Near to Blackpool Tower was the Big Wheel, which was huge and had lots of coaches attached to it. The customers only made one circle and then had to get off. Each coach stopped and filled up, then moved up and around a bit till the next coach was in position to be filled. So it continued until the first coach came down to the bottom again. The idea was to see the view and have the thrill of going up. It was an old ladies' type of thing. It wasn't too daring and I wasn't frightened of it, but it made Mother poorly and she had to sit on the floor of the coach, away from the windows.

The main thing I remember about Southport was the huge beach because the sea was a long way out. There was also a sizeable fairground, which was shabby and didn't have many customers.

In early August each year, to coincide with the potters' holidays, there was a fair in Hanley. It was called the Wakes and there was also one in Burslem. These fairs attracted crowds of people with money to spend because most of them didn't have enough to afford to go away on holiday. Until 1922, the Hanley fair had been situated in Parliament Row and Upper Market Square, but it had been very difficult for traffic to get through. So, from then on, it became sited on waste ground off Regent Road, near to Hanley Park, and it was mostly Pat Collins'. It was an important part of local life and I looked forward to it, even though I didn't go on much because I didn't like most of the rides. But I liked the atmosphere and wandered around, looking at what was going on and having an ice cream or two.

Teddy Anetts used to be sent by his father to get his supper beer and sometimes Teddy asked me to go along with him to, I think, the King's Arms on Cobridge Road, near to the crossroads. Teddy would take an empty bottle to the outdoor department and the publican would fill it before sticking a paper label over the cork and down each side of the neck to seal it because it was illegal to sell loose beer to children. As soon as Teddy got outside, he'd pull the seal off, while it was still wet, have a swig of the beer and then stick the seal back on! When he got back, his father would sometimes comment that it wasn't a good measure, but he wouldn't be able to tell if Teddy had taken a drink because in those days the publican would give extra to what had been asked for.

One of the tricks the lads used to do in Cobridge, when I was about ten or eleven, was to knock on front doors and run off. An alternative was to tie together the door knobs of next-door houses (which were only about three feet apart) and then knock on the doors and run off. Of course, neither door could be opened, so that the people would have to go out of their back doors, along the back entry, up the side of the row and then along the front of the houses to untie the rope! It was great fun for the lads, but not so funny for the people affected, especially if they were old folk.

Another trick, done in the dark, was to stick a pin in a front door or window frame, tie the end of a spool of cotton onto it and fix a small stone about four inches down the thread. If the lad was in Windermere Street, he'd then unwind the cotton from the spool until he came to the spare ground across the road. When he jerked the thread, the stone would tap on the door or window frame, but when the person came to the door in answer, he would be unable to see anyone because the lad and his friends would be lying on the ground!

It happened to me once when I was in the house alone. After going to answer the door tapping, I realized what was happening, so I quickly walked through our back yard, around to the front and onto the spare ground, where I caught the culprits. They looked sheepish, but nothing much was said and I took no action.

Every lad used to collect cigarette cards when I was about eleven. The cards were issued inside packets of cigarettes and on the back gave pictures and information about a great number of subjects. They were issued in sets of about fifty, so it was a challenge to get a complete set of as many subjects as possible. I had Dad's cards off him, of course, and I asked other men in the street if they had any to spare.

On Saturday afternoons, I used to wait in Waterloo Road for the crowd to come past from the football match at the Port Vale ground off Bryan Street, in Hanley, and I'd get a few cigarette cards from them. Most of Vale's supporters came from the northern part of the city and crowds rode on the trams and buses up Waterloo Road, while other supporters walked. But I don't remember any of the local men being Vale supporters.

It was difficult to get a full set of cigarette cards because we seemed to get a lot of duplicates. Sometimes, we could swap with other lads, though I didn't like to get dirty cards in exchange. We played games with the surplus cards. A card would be propped against a wall and then each lad in turn would skim another card to try to knock it down. Whoever did so would win all the cards on the ground.

About that time, I had a set of Meccano as a birthday present or for Christmas. It had lengths of plain, silver-coloured metal, which were cheaper than those in the painted sets. There were holes in the metal and there were lots of nuts and bolts. There were also a little spanner and screwdriver and a booklet telling me how to put it all together. I played with it a fair amount and used my imagination and made some quite different things. The set also had different-sized wheels and some of them had grooves on the outside, so they could be connected to other wheels and I made crude vehicles with them.

I used to do errands for my parents. We had a lot of groceries from Challinor's, at 432 Waterloo Road, which was on the corner of Portland Street. One lot of butter I brought home tasted funny, so I was sent back with it to try to get it changed. Mr Challinor said it was alright after he'd tasted it, but, after a while, he decided to give us a fresh supply, although only the same amount that we'd left. That didn't go down very well with my parents because we were good cash customers, unlike the many people who used to have goods on the slate, so I was never sent to Challinor's again. I shopped at Taylor's, on the opposite corner of Portland Street, at number 434, after that.

We had our newspapers from Samuel Smith's, at 410 Waterloo Road. Dad sometimes sent me there for cigarettes and, in appreciation for the custom, Mrs Smith would give me a few sweets in a paper bag. I was sent there one day on an errand with a pound note, which I unknowingly let drop from my fingers. When I got to the shop, I realized my hands were empty and I was in a panic because I believe a man's wages for a week at that time were between a pound and thirty shillings. I searched everywhere for the note, but had no luck, so I had to go home to report the loss. My parents were most upset and sent me back to have another good look around, which I did, but the money had vanished. As far as I can remember, I wasn't punished at all and I was lucky to have good parents because some fathers would have made me strip off and thrashed me with a leather belt.

One of the novelties that Smith's and other shops sold was kali, which was a sweet powder that could be eaten raw or made into a drink. For a period, two or three frames of movie cuttings of famous film stars were given away free with the mixture. These cuttings must have been sold off in bulk when the editors of the films had discarded them after selecting the final footage.

Mr Travis, our local butcher, had his wife and two daughters, Cissie and Edith, helping him out in his shop at 420 Waterloo Road. Cissie got very friendly with my uncle, Mo Wallett, and eventually married him. Later, Mr Travis bought a shop for them next to his, where Cissie sold tripe, pigs' trotters and cow heels.

Mo carried on with his job as a labourer in the marl hole in Cobridge. What a terrible job that was! He had to dig clay and push loads of it in tubs along railway tracks. The ground was mostly wet marl and, of course, his clogs and trousers got covered in it. He and the other men kept working even when it was raining and they had to dry their clothes out every night at home. Sometimes, I took his dinner to him there. It was nearly always in a pudding basin, covered by a saucer and tied around with a clean handkerchief.

The marl hole was between Leek New Road and Sneyd Street. The end of it was very near Leek New Road, just behind a wall, and I used to walk along the edge for a short cut to reach Uncle Mo. From there, I could see the bottom of the hole and it seemed to be about a quarter of a mile deep!

I also ran errands to the Burslem & District Industrial Co-operative Society's grocery store, at 328 Waterloo Road, on the far left-hand corner of the Cobridge crossroads. It was amazing how the assistants reckoned the goods up by adding each item aloud. Sometimes, there'd be thirty or forty items, but they never jotted them down. All the goods were wrapped in a large piece of brown paper and tied around securely with string off a big ball, which was snapped off with a quick snatch of the wrist. It was never cut. Payment was put in a brass cup, then screwed on to a brass top and powered up a wire to the office on the floor above. After a while, the receipt and any change came back down the wire. Included with the payment was our membership number, 18327. All purchases were recorded with a dividend of, I think, a shilling in the pound, which was paid out a time or two each year at the Co-op's head office in Newcastle Street, Burslem.

Sometimes, on special occasions, I was sent with a basin to get a steak and kidney dumpling from a pie shop at 90 Hope Street, which was the same building where Arnold Bennett had been born in 1867. Those dumplings and their gravy were lovely! On other occasions, I went to the Yorkshire Fisheries further up Hope Street, but on the other side. The shop sold the best fried fish I've ever tasted, but nothing else, as far as I know. It was owned and run by an old married couple.

At that time, we didn't have free-running table salt. We used coarse salt instead. Men with a horse and cart, loaded with block salt, came along our back entry. I seem to remember the blocks of salt were about three feet long and six inches square. A saw was used to cut a lump of salt off to sell to the housewives. We placed this on a table in the house and cut through as much as possible with a knife and then crushed it with a rolling pin and put the salt in a large jug. For use on the table, the salt was put in a tiny bowl, called a salt cellar, and we took a pinch and sprinkled it over our food.

An ice cream man also used to come in the back entry, pushing a barrow along and shouting, 'Ice Cream e oh!' The ice cream was held in a metal container, which nestled in chunks of ice to freeze it, and it was scooped out with a wooden spoon. Dad would send me out with a cup to fill and I had to ask for three wafer biscuits to stick in the ice cream. The barrow man was called "Ice Cream Joe" and the lads would gather around and kid Joe to put a bit extra in their cups, which he did if he was in a good mood. He was a little fellow, with squint eyes, and wore glasses, a flat cap and an apron. The ice cream was yellowish in colour and perhaps made of custard powder.

Another fellow came along the entry, pushing a contraption on a single bicycle wheel and shouting, 'Knives to grind!' He'd stop and upend the thing he was pushing and a grindstone and treadle would be revealed. People would come out of their houses with knives and scissors to sharpen. He'd start the grindstone going round by pressing on the treadle and would then sharpen the items on the turning stone, which would send a shower of sparks flying, to my joy!

A rag-and-bone man also came in the back entry, shouting, 'Rag bone!' He was after old clothes, which made fine quality paper, and paid for them with a balloon. The kids were very satisfied with that arrangement! I never saw anyone take bones to him, though it's possible they did. I know that pottery manufacturers used cattle bones to make bone china pottery and they still do.

Other tradesmen who came round were a fishmonger, a fruit and veg merchant and a pottery seller, who used to attract attention by ringing two plates together, which, at the same time, showed that the plates were sound and not cracked.

Norman Ball's mother brewed lovely drinks at her house in Mulgrave Street. There were two flavours: dandelion and burdock, and herb beer. The kids used to knock on her back door and ask for a bottle of one or the other, at a cost, I should think, of a ha'penny or a penny. The bottles were corked and had a piece of string tied around the neck and the cork because the contents were gaseous and tended to blow out the cork. Nevertheless, Mrs Ball had many a mess in her back kitchen when the corks did blow!

Just before Christmas each year, Mother made a couple of bottles of ginger ale, which I enjoyed. There always seemed to be a copy of the recipe about, but, unfortunately, I no longer have one.

Grandmother Kent nearly always gave me a tomato to eat when I went to see her and Uncle Ted would give me sixpence or a shilling, which was very generous. Next door to Grandmother's was Shore's newsagent's, at number 346, and they had two sons named Albert and Levi, with whom Sam and I used to play. Mr Shore owned a motorbike, which was a real luxury in those days, and every year he used to go to the Isle of Man to watch the TT races.

We used to play in a field off Lord Street (which was later renamed Etruria Road), opposite Etruria Park and across the canal from Wedgwood's pottery factory. It was where the bottom of the Odeon car park is now. The name we called it sounded like "Hoar Field", but was more likely to have been "Hall Field" because it was near to Etruria Hall, formerly the home of Josiah Wedgwood, the master potter. I was told that the grass had a very good colour owing to the chemicals that fell on it from the smoke from Shelton Bar! I used to tie knots with the long grass and think that anyone passing might trip over!

Burslem cricket ground was near to us, on Cobridge Road, and sometimes I stood outside with other lads, hoping I could get in for free. If we waited long enough, the gatekeeper would let two or three of us in at a time to view the game as long as we behaved. Billy Briscoe, the Port Vale footballer, was one of the Burslem cricketers and he later went on to keep the Black Boy public house, opposite the ground. He was a popular fellow and, when I was older, I went for a drink in the pub to have a look at him, as did other people. He had a hooked nose and was a burly fellow. He was serving because it was his pub and it was fairly scruffy, but no different to other pubs of the time.

There was an eclipse of the sun on 29 June 1927 and, to get ready for it, Dad smoked some glass by holding it over the open fire so that soot went all over it. He must have been aware that looking straight at the sun could damage your eyes. When the time came, we went to the end of the street to try to get a good view of the event, but there was a lot of cloud about and I can't remember if we saw anything.

Four doors away from Grandmother Kent lived her sister, my Great-aunt Jane, at 336 Etruria Vale. I was told that she was the boss of the cleaning staff at Etruria Hall, where the clerical officials of Shelton Bar worked. It was also said that she had £1,000 in the bank, which was a princely sum at that time! Her son, Fred Bryant, and his wife, Florrie, lived with her. Uncle Fred was only about 5 feet 1 inch tall and, like Dad, was a potter. Aunt Florrie came from Bradford and always kept her Yorkshire accent.

Uncle Ted on occasions talked about his war experiences. He'd volunteered for the army and ended up in France as a driver of a transport wagon, pulled by a couple of horses, which took supplies to the front. When he got back to base one day, he found one of the horses had half an ear missing, which must have resulted from it being hit by a piece of shrapnel. On at least one of his journeys, a bombardment started, so he jumped off the wagon and flattened himself on the ground. The horses then wandered off, but he must have found them again and carried on as normal, or else he may have been shot for deserting his post.

Once, he saw a dead German, who'd been crucified on a door, and, another time, he saw a Tommy strapped to a gun wheel, with his arms outstretched, as a punishment. He'd have stopped like that all day, regardless of the weather, but along came some Australians, who cut him loose. The Aussies wouldn't stand for punishments like that.

When the armistice was declared, Uncle Ted's unit marched into Cologne to occupy it, but there wasn't a soul to be seen. Everybody was hiding indoors in case they were shot or raped. Later on, when they saw there was to be no violence, the people started showing themselves and made the Tommies welcome. Uncle Ted developed a soft spot for the Germans because he made friends with some of them and visited them after the war and Dad went with him.

Uncle brought presents for my parents from Cologne, two of which I've still got. One was a lovely picture of Cologne Cathedral, which had a convex surface inlaid with mother-of-pearl. The other gift was a cut-throat razor, which had a picture of the cathedral etched onto its blade, but it had been made from Sheffield steel!

Uncle brought us home some other souvenirs, which were British, French and German bayonets and a German ceremonial helmet, with a spike on top. The helmet was minus its inside padding and so the clips holding the outside badges were uncovered. When I tried the helmet on, I had a job to get it off again because the fastening clips dug in my head!

Uncle had a head and shoulder silhouette of himself cut out in black paper and stuck on a card. He looked really good, with a cigarette stuck in his mouth and wearing his soft soldier's hat. Formerly, the soldiers had worn stiff hats, called cheese cutters, with a wire running around the inside of the top to keep them nice and round and flat. But, when they got in the trenches, they took the wire out and then banged the hats about, to soften them up and make them more comfortable.

When I was about eleven, I owned an air rifle, with which I used to practise in the back yard, on any old target. Sam also had an air rifle and once, when he was in a temper, I saw him shoot at a lad's legs! I never heard of the lad being injured, so perhaps Sam's aim was poor.

Around that time, I took part in a school play and had a few words to speak, which I can still remember, 'Truth often lies at the bottom of a well.' I don't recall what the saying was to do with or how it fitted into the rest of the play, so it hasn't been a great deal of use to me!

One hot day at school, I was one of three boys who were sent into the playground with a thermometer to see what the temperature was. The reading kept going higher and higher – I must have had my fingers over the bulb of mercury! But, luckily, the teacher came to fetch us in before the thermometer exploded!

When I was about eleven or twelve, Mr Travis, the butcher, bought a car and he was the only person I knew who had one at that time. It was a Wolseley open tourer, with a soft top, which folded down, and I can never remember him having it up. It was kept in a lock-up in a yard at the rear of Portland Street. He used to go out on Sundays for a spin with my Uncle Mo, who received driving lessons from him. At that time, there was no driving test and anyone of age could get a driving licence without any trouble. One day, Mr Travis hit a tram, but he just drove off! It seems at that time they didn't bother reporting accidents very often and there was no compulsory insurance!

Sometimes, Dad and I were invited out for a run and, of course, we sat in the rear seats. Mother and Aunt Cissie never came because in those days it seemed the women's role was to be at home. Dad used to offer payment to Mr Travis, but he always refused to accept it. It was a thrill having a ride in a car because I doubt if any of the other kids around our area had the same chance. It was cold sitting in the back, with the wind whistling around us, even though we were provided with a thick travelling rug to cover us. The furthest distance we travelled was to Lichfield, where we went a time or two. On the way, we'd stop outside a pub and the men would go inside while I stayed in the car and they'd bring something out for me.

One time, I was allowed to sit in the front seat, but a little lad ran out in front of the car. I made a grab for the steering wheel, trying to avoid an accident, but it was okay because Mr Travis had got everything in hand. Dad shouted at me for doing such a daft thing, but Mr Travis wasn't upset. He just said: 'It's alright, Will. Everything is alright.'

Mr Travis sometimes couldn't get into a higher gear, so he'd stop the car and try again! I understand that the car would have to have been going at a certain speed before a gear change could be made and, in addition, he had to double declutch. Also, at that time, there were no electrical windscreen wipers and Mr

Travis had to move his by hand through a lever inside the windscreen! That was very tiring and, as soon as he stopped to rest his arm, the windscreen was covered with rain! So it wasn't very satisfactory.

Mother was almost compelled to shop with Mr Travis because he gave us these occasional free rides and was Uncle Mo's father-in-law. But the meat he sold was tough and he bullied his customers by talking in a raised voice. If someone had missed buying from him for a day or two, he'd want to know why! But he wasn't all bad because I believe he gave some of his meat away free to very poor people.

The school encouraged the pupils to save money through a scheme enabling us to buy National Savings Certificates. At the time, a certificate cost sixteen shillings, which was a large amount, and, of course, no pupil had that kind of sum at any one time. So we could buy a sixpenny stamp and were issued with a card to stick it in. On filling the card with 32 sixpences, we'd get a sixteen shillings' certificate. I was one of the few "rich" children because I usually bought one or two stamps a week. For the poorest children, the sixpenny square on the card was divided into six squares so they could save odd pennies. The spaces were marked off by Mr Burgess, the teacher in charge of savings, and, when six spaces had been filled, the kids would get a sixpenny stamp. Heaven only knows how long it would take some of them to get a certificate and I would think most of them gave up.

I was pretty careful with my pocket money and must have accumulated quite a bit. I didn't know where to put it, but I was impressed with what Mr Burgess said about the savings certificates, so I started putting money regularly towards them. He gave me the job of going around the different classes to collect the money in and I also went to Cobridge Post Office, in Elder Road, to get the certificates when enough had been saved. I bought my first certificate on 12 March 1928 and its number was H27839789 in the third issue. I saved up enough to buy three more before I left school.

One of Mother's sisters, Aunt Hannah, was married to Jack Palin, who, I believe, came from Newcastle upon Tyne and was a foreman mechanic at Brown's Buses in Scotia Road, Burslem. They lived with their two sons, Aubrey and Stan, at 1 Hunt Street, Tunstall, but later moved to 6 Summerbank Road, a new semi-detached house, about half a mile away. We had quite a lot to do with their family and they invited us for tea on Sundays and to Christmas parties. I really enjoyed myself, especially since there were two lads to play with. At Christmas, Aubrey and I would supply the music, playing popular tunes of the time from sheet music. I'd play the piano and he'd be on the violin. To get there, we'd take a bus or tram. It was a thrill riding on the tram, although the bus was more modern. We got on at the corner of Waterloo Road and Cobridge Road. The stop was called North Road, but I don't know why because that street was nearly half a mile away.

When I was about twelve, the lads in my class at school had to take woodwork classes at Moorland Road County Junior School, in Burslem. We had to make our own way there, by bus, tram or train, if we could afford it, or by walking if not, because there was no school bus supplied. A few of us went by train from Waterloo Road Station and got off at Burslem Station, which was quite close to the school. The journey was quite exciting, but dangerous and, on one occasion, the last lad onto the train accidentally slammed the door onto Billy Anett's thumb!

Billy yelled and we opened the door really quickly. His thumb was flat, but, by a miracle, it had not burst or broken.

One of the woodwork teachers was named Mr Wallace, who was a big fellow and rather abrupt. During one session, he called me over and said I'd stolen a chisel off his bench. I denied that, so he clouted me across my jaw. I couldn't close my mouth properly for weeks and I think I must have had a slightly dislocated jaw. He must have got worried because, after playtime, he came to me and said he knew who'd taken the chisel, but I think he'd misplaced the tool.

On occasions, I used to go with my parents to Trentham Park, which I thought was wonderful. We used to travel on the bus or the train to Trentham Park Station, which was at the Hemheath side of Stone Road, near the end of a branch splitting off from the main line just before Trentham Station. Both stations are now demolished. The line was going to be extended to Newcastle, but it never got that far. A bridge was built over Stone Road, but the track only went a few yards further on.

I loved to wander in the park, where the springy turf allowed my feet to sink in. We'd take sandwiches with us or buy some and a cup of tea from a wooden refreshment house near to the entrance. Afterwards, we'd climb up the hill through the ferns, which were waist high. At the top, we saw a herd of deer to our left more than once and straight ahead was Jacob's Ladder. This was a series of wooden steps, about seven feet high, placed either side of the boundary wall, that you could climb to get onto the road to Eccleshall. Along the road, you could get to Beech Caves.

Around that time, Dad and Mother bought me two pairs of boxing gloves as a present. I didn't use them a lot, though I had a spar or two with Dad. Uncle Mo and Dad used them one day in our back kitchen to do a bit of sparring, but Mo lost his temper and started hitting out hard at Dad, who shouted at him to go steady. I was watching them with some apprehension, but they took off the gloves and made friends. Some time later, I was bought a punchball, which was fixed in the doorway of my bedroom so that I could have a knock when I wished. I also had a small-sized billiard table, which fitted on top of the kitchen table. It was a novelty at first, but then I lost interest, perhaps because I wasn't a very good player.

The Deep Pit in Hanley supplied Shelton Bar with coal by railway trucks. The track ran from the pit off High Street (which was later renamed Town Road), through an area of rough ground called the "Hollies" and across Waterloo Road between Portland Street and Mulgrave Street. It then went under Brook Street (which later became Century Street), across Cobridge Road, just before its junction with Etruria Road, and into the far side of Shelton Bar. There was a path from Windermere Street going across the track to Portland Street and we could wander along the line for quite a distance because there was no fencing. A time or two, when an engine was coming, with perhaps thirty trucks behind it, we put nails on the line to see what would happen. Of course, the nails didn't stop the engine, but the train flattened them to almost paper thinness.

At the end of Windermere Street was a lot of spare ground we could play on, which stretched to Cobridge Road, Portland Street, Rutland Street and Brook Street. On some of the ground were allotments, pigsties, stables and other temporary constructions. At the Brook Street end was the remains of an old church, made of wood supports and corrugated iron sheets. The timber was in great local demand for firewood and some people requisitioned it for their home fires. However, they weren't very careful because they pulled away vital supports and so part of the church fell on top of them, hurting one or two of them!

In front of the church was a pond and beyond that a football pitch, where Cobridge Alexandra played. Dad was their manager and they wore red shirts and white shorts. Uncle Mo was, I think, their centre-forward and Dad said he might have made a pretty good player, but, when he went for trials at some semi-professional clubs, he became greedy and asked too much for expenses, so they didn't ask him back.

One goal was right in front of the pool and, when anyone shot at the goal, the ball usually landed in the water because there weren't any nets to stop it. Also, the goalposts had to be dismantled after every match in case the wood-requisitioning people got their hands on them! Of course, the sockets that the posts went into were usually filled with bricks and stones by the next match by the local hooligans!

On the other side of the football pitch was Holden Lane (which was later renamed Edgware Street), but there were no houses on it. At that time, Mulgrave Street only went as far along as Windermere Street, but it was later extended to join Cobridge Road. Beyond Holden Lane, there was a fair-sized area of allotments, which stretched up to Derwent Street.

My uncle, George Wallett, his wife, Ada, and their three children lived in Cobridge Road, just below Burslem Cricket Club. There was a story that Aunt Ada asked a next-door neighbour to take all the food out of their pantry. It seems the idea was that Aunt was then intending to go to the police to tell them that Uncle George was starving her and their children, so that he'd be prosecuted. Apparently, the neighbour refused and so Uncle was saved. He was a nice fellow, as were all the male Walletts, but he was meek and browbeaten by Aunt Ada.

Uncle Fred Wallett bought a horse and a flat truck and went out around the streets trying to sell coal. I went with him once and we got as far as Tunstall. It seemed ages getting there because we only travelled at walking pace. The horse was kept in a stable in a building across the back entry from the Black Boy pub. I don't think this venture lasted very long.

I went with my cousin, Aubrey, to Tunstall Baths a few times. Once, when I was about twelve, a couple of bigger lads caught hold of me and were going to throw me into the pool. I was terrified I was going to drown, so I shouted at them to put me down as I couldn't swim. After a while, they let go of me, much to my relief. Another time, somebody tried to duck my head under the water and, unfortunately, I didn't learn to swim at that time because I was scared of the water.

One day around then, Aubrey got a couple of fags out of his pocket, which he said he'd had out of his father's cigarette box. When darkness came, we went to a space next to the Gospel Mission, with some matches, and lit up. I then saw someone and whispered, 'Hey up, a man's coming,' so we hid the cigarettes behind our backs until he'd gone. I didn't care much for the taste of the tobacco, so, after a few puffs, I threw the cigarette down and put my foot on it, and Aubrey did the same.

Aunt Hannah had a black and white cat called Bingo, which she gave to us, and I had the job of going to get it. It was put in a cardboard box and I took it home on the bus with very little trouble. It used to jump on our shoulders, from a standing start, while we stood up! At different times, we also had a couple of pups, a tortoise, a white mouse and a canary.

Mother and Dad gave me a great, thick hardback *Chums 1927-8* book for my birthday or as a present for Christmas. It was a weekly magazine for boys that the publisher had bound together. It was 832 pages long and had all kinds of adventure stories, information and tuition on how to do things, like box and compete in athletics. It also had illustrations and some of them were in colour, so it must have cost quite a lot. It was a great gift because it was just what I wanted and I was into reading then. I really took a fancy to it and in later years, even when I was middle-aged, I used to get it out from time to time and have a read of it. It was my favourite book and it's still one of my favourites now.

A bit later, I had *Grimms' Fairy Tales*, which was fantasy and out of this world, but the pages of the book kept coming loose. I also had a copy of Hans Christian Andersen's tales, which were intriguing and it was amazing what the imagination had brought up. I particularly remember the story of *The Emperor's New Clothes*, in which a ruler was kidded into buying an "invisible" new outfit and parading naked in front of his people as a result, but nobody dared say anything until a child cried out that the emperor had no clothes on. I read both books from time to time and occasionally much later.

I was still having my piano lessons from Miss Trigg and, in March 1929, I took a Junior Division exam in Pianoforte Playing with Trinity College of Music, London. The college was famous and people were singing its praises at that time. The exam was held in Gordon Chambers, in Cheapside, Hanley. I walked there on my own and I was nervous. A piano was set up and the examiner told me to play one or two pieces of music, but my hands were sweating and my fingers stuck to the keys as I played. I must have done pretty well, though, because I passed with honours.

I was in Teddy Anett's house one day, when I was about thirteen, and he told me that he listened to dance music. He switched on the wireless and on came, I think, Jack Payne's dance band. I liked the music so much that whenever I got the chance, I listened to the programme myself.

As well as listening to the wireless, I started going to the pictures in Hanley, largely on my own because I liked my own company. I gave up Cobridge Picture Hall and mainly went to the Capitol, in New Street (later renamed Goodson Street), and the Empire, which was between Brunswick Street and Trinity Street, where the shopping arcade is now. The front rows of the Capitol were right against the screen and you had to lift your head right up to see! These were cheap seats, which I went in sometimes.

I mainly went to see slapstick films and anything with adventure, especially Westerns, but I avoided romantic films till I got older. At first, the pictures were all silent, with the words of the actors printed at the bottom of the screen and it was a nuisance to have to read them while I was trying to follow the action.

During the films, there was always somebody playing an instrument at the side of the screen or in an orchestra pit. Depending on the class of the cinema, there might be a pianist or a small orchestra making background music to accompany the film. They played according to what was happening on the screen and they were experts at it. They'd play fast and loud if there was action, but soft and low if something romantic was happening. If there was an explosion, they'd bang out the lower notes! I didn't think much about it because it was just part of the setup at that time.

I particularly enjoyed Laurel and Hardy and laughed at them and their expressions. They were silly, but they had the touch. Hardy was a bully and Laurel was his stooge and they made comedy out of that. They got themselves in tangles in the films and I remember them making such a mess of trying to get a piano up a lot of steps to a house in their 1932 movie, *The Music Box*.

I also liked Buster Keaton, who was famous for his stunts on the top of high buildings. What intrigued me was the amount of traffic that could be seen down below in the streets, which was much more than exists in Stoke-on-Trent today!

I didn't go for Charlie Chaplin much because how he shuffled around and twiddled his stick was very exaggerated and didn't seem right. There were no real characters around like that.

In June 1929, I took another Trinity College music exam at Gordon Chambers, this time in The Theory of Music. Again I went on my own and I think I took a written exam, but I can't remember it. Once more, I passed with honours and on that occasion it was in the Advanced Junior Division.

I started going to see films at The Regent, in Piccadilly, Hanley, which had opened in February. It was a lovely place, posh and all up to date. There, in July, I saw the first talkie to be shown in The Potteries, which was *The Singing Fool*, starring Al Jolson. It was marvellous to hear the voices of the actors and I didn't have to spend time reading the subtitles! The other thing I remember about the film was the song, *Sonny Boy*, sung by Jolson, which was sentimental and pretty catchy.

A cousin of Aunt Cissie, named May Travis, used to visit her at times from one of the villages outside the city. She wore glasses and her hair had a pigtail style. She liked me a lot and kept coming after me, but I didn't really like it. Mother looked on her favourably, but it was considered sissy for a lad to have a girlfriend at that age.

About 1929, Mother, Dad and I had a week's holiday on the Isle of Man. It was exciting, but the crossing from Liverpool was rough and, being inexperienced at sea, we were below deck, feeling seasick. After suffering for a couple of hours, I staggered up on deck, where I immediately started to feel better, with the cool sea breezes blowing in my face. When I'd found my sea legs, I went below to look for my parents. They hadn't moved from where I'd left them and they were feeling very sorry for themselves. That was understandable because the atmosphere was clammy and the stench of vomit nearly made me feel nauseous again. I managed to persuade them it was much better on deck and, after they'd been on top for a while, they agreed!

I remember that crossing much more clearly than the holiday itself, although I know we stayed bed and breakfast in Douglas, the main town. The only other thing I recall is that I loved riding on the horse-drawn trams along the promenade, which were a real novelty.

Grandad Wallett had a bicycle, which he said was a racer, but it didn't look like one. It had upright handlebars and wheels which I think were made of bamboo cane. The brake in the hub of the back wheel was operated by pedalling slightly backwards! A normal brake was added on the front wheel, but you had to be careful with it because the brake blocks operating on the non-slip wooden rims caused the wheels to lock and tended to throw you over the handlebars! When I was about thirteen, I asked Grandad if I could borrow the bike, even though I couldn't ride one. At first, I used it like a scooter by putting one foot on a pedal and pushing along with the other foot. Grandad then came with me and steadied the bike while I learned to balance and, after a while, I was able to go out on my own.

Along Belmont Road, in Etruria, was a place where bicycles could be hired out. I went along there once with some lad to have a look at them. They were ramshackle, but we paid for one hour's ride and off we went. The brakes on my bike were poor and I found out, after a few minutes, that one of the tyres was flat, so we went back to the owner, who pumped it up. Then off we went again, only to find that it went flat again shortly afterwards, so we returned to the owner once more. This went on all through the hour and I wasn't very happy about the situation, but the owner gave me and my pal an extra half an hour free!

At that time, a lot of the roads in Stoke-on-Trent were made of cobblestones, which gave a joggy ride, especially if you were on a push-bike. Also, the grids were badly laid out because the spaces in between the bars ran parallel with the roads and so cyclists had to be careful not to run their wheels in and get thrown off. Eventually, new grids were fixed that ran at right angles or semi-right angles, which solved the problem.

There was a greyhound racing stadium in Sun Street, Hanley, and in 1929 the owners made a cinder track inside it for speedway. On the opposite side of the road was a dirt tip, which I climbed, along with other people, to look down at the motorbikes racing and see what was going on. If I remember rightly, the track owners used to shine searchlights into the faces of these non-payers! One of the riders who raced there was the famous daredevil, "Skid" Skinner, but I wasn't very impressed by the sport because when you'd seen one race, the others looked very much alike.

Dad had injured a knee playing football and it had left him with a kneecap which came out of place on odd occasions as he walked along. When this happened, he had to stop and pull his foot and leg right up behind him to get his kneecap back into position. One day, it occurred when he was in the middle of a road and he had to hop across to the pavement to fix his knee! In those days, we had quite regular fogs and one tea time there was a peasouper – you could hardly see a hand in front of you. Mother and I were expecting Dad home from work and he was late. I started worrying about him and thought his kneecap might have come out of place as he was crossing one of the busy roads and that a bus, not spotting him, might have knocked him down. As time went on, I was getting frantic with worry, but then he came in through the back door. I've never been so glad to see anyone as I was on this occasion!

One Monday, one of Dad's workmates said he was broke and asked Dad if he could lend him a shilling till the Friday when he'd be paid. Dad handed the shilling over and, sure enough, the loan was repaid on time. But the following Monday, Dad's workmate borrowed the shilling again and paid it back on the Friday. This arrangement went on for several weeks till Dad told the fellow: 'Keep it. It's more in your possession than mine!'

Dad told me a story about a youth when he'd been a young man. The youth released the brakes on several railway trucks, which crashed at the bottom of an incline. Fearing the consequences, he went straight away to the local army recruiting centre and volunteered to join up. Because he'd done so, the police decided not to arrest him and considered that serving with the colours instead would be sufficient punishment! The army was then thought to be very lowlife.

The last year at school was called class eight and its teacher, Mr Burgess, was good and strict. The class was divided into three parts. The top part had only two children in it, a boy and a girl. The next section had a few more children in it and I was one of them. We had a certain amount of work to do and, when that had been done, we could do more or less what we liked, provided that we were quiet. That left Mr Burgess with just the third part of the class to deal with.

He was also the sports master for the boys. He played with us a game that we called rugby. We ran, holding a football, to try and score in a goal, which was part of the playground wall. There was no throwing anyone on the Tarmac surface, of course, and we just tried to stop an opponent by holding onto him. It was good to grab Mr Burgess' jacket as he ran past with the ball.

The best footballer at the school at that time was no doubt "Nobby" (Freddie) Steele, who went on to become a famous Stoke City and England centre-forward. Also, there was talk of him being very good at the long jump, but he was a little younger than me and I don't remember him from school.

At the back of Burslem cricket ground was a very large area, called Macalonie or the Grange, where all the kids from Cobridge used to play, go for walks and explore. It was a wonderful place. It stretched from the back of Cobridge Road and the rear of Waterloo Road to Middleport and Wolstanton and bordered on Shelton Bar. Our entrance to it was down from the cricket ground at the end of a row of terraced houses. The end house was a shop that sold sweets and ice cream and must have done good business because there was always someone walking on Macalonie.

Along the path, on the left-hand side, were always some parked railway trucks at the end of a siding that led to Shelton Bar. The lads would go over to the trucks, open up the grease boxes, get out a handful of grease and fool about with it. When we stood by the side of these wagons, they towered above us.

Just past there were fields with lovely long grass in them and some of them contained horses. I saw larks hovering above and there we tried to catch butterflies and bees with our jackets, by throwing them on the insects when they settled. It was alright rolling our jackets back and bagging the butterflies, but, when we tried to pick up a bee that appeared dead, it would give us a nasty sting.

The path then forked, with the right branch leading to the back of Waterloo Road and the left towards Wolstanton. A short way along the latter path was a lovely country cottage and on the left was a field, which ran down to Shelton Colliery. Later, pylons were erected that took buckets of coal waste overhead and tipped it on the bottom of the field, which ended up as a huge waste tip.

The path from there went downhill and towards the bottom was a pond, which had frogspawn and "Jack Sharp" fish in it. I don't know the correct name of the fish, but we called them that because of their quick movement. I made a fishing rod out of a stick, a piece of string and a bent pin, but I never caught anything with that contraption. I did, however, manage to scoop a fish or two out with my hand and put them in a jam jar to take home. I also collected some frogspawn and took that home too.

Further along, the path went under a mineral railway bridge and then went over the Trent and Mersey Canal on a footbridge, which was used as a diving platform for young swimmers! The water was warmed by waste liquid from Shelton Bar, which polluted the canal. On a nice summer's day, quite a few lads took part in the swimming, some of them in the nude, but I wasn't one of them because I hadn't learned to swim. There were also a few spectators, who acted as lookouts for canal officials. Apparently, as soon as the warning was given, the "criminals" would be out of the water in a flash, grab their clothes and run off, although I never saw this happen myself.

Just beyond the canal was a railway embankment, which carried trucks containing molten slag from the furnaces at Shelton Bar. The bodies of the trucks contained very strong metal buckets, which swivelled so that they tipped sideways, emptying their red-hot contents down the side of the embankment. The molten slag usually dropped out in one huge lump and came to rest dangerously close to the towpath, with some bits finishing up in the water with a big hiss. When they tipped there during darkness, we could see the glow in the sky from Windermere Street! At times, the slag was reluctant to come out of the trucks and workmen would have to bang on the containers with sledgehammers to release it. When the containers swivelled to empty their load, the weight lifted the opposite wheels of the trucks off the track a few inches and it seemed to me that it only needed a bit heavier load to tip all the lot down the embankment!

The path on the far side of the embankment led up to Wolstanton and I walked it a time or two. It went under the main railway line between Etruria and Longport and then up a steep hill.

While I was playing with some lads in a field in Macalonie, we were being watched by two men. They came over and accused us of doing damage, which we denied. They looked like detectives and asked us for our names and addresses. I was afraid of being taken to court, but we never heard any more and I suppose they were trying to frighten us off.

On 5 October 1929, Trinity College presented certificates and prizes at the Victoria Hall, Hanley, to those pupils who'd passed its exams over the past year at its local centre in Cheapside. The Stoke-on-Trent Lord Mayor, W. T. Leason, was the chairman of the proceedings, which started at 2.30, and the college principal, Stanley Roper, gave a talk. My name was listed in the programme for my achievements in passing both the practical and musical knowledge exams, but I can't remember anything about the occasion! My parents were very pleased with my success, especially as they'd forked out a lot of money for my piano, and so we must have been there. The programme cost threepence and I've still got it.

One night, when I was about thirteen, we heard a cooing noise, so Dad went outside to check it and saw two pigeons perched on the back kitchen roof. He expected them to fly away, but they kept still. He got out a pair of steps, climbed partway up, put his hand up to the birds and stroked them and they still didn't fly away. They must have been exhausted from flying a long way. Dad asked me, 'Shall we keep them?' and I said right away, 'Yes!' He then wedged a stick between the walls of the coal house and put the pigeons on this perch. We bought some pigeon corn and fed them and then closed the door for the night. When I went to bed, I could hardly go to sleep for excitement!

We fed the birds the next morning and then opened the coal house door, allowing them to fly out. Dad said: 'They won't come back again. They'll go back to their own home.'

But, after a while, they returned and landed on top of our house and we coaxed them back in the coal house with more pigeon corn. Dad told me that they were tippler pigeons and I noticed that they had an unusual flight because every now and then they would tumble, or tipple, downwards for a short distance. I can't remember how long we kept them or what happened to them, but there was some talk about the landlord not liking tenants keeping pigeons because they were supposed to peck all the cement out from between the bricks, which may have been untrue.

Dad bought a bellows-type camera from Uncle Ted, which could be pushed into its own case and closed up, and was small enough to be put in a large pocket. It was a quarter-sized plate camera and, instead of using a roll of film, a glass plate was slid in at the back of the camera. It was quite good, but I was never told properly how to use it and my results were limited.

Dad showed me how to develop and print my own films. After the plates had been exposed, I took them into a dark room, the pantry, which was lit by a dim red light because a white light would have ruined the images. I then put them in a celluloid dish containing liquid developer. The dish was shaken gently and, after a while, an image would appear on the plate. When I considered the image had formed sufficiently, I put the plate in another dish, which contained a fixing liquid. After this, I washed the plate under the tap and stood it on its end to dry. When dry, I put the plate in a kind of picture frame, in the dark room, with a sheet of printing paper on top of it and then fixed on the back of the frame. Then, depending on the type of frame I was using, I either held it in front of a gaslight or took it outside and held it towards the light. Afterwards, I took the frame into the dark room and put the print in a dish of hypo, which fixed the image on the print. I also learned how to mask a print, which was to cut out parts of the image.

Each year, when Armistice Day, 11 November, was a weekday, the lads at school used to say, 'I wonder if Burgess will tell us a war story.' He usually did, without glamorizing things because he'd been in action himself. In those days, two minutes' silence was always held nationwide at eleven o'clock and Mr Burgess would finish his story a few seconds beforehand. The class would fall silent, awaiting the sound of the pottery works' buzzers, which signalled the commencement of the official silence. All the traffic stopped, all machinery was switched off (excepting absolutely essential things) and people stopped in the streets. It was a dramatic time, but, after two minutes, the buzzers blew again and we all went back to our normal work.

When I came in the house one day, I found several rolls of wallpaper lying around and Mother busy with a pair of scissors. It seems that wallpaper those days had about half an inch of waste on each side and so one side or both had to be cut off the length of the roll in order for the pattern to be matched. It was a laborious job and, if you removed both waste edges, but cut into the pattern, it would leave a gap when the two pieces were placed together. To prevent that, most people only cut off one side of the waste, but then the cut edge had to be pasted on the waste part of the adjoining piece of paper. That made a double thickness, which didn't look very good. Mother asked me to help, so I started cutting away, but it took me ages to finish a roll and it wasn't very straight at that!

One Saturday afternoon, a couple of youths from Dad's works knocked on our door and told him that he'd won the first prize in a raffle that had been held at the firm. He'd come home before the draw had been made and so they brought the prize to him in a box. When they opened it, an Angora rabbit was inside. Dad and Mother weren't very pleased, but I was! There was some talk in the family about getting wool off the rabbit to make a pullover eventually, but Dad later gave the animal to Jack Pinner, one of the youths who'd brought it to him.

As Christmas approached, when I was thirteen or so, I joined a Christmas club run by one of the Grittons' daughters and, for a number of years, gave my custom to her. I'd borrow a catalogue from her and feast my eyes on the pictures of all the mouth-watering chocolates that were on offer. After a couple of days, I'd choose something modest that I wanted and could afford. I'd then take the catalogue back and pay a penny or so, which would be recorded on a card that I kept. Every so often, I'd make another small payment until I'd paid up and then at last I would be given my chocolates, which I'd put on one side until Christmas Day. It was really exciting!

On 14 December 1929, I became fourteen and left school for good the next Friday, the 20th, when I was presented with my Leaving Certificate. It was pretty good and even Mr Wallace, the woodwork teacher, wrote that I was, 'A very sensible & capable boy.' The headmaster, Mr Thorley, put in his remarks that I was 'a sharp, intelligent boy . . . always interested in his work . . . well behaved & can be relied on to serve with truthfulness & fidelity.'

When I left school, I was confused because I was no longer a child and Dad told me that Uncle Ted had fixed me up with a job at the pottery factory of Josiah Wedgwood and Sons Limited, in Etruria. So I was about to go to work, which I realized would be very different, and I didn't know what to think about it.

In the middle of all that, on 16 December, the R-100 British airship flew right above us in Cobridge. It was on a trial flight and what a sight it was! It was a huge cigar-shaped thing sliding noiselessly overhead. Everybody came out to have a look at it and to compare it with the German zeppelin that had flown over during the Great War. It was very unusual to see aircraft at that time and, when any did appear, people rushed outside to have a look. Only a few years before, people had used to dash out to see a motorcar go past!

2 Perspiring In The Pot Banks

I started work for the very first time after Christmas in 1929, probably on Monday 30 December. Overall, I was glad to have got the job at Wedgwood's because some of the local lads weren't able to find work. The Wall Street Crash had taken place two months earlier and trade began to slow down, so fewer workers were needed and things became grim. Eventually, there was high unemployment worldwide.

Dad told me I was to be an apprentice turner. I'd be following in his footsteps because turning was his trade, but he turned electrical porcelain insulators and I was to turn cups. I had to report to the factory in Etruria at the unearthly hour of eight o'clock and so I called on Uncle Ted and my cousin, Sam, on the way because I'd be working with them in the earthenware department. We walked down Lord Street and over the canal bridge to arrive at the factory on the right-hand side. Uncle was the head handler of the department, who stuck handles and spouts on pots and was a talented worker. Sam was an apprentice. My weekly wages were to be fourteen shillings, which were two shillings more than an ordinary lad, without relatives to influence the boss, would get. That was, I suppose, a favour to Uncle Ted and, of course, it was paid in cash. Mother said I could keep one shilling and sixpence for pocket money out of my wages.

In those days, you had to supply your own tools and protective clothes, so Mother had bought me a white jacket and apron to wear, to shield my clothes from the clay dust. At first I worked in short trousers, the same ones I'd worn at school, and I had to wear them out before Mother bought me a pair of long flannel trousers some months later.

Uncle Ted showed me how to clock on and then we went to see the foreman of the department, Billy Jenks, with whom he used to go out drinking. Mr Jenks took me to see an apprentice, Eric Weller, working. He'd been there a couple of years and, for a while, I watched how things were done, did an errand or two, familiarized myself with the surroundings and had a word with Uncle Ted and Sam. Eric tried to take the mickey out of me by asking me to get a barrow full of steam, but that was too silly a request for anyone to fall for. Then he told me to pass him the dog hook, so I smiled, thinking it was another daft demand. But there really was a dog hook tool, which was a heavy cast-iron hook that was bent over at the top and held the lathe spindle while the chock was removed or tightened. A chock was a block of wood shaped to fit inside a cup.

Mr Jenks then took me to a bench where there was a lathe for turning. He demonstrated how to use it and then ordered me to try my hand. The lathe was operated by a foot treadle. When the treadle was pressed, the lathe reversed and when the treadle was released, the lathe turned forward. A cup was placed on the chock and, with the lathe in reverse, the cup was trued with the fingers of both hands. The lathe was then turned forward and a cutting tool shaved the bottom of the cup. After that, a foot, a kind of extra bottom, was wet and rubbed on a flat stone, to make it flat and stick. Then it was placed on the bottom of the cup and was slid around until it ran true. The foot served no practical purpose, but was for extra decoration. Unfortunately, the foot often stuck to the cup before it could be trued and so the whole thing would have to be thrown away. But that was still the easiest kind of cup to process.

I must have looked awkward working right-handed and, when I told Mr Jenks, as he was watching me, that I was left-handed, he wasn't very pleased. He said, 'I didn't know that!' Anyway, I must have made an improvement because I kept my job and went on to turn other shapes of cups.

We turners made our own tools from pieces of sheet mild steel supplied by the firm, often already cut down to convenient sizes. We had a bench that we'd make them on and we'd put the sheet in a vice to enable more pressure to be exerted when shaping it. Then we'd file it down to suit the shape we wanted the cup or foot to be. After a while, the tool would wear out, so we'd fasten another piece of shaped steel to the end of it. But, eventually, even that would wear out, so we'd then have to start again and make a completely new tool.

The end of the working week came at one o'clock on Saturday and, to knock the clay dust out, I gave my white coat and apron a beating on a special post, which was set in the ground outside. I then rolled up my clothes and took them to Mother to wash. I found out that Wedgwood's had bathrooms in the factory for the workers, so I started to use them and they were really good. So there were no more zinc baths in the living room for me – instead, it was the luxury of a real bath, with hot running water! I think that was the first time I'd ever used a proper bath and it only cost a copper or two. It was a wonderful idea of the company and I never came across the facility at any other firm.

When the factory had been built, it had been level with the Trent and Mersey Canal, which ran alongside it. But the factory had slowly sunk owing to subsidence and, by the time I got there, there seemed to be about a ten-feet difference in the level between them. But it didn't matter much because the ware by then was being moved out by road. Nevertheless, the factory was more modern than most of those in the Potteries because the old buildings had been knocked down or modernized. Also, there was less dust about where I worked because there wasn't a lot of clay to cut off the cups compared with that from other items, like heavy insulators, which were manufactured in the city. The factory was well and fairly pleasantly laid out and I think I had a window to look through. The firm was pretty go-ahead, with some of the machine operations and all the lights powered by electricity.

After working for about three months, the firm told me to stop at home until they sent for me. Unemployment was still rising and I understand that there were few orders. I didn't receive any dole or other payment, so Dad had to keep me again. I then just mucked around at home, but, after a few weeks, I had my recall.

That year, 1930, was the bicentenary of the birth of the renowned Josiah Wedgwood, the company's founder, and the firm celebrated it with an open-air show in Hanley Park, amongst other things. In the park, scenes from the old days were enacted and I took a very minor role in them. I went to the firm's stores and was issued with my costume, which consisted of a potters' placer's shirt and a pair of ladies' blue bloomers, representing knickerbockers! I didn't have much to do, but was involved in the crowd scenes and was told that I was on a news film being shown at the pictures. Apparently, I was briefly seen walking at the back of a group in one scene, but I never saw the film myself. I think the bicentenary was important in bringing orders in and Uncle Ted told me that Cadbury's had placed a big order for mugs, to be given away in a publicity stunt.

The firm employed someone to test that the handles were fired onto the cups firmly. That was done by striking the handles with a mallet. After a while, the losses were reduced, so the tester got into trouble for not hitting the handles hard enough!

Billy Jenks and his friend, Fred Ellis, the mould makers' manager, got jobs in Spain and so I didn't see them again. I was informed that Mr Jenks had been given the sack for fiddling. He was replaced as the foreman by Harry Longshaw and I soon got into trouble with him. I wanted him to count and record some cups I'd made, but he was walking away from me, so I gave him a whistle! He ignored me, so I had to go after him and he told me, 'Don't whistle me like a dog!' I hadn't meant to be offensive, but I suppose I deserved the rebuke.

Sam Kent decided to get a racing bike, so I had his old one, a Raleigh Tourer, and I suppose Mother and Dad paid for it. It was a good bike, but maybe on the heavy side. It was very exciting having a bike of my own, a bigger thrill than when I eventually bought my own car, and it meant I didn't have to walk to work any more. It was great freewheeling down Cobridge Road in the mornings, but, on the return journey, it was hard going upbank.

One day, I was cycling on a dirt track, known as Holden Lane, which started opposite Burslem cricket ground and ran down to Portland Street. A young man approached me and asked if he could borrow my bike because he was late for an appointment. I was dubious about lending it to him, but he seemed genuine, so I let him have it! He said he'd be back in half an hour, but, as soon as he'd gone, I thought to myself what a fool I'd been. As time went by, I became increasingly apprehensive, but he turned up more or less on time. He thanked me and said he'd arrived on time for his appointment. I was just overjoyed to get my bike back!

On another occasion, I decided to go on a bike run to Rudyard with Uncle Mo. He borrowed Grandad Wallett's bamboo-wheeled bike, but, when we got to around Dunwood, we got too close to each other and one of his pedals caught the spokes of my front wheel and ripped a few of them out. That put my bike out of action and it looked as if I had a long walk home coming. So I lifted the damaged end up and started wheeling the bike down the road. We got to the Black Horse Garage at Endon, where I intended to leave it to be repaired, but the mechanic said he'd put new spokes in for a shilling there and then. I didn't have any money with me, but I borrowed it off Mo and so had the job done. We then decided not to continue to Rudyard and made our way home.

Mo had to wait some days for repayment while I got the cash together. I think he was annoyed because he was short of money, but I didn't want Mother and Dad to know about my debt because if I'd borrowed from them, it would have made them short.

When the fancy took me, I went to watch Stoke with Dad and we stood on the Stoke End, behind the goal, about halfway back. I remember Bobby Archibald, a little fellow with bow legs, who caught the eye with his dribbling, but fiddled about on the left wing. There was also Bob McGrory, who was a solid, hard-working defender. He looked dour and Stoke's opponents could hardly get past him.

Dad used to have *John Bull* magazine fairly regularly and I used to read it. It had all kinds of interesting things in. It advertised books for sale and sometimes one would take my fancy, so I'd order it through the post. One I bought was

Wonders of the World, which was 744 pages long and had a lot of photographs of marvellous places that existed. I've still got it.

Around that time, *John Bull* had an offer on for a blue box camera, so I acquired one. The camera was very simple. It was just a box, with a single shutter speed and an attachment for taking close-ups. This was a piece of glass, which was screwed into the box and swivelled down in front of the lens. The back of the camera opened up, to enable a roll of film to be inserted. I used it whenever I felt like buying a film, but the results weren't very good. I suppose the camera was alright, but the photographer wasn't very experienced!

Billy and Teddy Anett's father had an allotment at the rear of Mulgrave Street and Teddy told me that they'd bought a spade from F. W. Woolworth & Co. Ltd., 7-9 Upper Market Square. I could hardly believe him because there was nothing sold in the store at that time for more than sixpence. It was well known as a threepenny and sixpenny store, but Teddy said that the handle and the blade had been bought separately for sixpence each, so the total cost had been a shilling.

A lot of Hanley's adolescents used to parade up and down Piccadilly and Brunswick Street on Sunday evenings and I went along with some of my Cobridge mates to join in quite a few times. In the early thirties, it was fashionable for youths to wear cloth caps and so I decided to get one from George Chawner, the outfitter's, at 70-76 Hope Street. I tried several on and stood in front of a mirror posing till I found a cap I liked. The following Sunday, I was there, with my big hat, set at a rakish angle in the contemporary style, flaunting it like a peacock, but I don't think I wore it for very long.

One day, Mother told me to go to Aunt Hannah's and collect a pup. A married couple she knew had bought the animal for their youngster, but the man was out of work and, when the pup had reached six months and needed a dog licence, he found he couldn't afford it. Even at that time, it was the tidy sum of 7s. 6d. So he decided to give the pup away rather than risk being prosecuted by the police.

I was very excited and, inside their house, I was greeted by the most beautiful pup I'd ever seen. She was a bundle of white fluff, with brown-tipped ears and a brown nose. She kept jumping up as high as my shoulder as if to demonstrate how pleased she was to see me. Her name was Floss and what joy we were to have with her in the years ahead. I quickly got her home and she ran all over the house to familiarize herself with things. She soon settled in and followed me everywhere. Mother and Dad were also delighted with our new possession, but I wonder what heartache Floss' previous owners must have felt in losing her.

I took Floss for runs, mainly in Macalonie, and had great fun with her. I trained her to 'Stay' and, on the command, she would whimper and shuffle about. I'd then go a long distance, sometimes out of sight, and shout, 'Come on!' She'd run like lightning, with great excitement, till she found me and then jump up nearly shoulder high! I played the same game with her at home, sending her up to the top of the stairs and then hiding, but she always found me.

Once, she stopped and rolled on some soft dog muck in Macalonie. I tried to clean her up with handfuls of grass, but that wasn't much use. Then I thought it would help to get her in the canal, but I didn't want to handle her and have my hands covered in muck. I was also worried that, if I threw her in, she might drown. So I told her to stay on one side of the canal while I went, over the bridge, to the other side, some distance away. Then, when I was opposite her, I called her to come to me and expected her to jump into the water. Instead, she took the long way round, over the bridge, and rejoined me on the other side! There was nothing more I could do, so we wandered back home, where Mother had the horrible job of getting her clean. Even now, I can remember the look on Mother's face!

Wedgwood's ran a rail trip to London one day, so Dad and Uncle Ted took Sam and me on it. We visited all the usual sights and went into a big store, where we had a ride on its moving staircases (escalators). I'd never seen any before and when I got home and told the lads about this wonderful experience, none of them believed me!

A strange incident occurred when we were outside one of the foreign embassies. A crank came running up to us, shouting and raving, but Dad and Uncle Ted just walked off, with Sam and me close behind. Then, when it was nearly midnight, we walked onto Tower Bridge and it was deserted. I was some way behind when a man appeared from nowhere and ran at me, which was frightening, so I hurried to catch the others up. I told Dad about the incident, but, when we turned around, the man had gone!

One day in 1931 or 1932, a door-to-door salesman called at our house and sold my parents a copy of *Virtue's Simplified Dictionary*, which was also an encyclopedia and had 1,466 pages and 3,000 illustrations, including some in colour. It must have been pretty expensive and I suppose they had me in mind when they bought it. It proved to be a good buy because my parents and I used it hundreds of times for checking spellings, mainly for letter writing. We occasionally found some parts of its encyclopedia useful, like the atlas, the list of historical dates and the sections about signs and symbols, persons and places, and the Christian names of men and women. Much later, my son, Jeff, used the dictionary and it helped me to check my spellings when I wrote this book! I still use it on occasions even now and I keep it handy in my sideboard.

Unfortunately, in 1931, when I was nearing sixteen and the effects of the Great Depression were getting worse, the prospects at Wedgwood's didn't seem too good. So Dad got me a job at Taylor Tunnicliff as an apprentice electrical porcelain turner. I walked to work with him and the boss of the clay department, Tom Reeves, put me on a bench and lathe next to Dad, which was where I stayed. The turning shops were dirty, with plenty of dust flying around because there was more clay to cut off in making heavy insulators than there'd been at Wedgwood's in manufacturing cups. Dad had a window right in front of him, but we couldn't see through it because it was so filthy. Even if we'd been able to, all we'd have seen was a wall with filthy windows opposite.

Our benches were lit by gaslight and sometimes when bits of clay flew off our turnings, they broke the mantle on the gas jet, which would then have to be replaced. But, after a while, the gaslights were replaced by electric bulbs. Also, the power to drive the ten or so lathes in our shop was produced by a gas engine, which, in turn, was replaced by an electric motor.

There was a long steel shaft running the length of two shops about ceiling height and it was fitted with a pulley for each lathe. The pulley and lathe were connected with a leather belt, which drove another pulley on the workbench. That pulley was connected to the lathe by a leather rope, which drove it. When our belts and ropes broke, we had to repair them ourselves. To re-fit the belt, we passed it over and around and then fastened it onto the revolving shaft. Next, for safety, we ran the belt onto a loose pulley before guiding it to the fixed pulley. It paid to watch that you didn't get your fingers or jacket sleeve under the belt as it ran onto the fixed pulley because you could be dragged around the shaft. Some years later, the loose pulley was taken off the shaft, which made the belt fixing very dangerous. The machinery could have been stopped while the repair was done, but that would have meant the men and lads stopping work and losing money because we were all on piecework.

Mr Reeves started me off with a very small insulator, about three-quarters of an inch in diameter and around three-eighths in height, with a small hole straight through the centre. First, I had to make my own tools from pieces of mild steel. Next, I had to get a spindle from a storage rack and screw it to the lathe via an iron socket. I had to adjust the spindle with a bit of padding, so that it ran true, before I pushed a tube of clay, about eight inches long, onto it. After that, I turned the tube, with a square cutting tool, to the correct diameter and then shaped several identical articles, of the required size, from the tube with a shaping tool. Next, I had to separate each article from the whole block with a tool called a bandie and completed the process by rounding off the rough edges touching the spindle with a countersink tool.

The normal payment for turning a gross of these articles was sixpence plus fifty per cent, which came to ninepence in total. But, as I was a half-price apprentice, I only got threepence plus fifty per cent, which meant I received fourpence ha'penny. Apprentices were a type of cheap labour, but my pay built up over the years as I became more experienced. When I reached eighteen, I became a one-third apprentice, so that I was paid two-thirds of the full wages plus fifty per cent. That gave me sixpence for turning a gross and finally, at 21, I went on to full pay. However, if I had a mechanical breakdown or there was an electrical fault or there were no available turning tubes, I didn't get paid for the lost time!

Also on Hampton Street was the factory's testing station, where the big insulators were tested at three times the working load of electricity. I heard that the station could produce a million volts!

On my first day with the firm, the next youngest apprentice, Bill Street, a tall, athletic fellow, came to me and handed over his job as tea boy to some of the men. Three times a day, I had to take the men's teapots down about 25 steps outside and then across the "bank" (the factory) to the cookhouse, where two ladies boiled water in saucepans on a gas stove for tea. There, I queued for the boiling water, with other tea lads and wenches, and then had to take all the full teapots back up the steps, which were slippery and dangerous in the rain, to the men. I lost out on this because I was on piecework and, when I was not producing the ware, I was earning no money! However, the men gave me a tip at Christmas. About a year later, a new apprentice started to work in our shop and I happily handed the tea-making job over to him.

One of the turners I remember was Joe Reeves, who was known as "Uncle Joe" and whose wife kept a toffee shop in Stoke. Another was "Boss" Hollison, who didn't have much to do with anybody. Then there was "Sheriff" Machin, a little chatty fellow, with a moustache, who extruded the clay for the turning tubes. There was also the looker for our shop, Fred "Jabber" Allerton, who'd got his nickname because he kept chattering. He carried clay to the throwers, for it to be thrown into a rough shape, and then brought the resulting piece to the turners.

From time to time, I had to go down to the bottle ovens to get some wooden boards to put my turned ware on, so that it could then be dried in the greenhouse. There, I saw the placers, who stacked pottery inside the ovens by climbing ladders. The pottery was put in containers called saggars, which were made of rough pieces of fired clay. The placers balanced the saggars on top of their heads to keep their bodies compact in the confined space, so that they didn't injure themselves or fall off the ladders. To help relieve the pressure on their heads, the placers put rolled-up stockings on top of them. At the top of the ladders, the placers put their ware on top of the pile of similar saggars in the ovens.

The hardest part of the placers' job was to "draw" (remove) the contents after the firing of the ovens, which would still be red hot. The quicker the ovens were drawn, the less the time that was needed to set them up again and the more the money that could be made. The placers put the ladders inside the ovens and climbed up, so that there were three or four men at different heights. The top man would swing the saggars to the fellow below him, who would hand them to the next man and so on. The saggars were so hot that the placers used cloth pads on their hands to try to stop them from burning, but they got scorched just the same. The placers moved the saggars on so quickly that they hardly touched them, but the speed of unloading was so great that sometimes a man would drop a saggar onto the fellow below, causing injury. I didn't fancy that job!

At one time, the throwers, lookers and turners hadn't been paid on what they'd produced, but only on what had finally come out of the ovens after all the processes had been completed. But, when I started, things had improved because we were paid for what was left after the fettlers, who were all women, had done their job, which was to smooth the rough edges of the pieces.

Once, a young apprentice turner, who'd only recently started, spent two weeks turning small balls with a hole in them and assembled a great number of grosses. They were awaiting passing by Tom Reeves in the greenhouse, a storage area, so named because the ware went green after the added water had dried out. Mr Reeves measured a sample of the balls from each batch and found out that they were all a 64th of an inch out and so he condemned the lot! That meant that the lad, who was, of course, on piecework, didn't get a penny for his efforts. He didn't come in the next day and I never saw him again. His heart must have been broken.

The throwers had a really good job because they were getting, so the rumours went, fabulous wages of around five pounds a week! There were only four of them in the whole factory and if they'd stopped work, it would have brought chaos, so they took advantage of the situation to make sure they were well paid. The throwers had a high reputation in the pottery industry in general and seemed to rule the roost. I was told about the former head thrower, Bernard Watkin, who, apparently, had been drunk half the time, but had been able to get away with it. The managers were very concerned about the situation and successfully plotted to break the throwers' stranglehold. They experimented in secret with making a new machine, the "Iron Man", which was worked by two labourers and was highly successful. It could throw all the big insulators, which the manual throwers had been paid big money for.

At 8 a.m., the streets were crowded with people going to work and likewise after 5.30 p.m. with people going home. Like every other pot bank, Taylor Tunnicliff had a steam buzzer, which sounded at 7.55 a.m., telling their workers to hurry up, and it sounded again at eight o'clock when they were required to be "on the bank". The lodge man would be standing at the gates and would turn late workers back till dinner time, so they'd have to trudge all the way back home. The throwers and turners were exempt from that rule and allowed to go onto the bank at any time. Just imagine the feelings of the workers being sent home, who saw the late throwers and turners strolling in, with nothing being said to them. The reason for this privilege was that earlier in the Depression there'd been few orders and so the throwers and turners had been allowed to come and see if there was any work for them. Sometimes, it had only amounted to an hour or two and so they'd been permitted to do it when it had suited them. When full-time work recommenced, the privilege remained.

Our meal times were taken at our workbenches, among the clay dust and dirt, because we had nowhere else to go. We had breakfast about 9.30, for around a quarter of an hour, and Dad and I often ate jam sandwiches or something like that. Dinner time was from 12.30 to 1.30 and we'd usually have cheese or ham sandwiches, except on Mondays when we'd finish the leftovers from the weekend's joint of meat. To follow, we'd have something basic, like cake or fruit, and all the food that Dad and I had was, of course, prepared by Mother. Then there was a tea break in the afternoon of ten minutes or so.

At 5.30, when we finished work, there'd be children outside the pot bank, asking us for bread. If the workers had any sandwiches left from their meals, they'd give them to the kids. Some of the kids asked me, 'Have you any bread, Mister?' That made me feel grown up. How lucky I was to have caring parents, good clothes, nice food, a comfortable home, a job and good health. At that time, only the directors and the general manager had cars, but later Tom Reeves and his son, Eric, who was a thrower, bought one together. I never, in my wildest dreams, thought I'd ever possess one!

When I started working at Taylor Tunnicliff, they had over 17,000 different patterns and each turner had an order book, in which Mr Reeves pasted printed orders. These details gave the number of the pattern, the glaze required, the type of the body wanted, the quantity needed and the amount of electrical charge the insulator would have to stand. The turner then had to decide how the thrower should throw the crude article and how he himself should turn it. The blueprint for the larger insulators was often complex and had to be studied by the experienced turners before work could begin. I saw Dad many times put a pattern on his bench, light up a fag, stand with one leg propped up on a board, lean on both elbows and study and plan a job.

Not all the insulators were turned. Quite a number were pressed in "dust", whereby clay was mixed with paraffin, or something like that, to leave granules. These were then put in a metal mould and pressed into shape by a hand press. Also, a few were cast by making plaster of Paris moulds and pouring slip (liquid clay) into them, which left the shaped articles after part-drying out. Had they been allowed to dry out fully, it would have been hard to have got them out.

Every Wednesday was settling day when all the turners separately went into Mr Reeves' office to discuss their wages. New patterns had to have a price fixed and small orders of old patterns were paid at a larger amount than normal because it took proportionately more time to turn them, so there was a lot of haggling. We were paid for everything that the fettlers had processed, but anything that was in the greenhouse or Mr Reeves hadn't passed was put on the debit side of our settling book. The visits to the office were done on the basis of seniority, so that, when I joined the firm, I was the last to settle. We then had to go to the office a second time, to have the workings and the amount of wages entered into the general office's books. We finally got our pay two days later, on the Friday.

In those days, there was no holiday pay. If you wanted to go on holiday, you had to save the money out of the rest of your wages. A lot of the workers couldn't do that, owing to the low wages, and so they never went on holiday.

On 20 March 1932, I went to the King's Hall, in Stoke, to see Oswald Mosley at a public meeting organized by his New Party. I was growing up and trying things out. I wasn't into politics, but I went to see what it was all about. The hall was full or nearly and there was a lot of bustle and excitement. Mosley came on stage and his voice was blaring out through his microphone. You couldn't hear yourself talk because of the noise and I suppose it was deliberate because no-one could get a protest in. I can't remember what he said, but he was like Hitler, ranting. Mosley had plenty of supporters and they made a lot of noise, but most people seemed stunned. One or two were thrown out, perhaps for shouting against him, but I can't remember seeing any violence. It didn't turn me on and I didn't go to anything like that again.

Two nights later, I went to see a future world heavyweight boxing champion, Primo Carnera, in action in an exhibition at the Palais de Danse, in Albion Square, opposite Hanley Town Hall. Carnera was a giant Italian, weighing just under twenty stones, and sparred with four local heavyweights. One of them was Sam Pearson, who later became the leader of Summerbank Youth Club, and he was made to look ridiculous. It was a thrill to see the boxer who became the best in the world the following year, even though Carnera was a poor champion. However, on 14 June 1934, he lost his title to Max Baer when the contest was stopped after Carnera had been down eleven times!

Bill Street, Stan Johnson (another Taylor Tunnicliff apprentice) and the latter's brother used to go camping at Rudyard at the weekends. I thought I'd like to go with them, so Dad bought me a second-hand tent from a business in Brook Street, Cobridge. It was six feet by three feet and he offered them a pound for it, which they accepted. I was proud to become its owner, but later found out that it had a slight leak, though it didn't matter a great deal.

The next Saturday afternoon, after we'd finished work, Bill, who lived in Stoke, called for me on his push-bike. I was ready, with my tent, groundsheet, blanket and eating utensils loaded on my bike, and off we went to a farm about half a mile from Rudyard Reservoir, where we met Stan and his brother. The farm was on a lane just off the main Leek to Rushton Spencer road and had very little passing traffic.

We paid the farmer the rent for the use of a field and a loft in an outbuilding to store our camping equipment when we weren't using it. The field was around half a mile away from the farm, on the other side of the main road, and had a stream running through it, from which we got our drinking water. The farmer also used the field to graze cows and so there were cowpats around, which must have got into the stream, but we boiled the water when we made tea! We made a fire from twigs and branches and the smoke from the damp wood went into the boiling water and gave it an unpleasant taste. Bill put a twig in the water and maintained that it took the bad taste away, but I didn't think it did. Nevertheless, it was great cooking bacon in a frying pan on a wood fire on a Sunday morning, if it wasn't raining!

We spent most weekends there from Easter to September for a couple of years, which made a nice change from being at the potters' shop. On Saturday nights, we'd walk to Leek and wander around and on Sundays, after breakfast, we'd go down to and walk along the side of Rudyard Reservoir. Once, Bill stripped off his clothes, put on a swimsuit and dived into the lake, but I didn't join him because I couldn't swim then. At that time, the lake was very popular and boats were hired out. There were also trips on power-driven pleasure boats and there was even a small fair at the village end of the reservoir, which we visited, but at tea time we'd sadly make our way home.

After I'd joined Taylor Tunnicliff, I missed the weekly bath I'd had at Wedgwood's, but I found a replacement at Hanley Baths, which were at the top of Lichfield Street. As well as the swimming baths, they also had bathrooms, which I started to use.

At that time, the standard was for men to wear hats and some of them even did so at work. But youngsters were rebelling against it and I followed their fashion. I felt better without a hat and, when I went out, I didn't have to think about where I might put it down. One day, Tommy Johnson, who was a turner at Taylor Tunnicliff and about Dad's age, shouted to me, 'At they in the hatless brigade?' He smiled, as though he thought it was ridiculous not to wear a hat. I smirked and carried on working. But Mother and Dad never said anything to me about it.

About the same time, I started to wear my shirts open-necked at work because the young generation stopped wearing ties except for smart occasions. Until then, I'd usually worn a tie at work. I suppose the old workers looked in disgust, but they didn't say anything.

Among the sideshows at Hanley Wakes were boxing booths, where their owners asked for volunteers to try to stand up to any of their tough bruisers for three rounds. Anyone who survived would be paid a few shillings. I went in to see these bouts a few times and, at close quarters in the tent, they seemed brutal. No-one ever won any money when I was there. One of the booths was run by the family of "Gas" Hickman, perhaps so called because he could supposedly punch with the power of a gas engine! He'd been a great bare knuckle fighter, but had been crushed to death by a carriage. The booths also had women boxers, who'd fight men, but I didn't see them in action.

I started watching boxing fairly regularly at the Victoria Hall on a Tuesday night. The ring was in the middle of the floor, but I went in the gallery because it had the cheapest seats, which were usually sevenpence. The ringside seats were expensive and full of the top nobs and the real enthusiasts.

There were a lot of good contests by some quality boxers and we had two local world-class flyweights at that time, "Tut" Whalley and Leek's "Tiny" Bostock. In 1938, Tut beat Tiny in a contest at Port Vale's Old Recreation Ground and then won the British Northern Area championship at the same venue. He was ranked second in the world when the war broke out the following year.

The Fitzgeralds were a local boxing family, the oldest active member of which was Jack. He had a fair number of bouts, but never got anywhere. When he gave up fighting, he became a manager and one of his boxers was his brother, Dennis, who wasn't very good and took a lot of punishment. After he'd lost one particular bout at the Victoria Hall, which I was at, Jack threw the towel on the floor in disgust, but Dennis couldn't help having been beaten. I thought it was terrible, humiliating him like that. One day, I passed him outside the Duke of Wellington pub in Fenton Road (which was later renamed Lichfield Street) and I was shocked to see the state he was in because he walked as if he was drunk and he was very unsteady. That was because he was punch-drunk through the battering he'd had on his head. Despite that, he later became a boxing promoter.

My favourite boxer was Pat Haley, a stylish welterweight, who won the Northern Area championship. He was paid fifty pounds for winning the title and that was a lot of money at the time. He had a broken nose, which had been more or less flattened. Like most professional boxers at the time, he topped up his earnings by working in touring boxing booths. I went to see him fight quite a few times.

In September and October 1932, letters were put in the *Evening Sentinel* by people unable to swim, indicating that they'd like to learn, but didn't know how to go about it. There was quite a bit of correspondence until someone called "Just Steve" wrote and offered tuition in return for donations to the North Staffordshire Royal Infirmary. A meeting was arranged on 10 October at Hanley Baths, at which fifty people turned out, so a club was set up and arrangements were made to hire a pool on Tuesday nights. Steve's Learners' Club proved to be pretty popular as the news got around and eventually two pools were hired and there were two or three instructors.

A few weeks after the club had started, I saw a notice in a window at the baths that swimming lessons were being given each week. It interested me because I hadn't learned to swim, so I joined up on the next available night. I was told to change into my costume upstairs on the spectators' balcony. That was because there were insufficient changing cubicles around the pool, so these were allocated to the women and girls. I trudged upstairs and found the conditions were primitive. There were no separate changing places, just the spectators' wooden forms to put my clothes on, alongside those of many other males. There were canvas curtains drawn across the front, which didn't fit properly, but that didn't bother me too much. There was no supervision of, or security for, our clothes and valuables, but I never had anything go missing, nor did I hear of any items going astray, in all the several years I attended the baths.

Having got changed, I gingerly walked barefooted along the wet wooden floor and down some iron steps to the side of the pool. I looked around and saw a mixture of people doing their own thing. Not one seemed as if they would do me any harm! That gave me confidence, so I walked down the steps at the shallow end and into the water, but that first night I just got used to being there. Over time, I improved my performance as my confidence got better, partly because nobody tried to duck my head under the water, as had happened at Tunstall Baths when I was a boy.

After a few attendances, I could swim several strokes and then I tackled a dive. I did that by standing on the second step of the pool, in the shallow end, and trying to dive in. I gradually got higher up the steps and then learned how to dive in from the side. I also tried a shallow dive, to see if the momentum would carry me to the other side of the pool and it did eventually after I'd practised it.

Finally, I was able to dive in from the top diving stage, though I wasn't too happy about it. I had to remember to turn my fingers and wrists upwards immediately they entered the water, which brought me to the surface because the body follows the upward curve. If you don't do that, you'll go straight to the bottom. I once made a mess of it and my nose pressed hard on the bottom of the pool as I came out of the dive. If I'd gone a fraction deeper, I'm sure I would have broken my nose.

The swimsuits we wore were full length. It didn't seem decent to wear just trunks in the company of women. In male-only sessions at the baths, though, it was different because garments were hired out at a penny or two and these turned out to be just a couple of pieces of cotton cloth tied around one's waist. But, sometimes, young lads would swim in the nude at these sessions owing to their lack of funds. There were also daredevils, who broke the rules by climbing onto the balcony rails and jumping into the water when the attendants were absent.

At that time in the city, we had two marvellous swimmers, Norman Wainwright and Bob Leivers, who both represented Britain in the Olympic Games and competed against each other at a variety of distances. It was a great pity that they happened to be around at the same time. On odd occasions, Wainwright was still in training with his coach at the baths when our sessions with Steve's Learners' Club commenced. I watched him and was fascinated by his swimming. He'd stand at the shallow end and then take a tremendous shallow dive, so that he hit the water almost flat. That would take him to about halfway up the length of the pool and with six strokes he'd reach the other end. Then he'd do a quick turn and push off so strongly that again he'd reach about halfway. He'd be back at the shallow end with a few more strokes. He broke fifty British records and was the leader of the British swimming team at the Olympic Games in 1948, but, amazing though he was, he never won an Olympic medal.

One Sunday, Mother asked me if I'd go with Dad to look at some new small semidetached houses that were being built in Leek Road, Shelton, on the Joiner's Square side of Poplar Grove (which was later renamed Mawson Grove). She told me to try to persuade him to go in for buying one. I don't know why that was because she seemed happy enough in Windermere Street. Anyway, I went with Dad and we measured the different rooms in one of the houses that had been completed. He must have pondered taking such a big step because he was in his forties, jobs weren't secure and he'd have a millstone around his neck in monthly payments till he was well into his sixties from a twenty-year mortgage.

Nevertheless, my parents rapidly decided to take the plunge and fork out a staggering £420 for one of the houses, which was in the course of being built and became number 472 Leek Road. That amount sounds like a fleabite nowadays, but then it was a very large sum of money. On 2 November, Dad went to F. Collis & Son, the solicitors, at 9 Brook Street, Stoke, and signed an agreement to buy the house from the nearby estate agents, Holloway & Co., of 5 Church Street. He paid a deposit of £53 8s. and took out a mortgage for the rest of the amount with Halifax Building Society. The house was completed around the end of the month and soon after, in December, we moved in. Dad made the first monthly mortgage payment of £2 7s. on 20 January 1933.

Our coal man, Mr Evans, moved our furniture for us, but not in his coal wagon! He had a lorry that he must have been using for removals. Mother and I travelled in his cab, but Dad wasn't with us, being, maybe, at work. Mother hadn't told many people we were moving because she didn't want them to know our business, so some folk were surprised.

We all settled in pretty well and it was marvellous to have our own bathroom, with running hot water, though it took a long time to heat up. That was because the system relied on a coal fire to heat the water in a boiler at the back of the grate. It went through a pipe from there to a hot water tank in the bathroom. It wasn't too bad in the winter, when we had the fire on regularly, but in the summer, we had to light the fire and wait an hour or two before we could have a bath and sometimes that made us too hot in the lounge!

Also, it was nice to have electricity instead of gas and it was a novelty just turning lights on and off, especially on the stairs, where the light was switched on at the bottom and off at the top and vice versa. Dad got himself a wireless that plugged into the mains, to replace his old accumulator-powered one.

Mother also got in on the act and bought an electric iron, which was a big improvement on the previous one that had had to be warmed up by placing it on the coal fire! Of course, the new iron had its limitations because in those days there was no thermostat and it was hard to judge the correct ironing heat. If left on, the iron would get hotter and hotter, so that Mother had to use the on/off switch no end of times.

Later on, we acquired an electric coal-effect fire, which had a flickering light feature in the latest style. We used it in the kitchen and, when Uncle Mo visited us, he was baffled by this modern technology. He flicked his cigarette ash into the fire and couldn't understand what the problem was when Mother told him not to do it. Therefore, when he sat in front of the real fire in the lounge, he flipped his ash into the hearth and so Mother had to sweep up after him!

We had two electric meters, one for the lights and another for the power. The light tariff was more expensive and so some people lit their houses by plugging lamps into their power sockets!

Our new house was a bit smaller than that in Windermere Street and had two main rooms downstairs. The lounge was at the front and looked down, over the front garden, onto Leek Road from a bay window. It had a fireplace facing the adjoining property and a small carpet, which was a luxury in those days, but it wasn't fitted. Otherwise, the floor was covered with linoleum, which we had put down.

Behind the lounge was the kitchen, with red floor tiles and a window looking out directly onto the back garden. We used the kitchen as the main dining room because it was big enough to fit a table and chairs. Off the side of it were a small pantry, with a sink, and the coal house, which was under the stairs.

Upstairs were two bedrooms and our modern bathroom, with a small sink and a flushing toilet, as well as the bath. Mother and Dad slept in the front bedroom, which had a fireplace, but they only ever used the fire a time or two, when one of them was poorly. That was because it was dangerous, with very little space between the fire and the bed. The back bedroom was mine and all the upstairs floors were covered in lino.

The ground at the front and back of the house had been left rough by the builders and we got no end of rubbish out of it. At the back, the ground came to within about three feet of the kitchen windows and was only a foot or two below them, so Mother asked Uncle Mo, who was out of work at the time, if he'd dig the soil back about three feet. I think Mother gave him half-a-crown and his meals for doing the job!

At the back of our land was a fence, separating the property from a council storage ground for cobblestones, which had been taken out of roads and piled up. Cobblestones went out of use as roads were Tarmacked, so eventually the ground grew over with vegetation and became a field, which it remains today. From our house, we could see trees in Hanley Park on the other side of Ridgway Road, behind the store ground.

There was also a fence at the front of our property, adjoining the pavement. We had a wooden front gate and concrete steps led from it to the front of the house.

There were no buildings opposite us. There was just an open space, which went right down to the River Trent. The only things there were electric pylons, underneath which was good and accessible soil, so people dug it up to put it on their gardens. I got some myself for our gardens, but I wondered at times whether the pylons would topple over if sufficient soil was taken away!

Hanley Sewage Works was just along from us, on the opposite side of Leek Road, stretching all the way from Poplar Grove to Boughey Road. Our neighbours were always on about the smell from it, but it was occasional and probably depended on the direction of the wind. I didn't think the smell was all that bad and accepted it for what it was. I can't remember my parents complaining and Mother used to say: 'Take deep breaths. It'll do you good!'

On the other side of the River Trent and Victoria Road were Berry Hill Collieries. I can remember them building a metal incline, with legs underneath, for trucks to go up to tip coal waste. From time to time, I watched them go up and down and the tip kept getting bigger and became cone shaped. Eventually, it was like a little mountain! Every so often, internal combustion would make it smoulder and they'd have to damp it down with water from a pipe. I suppose it was an eyesore really, but it just happened to be there. It was almost a normal part of life at the time.

Mother and Dad decided that we should have a name for our new house and sent me off to get one. I went to R. Weston & Sons, the sign writers at 23 Marsh Street South, Hanley, and had a look in their window at some ready-made signs. I fancied one with the name *Brendon* on it, not realizing that I could have had any designation put on. So I went in the shop and told the fellow what I wanted. He was amazed that he happened to have just the thing in his window! I don't remember what my parents said when I returned with it!

At that time, it was easy to communicate with the other people who lived near to us on Leek Road because the front gardens were more or less open. So we got to know everybody in the row from Poplar Grove to the path that led to Ridgway Road and they were all pretty friendly.

At the Hanley end of the row was a detached house, number 458, which was owned by George Sherratt. It had stables at the back, where he housed horses.

He was a horse dealer and kept them there in between buying and selling them.

On 24 February 1933, there was the worst blizzard for over thirty years and, when we got up, the stairs were covered in snow, which had blown in through the letter box! Outside, the snow had drifted and formed into mounds, which stopped all the traffic for a while. Locally, there were drifts up to nine feet high and quite a number of buses were abandoned. The *Sentinel* published the tale of a driver and conductor, who abandoned their bus between Leek and Endon and struggled through the blizzard to phone for help, but found that the bus had vanished under the snow when they returned!

Grandmother and Grandad Wallett had moved to 6 Washerwall Lane, a small stone cottage in the hamlet of Washerwall, near to Werrington, which was quite isolated at that time. The cottage only had two rooms, one downstairs and one upstairs. I think they had a cold water tap, but there was no gas or electricity and so for lighting they had oil lamps. There was no rear way out and the back window looked onto a field where cattle grazed.

Next door lived Grandmother's sister, whose husband owned a small piece of land, enclosed by a wall, the stones of which he was selling. As we required something to hold up our sloping front and back gardens, Mother and Dad decided to buy some of the stones and I was put in command of the operation. Mr Evans, the coal man, was pressed into service again and we loaded up his coal wagon. I started throwing all the big stones on, but the owner told me that I also needed smaller stones to make a wall. I thought he was trying to get rid of them, but I suppose he was right. Anyway, we got the stones back and built walls at the front and back of the house to terrace our gardens.

Dad got into partnership with William Evans, our next-door neighbour at number 474, to get some fancy white and pink stone to put around the edge of the front path and at the side of the steps. Mr Evans was a postman and finished his delivery about dinner time, so when the stone was delivered, he had the first pick and chose the best blocks, leaving us with the smaller pieces!

Dad and I gradually built our gardens up. First, we had to clear rubbish, like bricks, cement and cobblestones, out of the ground and then we put hedges in along all the boundaries, including alongside the fences. Eventually, we put plants in and seeds down for lawns in the front and back gardens.

After we'd moved to Shelton, I quickly lost touch with my Cobridge mates and so on Saturday nights, when there was little to do, I'd walk on my own around Hanley's Market Square, where anyone who had something to say could speak. Men brought soapboxes to stand on and delivered speeches on all kinds of subjects. People gathered around and listened or sometimes laughed or jeered. At times, there'd be a policeman standing around listening, maybe in case the orator slipped up and said something offensive or illegal. I didn't take in much of what the speakers said, but I liked the atmosphere.

One of the regular speakers was a fat man, who claimed he weighed twenty stones. He said he was out of work, but he lived fairly well because he was able to buy meat cheaply. That was maybe because the butchers in the market in Tontine Street cut the price of their unsold meat, so that it wouldn't go bad while it was on their hands. They didn't have fridges then to preserve it, so they'd continue to reduce their prices until all their surplus meat had gone.

Another regular speaker was "Aero" and his speciality was politics. What he said seemed reasonable, but he didn't stir me into action.

Also, wandering around town was the local legend, Vincent Riley, who used to get drunk on methylated spirits, which was easily obtained and cheap. He'd fought in the Great War and claimed to have been awarded the Military Medal for bravery, but had then become homeless and, from time to time, used to sleep by the walls of bottle ovens, which were nice and warm. He was regularly put in prison for being incapable and disorderly while drunk.

Sometimes, there'd be a one-man show going on and so, after listening to the speakers, I'd usually go over to have a look. There was an escape artist, who'd ask for a volunteer to fasten chains around him. He'd escape from them within minutes and then come round with his cap, collecting coppers.

While I was there, I often went over to the mobile baked potato machine, outside the Angel pub, at the bottom of High Street, which was operated by a fellow named White. The machine was a kind of barrow, with a coal-fired oven on top. He sold bags of big, soft potatoes, served in their skin, with some salt in a twisted piece of cellophane. There was always a stream of customers and partaking of the lovely baked delights was part of Saturday night out in town.

After that, I'd usually wander around the shops, especially Woolworth's, which would be packed with people. It would take me all my time to push my road through, but it was an interesting way of passing time and it didn't cost anything.

Also in the same area, some years earlier, Dad had bought a German banknote for sixpence. It had become worth thousands of marks during the time of inflation in the 1920s!

Around Easter in 1933, I started camping again with Bill and Stan and one weekend we were joined by my cousin, Aubrey. But, eventually, the expeditions faded out. Bill got a girlfriend, which mucked things up, and Stan found his sister-in-law dead one day. She'd gassed herself. From then on, he became rather strange and hardly spoke to anyone. Unfortunately, it affected his mind and he never got over the tragedy. So I tried camping on my own once, but it just wasn't as good.

Arthur Kinsey was a veteran turner at Taylor Tunnicliff and had completed fifty years' work for them before I started there. I was told that he'd therefore been to see one of the firm's directors, Percy Cooper, and explained his achievement with pride. Arthur was then 63 and had worked for them since he'd left school at thirteen. Apparently, Mr Cooper had then said to him: 'Very good. Come back and see me when you've done sixty years with us!'

I was working in the factory when Arthur completed his sixty years' service and so, full of expectation, he returned to see Mr Cooper, who reputedly replied, 'You were paid, weren't you?'

Arthur worked a little longer and then retired, supposedly without a thank you from the bosses. He went to live with his daughter because his wife had died. Some time later, Mr Cooper had second thoughts and contacted Arthur's daughter, offering to pay for a rocking chair for him. She refused point-blank and simply told Mr Cooper what he could do with the chair! I think the story must be true because I heard the same version from a number of people over the years.

Around that time, I got friendly with a girl at the factory named Sally, who was a fettler about two shops away. She was slim, but not particularly good-looking and I think she was older than me. I bumped into her from time to time and we got talking. I was daring and asked her what she was doing one night. We then went out for a walk around Joiner's Square a time or two, but it was just an experiment. I didn't want it to continue after that because I'd be committing myself and I was frightened of later having to say, 'I've had enough.' So I let it drop.

We had the bread delivered to our new house by a horse and trap from Boyce Adams & Co., the baker's, at 32 Piccadilly. Their shop was just down from the junction with Brunswick Street, on the right-hand side. The driver/salesman was only a little fellow, so he must have had a hard time getting in and out of the trap because it was high off the road. Its two wheels must have been six feet in diameter and the driving platform was at hub level, at about three feet off the ground. He had to clamber down and back up every time he dropped off a loaf and he left the horse and trap unattended while he made each delivery. There didn't seem to be any brakes on the trap, and, if there were, they were not used much, so it was marvellous the horse didn't bolt when it was startled.

At the time, there was very little wrapped bread, which was a new thing. Wrapped loaves were a penny extra, so most people didn't have them. The unwrapped loaves must have got grubby, with many people handling them. I suppose sometimes they were dropped on the road, in all kinds of filth and muck, and the bread man would just dust them down and deliver them! There was no sliced bread sold at that time, so housewives had to slice their own loaves to make sandwiches, which were commonly taken to work because there were very few canteens then. It was a laborious task, which had to be done every working day, and it was a dangerous one too, with the risk of the knives slipping and cutting the housewives' fingers.

We also had our milk delivered by a horse and trap, which was driven by a lady from the shop of John W. Cannon, at 43 Tintern Street, Hanley. Mother would take a jug down to the trap, where milk would be ladled out of a churn with a pint or half-pint measure. But, if a wind was blowing, dust would settle in the milk containers, so it was not very hygienic. However, the delivery woman helped us out once, when Dad received a cheque from a matured insurance policy. He didn't know what to do with it and mentioned it to her. To Dad's relief, she immediately gave us cash for the cheque!

We even had fruit and veg brought to the front gate, by a youth pushing a barrow along. He was about my age and was named Norman Banks. He was quite thick set and had the gift of the gab. He was the son of a greengrocer, who had a shop at 40 Fenton Road, below the canal bridge, on the left-hand side going up to Hanley. It was in the middle of a terraced row, which also included a chemist's and W. H. Nagington, the butcher's, at number 34, and round the corner was Harry Hall, a hairdresser. I got to know Norman, who was nicknamed "Monty" after the film star with the same surname, and we became mates.

After a while, Norman's father bought him a pony and cart to make things easier and to carry more goods. The pony was stabled in a place at the end of Hampton Street, opposite the Duke of Wellington pub. Norman was cruel with it and aggravated it by rapping its feet with a brush, which would make it lash out with its hind hooves. If Mr Banks had seen his son's tricks, I'm sure he'd have laid the brush around his backside!

Norman got to know about my boxing gloves, so he invited me and quite a few of the lads from Joiner's Square round to his house for a spar. There was a storeroom, up a flight of wooden steps, at the back of his father's shop and it became a kind of gymnasium. I did pretty well against most of the lads until one youth came up and kept sticking his left glove on my nose. He was so quick with it that I couldn't get out of the way and finished up with my nose pouring with blood. The same lad came to the gym another time and I had the usual three rounds with him, unfortunately with the same result. It was humiliating. Later, he returned, full of confidence, for a third encounter, but this time I got the measure of him and it was he who got the bloody nose. He went home with his hand over his face and he never came to the gym again.

Norman then must have gone telling the youths around Joiner's Square how good I was with the gloves because one night three tough-looking characters came in the gym and looked me over. I thought to myself, 'I'm in for a good hiding tonight,' but, fortunately, they didn't stop for many minutes before they drifted away.

A month or two after I'd been out with Sally, I did something similar with another girl at work, who was also a fettler, I think. She was named Joyce and was just an ordinary girl. I wasn't really interested in girls, but going out with them was the thing you did at that age. We went for a walk a couple of times and I took a photo of her on a canal bridge, but it fizzled out. For quite some time after that, I didn't bother with girls.

One day, a policeman came to our house and told us that they'd arrested a man who'd stolen Dad's overcoat. As the weather was warm, Dad hadn't noticed it was missing. Apparently, the fellow had just walked into the back of the house and taken the overcoat from its hook! Dad got the garment back and that was the last we heard about it.

Dad decided to have a concrete path around the house, so he ordered a load of cement, sand and gravel. The concrete was mixed and laid by the brother of Lizzie Halfpenny, who lived with her husband, Fred, next door, at number 470. Fred then got a joiner from Wedgwood's, where he worked, to construct a wood partition between our houses, to stop people from walking round the back. Also, when I got the chance, I fixed my punchball up in our back yard, securing it with hooks to the path and a permanent wooden surround, attached to the house and the fence.

Fred was a thrower at Wedgwood's, which made him almost divine, and he had quite a bit of publicity in the *Sentinel* when VIPs visited the works. Pictures were taken of him demonstrating his skills to the visitors and I think it all went to his head. He was very careful not to knock or scratch his hands when he did jobs at home because he thought his work would suffer if they weren't nice and smooth. He always wore gloves when he was working in the garden or with a hammer and Lizzie was always telling him to be heedful. She used to do some of the jobs for him, but we used to laugh at him because it wasn't very manly to use gloves for working!

Stoke had won the 1932-1933 Second Division championship and been promoted to the First Division. Dad became a season ticket holder and went to the matches regularly. Sometimes, I went with him. A Chinese half-back, "Frankie" Soo, started playing for Stoke and it was strange to see someone with a yellow face at that time. He had very good ability and became one of the best players in England.

I was taking Floss for a walk nearly every day and we went where her nose took us! We mostly went into Hanley Park, where she could have a good run. I didn't put her on a lead very often because she was pretty good at sticking to me and doing what she was told. One day, though, Mother shouted to me that Floss had got out of the house and gone across the road to another dog. I dashed out and found a mongrel trying to mate with her! I shouted, 'Come here!' to her, but she wasn't having it, so I shooed the other dog off. I don't know if they'd already mated, but no pups were ever born!

At Hanley Baths, I'd got friendly with a few people, especially two lads named Ron Finan and Tom Hall. Ron was nicknamed "Harry Roy" because he was crazy about the band leader of that name. Ron was a little fellow, but was cocky and used to pick an argument over nothing. He lived at 153 Etruria Road and was a printer. Tom was quiet and I think self-conscious because he had prominent teeth and a limp, which put girls off him. Although it was wrong, that made me self-conscious about being with him.

Norman Banks and I started to go to watch plays and shows, with singers, dancers, musicians and jugglers, at The Theatre Royal, in Pall Mall, Hanley. The shows were very enjoyable and some famous stars appeared in them. The Grand Theatre, on the corner of Trinity Street and Foundry Street, had put on similar shows, but had been destroyed in a fire on 11 May 1932. Those kinds of places were on the way out and being replaced by the pictures (as films were then called). The Grand had been converted to a cinema three months before the fire and reopened, showing films, in 1937, under a new name, the Odeon.

We used to go in the balcony at The Theatre Royal, which was the highest of four viewing levels. It had the cheapest seats and was nicknamed the "Gods". This top shelf was very steep and, as you walked to your seat, it felt as if you were going down a mountainside! When you sat down, your feet came level with the top of the seat in front. I always marvelled that nobody felt giddy and fell off to the stalls below! Beneath the "Gods" was the second circle, with the first circle below that. On the ground floor were the orchestra stalls at the front and the "pit" behind them, at the back. Between the ground floor stalls and the stage was the orchestra, which provided a spectacle.

There were two prices in the balcony, for early door and late door seats. We usually went late door, which was a shade cheaper, but risked the best seats having been taken. The late door people queued in a side entry and then, about five minutes before the performances began, we were let in. A commissionaire kept order outside the theatre and kept shouting, 'Early door!' until the allotted time of late door. While we were waiting, we were entertained by buskers in the street doing their stuff, singing, playing and juggling, and they were nearly as good as the people performing inside. They'd put a cap on the pavement, which people threw coppers into if they liked the act.

It was said that we could have a night out for only sixpence: threepence for the show, tuppence for half a pint of beer at the bar and a penny for a fag, which could be bought, with a free match, at some shops. There was a fish and chip shop next to the theatre, from which you could have a tuppenny split, that is chips and peas, on a plate.

I saw a body-building correspondence course advertised in one of the papers and took a fancy to it. It was called Strongfortism and was run by the Lionel Strongfort Institute, which claimed to be 'The Foremost Physical Culture and Health Correspondence School'. Strongfort was a world-famous German muscle man, whose real name was Max Unger. I signed up for the course in February 1934 and sent off my money. In return, I received six lessons, with quite a number of different exercises to practise, each with a photo of Strongfort showing how to do them. The correspondence also gave advice on how to be healthy and recommended cold baths, massage, walking, drinking water and eating green salads, fresh eggs, raw or lightly cooked vegetables, wholemeal bread and plenty of fruit, but I didn't take much notice of that! I glued all the materials in a book and started doing the exercises in my bedroom, but I expected too much too soon and thought I'd suddenly become a muscle man. Obviously, I needed to concentrate on it and be persistent, but it got to be a bore and I packed it in after a while.

On 3 March, Dad went to watch Stoke play Manchester City in the quarter-finals of the FA Cup at Maine Road in front of a crowd of 84,569. That's still the highest attendance at a club game in England outside of cup finals and semi-finals. Stoke lost 1-0 and Dad said he got crushed in the crowd.

Norman Banks was a smoker and, when he pulled a cigarette out, he'd offer me one. I used to refuse, but he kept on asking me till I tried one to shut him up. But he continued to offer me a fag and I fell for it. After a while, I felt compelled to buy some Woodbines to offer back to him and so I began to smoke regularly.

I always wore a collar and tie to go out in at night, except in the summer when I'd have an open-necked shirt. I'd also generally have on a made-to-measure three-piece suit, which was normal in those days. I bought a new one every year and, when it wore out, I went to work in it. When it was cold at work, I also wore an old jumper. I always had a sports jacket and they were more jazzy. I had an overcoat to keep me warm and a raincoat I put over an arm, nicely folded up, but I can't remember putting it on. I was swanking. Real posh! Also, I always went out in smart shoes and had pointed ones when they were in fashion, but I was still one of the "hatless brigade"! When I was being casual, I wore baggy plus fours and, in the summer, baggy khaki shorts.

Mother and Dad started to have a holiday in June, as well as taking one during the traditional week at the Wakes. Dad was able to take this time off work with the consent of Tom Reeves. It may be that the opportunity was there for other workers in the factory to do the same, but perhaps they didn't relish losing the pay. When my parents went away, I was left in charge of the house and Floss. One night, we had a terrific storm. The lightning was so severe that it seemed to be striking all around me and the thunder was crashing. It seemed as if I was in the middle of a battle. I couldn't sleep, so I went downstairs to have a look at Floss. She was terrified and all of a tremble, so I tried to comfort her and stayed with her until the storm moved on.

My cousin, Sam, told me that he, his friend Albert Deaville and another youth from Wedgwood's were cycling to Southport and camping there during the annual holiday in August. I decided to join them and, a few days before we set off, we sent all our camping equipment off by train.

The day of our departure was a Saturday and I got out of bed about six o'clock. Whiskers were beginning to grow on my face, so I decided to have a shave to make myself look more presentable. I'd never used a razor before, but I decided to borrow Dad's. However, being inexperienced and in a hurry, I cut my face to ribbons and it felt really sore! But I mounted my bike and rode to Sam's house in Etruria, where we all met. We headed out of the Potteries through Kidsgrove and reached Southport in pretty good time. We picked up our equipment from the railway station and then went to the campsite. It wasn't very glamorous and, although there was a small swimming pool, the springboard was roughly made and was partly collapsed. Mother and Dad came to visit us one day, perhaps because they were worried and it was a trip out.

On the sands was a biplane, so we went to have a look at it. The pilot was giving short trips around the coast. Business didn't seem to be very good, so he came over and offered to take us up for five shillings each. The plane didn't look very strong and I got the impression that it was held together with wire! We refused his offer, but I wish now that I'd taken a risk, even though five shillings was a lot of money then.

I began to get interested in dancing. During one of Aunt Hannah's visits to see us, she mentioned that Aubrey was going ballroom dancing in Tunstall, so I decided to accompany him and try it out. The next Saturday night, I travelled by bus to his house in Summerbank Road and he took me to a hall along the road, towards the town. Inside was a jazz band playing and youths and girls were dancing, going strictly anticlockwise. After a while, the music stopped, the girls sat down on chairs placed around the outside of the hall and the lads went and stood at the opposite end of the room from the band. The youths talked and acted tough, something like the Yanks did on the pictures, and the girls giggled and tried to look glamorous like the film stars.

When the next dance was announced by the MC, Aubrey left me standing, saying that he was going to ask a girl for a dance. I watched him and other youths doing their stuff, swinging their partners around, and I wished I had their ability. After three tunes had been played for a particular dance, the band would stop and the couples would go back to their respective places to await the start of a different dance. I asked Aubrey to take me on the floor, to give me an idea of what it was all about, but he refused, telling me that the MC didn't allow two lads to dance together, although the girls were permitted to dance in couples. Convention frowned on males dancing together and it was unthinkable that a lady would lower herself and ask a gentleman for a dance. So if a woman wished to dance, but wasn't asked by a man, her only option was to dance with another woman. However, a man could move around the floor and ask any lady for a dance, but had to risk the humiliation of a refusal.

Most of the girls in the hall wore floor-length evening dresses and they looked very nice, but I stood around all night, not daring to ask for a dance, and then got a bus home. However, the following week, I went early for the learners' session before the dance proper and the MC led me onto the floor and took the lady's part, showing me the basic steps to the waltz. The dance was performed to triple time and you had to put your left foot forward on the strong beat, then move your right foot in front, as though you were walking, and finally bring your left foot to the side of your right. The pattern was repeated on the following three beats, but this time, the lead foot was your right. The sequence remained the same even when you were turning. I was very awkward when I tried it, but I suppose all the beginners were.

After that bit of practice, the room filled up and the dance proper commenced. I stood around for ages, looking and wondering which unlucky girl I'd dare to ask for a dance. I was in dread of being refused, so I thought I hadn't better approach a good-looking girl. Eventually, I selected a plain girl, about six feet tall, who'd hardly been asked to dance, which I suppose was because of her height and looks. I pulled myself together, walked across, asked her for the next dance, which was a waltz, and told her I couldn't dance. She smiled and got to her feet and I made an effort to take her around the floor. I tripped and trod on her toes a number of times, but she didn't complain. When the music stopped, to signal the end of that particular dance, I thanked her and walked back to the end of the room, thankful I'd got over the first obstacle. I told Aubrey about the experience and he nodded and smiled because he'd gone through it before.

The band also played tunes for the other main dances of the time, the quickstep, the slow foxtrot, the tango and the rumba, but I thought I'd be best to concentrate on the waltz because that was the only dance I'd attempted. So I had to wait a while until the next waltz came up, when I tried again with another girl and I was slightly better that time. I had one more attempt before it was home time.

I persevered for some weeks and my dancing gradually improved. As I began to take it more seriously, I bought a pair of black, shiny, lightweight plastic dancing shoes from William Timpson Ltd., at 8 Market Square, Hanley, which enabled me to move about the floor better.

One night, I was hanging around at the top of Piccadilly, when Ron Finan came up to me, complaining about a fellow, whom he wanted me to sort out. Flipping heck! I went with Ron to where the fellow was standing and stood next to him, intimidating him. We had a word or two and then fortunately it became friendly and all broke up.

Another night around that time, I was walking along Bethesda Street, in Hanley, when I heard and saw a couple quarrelling. While I was looking, the man hit the woman across the mouth. She came across the road and said to me, 'You saw that, didn't you?' While she was speaking, blood was running down her chin. I told her I'd seen the incident and she then wanted to go to the police station, which was nearby, in the town hall buildings. I didn't want to get mixed up with anything, especially as the man started raising his voice and getting nasty, so we walked around the streets for a few minutes, to Lichfield Street. I put my arm round her to try to calm her down, but, at the same time, the man was telling me to 'Buzz off!' After a while, she pulled herself together and became more friendly with the fellow. Then they went off together, to my relief!

A few days later, I saw them coming towards me, up Lichfield Street, near the canal bridge, quarrelling violently! I was hoping that, when the woman saw me, she wouldn't want to go to the police station about the previous incident and, fortunately, neither of them noticed me.

In 1935, I saw an advert about becoming a customs officer or a coastguard. I wrote off for details and it turned out that there was a correspondence course offering training for a civil service entrance exam. I signed up and made a payment. I was sent a book on arithmetic and one on geography, called *The World*, by L. Dudley Stamp, which I still have. I was supposed to read the books and answer a list of questions that I was sent. When I'd answered them, I posted them back and then had them returned with comments. It carried on like that for a month or two and I sent several lots of answers off, most of which I got right, but I was mainly copying from the books, so it didn't appear to be how it ought to have been. It didn't seem proper schooling because there was no teacher and nobody to explain things. The firm running the course was supposed to tell me when I was ready for the exam, but I lost enthusiasm and packed it in.

About that time, I went along, with Norman, to the Co-op Club in Lonsdale Street, Stoke, which was in an upstairs room near to the football ground, but on the other side of the road. Meetings were held at the club for young people for the purpose of improving the image of the movement in their minds. What we went there for was to partake in their dances, football matches and cycling activities.

There was no band at the dances that were held there, but I think there was a pianist and you could make your own rules up because it was quite relaxed. They also used to let the room out for parties and things like that.

I danced with most of the girls there, including Norah Burt, who lived in Hanford and whose father was a gravestone maker. We went for a bike ride together around the lanes there and another time we had a walk, but I then let it drift because I didn't want to get too involved.

I played right-back for the Co-op Club's football team for a season or two, but we didn't have a ground and all the games were friendlies. We played on Saturday afternoons and, after each match, the club secretary phoned the *Sentinel* the result, which would be in the stop press that same night. Most of the time, we got beaten, but I remember one game we won, against some very young lads. All our team except our goalkeeper and me were up the field trying to score, but all they got was three goals when they should have scored twenty!

I also joined the Co-op cycling club and rode with them to a good many places around the area. By that time, I'd bought a second-hand racing bike from a lad in Etruria, Alec Clacker, who worked in the fitting shop at Taylor Tunnicliff. I was told that to make one of his cycles lighter in weight, he drilled so many holes in the saddle column that it collapsed under him!

The captain and the secretary of the cycling club when I joined was John Smith, who worked at Densems gent's outfitters at Gray's Corner, Stoke. That was what the junction of Liverpool Road and High Street (which was later renamed Church Street) was known as at that time. John was a weedy little fellow and had a habit of sniffing up snot that came out of his nose!

Also in the club was Norman Gifford, who was in his mid-teens and whose father was the superintendent of Hanley Baths. Norman seemed to think himself superior to other people.

Then there was Billy Woodvine, who was a young teenager and whose father ran an estate agent's in Stoke Road, Shelton, virtually opposite Cauldon Road. Billy was gabby and always showing off.

Amongst the female members was Eva Thorpe, who was 6 feet 1 inch tall and not very good-looking, so the lads tended to avoid her. In one of the dances at the club, when the music stopped, you had to kiss the nearest girl and all the lads tried not to end up next to Eva!

On one of our cycle trips, a few of the youth members and I had a swim in a country canal. I must have taken my costume to wear because I wouldn't have swum naked. It was cleaner than the canals around Stoke, but, when I think about it now, it seems a daft thing to have done! I also had a swim at Ellesmere, on one of our runs, but I found it cold and got cramp, so I came out of the water as quickly as I could. However, the coldest water was at Market Drayton open-air baths. The day we were there, there were only two people in their swimsuits, apart from our cycling club crowd, and I soon discovered why. I dived in and the shock of the water nearly paralyzed me. I was in and out in ten seconds flat! I was already shivering, so I quickly dried myself and put my clothes on.

We also went to Buxton a time or two. It was different to what I'd been used to around the Potteries. I never expected to see hills like that! At Upper Hulme, we had to dismount and push our bikes all the way up the hill to Ramshaw Rocks, but, when we got to Buxton, we had an ice cream and a walk around the town. On the way back, it was hair-raising freewheeling down the same hill and I was worried about what the younger members might do!

I saw an advert in the *Sentinel* about the Cunningham Holiday Camp in Douglas, on the Isle of Man, and told Mother and Dad about it. Dad had been there some years previously and they agreed it would be a good idea for me to try it for my annual holiday. I wrote off to the camp for some literature and discovered they were offering three types of accommodation: under canvas in a bell tent; in a hut or in a so-called "mansion", which was a concrete building divided into rooms. I decided to try one of the huts, so I sent off my five shillings' deposit towards the 25 shillings' full board for the week.

When I mentioned to Ron Finan and Tom Hall that I was trying Cunningham's camp that summer, they told me they were going too and said we could pal up together. When the time came, everybody at Taylor Tunnicliff finished work early, at about 4.30 on the Friday, as soon as our wages had been paid. We piled up our unfinished clay ware on the floor of the workshop, gave it a good wetting and covered it with thick press cloth, to help prevent it from drying out, so that it would last over the week.

I then went home, where Mother made my tea while I got ready, but I was so excited that I kept going to the toilet! Ron came for me in good time, even though he'd lugged his suitcase all the way from Etruria. We then had to carry our luggage to Stoke Station, which nearly killed me! It was alright for the placers, who carried their cases with ease on top of their heads, just as they did the ware saggars in the pot banks! We met Tom at the station, where there were crowds of holiday-makers, waiting for their various trains, but there were nowhere near as many people as there would have been the following morning. There was a queue for tickets and boarding, which stretched about 25 yards down Station Road in both directions! Every so often, an announcement was made by one of the staff for those people getting on the next train to go onto the platform and, when our train to Liverpool came in about seven o'clock, there was a rush to get a seat and put our luggage in the rack above. The train didn't have a corridor, so we were stuck in the same compartment until we arrived at our destination. There were no toilets on the train either, so Ron, Tom and I relieved ourselves before we got on, which was normal practice in those days!

There seemed to be a lot of hold-ups on the way, perhaps due to the amount of traffic about, but we eventually got to Lime Street Station, where the passengers spilled out on the platform. We had to wait a bit outside the station for a tram and, when one turned up, it clanged and banged along as it took us to the pier head. We then joined a big queue for the boat, shuffled slowly on board with the crowd and tried to find a place to sit, but it was impossible because all the seats had been taken. Therefore, we had to sit on our suitcases, which were stood on end, and it was very uncomfortable, so we took it in turns to have a walk around. But the sea was fairly calm, so we had a good trip.

We docked at Douglas in the early hours of the morning and made our way to Cunningham's, still lugging our suitcases with us. We were allowed to enter and, I think, were given food and drinks. Ron and Tom were in different accommodation from me and I shared a hut with three Scottish lads. It was rough, but clean, and I had an iron bed. As soon as our quarters were empty of the previous occupants, we dumped our suitcases and went down to the promenade. We strolled around, looking at the sights and the girls and then we boarded a horse-drawn tram, which took us back to the camp for dinner time.

We ate in a big dining hall, where we were allotted a table and a waiter for the week. There were three good meals a day and something for supper, if we cared to go in for it. We could, and did, have second helpings and some of the campers had never previously had meals like those!

The camp was all male, with not a female in sight, and it was like an army camp, without most of the hassle. But, at night, there was a dance in the camp, which girls could attend. A very good dance band played, all dressed in dinner suits, and they rendered *Tiger Rag* by Harry Roy very well, which delighted Ron! Of course, I took the opportunity to continue my dancing and Ron and Tom got on the floor too. I'd bought some stink bombs, from W. J. Wood, a newsagent's at 58 Marsh Street South, in Hanley, and dropped one on the dance floor, which was a daft trick, but you should have seen all the lads and girls rush away!

Along the front at Douglas were several open-fronted singing booths, where people could go in to learn for free to sing the very latest songs, played by a pianist, and buy the sheet music of them. I loved that and it was great to hear everybody join in and let themselves go. I sang one or two new jazz songs and bought copies of the music, but the sheets were fairly dear, at sixpence a copy.

There was a pretty good rail system on the island and so we bought a season ticket each, which entitled us to go anywhere we liked at any time. So we had a good look around on different days at the island's lovely scenery.

One day, probably on the Sunday, we went to Kirk Braddan, a church just outside Douglas, where an open-air service was held. We went along to have a look at what was going on and there were hundreds of people in the congregation in a field above the church, although I suppose many of them were tourists.

Another time, we went to Onchan Head, which was to the northeast of Douglas. There was a lovely view of Douglas Bay from there and there were cliffs and rocks in the sea below.

One morning, somebody suggested us having a dip in the sea before breakfast, to give us an appetite. We ran down the beach into the water, but, unfortunately, I stubbed my toe on a rock and the sea was perishing. I wasn't in the water many seconds before I was out and there were no more early morning dips! Later, I leaned on the rails of the promenade and looked down at the full tide, about ten feet deep. The water was beautifully clear, unlike that at the other seaside resorts I'd been.

We met two girls at the camp and I got my picture taken sitting with my arms around them. That was a stunt that my friends and I started to pull on holiday because it would make us look good, especially when we got back home and showed off our photos!

The police in Douglas were a rough lot and didn't seem to like youngsters hanging around. I saw a sergeant put his shoulder in a youth when he didn't move quickly when told to do so and, of course, the birch continued to be used for a good many years after it had been discontinued on the mainland.

All too soon, the week passed by and the next Saturday we left a two shillings' or half-a-crown tip for our waiter after having our last breakfast. We then made our way to the pier and joined the queue of hundreds of people to board the return boat. The journey was pretty smooth and I arrived home in time for tea. Afterwards, I walked to Hanley and had a stroll around the big stores, carrying my dance shoes in a brown paper bag under my arm. I then made my way to the Ideal Ballroom in High Street, to which I transferred my custom because it was nearer home than the hall in Tunstall. All the regulars, who'd been away for the week, were present at the dance, showing off their suntans!

The ballroom had once been a chapel and next to it was a graveyard. Both were later destroyed to make way for the Hanley bypass. Fred Hackney, a thrower I knew from Taylor Tunnicliff, used to dance there and, during the fifteen-minute or so interval, I'd go with him and his mates for a drink of mild at the Golden Cup, one of six pubs along the road. We also played skittles there and Fred was pretty good at it. I was told a story that he'd lifted a cast-iron table up, in a pub, with his teeth! It sounded far-fetched, but he might have done it.

After some weeks, on Saturday evenings, I started to patronize the superior Majestic Ballroom, which was in Pall Mall, opposite The Theatre Royal. The entrance fee was a shilling. It was more imposing than the Ideal and attracted better-class people. I used to go alone most of the time, but sometimes I went with Ron or Norman. I didn't take any girls home because I didn't fancy walking back from wherever they lived. Also, I didn't wish to get entangled with that almost unknown quantity!

All the main dances of the time were performed there, but, every so often, a new one was demonstrated by the MC, Harry Clarke, and his wife. They were both about sixty and he was slim, but with a drawn face, whilst she wore thick make-up and dyed her hair dark, presumably trying to hide her age. One of the new dances they introduced was the Lambeth walk, which became popular. It was a line dance, where you walked side by side, hand in hand, with your partner. Other dances I remember that they presented were the Blackpool walk and one to the tune of *Under the Spreading Chestnut Tree*. Another popular dance was the Paul Jones, where the girls went round in a circle and the fellows did the same the opposite way, outside them. When the music stopped, the lads would grab the nearest girl and they had to dance to the tune that followed. The two circles would then form again and the process was repeated.

The LMS Railway ran cheap trips to Blackpool on Saturday evenings about September for a year or two, with free entrance to the Tower Ballroom or the Winter Gardens for just 2s. 6d. The trips were fantastic value and I took advantage of them a few times, as did some mates and girls from the Majestic. We'd leave Stoke Station about 6 p.m. and have around three hours on the marvellous Blackpool dance floors before returning home. The Tower Ballroom was under Blackpool Tower and the Winter Gardens were nearby. They were both huge and had balconies all around, from which spectators could watch. The wooden block dance floors were easy to glide around, with no resistance to your feet, but they were difficult to walk on because they were waxed and polished. The Tower floor was especially beautiful, with a pattern created by different coloured blocks. It was great fun, even though it was late when we got back.

I was kept pretty fit by my different activities at that time: football on Saturday afternoons, dancing on Saturday nights, cycling on Sundays, swimming or watching boxing on Tuesday nights, dancing at the Co-op Club on one of the other nights and a bit of boxing at Norman's. Then, when the cycling had finished for the winter months, I went swimming at Hanley Baths on Sundays. While I was there, I did some practising with the Hanley water polo team, although I never played for them. I found it to be a hard game. Your feet weren't allowed to touch the bottom of the pool, you had to sprint after the ball and the force the players could throw it with had to be seen to be believed. It took me all my time to get out of the way of its flight! The trick was to press the ball under the water and then flick it out with a backward movement, which made it go like a rocket.

A new open-air baths was constructed at Trentham Gardens, which was in a lovely setting, and I went there a few times with Norman and with Ron. Unfortunately, the cement around the side of the pool hadn't been put in properly, so it was flaking and rough on your bare feet. I tried the springboard, but it seemed awkward to use. I never did master the technique of using it because it was embarrassing to practice in front of lots of spectators sitting around on the seats provided.

Ron and I decided to join a PT class, which was being run by the council's Education Department in the evening at a school in Penkhull, and we went a few times. We took part in different exercises, such as doing somersaults and jumping over a vaulting horse. I once made a mess of the latter and my leg scraped down the side of it and started to bleed. Looking on the floor, I noticed about twelve square inches of paper-thin skin lying there and, when I picked it up, I saw hairs sticking out of it! It made me feel a little queer.

All the big pot banks had their yearly hop. I think the Taylor Tunnicliff dance was held at the Grand Hotel, in Trinity Street, on a Friday night and finished at 2 a.m., but I left about 12 because I had to go to work the following morning! I still felt washed out when I woke, but I only had to labour from 8 to 1, so I managed it.

On Christmas Eve 1935, the Majestic Ballroom held its usual dance and I was there. The room was decorated with balloons and paper streamers and there were prizes for the winners of novelty dances. There was some kissing as couples wished each other a merry Christmas, but I didn't partake, as far as I can remember. The dance finished at midnight because it wasn't allowed to continue into Christmas Day. I went to it regularly and was always at the Majestic's New Year's dance, at which the opposite sexes celebrated the magic hour with a kiss on the lips, but I can't recall indulging in that either.

We only had two days off for Christmas and it was work as usual on New Year's Day, so we always felt tired when we went in. After the festivities, the cold, dark days of January and February were depressing and the next holiday wasn't until Easter when we had the Monday off.

The king, George V, died on 20 January 1936 and his eldest son was proclaimed his successor as Edward VIII. George hadn't been regarded as anything spectacular and I never gave it a thought as to whether things would be any different after he'd died because the monarchy was just one of those things that carried on. But his death and funeral and the crowning of the next king meant the media could make the most of the occasions and they gave people something different to talk about in their drab lives.

In February, the potters' union, the National Society of Pottery Workers, put in a claim for a 7½ per cent pay increase. Work was picking up and unemployment had dropped in the industry, from 36.3% in 1931 to 22.3% in 1935, so the bosses agreed to a rise, which worked out at about 3½ per cent. I was quite pleased with that under the circumstances.

On 7 March, Germany reoccupied the Rhineland, which had been taken off them by the 1919 Treaty of Versailles after the Great War. I was aware of the situation through the newspapers and it appeared dangerous because our government and the French made loud noises about it, but it seemed a long way away. I didn't want to get involved in any problems and hoped it would go away, which it did because it quietened down after a while.

Cutting our lawns was my job. I used hedge clippers because we couldn't afford a lawnmower. I made a good job of it, but it took two evenings to do. After a while, we heard that some of our neighbours had got together and bought a lawnmower and made a separate roller from an oil drum filled with cement. Dad approached them and succeeding in joining their ownership, which made my job a lot easier. But there was a snag. Whenever I wanted to use the appliances, I first had to find out which neighbour had them. I then had to roll them down their steps and along the pavement and haul them up our steps. That was okay with the mower, but the roller was an enormous weight and was a real struggle. Also, I obviously had to clean them after use and Harold Bentley, at number 464, was forever moaning about them not being clean.

It was in the newspapers that the Italians had invaded Abyssinia the previous year, but they'd found it hard going to defeat the African army. So they used poison gas and two of the sons of the Italian dictator, Benito Mussolini, were sent with the air force to do some bombing of the Abyssinians. One of them, Vittorio, thought that dropping bombs was a beautiful sight and described them as 'budding roses'. He said that killing the natives was 'exceptionally good fun' and treated it all like it was a sporting event! I objected to that when I heard about it because it just wasn't right. On 5 May, the war ended and the Abyssinian emperor fled to England. Mussolini then made Abyssinia part of his empire, but I thought that it was all wrong for a stronger country to take over a weaker one like that.

There was news of something big happening in our country on 27 May when the huge new ocean liner, the Queen Mary, left Southampton for her maiden crossing of the Atlantic Ocean to New York. It was headlines in the *Sentinel* and the ship was described as a 'wonder of maritime engineering'. The liner looked good in the photos and I was proud that we'd built something so impressive. Also, constructing it had created a lot of work for ship builders when it was badly needed.

One lovely warm summer night, I was talking to Fred Halfpenny and mentioned I had a tent. He said it would be great to camp on the lawn in it, so I told him I'd fix it up, which I did. He went into his house to get his blankets, but, about a quarter of an hour later, he came out looking sheepish and made an excuse not to sleep outside! Seeing as I'd put my tent up, I spent the night on my own under canvas on our lawn, which made a nice change as I hadn't been camping at Rudyard for a year or two.

John Smith got himself a grocer's shop and left the cycling club about twelve months after I'd joined. Then, by popular demand, I replaced him as captain and secretary, with Norman Gifford becoming my vice-captain. Norman and I had to go to a weekly meeting at the Co-op Club, where the activities for the coming week were planned, in a sloppy fashion. But Norman and I more or less decided where we'd cycle to the following Sunday and then we announced it to the other members later. I advertised our outings regularly in the *Sentinel*, to inform the members and to encourage other people to join, but for me to do that we had to have a name, so we started calling the club Stoke Circle Wheelers.

About that time, Guy and Hannah Bradbury and their daughters, Nancy and Kath, came to live next door, at number 474. Nancy was fifteen and had a cycle, so Mother suggested I ask her to join our club, which I did, and she accepted. On one of our runs, some while later, Nancy and another girl rode off from us without saying a word. They simply disappeared and it was no use looking for them because they could have been anywhere. I suppose I was responsible for them and I didn't think their behaviour was correct, so I suspended them for a couple of weeks.

Ron, Tom and I booked up at Cunningham's camp again for the Wakes holiday, but, on this occasion, we stayed in the more luxurious mansions, which had three or four iron beds to a room, although the accommodation was quite basic really. The crossing was pretty smooth again, but the holiday was more routine that year because we knew the ropes. We spent plenty of time wandering along the prom, watching the girls, but we were shy of talking to them. While we were there, I bumped into some old pals from Granville School and one of them, Bill Bowcock, spent some time with us.

For a change, I tried a different dance hall in Hanley, in Lower Foundry Street, which, I think, was a church hall. It was alright, but not in the same class as the Majestic, so I only went two or three times. Also, there was the City Arcade in Hanley, which had opened in 1933 and ran in a kind of crescent from Lamb Street to Stafford Street. Off the middle of it, on the right-hand side, there was a pretty posh dance hall, which I tried a few times. It was more expensive than the Majestic and so once more I returned my custom to my old haunt.

I was a member of the National Society of Pottery Workers, at the cost of a shilling a week, I think, and I even went to a few of their meetings, in a room in Hanley Town Hall, but they were a bore. Only about twenty members would go along because few workers wanted to bother with the union.

One of the representatives at Taylor Tunnicliff was Jim Biddulph, a turner, who later became the president of the whole union. He had a brother living in Canada, who told Jim that the firm he was working for wanted young turners. So Jim asked one or two of us if we were interested. It seemed a novelty, so I volunteered, as did Bill Street. Jim wrote to his brother and later somebody told me that Bill had been selected. After a few weeks, Jim came back to me and said

Bill had withdrawn because his girlfriend didn't want him to go. Jim then offered me the job, but I said: 'No. You didn't pick me in the first place, so that's it.' I didn't really want the job anyway and Dad had told me that Mother would be really upset if I left home to go there, so that pulled on my feelings.

On 18 November, England beat Ireland 3-1 in the first international to be held at Stoke's Victoria Ground for 43 years. In the England team were two Stoke players, Freddie Steele and Joe Johnson, and it was big news in the *Sentinel*. The match was played on a Wednesday afternoon, so I couldn't go along because I was working, as were many others.

The king planned to marry an American woman, Mrs Wallis Simpson, who was getting divorced from her second husband at the time, but the prime minister, Stanley Baldwin, told the king he was totally opposed to the wedding and that he and his government would resign if it went ahead. No-one knew what would happen next, but Edward eventually gave way and abdicated on 10 December.

I was disgusted at the king stooping so low and having the stigma of associating with such a woman, but, if he hadn't stepped down, the situation could have been very serious and there might have been a civil war. If that had happened, I don't know which side I'd have gone on. So it was a very good thing that he abdicated and his brother, who succeeded him as George VI, was more stable and had a family with children, which was more in keeping with the British way of life. Also, Edward later associated with Adolf Hitler and if he'd stayed as king, he might have been a traitor to us.

As my twenty-first birthday drew near, I began to feel rather old. Mother and Dad asked if I'd like some money or a party to celebrate my coming of age. I hated the thought of people getting drunk on my parents' hard-earned savings and so I chose to have the money. When my birthday arrived, on 14 December, I didn't feel much older after all, but I did become a journeyman turner, so I no longer had to allow the firm any of my wages. On 11 December, I drew £2 5s. 2d., but on the 18th I received £2 13s. 9d.

Dad suggested to me that we should buy a car between us. He'd seen a basic brand new one for £100 in the garage of John Pepper (Hanley) Ltd., 61-65 Piccadilly, which was at the bottom of the road and ran through to Albion Street. I didn't fancy paying all that money out because a car wouldn't have been much use to me. My week was already pretty full up, so I turned Dad's offer down.

I still wasn't a regular at Stoke's matches and I was working when they beat West Bromwich Albion 10-3 in the afternoon on 4 February 1937. It was a remarkable score and Freddie Steele got five of Stoke's goals. Everybody was talking about it.

I thought I'd like to join the police force because I felt it might be better than being in the pottery industry, so I made enquiries at Hanley Police Station, but it was no use because I wasn't tall enough. The minimum height required was 5 feet 10 inches and I was only 5 feet 9. But then I saw an advert in a newspaper, which said that recruits from my height and above were wanted in London. It seemed that they'd been forced to lower their requirements because of a shortage of applicants. I wrote off and got a reply saying that they wanted proof of my height. So I went to Stoke Police Station, in Copeland Street, and asked the constable behind the desk if he could measure me. He did and I was a fraction over 5 feet 9. He wrote that on my application form, which I posted to London.

Some time later, I got a letter back, telling me to report to New Scotland Yard, in Victoria Embankment in London, for an educational and physical examination. When the time came, I travelled by train from Stoke Station to Euston in the evening, after work. I then took the underground to a YMCA hostel, where I stayed the night, as recommended. I thought the tube was amazing and it was interesting to follow my journey along from the map on the ceiling of the train. I didn't see much of the YMCA, but there were several beds in a room. There was no-one else there when I went to bed, although there was another man in the room when I woke.

Early the next morning, I set out and joined a number of other young hopefuls awaiting the examination ordeal at the police headquarters. They told us that we wouldn't be given any explanation if we failed the examinations, which, unfortunately, I did. The only test I can remember was standing on two marks on the floor, so they could see if we were flat-footed, to check whether we could run or not. When it was all over, I got a train back to Stoke and arrived in the afternoon. I then went to work for the last couple of hours and informed Dad, who still worked next to me, of the situation.

For the first time in the pottery industry, in 1937, we received holiday pay. It was for a week's holiday and was the result of an agreement our union made with the bosses in April. The amount given depended on your age and sex and, as a man between 21 and 23, I got forty shillings. The pay enabled many people to go on holiday for the first time ever.

There was a sensation on 6 May when the German zeppelin, Hindenburg, burst into flames when it was landing at Lakehurst, New Jersey, in America. It was a big story in the *Sentinel* the day after. It was the biggest flying machine in the world and had used highly-inflammable hydrogen as its lifting gas. 35 passengers and crew died and the pictures of it burning were quite a spectacle. By then, it was becoming obvious that the Germans weren't on our side and I wondered if the disaster meant they'd cancel the production of zeppelins and not send any against us if there was a war.

Neville Chamberlain became the new prime minister on 28 May. I didn't follow politics and I didn't know what the implications of that were, but he didn't look a likely leader. He didn't talk the part either and he seemed feeble for a leader.

After Edward VIII had abdicated, he'd been made the Duke of Windsor. He finally married Wallis Simpson on 3 June, but I wasn't bothered either way about that.

My life went on as usual, with a lot of dancing, swimming and cycling. Floss was still happily trotting around and I still did a bit of sparring in Banks' storeroom, as well as watching the professionals boxing at the Victoria Hall.

Ron, Tom and I went to Cunningham's again for the potters' holiday and enjoyed ourselves, as usual. One day, for a joke, I had myself photographed bare-chested behind a small palm, looking like Tarzan in the jungle! Also, for our photo collection, I had myself shot sitting in between two Irish colleens, who were enjoying the sun on their deckchairs.

After the holiday, I decided to try dancing at Trentham Gardens Ballroom. It was posh and cost around two shillings to get in. There were tables and chairs all around the outer edge of the dance floor, but there wasn't enough seating for everybody. The girls commandeered the tables and chairs and left their handbags there while having a dance, but I don't remember anything ever being stolen. I got to and back from the ballroom on the buses, which were plentiful and ran pretty late, but the fares were an added expense, so, after a few visits, I mainly returned to patronizing the Majestic.

Dad purchased a wooden hut to put our gardening tools in and erected it in the back yard. Then it was decided to move our coal stock there from under the stairs to get the dust out of the house. We cleaned out the old coal house and had the walls plastered. We then had it decorated and shelves installed, so that it became a pantry, where we stored our food.

I was still on piecework at Taylor Tunnicliff and so my earnings varied from week to week. For example, on 10 September, I was paid £3 6s. 9d., but a week later I only received £2 11s. 9d.

Oswald Mosley had got on the political bandwagon and become the leader of the British Union of Fascists. He was copying the ideas of the Nazis in Germany and there was usually trouble when he had meetings. Although what he was doing wasn't affecting my life, I wondered what it might lead to if he got enough supporters.

I'd always avoided going to see dentists because they pulled teeth out, but about that time I had a molar that was aching. So I made an appointment with a dentist at the top of Broad Street, Hanley, who said it needed to be extracted. I decided to try gas to have it out because I'd had some horrible experiences having teeth removed under cocaine, which had seemed like a type of torture. This time, a mask was placed over my mouth and nose and I was told to breathe deeply. I did so and that's all I remembered till a receptionist told me to wake up and that my tooth had been removed. I thought it was a queer experience.

I saw the odd thing or two about Japan being at war with China, but I wasn't particularly bothered about it because it was happening thousands of miles away. But a big war might have started after the American gunboat, Panay, was bombed and sunk on 12 December on the River Yangtze near Nanking. British ships were also attacked by the Japanese. Fortunately, the Japanese government apologized and agreed to pay America two million dollars in compensation. Things then settled down and my life carried on as normal.

On 29 December, Ireland declared itself independent, which didn't seem right because I'd always thought of us all being British. I supposed it was alright if that was what they wanted, but it left the island split into two different countries. I wondered if it would lead to a civil war, but things continued to be more or less the same as they'd been before.

At work, Dad was having trouble lifting up his heavy insulators and reaming holes in them, which was a particularly awkward and taxing job. He had to grip each delicate article tightly between his knees and enlarge a hole by twisting a tool with both hands round the inside of it, whilst, at the same time, being careful not to damage it. He suffered from stomach ulcers and they played him up at times, especially when he was struggling with heavy items at work. He asked me to help him a time or two, which I did, and he offered to give me a ha'penny for every insulator I lifted for him. He was paid about a shilling for each item he turned, but I refused to accept any payment.

Although by that time, there were about 27,000 different shapes and sizes of insulators at Taylor Tunnicliff, I never got round to turning the big ones and neither were they done by any of the other young turners of my age. It seemed to be a deliberate policy of Tom Reeves to give the bigger and, of course, better-paid jobs to the older men, who mockingly called us "the lads"! I think it was a poor policy not to give the younger ones some encouragement to try to test their skills because the experienced men wouldn't be there for ever. Like the other youngsters, I only turned the lighter insulators, but I should have pushed myself to get some of the better-priced stuff. But, at the time, it didn't seem to matter much because I was pretty happy with my life.

3 Love And War

In the spring of 1938, I became aware of newspaper reports of events involving Germany and a leader named Adolf Hitler. I didn't bother with the papers very often and what I read about foreign matters didn't register much in my mind. Everything seemed so remote and I couldn't see why I should be concerned with that foreign lot and what they did. Germany invaded and took over Austria on 12 March, but I can't say that it specifically came to my attention.

Around the beginning of April, I saw an advert in the *Sentinel* for a job as a school attendance officer. I was interested in it because it would make a change from what I was doing and would get me out of the dust in the factory. The problem was that the council wanted references and I didn't know what to do about that. I felt I couldn't ask Taylor Tunnicliff in case I got the push or the employer took it out on me in some way. So I went to see our doctor, Jimmy Yates, at his surgery at Penton House, in Stoke Road. The building is now next to Signal Radio and extends round the corner into Queen Anne Street.

The only times I'd seen Dr Yates before had been when I'd collected a white liquid medicine from time to time for Mother. I never knew what it was for, but he'd just dished it out and I'd paid him half-a-crown a time. So I was almost a stranger, but he wrote me a reference on the spot and I think I paid him for it. He put that I was 'a man of high moral character, integrity, industrious and trustworthy,' but he mistakenly wrote my name as 'Cecil'!

I needed another reference, but I couldn't think of anyone else I knew who was influential. Also, I think I was supposed to write a letter of application, so the whole thing seemed a lot of trouble, especially as the wages weren't very good, so I lost interest and didn't apply for the job after all.

A newsagent's shop, owned by two distant relatives of mine, came up for sale. It was on Hartshill Road, at the junction with Shelton New Road. I went to have a look at it, but I didn't think it would suit me and I wasn't very enthusiastic about it. I wondered what would happen with the shop if there was a war and the owners didn't seem to be bothered whether I wanted it or not, so I left it at that.

I followed world heavyweight boxing a bit and the champion at that time was Joe Louis, a coloured American. His success was controversial because there was a lot of segregation in America and coloured people were considered to be inferior by white men, which seemed strange to me. Louis was supposed to be a very good boxer and I saw him a time or two on newsreels at the pictures. On 22 June, he fought the German ex-world champion, Max Schmeling, in a contest that was one of the most famous in history because it was a coloured fellow against a white man and America against Nazi Germany. I sided with the American (who won by a knockout in the first round), I suppose because the Nazis were being talked about as being the enemy, which was perhaps a silly thought because it was kind of our man's right, your man's wrong. But the world's still the same today and I suppose it always will be.

On 3 July, it was headline news that the engine, Mallard, had broken the world speed record for a steam locomotive, at 126 miles an hour, near to Grantham. In a way, it was just another fastest time because different vehicles were always racing one another, but the fact that Mallard had taken the record away from a

German engine seemed important to some people.

Norman and I decided to go to Blackpool for our August holiday that year. So we booked into a boarding house near to North Station, where I'd previously stayed with Mother and Dad. On the Friday afternoon before the holiday, I went through the usual rigmarole of wetting and packing up my clay to keep it in good order for a week. I then packed my case, but we didn't go on the Friday night, as I'd done to the Isle of Man, but got an early train from Stoke the following morning. The digs were just a short walk from North Station and, when we arrived, we were informed by the landlady of the rules of the establishment. The only one I can remember was that we should be in every night by 10 p.m., but we could extend that to eleven if we applied to her each time and she'd then let us have a key. Needless to say, we had a key each night!

In boarding houses in those days, there was only usually one toilet for a house full of guests, perhaps twenty or thirty of them. It was terrible first thing in a morning queuing up to use it! Guests were supplied with a jug of water and a basin to wash with in their rooms and, if they were lucky, warm water would be provided! They'd also be given a bucket for dirty water to be emptied into and, if a family was in a room, the water might have to be rationed between them!

Norman and I would stroll along the Promenade during the day and go dancing at the Winter Gardens or the Tower Ballroom at night. They were both very popular and so it took us all our time to dance round, trying to force a way through. As usual, I was up to my tricks and got Norman to photograph me between a couple of belles! Then, another day, we went swimming in the big open-air baths, by South Pier, which were crowded. I sat in the water with two girls we met and got Norman to take a photo of us with my arms round them.

On another occasion at these baths, the water was filled with bathers, but, when I came out of the changing room, I spotted an unoccupied area, so I took a running dive. But, as I was diving head first, I saw a sign, which read: 'DANGER 18 INCHES'! It was marvellous how quickly I reacted because I straightened out in mid-flight into a flat dive and made a big smack on the water. How daft and lucky I was. I nearly smashed my head in! I sat in the shallow water for a while to pull myself together and wondered what the spectators thought about it.

Later in the week, we met two more girls and I arranged to see one of them at an indoor swimming baths, maybe the Lido, on Lytham Road. She turned up and we had a swim together before exchanging addresses. She was smallish, with dark hair, lived in Bolton and worked in one of the cotton mills. When we got home, we wrote to each other two or three times and she wanted me to go there by train when Stoke were playing Bolton, but, by the time the match came round, my life had changed, so I didn't go. She was a nice girl, but, unfortunately, I can no longer remember her name.

By September 1938, war was in the air. There were reports of our prime minister, Neville Chamberlain, flying to Germany to see this Hitler guy and it made me a little concerned. Chamberlain came back with an agreement from Munich, waving a piece of paper in the air and saying, 'I believe it is peace for our time.' I can still see him now in my mind's eye, on the newsreel at the pictures. It seemed that he and the French had given away someone else's territory to the Germans. That was the Sudetenland in Czechoslovakia, which I knew nothing about at the time. I was a little relieved, even though I couldn't imagine us getting into a war situation. The Home Office issued instructions on how to build your own air-raid shelter, but Dad and I did nothing about it. We wondered what the neighbours would have said had they seen us digging a big hole in the garden!

One Saturday night, in about October, I was at the Majestic Ballroom as usual, in Norman's company, and we danced with various girls, as we always did. Towards the end of the night, perhaps seeing himself as a matchmaker, he asked me which one I fancied taking home. I pointed to a slim, dark-haired girl, with prominent teeth. I'd danced with her a couple of times earlier because she seemed a fair dancer and was attractive. But, I thought Norman was kidding because we'd never taken anybody home before and I think he'd already got a girl, Nellie Clarke, but that night he'd left her at home.

I had the last dance with the girl and, at the end of it, I asked if I could see her home. I don't think I'd have done so had Norman not put me up to it because I thought it would be too much trouble to walk a girl home and then have to make my own way back. I didn't want to get too involved and tied down because I was happy being free and enjoying my life. Anyway, the girl coyly said I could walk her back and, as she had a friend with her, Norman made up a foursome. I asked her where she lived and she said it was in Northwood. I was glad it wasn't too far because I wanted to get off home, but I didn't fancy going to Northwood because I had a preconception that it was a very rough area, where the men were fighting in the streets all the time. I was worried that Norman and I would have to battle our way out! I was therefore surprised when we arrived at the end of Rose Street that everywhere was quiet. We all stood there talking and I felt like a smoke, so I pulled out a fag, but found I had no matches. Just then, two youths came along and I asked one of them for a light, but he pulled his face and just said, 'No!' I thought to myself what a miserable so-and-so he was, but I discovered later that he was the girl's boyfriend, Levi Galley! Ever likely he felt sore.

In our conversation, I found out that the girl was called Nellie Middleton, but her real name was Helen. It seemed to me a silly idea to have given a child a nice name and then call her something else, but maybe her family thought the neighbours would jeer if her posh name was used. She was eighteen and lived at 12 Rose Street, with her father, brother, two sisters, brother-in-law and baby nephew. Time was getting on, so Norman said, 'Give him a kiss!' Helen was demure and refused, but I fixed up to see her again. She and her friend then went off up the street and Norman and I walked home.

I started going out with Helen on a regular basis. On Saturday nights, I'd meet her in the Majestic because she worked as a shop assistant at British Home Stores, in Parliament Row, until 9 p.m. By the time the staff had cleared out the milling crowd (most of whom were just having a walk around) and tidied the counters, it would be getting on for 9.30, so she was rarely away before then. At the end of the night, I'd walk her back to Rose Street and, after a time or two, she slipped her arm into mine and linked me. Then we naturally carried on doing that, but I don't think we ever held hands.

Soon, Helen and I were meeting two or three nights a week and I started to wait outside the rear entrance to British Home Stores for her to finish work on Saturday nights before we went dancing. On the other nights, we'd go for a walk. However, it was a while before I kissed her because she was on the shy side and it would have been regarded as being rather forward. Our first kiss eventually took place in an entry that ran behind Helen's house in Rose Street.

Another night, we were having a kiss in the entry when a policeman came up and shone a torch on us. He asked us what we were up to and I said: 'The girl lives here. This is her back gate.' He then drifted off.

I went into British Home Stores a time or two to have a word with Helen when she was working, but not very often because I didn't want her to get into trouble with the bosses. She was in charge of the hardware counter, which was near the New Street entrance, and sold nails, screws, hinges and other similar things. She also had to operate a key-cutting machine. Somebody must have shown her what to do, but she hadn't really grasped it. I suppose she must have got most of the keys cut right, but she also got some wrong and I saw a cardboard box full of rejected keys that people had brought back! It was on clear display for the public to see!

One night, Helen suggested that I should go on ahead to the Majestic, instead of waiting for her outside British Home Stores in the cold, so I did. We carried on with that arrangement for a few weeks. Then one night, before Helen had arrived, I had a dance with a girl and decided to take her for a cup of tea in the tea room during the interval. We were just going in when Helen appeared earlier than expected and I was shocked to see her. Of course, she wasn't very pleased!

She said: 'Right! You'll meet me at the back of British Home Stores again from now on! There I was, slaving away and you were enjoying yourself with a girl!'

I was just being friendly with the girl, but I was back to standing outside in the cold, waiting for Helen to finish work. Even worse, I had to pay for her to go in to the dance hall again!

In December, Mother suggested that Helen visit us on Christmas Day to share a meal. I passed on the message and Helen accepted the offer. When the day came, it went off okay and then we all trooped off to Aunt Hannah's for Boxing Day.

I was first invited to Helen's home at the end of January 1939 for a party to celebrate the fourth birthday of her nephew, Harry Poole Junior. Ron came as a bit of company for me and we both played a piano that the Middletons were storing for a neighbour, or rather we tried to play it because the instrument was in very poor condition and out of tune, with several notes not operating. There were quite a number of guests and, as we were sitting around, someone thrust a baby into my arms, saying something like, 'You'll have to get used to this kind of thing!' Almost immediately, the baby started to cry and it was taken off me when it was discovered that the poor little soul had a cigarette burn. I don't think that was my fault, but it could have been.

At home time, Harry Poole Senior said to me: 'You're alright now. You'll be able to come to the house without being invited.' What that meant was that instead of meeting Helen in the town, most of the time from then on I had to collect her from her home. The front door was always open, but, of course, I knocked and waited, though I was told just to walk in. I didn't like the idea of that, but, after the family had badgered me about it for a long while, I finally adopted the local custom and went in after knocking. But, mainly, I just went along with things because, at that stage, I didn't imagine getting really attached.

Helen's father, Ted, was tubby and jovial, with dark, curly hair, and was about medium height. He used to have epileptic fits, apparently as a result of his experiences as a soldier in the Great War. When he felt one coming on, he'd ask one of his children to hold one of his hands until he felt better and then he'd be alright. He'd been the head cod placer (the chief foreman of the placers) at the pot bank of Doulton & Co. Ltd., in Nile Street, Burslem. His weakness was drinking and, when he'd received his pay on a Friday, he'd go straight into a pub, where he loved to treat his mates. So before the night was out, his wages would be gone. However, he didn't forget his wife, Leah, because he'd take home some fruit and a bottle of stout for her.

Unfortunately, by the time I met him, he'd lost his job through modernization, which had made his work obsolete. So he'd become unemployed and was subjected to the means test. He'd had to face a tribunal and tell them how much money was coming into the house, even though it was almost all from his family. The inquiry had decided that his family was making enough to keep him, so he was given nothing.

Despite that, he still liked a drink and would scrape together one or two coppers as a "latch lifter", as he called them. That meant he could get into the Cross Keys, the local pub, just up the street, and order half a pint of beer for tuppence. He'd make that last for maybe an hour or more until somebody took pity on him and treated him to another half. With luck, that would go on until closing time at ten o'clock! Sometimes, he'd sit at home, with a bottle of beer by the side of his chair and take a swig out of it every now and then. I don't know if he preferred it that way or whether the family had no glasses.

Just after I first visited his house, Helen asked him what he thought of me. He said, 'Well, ay's orayt, but ay's a mingy bugger!' That meant I was alright, but I was stingy. The reason for his statement was that he used to remark to me that, if he had another penny, he'd be able to go and have a drink. That was a hint for me to part with my money, but I ignored him because I didn't like the idea of anyone drinking away my hard-earned cash.

Helen's mother, Leah, had drowned herself in the Caldon Canal at Wall Grange on 28 September 1931, the night before Helen's eleventh birthday. For a while, I thought that was because her husband was a drunkard, but I later found a report in the *Sentinel* and it seems there was something wrong with her. She was in Cheddleton Mental Hospital at the time and had been allowed out for a short while in the company of another patient, Florence Trigger, from 33 Bleak Street (now Orgreave Street), Cobridge. Unfortunately, the bodies of both women were found later that night in the canal.

Helen's elder sister, Vera, was 25 and was friendly enough. She wore high heels a treat, walking on them really evenly, unlike most women. She was a caster at Newhall Pottery, in Newhall Street, Hanley.

Her husband, Harry, was 27. He was slim and wore a moustache, which wasn't unfashionable at that time. He was a pleasant fellow, who was known as "Big Harry", to distinguish him from "Young Harry", his son.

Young Harry had a mass of curly hair, which everybody admired, but he just looked at you and hardly spoke. I don't know whether he was shy, but he was rather spoilt. Vera and Big Harry didn't chastise him much and he seemed to have a lot of his own way.

Helen's brother, Elijah, was tall and had dark, wavy hair. He was sixteen and an apprentice plasterer. He was alright, but I didn't have much to do with him, I suppose because I was quite a lot older than him.

Helen's younger sister, Leah, was thirteen when I met her and was still at school. She had long, dark hair and was a lovely-looking girl, more so than Helen, I'd say. She had a calm personality, but always seemed flush-faced, as though she was hot.

The Middletons were a poor family and had hardly got enough income to live on. Their house was rented and the furniture was worn out. Nails were sticking up out of one chair and were hammered down at times, but, as the seating wore through, more nails were exposed. Young Harry was allowed to try to knock them back in, so that made the problem worse. One night, when I had my best and only suit on, I sat on that chair very gingerly, because the fabric and stuffing were giving way, but, when I stood up, my trousers got caught in the exposed nails and ripped! It was very embarrassing and the family offered to sew the rip, but I refused to let them because I didn't want to sit trouserless in someone else's house. I don't know what my parents thought of the situation, but they never said anything.

The Middletons' house had only two bedrooms. Harry and Vera slept in the front bedroom with Young Harry, while the other four members of the family slept in the back. Ted and Elijah had one bed and Helen and Leah had another, with a curtain across the room dividing them! Also, their front door key must have been about six inches long and weighed around half a pound. There were no carpets in the house because they were too expensive to buy and the door from the parlour to the kitchen dragged on the quarry floor tiles.

There was no bathroom, so the family used a zinc bath in front of their coal fire, with hot water carted in from the boiler in their kitchen. The boiler was like a fireplace, but with a metal bowl on top, which was filled with cold water from their sink and then heated. Mother offered Helen the use of our bathroom, which she therefore took advantage of from time to time.

There was a parlour at the front of the house, where the stored piano was being kept, and there was some old furniture. The family dined and mainly lived in a middle room between there and the kitchen, which had a sink and a gas cooker.

The toilet was situated in a small brick building at the back of the yard. The pan was made from pottery, but the tank was cast iron and was screwed onto the wall. It was rusting and there was red rust in the water. It was all a mess, really, and, after they'd used the toilet, they had to wash their hands inside the house in cold water.

The Middletons also had a pantry, from which steps led down to a cellar. This wasn't used for anything because a rotten smell came from a grid that was in the floor of it. Beneath the grid was a hole, which went to the sewers, and I saw some liquid in it, but I was afraid to look too closely at what it was. It was all a health hazard and I didn't make many visits down there!

A boot scraper had been built into the outside of the front wall of the house, by the door. When the street had been built, there was no pavement, so people were walking in mud in wet weather. Before they entered a house, they'd insert their boots in the scraper and pull the soles back over a length of iron, which removed the mud, or most of it. There are still quite a lot of these boot scrapers about.

On 15 March 1939, Germany took over the rest of Czechoslovakia, but, like most other people, I lost no sleep over the latest development, which was happening hundreds of miles away. However, civil defence began to be organized and Dad was one of the first to join the air-raid wardens because he was more concerned than most people. They were supposed to look out for fires and report them to the appropriate authority, but it all seemed a bit of a joke to start off with. There were also other groups, like the Auxiliary Fire Service, which backed up the professionals, and the Observer Corps, a mob that watched for enemy aeroplanes. All these jobs were done voluntarily, of course, but some were made full time when things hotted up. Also, works' buzzers were banned, except as air-raid warnings, and trenches were dug at the top end of Hanley Park for people to jump into in the event of an air raid, but it was a question if the ditches were two feet deep.

Gas masks were issued to everyone, including babies (who had their own special version), in case the Germans attacked us with poison gas. The mask was a fiddle to put on and it made you look like a pig man from out of this world! You put your chin in first and then pulled the rest of it over your head. The idea was to have it with you at all times and put it on quickly if there was an alert, but people soon got browned-off carrying it around with them and stopped doing so. The cardboard boxes that the masks were in got soaked in the rain, so a nice little profit was made from selling plastic covers to put them in! I took my mask with me for a while, but then gave up, especially because it was a damned nuisance and once the "phony war" was under way, nothing seemed to be happening.

Anderson shelters were distributed to householders as quickly as possible. They were prefabricated and made of a corrugated metal arch. They were designed to be dug partway into the garden and covered with earth. Soon after getting ours, Dad and I installed it at the top of our garden. We dug some of the earth out and put in the shelter so that about half of it was in the ground. We then built a low wall of setts along two sides of it to protect it. The land our property was on had been owned by the corporation and used for storing road construction materials, so we used setts that we dug up from our garden. As the ground sloped quite steeply, the other two sides of the shelter were held in place by the earth. We put a stool or two inside for seating and wooden duckboards to put our feet on. For good measure, I also ended up helping Helen's family to dig in their shelter, when I turned up unexpectedly one day, and got my best clothes dirty in the process!

Young men were required to register at the local employment exchanges for National War Service, on different dates, according to their ages. I signed up at Hanley Employment Exchange, in Cannon Street, when told to do so and I was asked which branch of the Forces I'd prefer to serve in. It didn't take me long to decide when I thought of the horrible muck colour of the army uniform as against the blue Royal Air Force one, which sported a collar and tie and looked very smart. I also thought that in the army I'd perhaps have to live in a trench in the mud, with bullets flying around, whereas the RAF would have decent beds to lie in and good food to eat. I didn't fancy the navy at all because I didn't want to be in the middle of the ocean. I hadn't been a very good sailor going across to the Isle of Man, so I dreaded the thought of being on a sinking ship. So I said I'd like to be in the air force.

It was about that time that Ron lent me a famous novel about the Great War, *All Quiet on the Western Front,* by Erich Maria Remarque, and recommended that I read it. I did and was impressed with it. It was unusual because it was so basic and described how horrible war actually was, whereas everything I'd seen and read about it before had been glamorized and made it out to be heroic. Also, I was very surprised that it was about the enemy, the Germans. The book shocked me, but I don't think it made much difference to the way I thought about things. When you're younger, you don't realize what life's all about.

In the spring, I took Helen for a day out to Alton Towers on a train, probably from Stoke Station. She hadn't been anywhere much beforehand and I don't think she'd realized that there were places with things to do outside the city. There were just gardens at Alton Towers then and there was no theme park. There was an entrance just outside Alton Station and we had to climb a lot of steps to get in. We walked around and had egg and toast at the café, served up by a waitress, which was a bit of a thrill. Helen later went on about the day many a time, saying how nice it had been.

Sometimes, Helen would come with me when I was taking Floss for a walk and we went over to Berry Hill a few times. Whenever Helen and I stopped to have a kiss, Floss would come fussing around and want attention. But, as soon as Helen and I stopped kissing, Floss would go back to normal, running about!

Nancy Bradbury was going out with (and later married) a fellow named Fred Cadman and he was in the first lot of conscripts to be called up for training in May. That was only supposed to last for a few months, but Fred and thousands of others didn't get back to civvy life until after the war had ended. I saw him when he came home on leave and he looked fit and tanned. He talked about using the new Bren gun, which was a very good light machine gun that had been invented in Czechoslovakia.

Our neighbours, Harold and Annie Bentley, had a son named Derek and my mother used to do his dinner while they were at work. Once, she gave him pink rice pudding and he thought it was great, so he asked his own mother to make some. She asked us for the secret and was told that the colour came from hot milk swirled around a jam pot, empty except for the scrapings, and then poured into the pudding.

Around that time, Norman announced that he was getting married to Nellie Clarke, whom he'd met when she'd walked past his stable door in Hampton Street on her way to work at Taylor Tunnicliff. He used to stand there and watch the girls go by!

Norman asked me to be his best man and I accepted. He and Nellie invited Helen and me to their engagement party in Fenton, where Nellie lived, but Helen either couldn't or wouldn't go. She said I shouldn't go either because, 'It'll only be an all-night booze-up and you'll end up sleeping with Mrs Clarke!' She was Nellie's mother, who was a widow and young looking. Helen was jealous of her, but I don't know why. Helen looked ready to chuck our relationship up, so I thought I'd better not go. I wasn't used to that kind of pressure and I wasn't strong enough to resist it. Perhaps I should have taken no notice and gone anyway, but I made an excuse and didn't go. I thought it would cause more trouble with Helen if I was the best man, so I told Norman I was dropping out. I felt terrible, but he didn't say much, although I suppose he was disgusted. What a mess it was! I could kick myself now!

I don't think Helen and I went to the wedding. I'd offended Norman and we drifted apart as pals after that, although the war and the fact that he'd got married changed things anyway.

Despite the preparations for war, life went on pretty normally for most people and Mother and Dad asked if Helen and I would like to go away with them during the potters' holiday that August. We accepted and booked into a boarding house in Morecambe. I don't think Helen had ever been on holiday before, so it was a real experience for her. Mother and Dad went on the Saturday, but I had to wait for Helen because the British Home Stores staff had to work until about 9.30 that night. Their opening hours were 9 a.m. to 7 p.m., Mondays to Wednesdays; 9 till 1 on Thursdays, with half-day closing; Fridays 9 to 8 and Saturdays 9 till 9. In addition, each day, the workers had to go in for 8.30 for "staff training"!

Therefore, Helen and I caught a train from Stoke to Morecambe on the Sunday morning. We found Mother and Dad at the boarding house alright and things were okay, although the landlady was a tartar. Helen and I went to the outdoor swimming baths and did some dancing in a ballroom on the pier, where I particularly remember the popular tune, *Deep Purple*, being played by the band. The lights were dimmed and a purple light came on as the tune started. It was romantic.

We went on the beach one day and Helen wanted to have her photo taken on one of the horses on hire and then dismount. After the picture had been taken, the owner started to lead the animals off for a walk with us still in the saddle. Helen was furious because she was astride the animal and her skirt had been pushed up, revealing her thighs. When we got back to the starting point, she dashed off the sands. When I caught up with her, she was vexed with embarrassment and demanded her rail ticket home! I took no notice, but, when she insisted on having it, I pulled it out and offered it to her. That shook her because she didn't really mean to go home. Anyway, after some more palaver, she calmed down and decided to stay.

Later in the week, Helen bought me a nine-carat gold signet ring for fifteen shillings from a jeweller's in the town. I think it was partly to thank me for the holiday, but also it was probably to push things forward. I went along with it, although I didn't particularly want a ring. I don't wear it now because it's too small for my fingers.

While we were away, there was a trial blackout in Staffordshire, as the prospect of war increased. Then, on 24 August, Chamberlain warned Hitler that we'd back Poland if he started anything, but I just wondered why the prime minister hadn't kept his mouth shut! Things began to look increasingly serious and it was worrying to hear on the 31st that women and children were about to be evacuated from London. The following day, news came that Germany had invaded Poland, but I couldn't understand how we were going to get help to the Poles. The orders came that no lights should be seen from outside at night and that car lights should be dimmed. Mother's response was to go up to Hanley to get some material to make blackout curtains.

On 2 September, which was a Saturday, Helen and I went dancing as usual at the Majestic, but walked home in the blackout, which was a strange experience. It was very difficult walking about in the dark without streetlights, especially on a long, cloudy, moonless night in the winter. Some nights, you could barely see a hand in front of your face and, on one occasion, Helen bumped into a man smoking a pipe. It pushed into her face and burnt her. She'd seen no sign at all of him coming.

On Sunday 3 September, we were informed by the wireless that the prime minister had an announcement to make. I listened to Chamberlain's broadcast with Mother and Dad and, at 11.15, he told us that we were at war with Germany. It was a terrible shock, although the implications never occurred to me and I didn't realize that I'd have to go in the Forces. It was a nice morning and, of course, we went out into our garden and discussed the situation with our neighbours. While that was going on, Ron called and said he was going to Hanley to join up. He asked if I was going along with him and, reluctantly, I said I'd accompany him. On the way, he told me that he was hoping to get into a trade in the RAF connected with his current job in the printing industry and so avoid any of the shooting. I don't know where I came into the scheme because I knew nothing about printing! I never gave any thought as to what my parents were thinking, but I bet their hair was turning white with worry.

The RAF recruiting office was in Upper Market Square. The fellow inside looked as if he'd had no sleep for about three days because his eyes were all bunged up. I suppose things had been very hectic for him with the build-up of the war situation. Ron explained to him the job he wanted, but the officer said there was none such and that it would be better for us to wait till we were called up. I came out of the centre very relieved! We then decided to go to Helen's to tell our story, which we did, and her family must have thought what fools we were.

Everybody was issued with a National Registration Identity Card, which was made of thick paper and was about 5 inches by 3¼ in size. I think I got mine from Cauldon Road School. It gave your identity number (mine was ONEP/131/3) and you had to fill in your names and address and sign it. There was a warning on the card to carry it at all times and produce it on demand by a police officer or a member of the armed forces. It also said that failure to do so was punishable by a fine or imprisonment or both. It was obviously supposed to be used as a measure for preventing German spies from wandering about, but I can't remember anyone ever checking my card! I carried it for a short while, maybe a few weeks, but I had to keep transferring it from one pocket to the next when I changed clothes. So, after a while, I forgot about it, as did most people!

We had one or two air-raid alerts soon after war had been declared and their wailing sirens terrified us at first, but we got used to them after a while. When the alert sounded, workers were told to go into the cellars, which we did, and we'd stay there until we heard the continuous tone of the all clear. At the time, all the Germans did was to have a few planes flying around the country to keep the workers in shelters and stop production. Millions of man-hours were lost at a cost of a few gallons of fuel to the Germans! There were no bombs dropped around Stoke-on-Trent at that time.

When we were at home and there was an alert, we'd rush to our shelter, taking Floss with us. It wasn't comfortable to sit in for long, especially in the winter because there was no form of heating, except for a hot-water bottle or a flask of tea, and the only lighting we had was a torch. I bet Floss wondered what silly game was going on when we could have been sitting around the coal fire! We'd strain our ears until they'd almost burst with listening for planes. When one came over, we'd pick out the drone of its engines and, as it gradually got louder and nearer, we'd discuss whether it was one of ours or theirs. We did so in whispers in case the pilot could hear us! Then, we'd listen for the sound of a bomb whistling down, but we were told that just after a plane had gone overhead a bomb could no longer hit us. We hardly believed that and didn't feel safe until the plane was a long way past. If there was a quiet spell, one of us would nip into the house and make a cup of tea for everybody. However, because of the discomfort of the shelter, my parents and I didn't use it many times. Like most people, I became complacent and went out many a time when there was a raid on, while Helen's father didn't even bother to get out of bed in the night when the alert sounded!

Overall, life carried on pretty much as normal for most people and Helen and I continued to enjoy our dancing at the Majestic, where the band played the most popular tunes of the time, like *Roll out the Barrel* and *We're Going to Hang out the Washing on the Siegfried Line*. Those were very nice songs that you could sing along to.

Helen was taking over my life and I couldn't have any time off from seeing her. She expected me to meet her every day. She told me that either I'd have to buy her a bike, so that she could come out on rides with the cycling club, or I'd have to pack it in. Things weren't the same anyway as the club was breaking up because of the war, so I gave it up. I don't think Helen was serious about cycling in any case.

1940 started off very quietly, with the Yanks claiming that there was a "phony war" because there'd been very little activity since Poland had been overrun in September. Despite that, bacon, butter and sugar were rationed from 8 January. Mother never mentioned any problems in getting hold of those items, but she provided whatever there was and Dad and I just ate it. We had to get on with it and make the best of things.

Helen was getting on well at British Home Stores and was sent to London to do a week's training to become a supervisor. She was nervous about going to the big city, but she met a fellow at Stoke Station, who escorted her to London. What she did there was successful and she was upgraded to her new position, although she still had to work the same long hours. The job really suited her, though, because she found that she was very good at telling people what to do!

By that time, I'd met Helen's Aunt Sally and Uncle Bill, who lived at 29 Rose Street. They both worked at J. and G. Meakin's Eagle Pottery in Ivy House Road. Sally was a caster (who poured slip into a mould to make the shape of an item) and Bill was a foreman of labourers. They'd wander into Ted Middleton's house whenever they felt like it and if Sally wanted to warm herself in front of their fire, she'd say: 'Hey up! Let the dog see the rabbit!' Bill was also a football referee and officiated as a linesman in some Football League games. He'd played for Meakin's in his younger days, but had failed his medical in the First World War because he was told he only had one lung. That was strange because he was able to do heavy work and play football!

On 9 April, the war really got moving, with the German invasion of Norway and Denmark and both countries were quickly overrun, with little resistance. British forces were then sent to try to push the Germans out of Norway, but they weren't successful and withdrew, so we were humiliated. I wondered what would happen next.

The "phony war" truly came to an end on 10 May when German armies attacked the Netherlands, Belgium and Luxembourg before quickly pushing on into France. We were then told that Chamberlain had resigned and that Winston Churchill had taken over his job. On the 13th, Churchill stood up in the House of Commons and said all he could offer us was 'blood, toil, tears and sweat'. As usual, I became aware of that through the wireless and newspapers and, at the time, I felt a surge of patriotism go through me. Churchill was an expert at getting us going.

The following day, there was an announcement on the wireless by Anthony Eden, the new Secretary of State for War, that a new citizens' army was to be formed, called the Local Defence Volunteers. The reason seemed to be that there were reports that paratroopers were being dropped in the Low Countries among the refugees and causing havoc, especially as some of the Germans were supposedly disguised as nuns. It was thought that the Germans might do similar here and it was announced that volunteers for the new force should register at a police station.

After hearing the broadcast, I decided to join up and so I strolled up to Hanley Police Station to offer my services. The officer behind the desk didn't look too pleased when I told him what I wanted to do. He said that one or two people had already called in, but that he knew nothing about what was going on. He pulled out a piece of paper, with a short list of names on it, and added mine. I thanked him and left. Every day afterwards, I looked to see if the postman had called with some information, but there was nothing. As things were looking bad on the other side of the Channel, I thought there might have been some urgency, but it seemed not.

By the end of the month, our army was hemmed in around Dunkirk and it looked like the end for us. It didn't seem as if our troops could survive and I couldn't really take it in. I couldn't imagine Europe being overrun like that. It didn't seem real. I had a lifestyle and couldn't imagine it changing.

But a miracle occurred and we managed to evacuate most of our army to fight another day. Joe Machin, the son of the "Sheriff" at Taylor Tunnicliff, was one of those rescued. He'd been in the Terriers (the Territorial Army) when the war broke out and so had been called to serve right away. He later told me how he'd had to wade in the sea up to his neck to get to a ship. He was in a long line of soldiers hanging onto each other as they moved slowly forward. They were in the water a long time and some of them never made it to the ship. A lot of the soldiers hung onto their equipment, which was very heavy, and some became so exhausted that they gave up the struggle. I thought the Dunkirk rescue was a good show, but I'd expected our soldiers would get away because we were British!

After the evacuation was completed, a German invasion was expected, so Britain got its defences ready, which weren't much. On the east coast, barbed wire was strung along the beaches and promenades and steel girders were cemented in the sand to stop enemy tanks rolling up the beaches, which were mined. Inland, concrete pillboxes were constructed and anti-tank defences were stored on the grass verge of Leek Road, Shelton, by the Terrace Inn. I suppose the idea was that when enemy tanks were reported to be coming our way, these concrete blocks would be placed across the road and the LDV deployed behind them. Fortunately, it was never put to the test because that defence couldn't have lasted many minutes.

After a few weeks of waiting to hear from the LDV, I decided to go to see what was happening. So, following work one night, I went to the Ivy House barracks in Bucknall Road. I asked someone about the LDV and was told to go inside, where I found some civilians being drilled. There were no rifles that I could see, nor anything else military, except for the barracks itself, and it all seemed chaotic. I watched the disarray for a while and listened to conversation of the volunteer old soldiers, who'd fought in the First World War. Amongst other things, I heard that Shelton Bar had set up its own LDV, but had just three rifles and bullets! I was assigned to the Drill Hall, a barracks, in Victoria Square, Shelton, for my headquarters and, some weeks later, I was finally issued with the first part of my uniform, which was the armband, containing the letters "LDV"! At that time, they didn't have much stuff at all.

In the midst of the chaos, Helen's father joined the army, which gave him an income. He was based in Tarporley and Dunham Massey, in Cheshire, and Branston, just outside Burton-upon-Trent, and therefore had to live away from home. I don't know how he managed to enlist because he was fifty and not fit. But he wasn't in the colours for long before he was discharged owing to his lack of fitness.

After Dunkirk, increasing numbers of foreign troops appeared in the area. French and Polish soldiers camped out in Trentham Park, whilst some of the Polish army was in barracks at the Blackshaw Moor camp, near Leek. Also, Greeks, Cypriots, Arabs and Egyptians were stationed at Keele Hall and Park. General de Gaulle, the leader of the Free French movement, came to visit the French Light Mountain Division at Trentham on 29 June. One night, as I was walking along Stoke Road, I saw two unusual characters, dressed in khaki cloaks, standing in a doorway. I heard afterwards that they were members of the French Foreign Legion.

By that time, we'd got so used to the air-raid sirens sounding that, when we were at work, we didn't bother going any more to the improvised shelters that Taylor Tunnicliff had constructed. We just kept on working, which suited the firm and us!

On 26 June, the first bomb fell in North Staffordshire and hit a house in Gower Street, Newcastle. A four-year-old boy, John Stobart, was killed and several people were injured. John was the first of 71 people who died in North Staffordshire as a result of the Blitz.

A day or two later, bombs were also dropped on Hanley and caused a big fire at Sun Street greyhound stadium, as well as significant damage to Hanley Station, but I can't remember hearing anything myself. I suppose the Luftwaffe had been after Shelton Bar, which was very close by. The red glow from its molten slag would have been seen from miles away in the air at night and there was a big problem trying to mask it.

Shortly afterwards, the newly-opened nurses' home at the Royal Infirmary was hit and seriously damaged and an operating theatre at the hospital was destroyed. Fortunately, no-one was hurt.

Etruria had a very good air-raid shelter in an old tunnel, through which a footpath ran under a slag heap, at Tinkersclough, off Clough Street. By then, Grandmother Kent and Uncle Ted and his family had moved down Etruria Vale Road to a council house, number 256, and the shelter was handy for them, but I never heard about any of them, except Uncle Ted, taking advantage of it. But hundreds of people used it and chairs and even beds were taken in! However, on 29 June, a seven-year-old boy, William Shaw, of 70 Ladysmith Road, was killed and his parents injured when bombs destroyed a number of houses in the street.

In July, the LDV changed its name to the Home Guard and I was finally issued with my uniform, which was khaki in colour and made of denim. It was a sort of overall because we wore it on top of our normal clothes. It was the kind of thing real soldiers used to do dirty or rough jobs in. We were also given a glengarry cap, which we wore sloped on one side of our head. At night, we'd report to the barracks and march in squads, each perhaps of ten men, to Hanley Park to be trained. We were drilled and did military exercises, which included jumping into the trenches there and squatting down. We were watched a few times by Mother and Helen and I suppose they had a laugh!

At first, we weren't equipped with guns, but, after a while, we were issued with some .300-inch American First World War rifles. They'd been stored in grease since the Great War and were good weapons. However, there were nowhere near enough of them for everybody to have one, so we'd take it in turns to use them when we were drilling.

We also got a water-cooled First World War machine gun, a weapon which was in short supply. The old soldiers in the Home Guard loved to tell youngsters like me of the times when they'd been short of water for the gun in the Great War. To solve the problem, the squad had had to urinate into the gun's water jacket to cool it when it got hot with continuous firing! However, in the Home Guard, we hardly ever had any shooting practice as I suppose ammunition was being conserved ready for the big push.

At an order, in training, we'd come to attention and then shout together: 'Down, crawl, observe, fire.' That was to fix in our minds what to do in case we ever came across the enemy. We also advanced in lines towards the "enemy", with rifles at the ready, and every now and then said, 'Bullets,' dipping our rifles as we did so, as if we were firing. That saved a lot of ammunition!

The only times we actually fired bullets were on a couple of occasions at the back of the barracks. We were given miniature rifles, .22 calibre, which we aimed at targets after a bit of instruction. I was wary because somebody could have been killed if I'd done the wrong thing and I didn't know how hard the kick from the rifle would be. As it turned out, it was rather a thrill and there was only a small kick, but I don't know if I hit the target with the one or two shots I had.

By August, the Battle of Britain was at its peak, so Helen and I didn't go on holiday to the seaside. It would have seemed unpatriotic. Things were getting difficult owing to food rationing, but some people still went away. However, we did have one or two outings. One day we went to Alton Towers by train and enjoyed it, even though there were no amusements. The highlight of the trip was another meal of egg on toast that we had at the tearoom!

Helen and I got engaged, probably some time during that year, but I can't remember specifically when it was. It was what you did in those days when you'd been going out for a while. Helen had put hints forward, but I didn't really want to get engaged because I was happy with how things were and I didn't want any ties. Anyway, I went along with it and bought her an eighteen-carat gold ring with three diamonds, set in platinum, from Thomas George Shaw, the jeweller, whose shop was at 7 City Arcade. People in general didn't have engagement parties at that time and we followed suit.

Once I'd become involved with the Home Guard, Mother was often left on her own, except for Floss. Dad was out regularly with the air-raid wardens, checking for bomb damage and lights showing through windows, which were supposed to be reported to the authorities. When I wasn't on duty, I'd be out with Helen, so Mother must have been terrified when there was a big raid on because the alert would last for hours sometimes.

I was still doing piecework at Taylor Tunnicliff and, by that time, my wages were often over four pounds a week. On 11 October, I was paid £4 1s. and received £4 2s. 2d. the following week.

On 14 November, there was a massive German air attack on Coventry. More than 4,000 houses were damaged or destroyed, most of the cathedral was flattened and around 600 people were killed. In North Staffordshire, though, only one person died that night in an air raid and I suppose we were lucky because many cities suffered more casualties and damage during the Blitz than we did in Stoke.

In the afternoon on my 25th birthday, in December, I was having a bath when there was a big bang. I hurried to get dry and dressed, but there were no more explosions. I hadn't heard an air-raid warning, but sometimes German bombers slipped into our airspace without us knowing. The story went round that a land mine had been dropped on the end of a parachute. The idea was that it came down slowly and, as it touched the ground, exploded outwards with greater effect than a bomb would do through dropping at speed and burying itself in the ground before exploding.

It was later reported that a stick of bombs had been dropped on Chesterton and killed fourteen people and injured scores of others. There was no specific announcement in the press or on the wireless at the time and it was merely stated that there'd been a raid on the Midlands and that there'd been casualties. The idea was to deny the enemy information and all we ever knew at the time about such events was by word of mouth.

On 16 December, when I was on duty at the barracks, bombs were dropped nearby, killing five people at 29 Mount Pleasant and also causing extensive damage in Argyle Street. We were taken out and posted around the scene of the destruction, with rifles and bayonets, to keep out sightseers and looters, but we weren't given bullets. We might have killed somebody! People who lived in the cordoned-off area were allowed to enter, but it was very difficult to tell who they were! Some had their identity cards with them when I challenged them, but others said they'd left them at home, so I let them through and hoped for the best!

Helen and I went to the Christmas dance at the Majestic, as usual, and I won a goose as a prize from a spot dance, in which you had to be on the right spot when the music stopped. At the end of the night, I collected the dead bird and walked Helen home. We went in the entry behind Helen's house for a goodnight kiss, so I had to put the goose down on their back yard step. But when I picked it up again, there was a pool of blood on the step! I then made my way home, but couldn't hand the bird over to my parents because they were asleep. So I left it outside and, feeling pleased with myself, offered my prize to Mother the following morning. However, I was disappointed because she pointed out that we already had a turkey. So I went to see Grandmother and Grandad Wallett and presented it to them. Although they must have been overwhelmed, because it was doubtful if they'd ever had a goose before, they refused it as it was much too big for their oven. So I had to return home with it, but eventually managed to give it away.

On 16 January 1941, incendiary bombs were dropped around Etruria in clusters, causing many fires. I suppose the Germans were again after Shelton Bar. Some of these bombs fell on the gasometers along Etruscan Street and holes were punched in the top of them. The holes allowed gas to escape and it became ignited, causing blazing jets. The whole area became lit up and a clear target for the Luftwaffe. It was marvellous how the entire gasworks didn't blow up, taking Etruria with it. But some of the workers showed incredible bravery and climbed to the top of the gasometers to put out the fires by filling the holes with lumps of clay. There were no official reports broadcast about where there'd been damage, but word got around that St. Matthew's Church, in Lord Street, had been hit, so I had a look at it myself and noticed that lumps had been knocked off it.

My cousin, Bernard, was a messenger for the air-raid wardens at the time and was travelling along Belmont Road when the bombs started dropping. So he helped to put out fires on the ground by shovelling dirt on them and spraying them with water from a stirrup pump. Uncle Ted didn't like Bernard being involved with all that because, with his First World War experiences, he knew what it was all about. But Bernard carried on volunteering and Uncle must have felt ashamed when he reflected upon himself sitting in Tinkersclough shelter throughout that raid.

On the same night, a stick of bombs wrecked six houses and killed eight people in Basford. Also, during the same raid, a single bomb was dropped on Stoke Old Road, in Hartshill, which destroyed five cottages, killing nine people.

By then, Vera and Harry had moved to 9 Holdcroft Road, Abbey Hulton, to a council house they'd had allocated to them. Sometimes, I'd stop in with Helen, while she looked after Young Harry, so that his parents could go out for the night. On one of these occasions, we had a row and I walked out on her. When I went out of the door, instead of going left, as I usually did, I turned right. Helen came running out after me in the direction of my normal route and, in the blackout, she couldn't find me, so I was able to get off home without any trouble.

The next few nights, I went out on my own, dancing at the Rialto in Church Street, Stoke, amongst other places. On one of these occasions, Helen called at my house with a friend and told Dad the heel had come off one of her shoes. She said they just happened to be passing! Dad fixed it for her and, after some conversation, the girls went away. A few nights later, Helen again knocked at our door, but this time I was at home. My parents invited her in and she told us that her father had died the previous night (2 February). He'd gone to bed as usual, but, when Elijah had woken up in the morning, he'd found his father dead. Mother said to me, 'Take her home,' which I did.

As Helen and I were engaged and Ted's death gave us the opportunity of a house, we decided to get married. I wasn't particularly bothered about it because we were alright as we were, but I couldn't for shame stop it and it was all going that way anyhow. So I said something like: 'Well, that's it. I suppose we'd better get married.' Helen was agreeable, of course, but probably wouldn't have liked to have made the suggestion first. It's funny she hadn't pushed it more. I got the impression very few fellows wanted to get married because they'd get tied up. It seemed to be the women who pushed it.

It was agreed that Leah would live with Helen and me in Rose Street after we got married and Elijah would stay with Vera and Harry. While Helen and I planned our wedding, she, Leah and Elijah continued to live in Rose Street and I stayed in Leek Road.

I don't think Ted had made a will and all he'd got was about a shilling in his pocket. Because of the family's lack of money, he was buried in the third-class area of Hanley Cemetery, towards the canal, in the same grave as Helen's mother, at a cost of £1 4s. His funeral was on 6 February and, when we were leaving afterwards, I put an arm round Helen to comfort her, but she was so upset that she shrugged it off. Later, I made a wooden cross for Ted's grave, but it disappeared.

The king and queen visited Stoke-on-Trent on 14 February to see the wartime operations of local industries and inspect the area's civil defence efforts. Their visit was supposed to be secret and I didn't know it was going to happen, but a large crowd assembled to greet them on their arrival at Stoke Station! There was a military parade in Winton Square, where the king and queen had a cup of tea from a mobile canteen and chatted with people. They then visited Shelton Bar and W. T. Copeland and Sons' Spode Works, in High Street, Stoke, before leaving on the royal train.

I wasn't bothered about them and didn't go chasing after them myself. It was costing a lot of money to keep them living in luxury, but I suppose they were a rallying point, though I don't think their visit made much difference to anything.

A new munitions factory was constructed in a hurry at Swynnerton by hundreds of building workers, including Big Harry, who told me that they were bricklaying almost shoulder to shoulder. Harry wasn't actually a bricklayer, but had been a brickie's labourer, so he knew something about the job. His brother, Ern, taught Harry the ropes while they were working next to each other on the Swynnerton job and put him right as they went along.

The factory was completed in 1941 and it was huge. Railway tracks were laid down from the main line near to Yarnfield and a station bigger than Stoke was built at Coldmeece, as well as a bus station. At the peak of the factory's production, 23,000 people, mostly women, worked there on shifts and most of them had to be brought in from, and taken back to, the surrounding area each day. The night shift had to be done in blackout conditions, so care had to be taken not to let any light escape. Shell cases were brought in from other places where they'd been made, such as Radway Green, and were filled with yellow explosive powder, which seemed to be the main occupation there. The powder affected the workers' skin and, when they were shopping in Hanley, it looked as if we'd been invaded by the Chinese!

Our Home Guard unit was eventually issued with real and fairly comfortable khaki army uniforms, just the same as those of the regular units, and heavy boots, with studs in the bottom, perhaps to help preserve the leather. We were also given flashes to sew onto our shoulders. They were pieces of thin material, with the words 'HOME GUARD' clearly displayed. But, as far as I know, we weren't given helmets and I can't ever remember ever wearing one in the Home Guard. But I did get two stripes to sew onto the arms of my blouse (a short jacket, tight round the waist) when I was promoted to corporal. They were just dished out, but I was never put in charge of anybody or anything. Perhaps they didn't have enough corporals and I was making the numbers up!

One night, when I was on duty, I got into conversation with another private, who'd been to the same school as me, although I couldn't remember him, maybe because he was a little older. He was named Jack Green and was a small, quiet fellow, who lived at 32 Douglas Street, Cobridge. He worked at Myott's pot bank, which was on the same road. He worked on the kilns, I think as an odd man, a labourer, who mainly shovelled coal into the oven fire. It was very hot work! I got on well with Jack. His wife, Rose, was slim and nervy, as though she was ready to explode, which she did on occasions.

After a while, Helen and I started going with Jack and Rose to the Coronation Working Men's Club, in Hunter Street, Cobridge, on Saturday nights and became members for a small annual fee. Although it was in my old stamping ground, I didn't feel any particular attachment to the area. The entertainment consisted mostly of singers, accompanied by a pianist, and they were generally of a good class. A committee man would get on the stage and ask for complete silence. Even if there was only a little noise, he'd tell the audience that the show wouldn't commence until they quietened down. Most times, there was sufficient order to allow the singer to do his or her stuff, at least for the first minute or so!

One night when the alert had sounded, Helen and I went across to her Aunt Sally and Uncle Bill's and got in their shelter with them. No bombs were dropped, so, after an hour or two, they got fed up and went back into their house. The next thing I knew was that they were shouting to us that the all clear had sounded. We must have dropped off to sleep and it was 2 a.m., so I had to get off home smartish!

In the Home Guard, we had to police vital places, such as the electricity works in Ridgway Road and the gasworks in Etruria. The former was better because it was nearer to home and, after my night stint had finished at 6 a.m., I could go to bed for about 1½ hours before going to work. It was a very tiring business. The guard was done on a two hours on and four hours off basis. We'd try to get a bit of rest during the off period by lying on the floor of the power station, with a blanket wrapped around us. When I was on guard, I'd stand on my own outside the works' railings, with a rifle and bayonet, but no ammunition. However, there was an electric alarm button on the railings, which could be pressed if there was trouble and would alert our commander inside the plant.

If anyone appeared, I was supposed to shout: 'Halt! Who goes there?' If it was somebody on our side, he was expected to answer, 'Friend.' I don't know what my reaction would have been if anyone had replied, 'Enemy!' Not many people used that road in the blackout, so it was pretty quiet. I'd stand there listening in case someone came up to me and I wondered what would happen if paratroopers were dropped nearby. It was hard to judge by sound how far away passers-by were. I did challenge one or two people, who were just walking on the park side of the road and pulled out their identity card to show me. I'd look at it and pretend to read it, but sometimes I wouldn't even be able to see what it was they were holding! I should imagine that most people avoided the area in case they got shot, whilst some of those who went by would be laughing later when they recalled what a fool the guard was not to have seen that what was being offered wasn't an identity card!

I didn't like the gasworks guard because we were posted right under a gasometer in Etruscan Street. I used to look up at it, towering high above me, and think that, if it blew up, my body would be scattered all over the area. I was glad I hadn't been on duty there the night the incendiary bombs had been dropped! No civilians ever came along when I was on guard there.

One night, a Home Guard sergeant appeared to see how I was getting on. He was a First World War veteran and started to tell me about his experiences. The alert had sounded and, while he was talking, we heard a plane droning in the sky. As it came nearer, he shouted, 'Get down flat on your face!' I did that as quickly as I could, even though I felt silly, but the plane passed by in the distance, giving us no bother at all!

Another night, we were guarding the North Staffordshire Colliery Owners' offices, opposite the junction of Leek Road and Boughey Road, in Shelton. There was a meeting taking place inside and, as I opened the door to see how it was faring, an amazing sight was revealed. There was a banquet going on, with the tables groaning under the weight of food and drinks! What a farce it was. The ordinary people were on rationing and there were the bigwigs living it up!

Norman Banks had joined the AFS, to help back up the regular fire service in dealing with the large number of fires that were caused by bombing. He told me they had to go as far afield as Birmingham to give assistance. I didn't fancy that lousy job, being stuck on top of a ladder, with the Germans dropping bombs all around me!

Bill Street joined the armed forces and went in the Grenadier Guards, in which he got to the rank of sergeant. He fought in the western desert in North Africa, with the Desert Rats, but, unfortunately, had an arm blown off. I never saw him again after he'd left Taylor Tunnicliff.

On Saturday nights, I still went to collect Helen from British Home Stores after closing time. I'd wait for her at the rear entrance, along with a gang of fellows also expecting the arrival of their girlfriends from the shop. Because of the blackout, when the girls came out, they couldn't see a thing because their eyes were accustomed to the electric lights. When a girl appeared in the doorway, the appropriate fellow would reach forward, grab her by the hand and lead her into the street.

Helen's sister, Leah, was working at Taylor Tunnicliff as a presser. She hand operated one of the metal presses that shaped ware. The machine was constructed with the desired shape on its bottom and it would squash "clay dust" (a clay-type compound) into the required compact item. It was a very repetitive job.

There was some talk of us going on shifts. I have a feeling that the firm wanted us also to work at night, which was when most air-raids occurred. I didn't fancy it one little bit, but nothing was done, thank goodness.

One night, I was talking to a sergeant in the Home Guard about the heavy shipping losses we were suffering and the effect on food rationing. He told me he thought we were finished and that we'd have to surrender because we were near to starvation. That shook me because, although things were getting bad, I couldn't bear to think we could be beaten.

An American lodging in Stoke-on-Trent also thought we were in a desperate situation, but was fined two pounds for saying, 'We can't win,' 'I take my hat off to Adolf Hitler,' 'The Germans will win the war,' and 'Lord Haw-Haw is a better man than Churchill.' People listened quite freely on the wireless to Haw-Haw (William Joyce), who broadcast Nazi propaganda to Britain, but I can't remember hearing him because I was out every night.

By that time, there were very few eggs to be had, but part of the egg ration was some powdered stuff from America, to which water was added before it was cooked. It didn't look like an egg; it was more like a yellow oatcake and it wasn't very nice. We also had tinned meatloaf from the Yanks, called Spam, which wasn't bad at all. We were short of Virginian-type cigarettes, but some brands that the Americans smoked were available, like Camel. They tasted terrible, just like camel dung, and few Englishmen liked them.

British Home Stores got a bus trip fixed up to a dance hall in Liverpool, which Helen and I went on. We danced until late and then made the return journey to Stoke in the blackout. I thought we'd never get back! There were no motorways then and it amazed me how the driver got us back because he had to find his way with masked headlights and without signposts, which had all been taken down earlier in the war. We arrived in Hanley at about 4 a.m. and then I had to see Helen home. As I walked down Huntbach Street on the way back to Leek Road, I joined another fellow and we got talking. I couldn't see much of him, but it turned out that he was a bus conductor going to work. I don't know what he thought of me going home to bed!

Owing to the shipping losses, there developed a shortage of imported scrap iron, which was needed to manufacture new arms for the war effort. So an order came into force that iron railings were to be requisitioned and all over the country workmen were sent to do the job. Some householders had railings on the outside of their walls and those were cut down by an acetylene flame at first, but that took too long. So a sledgehammer was then tried and that proved to be a lot quicker because cast iron would snap with a heavy blow. Between Victoria Road (which was later renamed College Road) and Victoria Avenue, in Shelton, was a small grassed area, surrounded by railings, inside which was a First World War tank on display. But workmen came along and took the whole lot for scrap iron! However, the railings at important places, like the gas and electricity works, were left up to help stop intruders and saboteurs getting in.

Helen and I arranged our wedding for 21 June at St. Mark's Church, Shelton, which was impressive and like a cathedral. It seemed a nice time of year to have the wedding and, in those days, it was expected you'd get married in your own area church. So we went to see the vicar in Rectory Road and put the banns in. It was to be a white wedding and we arranged to have the choirboys singing. Helen wrote to her favourite uncle, Joe, who'd moved to Coventry, asking him to give her away and he said he would. I chose my cousin, Aubrey, to be my best man because I was very friendly with him and it was decided that Big Harry would be the groomsman. The bridesmaids were picked by Helen and they were her sister, Leah; her cousin, Edith Johns, and my cousin, Annie. Helen also decided that Young Harry would be the pageboy because he was her nephew, her favourite. Also, he was a nice little lad, with curly hair, and so would add a touch of glamour.

We booked rooms at Keelings Road Wesleyan Chapel, on the corner with Rose

Street, for our reception. We were doing our own catering because it was unusual at that time to have the professionals in or hire a hotel or restaurant. We were relying on people helping us out with food from their rations, plus whatever else they could get together, like tablecloths, crockery and cutlery.

We started to redecorate Helen's house because it was crummy. With getting married, we wanted it to look fresh and new, but I was struggling as a decorator at first because I had no previous experience and there was a shortage of materials, especially paper for the walls. We made the paste from flour and water and we mixed lime with water to paint the ceilings. That was a messy job and not at all satisfactory, particularly in the living room, where the ceiling was very dirty through the coal smoke. Then Helen's Aunt Sally came in and said I'd put the border strip on upside down, though it looked alright to me. When she offered further advice, I got annoyed and handed her the brush I was using! She was taken aback, but there was no trouble and I carried on working.

On 24 May, our biggest warship, the battle cruiser, the Hood, was sunk by the new German battleship, the Bismarck. It was reported in the press and was really serious, but I didn't realize it.

The same day, I was the best man at my cousin Sam's wedding to Hilda Baxter at Christ Church, in Church Terrace, Cobridge. Sam had joined the navy and wore his uniform. I offered to wear my Home Guard uniform, as a joke really, but I was turned down flat by Hilda! She was a van driver, which was unusual for a woman at that time, but a lot of jobs had been left vacant through many men being called up. I can't remember any details about the wedding, but I do recall the excitement of the chase after the Bismarck, which was sunk three days later.

On 2 June, clothing rationing began and coupons were issued for the purchase of new clothes, shoes and boots, but that didn't affect us a lot. We never seemed to go short and we managed with what we'd got.

The day of the big wedding, Saturday 21 June, finally came. I went to work as usual in the morning, thinking every bit of production would help to beat Hitler, even though some people talked about me, suggesting I was scratching about for money. I finished at 1 p.m. and I think the ceremony was at 3 o'clock. Helen had the day off. Aubrey called for me at home and we set off for the church in good time, chauffer-driven in a hired car. It was sunny and warm and there was a breeze blowing. Helen wore a white dress and a gold cross and chain, which I'd bought as a special present for her. The wedding went off okay, with the usual kind of ceremony, and I put the platinum ring Helen had selected on her finger when the vicar asked me to. When he pronounced us man and wife, I kissed her, as was expected. It all felt new and strange and I was a bit bewildered.

Unfortunately, we couldn't have the church bells ringing, as we'd have liked, because it was forbidden. The peeling of bells had been designated as the official method of telling the population that we were being invaded by enemy paratroopers. However, we did get a *Sentinel* photographer to take pictures when we came out after the ceremony. These were, of course, in black and white and the results were alright, but the photos were spoiled by a scruffy notice board at the side of the church entrance. One of the pictures was printed in the *Weekly Sentinel* on 28 June, but Helen was written as 'Ellen' in the accompanying caption. Also, there was a short report on the occasion in the *Evening Sentinel* on 26 June. There was quite a lot of interest in the wedding from friends, work colleagues and neighbours, who turned up to the church, along with the official guests, but, after the photos had been taken, Helen and I were whisked away in the car to the reception rooms.

The reception went off okay and was mainly a sit-down meal, served up by the family. I gave a little speech, thanking people for the food and other items they'd kindly supplied for the occasion. As soon as the meal was finished and the washing-up commenced, guests started looking around for the crockery and cutlery they'd lent us. Everybody had tied cotton round their own cutlery to try to distinguish it from other people's, so, when it came to it, nobody knew which was theirs!

We hadn't got a honeymoon planned, I think because we felt it would have been unpatriotic, with the war being on and people dying, and then there was the expense. But Helen's Uncle Joe, who'd given her away, came over and offered to put us up for the night at his home in Coventry. I was worried about the German bombers, which had given the town a plastering, but he said it was alright as they hadn't been around for a while and the last biggish raid had been on 8 April. Helen seemed okay about it, perhaps not realizing what might have happened, and so, after some hesitation, I agreed we'd go back with him and his wife, Florrie, on the train.

My Uncle Jack had a car and offered to run us all to Stoke Station. He was still a foreman mechanic at Brown's Buses and I suppose he'd picked up a bargain car, with knowing something about motor vehicles. He'd had it a year or two and had previously taken Helen and me a trip in it, to a big area of tulip fields. I think he'd also conveyed some of our guests from the church to the reception. The hire car had gone by that time, so we accepted Uncle Jack's offer. Petrol was rationed by then and he was obviously using up some of his limited supply to help us out.

I told my parents that we were going off for a bit of a honeymoon and I gave Vera a pound to buy a drink at the Cross Keys for any of the guests who wanted one. That doesn't seem much nowadays, but it was sufficient for all those who wanted to drink to our health.

The journey to Coventry was uneventful and darkness had fallen by the time we got there. Coventry Station was in semi-darkness and everything appeared strange. We seemed to be in another world. Uncle Joe and Aunt Florrie guided us onto a bus, which took us to their modern house at 39 Sussex Road. Inside, we met Aunt Florrie's mother, who was an old lady, and Uncle Tom, who'd been adopted by Uncle Joe's parents. They'd died when Uncle Joe was in his teens and he'd been left to bring up his younger brothers, Tom, Alf and Ted (Helen's father). So he'd had a rough time and it was a great achievement because they were hard days then, with no financial help available from anywhere.

Helen and I were given some supper and then we were allocated the best bedroom in the house. In the morning, there was a knock on the door and in came Uncle Tom with two cups of tea and the news that Germany had invaded Russia. I didn't really realize the implications of that and we got ready and went downstairs for breakfast, which was very enjoyable. While we were eating, they all told us about the Blitz in Coventry. They'd spent hours huddled under the stairs, while bombs and incendiaries rained down. They'd been lucky because the only damage had been to their roof and ceilings, which must have been repaired before our visit.

After breakfast, we were taken by bus to the city centre to view the damage. Of course, by then most of the rubble had been cleared away and things had been tidied up. Even so, it looked rather rough. Uncle Joe pointed to a building, which was all boarded up, and told me that it was Woolworth's. I thought it had been well put out of business, but, on looking closer, I saw a notice chalked on a board, which read, 'Business as Usual,' so the shop must have been open! Outside, there was a huge hole in the road, with an exposed pipe about four inches in diameter running across it! The state of some of the roads was so bad that there were still diversions. Uncle Joe said that, after the 14 November raid, the damage had been so bad that it had been hard to tell which street was which!

We got back from our trip in time for some dinner, which again would have been provided out of their food ration. We chatted for a while and Uncle and Aunt then took us by bus to the station to catch a train back to Stoke. From there, we walked along Leek Road to see Mother and Dad and told them about our brief honeymoon. We eventually made our way to 12 Rose Street, but it was strange going to live in another house with someone new.

The first thing we had to do was to look for a box of matches to kindle the gaslight. That seemed peculiar after simply being used to switching on an electric light. We'd bought a new bedroom suite, of light-coloured oak, for, I think, £25, but made do with the old mattress and springs. I found that the sheets had been arranged in what was called a French bed style, so we couldn't get into the bed! Therefore, we had to rearrange it and then shake the mattress, which was a kind of bag filled with flocks that had to be levelled out. Eventually, we got into bed, only to roll into a sag in the middle of it, where the springs had worn! It was most uncomfortable and, the next morning, I had to get up earlier than I had before because I had a much longer walk to make to Taylor Tunnicliff.

I had to sleep on the side of the bed next to the door. That was because, if there was an attack on us during the night by a thug, I'd be the more likely one to be on the receiving end of any punishment! I didn't think the arrangement was fair, but I put up with it from then on, to avoid being called a coward!

The conditions in the house were more primitive than those I'd been used to in Leek Road. I suppose in a way I'd moved down in the world, but I didn't give it too much thought and, of course, I was at work half the time. I took it in my stride, which you do more when you're young.

Shortly afterwards, I discussed with Helen the open-door policy of the house that had been in operation for years. I wasn't happy with it because I didn't want people walking in just when they liked. We decided from then on to keep it shut, so anyone calling had to knock. When Aunt Sally next came, she couldn't get in and wanted to know what was going on. When I explained the situation, she wasn't very pleased!

One night, when Helen and I were in bed, the alert sounded. I don't think any bombs were dropped locally, but the sound of the planes going over frightened Helen. She shouted to Leah, who was in the back bedroom, to join us, which she did. Perhaps Helen wanted us all to die together if we were hit.

We were having Young Harry stay with us overnight at times. Helen liked him coming and it was giving his parents a break. She thought he was wonderful, but I never got a word out of him. He just stared at me! Unfortunately, one night, when there was an air raid on, he developed toothache and wouldn't be pacified. Helen thought we ought to take him back home, so we got dressed in the small hours and set off. The German planes were going over in droves, in the direction of Liverpool, and there wasn't a soul about. Although no bombs were dropped on Stoke, it was really frightening. I carried Harry most of the way on my shoulders and, when we got to Holdcroft Road, we roused his parents and explained the situation. We then had to walk all the way back, with the bombers still going over!

The clothing coupons weren't sufficient for the girls and those at Taylor Tunnicliff used to rub sand from the firm onto their legs. That left a brown colour on them, so it looked as if the girls were wearing silk stockings. For effect, they finished it off by running a pencil mark right down the back of their legs. That gave the impression of a seam, which was fashionable then. One day, a director saw Leah taking some sand and asked her what she was doing. When she explained, he looked puzzled, but told her it was okay as long as she didn't take too much.

I was told that I had to go on a weekend course of battle training, along with other members of the Home Guard. I collected a rifle and bayonet to take home with me so that I didn't have to go to the barracks beforehand to get them. When Helen saw the rifle, she was terrified because she thought it might go off. I tried to explain that I had no ammunition with me, so I couldn't fire the rifle nor could it go off accidentally. But it was no use – the rifle had to stand in a corner of the parlour out of the way!

After dinner on the Saturday, I set off for Holehouse Lane (which is now Holehouse Road), Abbey Hulton, off which I found the camp in some fields. In charge was a sergeant major from the regular army, who took us to some bell tents, where we were to sleep the night. I don't think we did much for the rest of the day!

The following morning, we had breakfast early and then we were sent on an assault course, which had been constructed in a field. We had to crawl under, jump over and run round different obstacles in the quickest possible time.

The sergeant major later demonstrated the use of a sticky bomb, which was like a ball, about the size of two clasped hands, covered with a sticky substance and with a short handle attached to it. He told us that it was different from normal bombs in that it exploded *towards* the greatest resistance. To prove that, he ordered us to stand in a line, a few yards from, but facing, the bomb, and bend our heads down in case bits of dirt blew in our faces. He then stuck the bomb onto, I think, a metal sheet and pulled out the safety pin. After a few seconds, the bomb exploded exactly as he'd explained and the force of the blast went through the sheet and not in our direction, much to my relief!

In the training area was a shooting range, but I can't remember us making use of it, probably because we were preserving ammunition. The range was later commemorated when a new street built off Holehouse Lane was called Butts Green.

Helen was 21 on 29 September, so we had a little party at home to celebrate and my parents came along. By then, it was safer to hold events because there weren't so many air raids as the Germans were concentrating on their war against the Russians.

I got fed up of carrying around the big old-fashioned front door key to our house, so I went to see the landlord's agent at his office in Cheapside and got a

Yale lock from him. Fortunately, the man next door in Rose Street, at number 10, had a drill with the exact-sized bit required, so I was able to make a good job of fitting the new lock and we then only had to carry a lightweight key.

One of Helen's relatives let us have a second-hand wireless cheap. Its electricity was supplied by an accumulator. When the charge had run down, after a week or two, I had to take it to a nearby shop to have it charged up again. The reason for all that was that our house had no electricity supply.

Sometimes, Helen, Leah and I would decide to have a fish and chip supper. While the girls were cutting and buttering slices of bread and making tea, I'd make my way up to St. John Street, where there was a high-class fishery. I'd have to queue before asking for a couple of fish and some chips and give the owners a bowl to put some mushy peas in. I'd then hurry home, with our supper held close to me to keep it warm.

One morning, I had a letter from the Ministry of Labour and National Service, giving me the armed forces registration number HC2 2641 and asking me to attend a medical in a room at Bethesda Sunday School, in Bethesda Street, on 5 December. I duly presented myself to the North Staffordshire Medical Board and had to strip off all my clothes. After a bit of prodding and some tests, I was declared to be Grade 1. I was very pleased with that result because it made me feel quite healthy. Later, I realized that most lads examined got the same grade because the Forces needed men!

Following the Japanese attack on Pearl Harbor, Germany and Italy declared war on the U.S.A., on 11 December. I thought that was a crazy thing to have done. They should have waited to see what happened.

During my medical examination, I'd asked if I could serve in an aircrew in the RAF, with the "Boys in Blue", as they were nicknamed from their blue uniform. I wanted to do that because it seemed an exciting job, piloting a plane and shooting down Jerry aircraft! After a week or two, I had a letter, with a train ticket, telling me to report to a depot in Birmingham for a further medical and an educational test, which I did. One of the tests was to blow, I think for a minute, into a mouthpiece, attached to a dial, which indicated the pressure. Although I succeeded in that, I failed the overall examination. I was then told that I'd be put on the ground staff instead of serving with the "Brylcreem Boys", as the RAF pilots had become known because many of them used the hair cream. I should have been well satisfied with that, but I felt as if I wanted to go out there and do something. So I told the fellow that, but he defended the ground staff and explained how they fought back when the Jerries attacked aerodromes. Still I was adamant and told him I wished to go into the army and so that's what happened.

Rationing was getting tighter and cigarettes were hard to come by. I was smoking fifteen to twenty a day and having to try different shops to get any. Jack Green thought the government should stop tobacco imports, but I think it would have had a detrimental effect on the war effort because many people (including me) would have hated to have been without a fag. And how would Churchill have done without his cigars?

There were workers moving from place to place to do various jobs and they needed somewhere to stay. Some built bomb factories and other military establishments. There was a national appeal to take in a lodger and so, in response, Mother and Dad put up a girl from outside the area, who was working here. She was pleasant, well spoken and nice looking, with dark hair. She had a husband or boyfriend in the air force and said he'd had two eggs for breakfast on one occasion. Mother told Helen the story, but she disbelieved it because eggs were still rationed and there were very few about. Also, her brother, Elijah, was in the RAF and he'd never had two eggs for his breakfast! I think Helen was jealous because the girl was getting attention from Mother, so there was an unpleasant atmosphere in the house when we visited for quite some time. The girl's statement did seem exaggerated, but the Forces were issued with extra amounts when there was a glut of foodstuffs.

In the early hours of 15 March 1942, the Home Guard went on manoeuvres, against the regular army, an officer said. I never saw our opponents because I was stuck on guard duty at the Victoria Square barracks. I was standing halfway up the entrance passage, with my rifle and bayonet fixed. There were a number of people in the square watching and showing an interest. One fellow gradually worked his way up to me and seemed to be trying to sidle past to have a look at what was going on in the barracks' square behind. Very little was spoken, but he wouldn't go back, even though he wouldn't have known that I had no ammunition. I looked around for help, but the guard commander was out of sight, so I was on my own. The fellow was getting me a little annoyed because I'd got the tip of my bayonet almost up his left nostril and still he wouldn't move! I was contemplating sticking the bayonet in his chest just a mere fraction, to make him jump and go back, when I was relieved by the next guard. I don't know what happened then. I was just glad to be away from the situation.

On 5 April, the baking of white bread came to an end. From then on, we had bread something like wholemeal is today. We were told it was healthier, though everybody thought that was a con. But it tasted pretty decent to me.

The Yankee armed forces began to infiltrate the country. Some of them were stationed in a camp at Yarnfield. In their time off, they were driven to various towns in the area in "liberty" trucks. They were called that because they freed the soldiers from restraint for a few hours. The Yanks filled the pubs in Hanley and had plenty of money to spend, so a lot of the girls were attracted to them. They were as bold as brass and went around with a cocky attitude, like they did on the films that flooded our picture houses. They had sweets and chocolate, which were rationed here, to give to the girls. Nylon stockings were new on the market in the U.S.A. and, of course, the Yankee soldiers also handed them out to the girls, sometimes in return for favours! Children used to follow the Yanks around and ask them for chewing gum.

They had a lovely uniform made with the best material. They had shiny badges and buttons and even collars and ties. Our lads just had battledress, with a tunic which fastened around the neck. It was made of rough serge and looked like horse blankets! Our lads in the Forces couldn't compete with them and had very little money in their pockets, which caused resentment.

The Americans had a club in Hanley, at 18 Upper Market Square, which is presently occupied by Halifax. They had the Stars and Stripes hoisted over the building and, whenever I saw the flag, my blood used to boil because they'd taken over and my thoughts turned to how I could pull it down and replace it with the Union Jack!

Perhaps people didn't realize it at the time, but the Americans were an occupying force and they gradually took over. They swaggered around the place as though they owned it. The land they occupied became their land and they had guards to defend it. Anyone trying to get in their bases would have risked being shot!

Helen had an Uncle John, on her mother's side, the Simons. He was an insurance man, who was very well dressed and a snob. Aunt Sally had given him a bit of business, but, apparently, one time, when he was collecting money from her, she dropped a sixpenny piece on the floor. Uncle John put his foot on it and was going to claim it, but Uncle Bill saw what happened and told him about it. Uncle Bill couldn't abide him and referred to him as "Gentleman John"!

One night when there was a raid, there was an almighty crash just after tea time, I seem to remember. Helen, Leah and I dashed into the parlour, perhaps in panic, and I put my arms around them, pushing them into the corner by the front door. A bomb had hit Broom Street, which was just a stone's throw away from us, and I was expecting the next one to hit us, but, fortunately, nothing else happened.

One night, early in September, when I got home from work, there was a letter awaiting me, with 'OHMS' printed on it. It contained my call-up papers to the Territorial Army and a travel warrant. It told me to report to an army depot in Wakefield in Yorkshire on the 17th and to take my Home Guard uniform with me. That was because it was the same type of uniform as the regular army used. My call-up was a shock, even though I knew it had to happen some time, and Helen wasn't very pleased!

The next morning, Dad was already toiling away when I got to work. I threw the letter down on his bench and awaited his approval. He picked it up slowly and I could see he dreaded opening it. After he'd read it, he echoed my own thoughts and said, 'It had to come.' Only later did I realize what his thoughts were when he was told his only son had to go away, to what?

Since I'd been married, I'd carried on having my dinners with my parents during the week because their house was near to the factory. That day, I had to tell Mother about my call-up and she was very upset.

The works manager told me that he'd tried to hold on to me, but had failed. I informed Tom Reeves, our foreman, and he said, 'Come and see us when you're on leave.' I also told the office of the Home Guard, at the Victoria Square barracks, but they didn't break down in tears!

One night shortly afterwards, Dad knocked at our door and came in to offer Helen a home with him and Mother while I was away. She accepted because she and Leah would have been left on their own. It was then decided that Leah would go to live with Vera and Harry in Abbey Hulton.

Soon after, Vera came to us with a sob story. It seemed she had married friends who had difficulties with their living accommodation. She suggested we let them have our house until they found somewhere else. Like fools, we agreed because they were Vera's pals and we believed they'd vacate the house when I came home from the war. Also, Helen said she didn't want the trouble or expense of going to pay the rent every week, so we decided to hand the rent book over to them. I went to see the landlord's agent to get things sorted out, but he said that once they got in the house we'd have no chance of getting them out. But I was still in cloud-cuckoo-land and told him I was sure it would be alright. He said:

'Right. It's up to you!'

When Helen moved in with my parents, she couldn't take much furniture with her because there was no room to put it. So she left most of it at Rose Street and asked the new occupants to look after it until I was demobilized. I suppose she never dreamed that it would be another four years before I got home!

4 The Muleteer

On 17 September 1942, I made my way alone to Stoke Station in battledress, having stripped off my Home Guard flashes and my corporal stripes. I changed my travel warrant to a one-way ticket to Wakefield and wondered what would follow. It was a nice day and the journey was uneventful. The train came to a halt in the afternoon at Wakefield Kirkgate Station and I reluctantly got out. There seemed to be hardly anyone around and I was wondering what to do, but an army corporal appeared and took control. He seemed to be a decent fellow and told me he'd been on duty at the station all day, waiting for and directing new recruits. He took me to an army truck and drove me to Nostell Priory, on the edge of the town, which had large grounds and had been converted to an army depot.

I was taken to a fellow sitting behind a trestle table and he signed me into the army for the duration of the war. I was enlisted into the 37th Primary Training Wing, although I never knew that was what it was called. The fellow wrote all my particulars into a brown *Soldier's Service Book*, which he handed to me, with the words, 'Don't lose it!' I looked into it and saw that I had my very own number, which was 14287042. I thought it seemed rather big because there were never that many men in the whole of the services, never mind the army on its own. Later, I met a soldier whose number was in the eleven millions and he'd only joined three months before me. Perhaps they were trying to kid the Germans that we had a huge army!

There were some other new recruits as well and we were shown our sleeping quarters, which were in some old stables. We were each given a cloth bag, shaped like an empty mattress, and told to fill it with straw from some full bales. We then slept on our mattresses on the floor, but I rolled off mine several times in the night because I'd filled it too full! The next day, I emptied a lot of the straw out and made myself a much more comfortable bed.

On waking, we had to wash and shave in cold water in the wash house, which had a long table, with a trough running down the centre and a few taps hung over it. I wasn't used to that, so it felt a bit rough!

Then I had a medical, which I again passed A1. My description was put in my service book and the details were the same as those which had been written up in my Medical Examination Record by the North Staffordshire Medical Board the previous December: 'Height 5 ft 9 ins.; Weight 139 lbs.; Maximum Chest 36 ins.; Complexion Fresh; Eyes Brown; Hair D. Brown; Distinctive Marks and Minor Defects Scar L. Knee.'

The same day, I was ordered to report to the dentist. I'd already had seven teeth taken out and I fully expected to have a front tooth extracted as well because it had decayed quite a bit. But the dentist cleaned it up and filled it. He did the same with another tooth and then polished the rest. I hadn't realized till then that teeth could be repaired! I was very pleased with the result and, from then on, I had my teeth checked regularly. That must have worked well at least while I was in the army because I only had to have one more filling during the whole time I was a soldier.

We were issued with two uniforms, but because I had my Home Guard battledress, I had less to come to me than most of the others. The uniforms were covered with a white powder, which, we were told, resisted poison gas, but it wore off after a short while! The new blouse I was given was so big around the neck that it would have fitted two heads in, but a tailor made some chalk marks on it for alteration. We wore one of the uniforms most of the time, keeping the other for best, for guard duties and when we went out on leave, but neither was washed during the whole time I had them!

We were given a large kitbag, made of canvas, to put our stuff in – clothes, shoes, general belongings, anything. The idea was to keep it all together, rather than leave it lying around for anybody to pick up, and it made it simple to move things when we changed locations. I've still got it. One invaluable thing I kept in there was my housewife (a repair outfit of needles, a thimble, cotton and wool), which we were also allocated.

The next day (the 19th), I had an inoculation, known as TAB, for typhoid and paratyphoid fever, and another for tetanus. Those were the first of quite a number of vaccinations I had during my war service and I was later also immunized against typhus and cholera.

Every day, we had to clean and polish our boots (which were heavy and designed for marching) and shine our general service cap badge. We were general service soldiers until we got fixed up with a regiment, so our cap badge was designed with that in mind. We also had to blanco (or colour) our webbing belts and gaiters, make up our bunks and lay out our equipment. All that was for the morning inspection on parade, which took place after breakfast every day except Sunday.

After a day or two, we started to sleep in doubled-up bunks in huts. I had a lower bunk, but the one above me wasn't very high. At about ten o'clock, somebody, like the guard sergeant, would shout, 'Lights out,' which was the signal for us to get into bed. I woke up in the middle of the first night and panicked because I couldn't see a thing. I thought I'd lost my sight, so I quickly sat up and banged my head on a crosspiece of the bunk above. I saw a few stars, which brought me back to my senses and I realized that the problem was that the windows had been blacked out! I felt my head, which seemed wet with blood, but, as I couldn't see, there was nothing I could do about it. As soon as the lights came on in the morning, I dashed to a mirror, but, amazingly, found my head to be okay.

For the first few days, we weren't allowed out of our barracks because, as raw recruits, we'd have dented the army's image with our unsoldierly behaviour! I don't think I ever went into Wakefield, but I do remember one day walking for leisure along a country road with others from our group.

We were increasingly taught drill and how to march. I had it pretty easy because I'd been drilling in the Home Guard and didn't make as many mistakes as most of the others. There were about 125 of us and we were divided into four platoons, each of which was named after a general. Mine was Roberts Platoon, but we were never told which General Roberts that was, so it was just a name as far as I was concerned. Sergeant Dunn, who, with a corporal, was to lick us into shape, told us that at the end of six weeks there'd be a passing-out parade and we were expected to get the top marks from our commanding officer. Sergeant Dunn was pretty confident that we'd succeed because his last platoon had been the best of the four. He was a small, but cheerful fellow, who had the ability to show us how to do things. But when he demonstrated how to come to attention, he always made such a kerfuffle that his cap would fall off. The corporal, standing next to him, would pick it up and hand it back to him. We didn't laugh at that because we didn't dare, but we did smile!

There was quite a bit to remember. We'd assemble on the parade ground just before the appointed time and then one of our instructors would come along and shout, 'Squad!' That would bring us to attention. At the command, 'Right marker,' a pre-selected rookie would march to a spot facing the instructor and come to a halt. The 'Fall in' order would then be given, at which we'd smartly march to the left-hand side of the right marker and organize ourselves in three ranks, with about ten fellows in each. There was no pre-decided position. You just found a place and it soon sorted itself out.

The roll call had to be taken in case anyone had decided in the night to go home! We'd then get a series of orders, which we often made a mess of. Some of the main ones were:

'Stand at ease,' according to which, we were to clasp our hands behind our backs and move our left feet a step to the side;

'Stand easy,' meaning we were supposed to keep our feet still, but could move our bodies a little;

'By the left, quick march,' which meant we should start on our left foot and keep in line with the man on the left in the front row;

'Left turn,' when we were required to turn to the left and vice versa if we were to change direction to the right;

'About turn,' whereby we should turn back to the way we'd come;

'Left [or right] incline,' as a result of which we were supposed to bend slightly to the left (or right), but the manoeuvre could end up in a shambles;

'Halt,' which actually needed a bit of a shuffle in the process and it was marvellous how everybody eventually learned to come together;

'Change step,' to achieve which we had to do a little skip from left to right or vice versa;

'Slow march,' when a funeral-type march was wanted, but there was no exact timed pace;

'Eyes left [or right],' whereby we should turn our heads in the required direction;

'Dismiss,' at the end of the parade, after coming to attention and turning right, and saluting when an officer was present.

Sometimes, we paraded with rifles and were given different orders, such as:

'Slope arms,' as a result of which we were to put our rifles on our left shoulders;

'Order arms,' which meant we had to rest our rifle butts on the ground, with the muzzles pulled in towards us;

'Present arms,' whereby we were to hold our rifles in front of us, with the triggers facing forwards;

'Fix bayonets,' when we were required to take our bayonets from their sheaths and attach them to our rifles;

'Unfix bayonets,' which obviously meant we were to put them away.

As you can imagine, half the time we were running around in circles, but our drill improved every day and, after a couple of weeks, we were beginning to look like soldiers.

By then, Sergeant Dunn had become impressed by one of our fellows, who seemed to walk about with his nose in the air. So he told the recruit that he was going to recommend him for a commission. I don't know what came of it, but the fellow had officer style written all over him.

The rifles we used were Short Lee-Enfields, which had been popular in the First World War. They had an adjustable rear sighting and were very accurate. We did fire them occasionally, but were only given about four rounds of ammunition because bullets were in short supply. Their barrels were shorter than those of other rifles, but their bayonets were on the long side.

We didn't have our own rifles. They were kept in the armoury at the barracks and brought out for exercises, so I ended up with different rifles at different times. It was rather sloppy and it was the same the whole time I was in the army.

At the end of each week, we had to queue to get our pay from an officer, who had a pile of cash on a trestle table. We had to stand to attention and salute before receiving it and the officers didn't like us counting it! My first payment was eight shillings. That may have been for a short week, but I didn't get a lot more afterwards. Being married, an allowance was taken from my wages by the army and sent to Helen, but included in our pay was a small amount for cleaning materials, such as boot polish, metal polish, blanco and cloths, which we had to buy ourselves.

One day, Sergeant Dunn asked, 'Anyone play the piano?'

I held back because I'd heard old soldiers say, 'Don't volunteer for anything!' But two or three of the lads said they could, so the sergeant ordered them to run up the road and back while the rest of us stood and watched them! There was no point in it. He was just taking the mickey.

Later in our training, we were introduced to the Bren gun. I think there was one per platoon. We practised firing it without any ammunition, which again was scarce, so that saved us from having to set up on a firing range. We just pulled the trigger and pretended that it had fired! We also took it apart and put it back together again. That was to learn how it worked because it would quickly get hot when being fired and the barrel would have to be changed every so often.

I wrote to Helen nearly every day and to my parents to a lesser degree. I soon noticed a fellow who appeared to be looking over my shoulder at my letters. I took no action at first, but then I got annoyed because I thought he was kinky, so I asked him what he was up to. I got a surprising answer – he could neither read nor write. I felt sorry for him right away and asked if he'd like me to write him a letter to his wife. He was pleased and accepted my offer, but he wasn't the least bit helpful when I asked him what he'd like me to put. He told me to write whatever I liked! I did my best, but it was funny writing to a woman I'd never met and trying to put in some warmth and love. He told me that he normally worked in an abattoir, receiving five pounds a week for killing animals, which was more than I was getting at Taylor Tunnicliff. I wrote about three letters for him, but I can't remember seeing him again after that.

On the day of our passing-out parade, we put on our best battledress and boots and gave everything an extra polish. All four platoons assembled on the parade ground in front of some officers. Each platoon did its drill and the officers then got together to decide which was the best. Naturally, it was Roberts Platoon and we and our instructors were very pleased.

We recruits were also tested on our ability to do different things. The first test was to try to thread a needle and it was surprising that one or two of the fellows couldn't do it. Then there were things which had to be put together or taken apart. The tests got more complicated, so that the last puzzles were mind benders. I got about halfway through. I think the fellows who hadn't been able to thread their needles were put in the pioneer corps, the pick and shovel mob!

Then came interviews and mine was conducted by a private. He asked me what branch of the service I wanted to be in. I was still enthusiastic and said I'd like to be a tank driver, but that I supposed they already had plenty of them. He said, 'Oh no, we want some more.' So I thought I had a good chance and was pleased. We were told to keep our eyes on the notice board to see where we'd be posted to. Eventually, my name came up and the order stated that I was to be sent to the 25th Medium and Heavy Training Regiment of the Royal Artillery at Marske-by-the-Sea in Yorkshire, a few miles from Redcar.

I arrived in Marske on 28 or 29 October, along with some others. I heard there'd been a bombing raid on the camp on the 16th, which had caused some damage. We were interviewed and asked what we wanted to do. I said I wanted to be a driver, but was told that there were a lot of them, so I'd have to be a gunner! We were billeted in long wooden huts and had the luxury of sleeping in single bunks!

Our guns had a six-inch calibre and were classified as medium size. They could also be used as howitzers to shoot over an obstruction, such as a small mountain, and drop a shell on the other side. The shells were very heavy and it must have been really tiring to have loaded them when firing went on for hours. We soon got training with the guns and had a bash at all the necessary tasks involved, including laying, which was pointing them in the right direction. In most cases, the target was out of sight. Again, it was all done without ammunition because it was too expensive to use, so we had to pretend we were firing the guns! I think I only once picked a shell up and that was a dummy. My army service book says I was also trained on 4.5-inch guns, but I can't remember those!

We practised shouting messages as part of our training. We were spread out around a large field, about twenty yards apart. An officer gave a message to the gunner next to him and told him to shout it to the next man and so on until the last fellow shouted it back to the officer. The message he received was entirely different to the one he sent out and, though we tried several times, the result was always the same! I shudder to think what would have happened had we had to do that in action.

We were given an artillery badge for our glengarry caps. It was not a full-blown one, in the shape of an artillery piece, but was smaller and depicted a bursting bomb. It was more suitable for our loose caps because of its size. We were also issued with a lanyard each, for show because it served no useful purpose. We put it under our left epaulette and armpit, to thread through a loop in the cord to form a circle and then the end of the lanyard was tucked into the left breast pocket. It had originally been used to thread though the triggers of artillery pieces to prevent injury from the firing recoil. We were issued with khaki-coloured ones, probably for camouflage, but we replaced them with nicer-looking white ones, which we bought from army and navy stores.

One day, our PT instructor asked if any of us would like to do some boxing.

Several of us said we would. Every morning, at about 6.30, he'd stick his head into the huts and shout, 'Boxers out!' We'd don vests and shorts and tumble out to go for a run for about twenty minutes. One morning, it was snowing and I regretted having volunteered when I could have been nice and snug in bed! Later in the day, we'd do a bit of boxing among ourselves, whilst being coached by a fellow with a broken nose! We were told that we'd be fighting some lads from another regiment in a tournament, but, when it came to it, the instructor was unable to fix me up with a bout. He said he'd see if he could get one of our lads to take me on, but I didn't want to fight one of my mates, so I wasn't involved in the tournament.

In our time off, we were allowed to wander into Marske and onto the sea front. We couldn't get down to the sands because barbed wire was strung all the way along and behind that defence were signs reading, 'Beware Mines'. We also went, by train, I think, to Saltburn-by-the-Sea, which was quite small, and Redcar, which was bigger and a proper seaside resort in peacetime. We went to the NAAFI canteens for char and a wad (a mug of tea and a bun), which made a change from the camp cookhouse, where we had to queue to be served more or less whatever they had in.

On 26 November, we were tested in a gas chamber, which was a big hut, in a field, filled with DM gas. We were ordered to put on our gas masks and walk and then run around in the chamber before taking the masks off. We then spent about half a minute in there, breathing in the poison, and we were soon gasping for breath. Afterwards, we were ordered outside, where half the fellows spewed up their guts and I wasn't very happy myself!

On 16 December, to celebrate our passing out from gun training, we actually had to shoot one of the guns! I wasn't in the firing team and so went along with many others to watch the proceedings. The gun was towed up to a cliff top, placed facing out to sea and fired. It was entered in my service book that I'd fired a six-inch howitzer, though I never did!

A sergeant told us that we might be getting leave at Christmas, but it seemed to be a tale because some lads had been in the army for years and had never had furlough during the festive season. However, we'd done three months' service and so were due for a holiday. Soon after, to my delight, confirmation of our leave, from the 22nd to the 30th, was posted on the notice board. When the time came to go home, I collected my travel warrant and some pay and food coupons and made my way to the railway station with the rest of our mob.

I travelled back via Middlesbrough, which wasn't very pretty, and, I should imagine, Manchester. On arrival at Stoke Station, I had to show my leave pass to the "redcaps" (the military police), who were always hanging around looking for trouble. I walked along Station Road and then Leek Road, past their office at number 652 (now 139), but I didn't call in! I had a good Christmas back with my family, though Helen and I only had my old bachelor's single bed to sleep in owing to the difficulty of accommodating our furniture from 12 Rose Street.

Helen had started going to Shelton Church, which was fairly convenient for her to get to from Leek Road. I suppose she also went there because it was where we'd got married, but I didn't go with her while I was on leave because I wasn't interested.

When I'd first met her, she was attending Hanley Gospel Mission, in Majolica

Street, Hanley, with her Aunt Sally and Uncle Bill, and had been going there regularly from when she'd been in Sunday school. I suppose she'd decided to transfer her allegiance to Shelton Church because the mission was now some distance from her new home. The mission was eventually demolished to make way for the bypass in Hanley.

It was a wrench to leave home again after Christmas and have to return to Marske, but, as I'd completed my training, I was only there briefly. On 11 January 1943, I was transferred to the 3rd Reserve Medium Regiment of the Royal Artillery, which was based in Watford. Along with some others, I was sent to a depot there and I suppose we travelled by rail. Unknown to me, we were awaiting transfer to a frontline regiment.

While we were in Watford, we attended lectures and went to cinemas, where films were shown on things like how to kill Germans and how to recognize different tanks and military objects. One of the films demonstrated how to get behind a sentry, slit his throat, kick him in the ribs when he fell to the ground and then kick him hard in the head to make sure he was finished off.

I wrote to Helen, making arrangements to phone her. On the agreed night, she'd be near a telephone because she'd be fire watching with a colleague at British Home Stores, ready to report any flames to the fire brigade. At the appointed time, I went into a phone box and asked the operator to connect me to Stoke. He told me to put some money in the slot, which I did, but he didn't believe that I'd done so. As it was about 10 p.m., the shops had closed and so I had to chase around to get some more change. I was lucky the second time and got through. Helen answered, but didn't believe it was me, perhaps because my voice didn't sound the same! We had a few words, but found it was hard to communicate. To us, it was high technology and I doubt if either of us had ever used a phone before.

After I'd been at Watford for a week or two, I was informed via the notice board that I was being posted to Beauly, near Inverness in Scotland, to join 454 Battery of the 3rd Mountain Regiment of the Royal Artillery, which was part of the 52nd (Lowland) Division. The regiment had been formed on 1 December and its commanding officer was Lieutenant Colonel J. S. W. Tremenheere, but the leading officers were remote, like gods, so I rarely saw him in the three years that I was with the regiment. But I don't suppose he ever came across me at all!

I wondered how the hell the regiment got guns up mountains, but a fellow told me that he thought they had mules. I couldn't understand how mules could possibly tow a gun and limber up there, without it tipping over or getting bogged down. My mind just boggled with the thought, but no-one seemed to know much about it, so I had to wait and see.

On 1 February, a few of us from Watford travelled by train to Beauly, which had a station, even though it was only a village. Having detrained, we checked in at the regimental camp offices on the outskirts of the village. We were then shown to our Nissen huts and allocated single bunks. Each of the huts was heated by a coal-fired stove, located in the middle. I discovered that it was roasting by the stove and freezing at the ends of the hut, but, fortunately, I was placed nicely in between. Unfortunately, the toilets left something to be desired. They were like wooden boxes with a hole in the top and there was a sanitary orderly, who was responsible for emptying them. Everybody wanted his job because he was his own boss. He didn't have to go on parade; he only had to look after the toilets.

From the conversations going around, it seemed that the regiment really did have mules. About 6.30 the next morning, we paraded on a square behind the Beauly Arms hotel, which was where the officers slept. A sergeant named Lark, who was pudgy and had a false smile, called us to attention in a sloppy way – with a regular unit, the discipline was more relaxed. He then did a roll call before shouting, 'File them out to water!' Behind the hotel were some stables and inside were the mules, which he meant we were supposed to lead for a drink from a trough. When I saw them, my heart sank because they were a completely different kettle of fish from flying an aircraft or driving a tank! I'd only ever seen one mule before and that was pulling a cart in Huntbach Street, Hanley, many years previously.

I was told to grab a couple of the animals, whom I later named Susie and Sandy, so I went gingerly into the stables and carefully untied them. I took them to the trough, where they had a drink as planned. I then led them back into the stables and tied them back up, head first, alongside the others, who'd also had their fill. Unfortunately, a nosebag full of feed was put behind the animals, which made them snort, move about and kick and bite one another because they were hungry. So, after tethering my two, my heart was in my mouth as I passed by their rear and saw what vicious weapons their hooves were. At the command, 'Feed up,' I carefully walked past the back end of my mules again and put on their nosebags before running the gauntlet once more as I came away, fully expecting to get kicked. But I was lucky!

After that, we went back to the barracks to make our beds up and lay our kit out in the prescribed manner (ready for inspection), to wash and shave and to polish our equipment. Finally, we had our breakfast from the cookhouse and could go to the toilet. The food was pretty decent because the army had to look after the troops, but it was annoying having to wait until after the mules had had theirs, as was the strict rule. Our breakfast usually consisted of porridge, followed by bacon, sausage, an egg and maybe baked beans.

We then had to groom the mules, with a big brush, to get muck and dust off their coats. During the night, when they'd been tethered, they had to defecate and urinate where they stood and, if they felt like lying down, they just lay in the stuff. So they'd be covered in filth by the morning and sometimes we had to loosen it with our hands. The brush would get so full of it that from time to time we had to draw it across the teeth of a currycomb. So I had a bash at grooming my mules' coats, while making sure I didn't get too near to their hooves.

Then we had to groom their hind hooves and the procedure was to stroke the mule from the withers to the rear quarters and then grab its tail, pulling it towards you, whilst pushing its backside with your shoulder. That forced the mule to push back to keep on its feet, but the tail pull kept it off balance, so that if it kicked out it would be liable to fall over. But Susie was very touchy when I tried to brush her hind hooves and kept trying to kick me, so I just ran my fingers over any trapped muck to get the thick off. I was always careful with her, but on a later occasion came across a fellow (who'd ridden her while I was on leave) brushing her hooves without any trouble!

When we'd finished, we got a horse blanket, folded it into four and placed it on each animal that was to be ridden, for comfort because the mules' backs were bony. The blanket was secured with a surcingle, which fastened it around the mule's body. The mules were then taken out of the stables, doubled up and tied together, but about two feet apart, with a rope. A bridle, with reins attached, was put onto their heads in order to control them. We new lads were handed the reins and I took mine with some trepidation. The orders, 'Prepare to mount,' and, 'Mount,' were given. I tried to comply, but couldn't make it because there were no stirrups to put a foot in, the animal was moving about and its back was too high. I can't remember whether it was Susie or Sandy, but it may well have been the former because she was about a hand taller. Eventually, I was given a lift up. Then the order, 'Walk march,' was shouted by the officer in charge, which meant get started, and he led off on his magnificent horse, with its saddle and stirrups all polished up. That was typical because I can't remember an officer ever stooping so low as to ride a mule!

I fitted my animals in the column and we clattered out of the small parade ground and turned left into the main street and then left again, up a side road. It was fairly comfortable sitting on the mule's warm back and I began to feel a little more confident. About three-quarters of a mile up the road, the officer shouted, 'Trot,' and those immediately behind him did so. It wasn't long before they were out of sight. The fellow at the front of our remaining mules had deliberately held back, but, when he was ready, he dug his heels into his animal's ribs and went cantering down the road, with the rest of us following him. It was like a charge of the U.S. cavalry in the films and one or two of the men even gave war whoops! I was being jogged about, slipping all over the place and hanging on like grim death. Eventually, we caught up with the others, much to my relief! It had all probably been pre-arranged by the longer-serving riders just for the pleasure of seeing newcomers hit the deck. I later learned that a couple of the fellows had fallen off on the road, but they weren't seriously injured. Nevertheless, I'd been lucky.

When we returned to the stables, we had to water and feed the mules and sweep up the muck and straw, which was replaced regularly. We were then allowed to have our dinner! That normally comprised potatoes, meat and veg, which was enjoyable.

Afterwards, we new fellows were given two sets of equipment, one for each mule we were in charge of. That consisted of two bridles, saddles and sets of reins, as well as other bits and pieces. The saddles weren't for riding on, but for carrying loads. As Beauly was the regimental headquarters, we carried office equipment, maps, documents, radio transmitters and whatever else was needed. We were ordered to keep all our equipment clean and the metal parts had to be sandpapered and polished so that they shone. Any parts of the leather which touched the mules' coats got covered in grease and had to be scrubbed clean. Then saddle soap had to be applied to make it supple. Each set of equipment was stamped with a different number so that items couldn't be swapped by unscrupulous fellows! It was all inspected at least once a week.

So, along with the other new lads, I became a mule driver. The old hands continued to look after the guns and were the elite. A lot of them appeared to be Geordies, as did the sergeants, who'd picked them. None of the new recruits, as far as I know, handled the artillery.

On my second morning, we again went out for a ride and once more a group trotted off with the officer, leaving the rest of us behind. But this time, when the cavalry charge took place, I was thrown off my mule and crashed onto the metalled road. I was lying there as the rest of the group and my mules disappeared into the distance! Nobody seemed concerned, but, amazingly, I wasn't injured. I walked after them and, when I eventually caught up, some of the fellows were amused!

We only rode the mules to give them some exercise. Most of the time, they carried artillery loads because that was the purpose of having them. We'd walk alongside them, holding their reins and trying to keep them in control. My animals usually carried two boxes of ammunition each, one on each side. When we mounted the mules, we always approached them from the nearside and therefore it was standard procedure for us to ride the mule on the left of our pair. I only rode Sandy once because he was used to being on the right and kept trying to get back there, which caused chaos. So, other than that, I rode Susie and had Sandy fastened on.

After a day or two, we were given a new uniform. The tunics were service dress, with brass buttons down the middle and one on each pocket. The trousers were riding breeches, with the inside upper legs covered with leather to extend their life and give a better grip when riding. Wound round our lower legs were puttees. Our hats were cheese cutters, with a full-blown metal badge in the shape of an artillery gun. We were also given a pair of blunt chrome-coloured spurs, which fastened round our boots with a strap. The spurs were only for show, for dressing up on parades on odd occasions, and we never used them when riding the mules.

I was also given a jackknife, which was supposed to be for cutting things and fighting with. Its black plastic handle was roughened, to give it a good grip, and it held two other metal implements: a tin and bottle opener and a curved kind of hook for picking stones out of mules' or horses' hooves and splicing ropes. I put the knife away in my kitbag and never used it, although I've still got it!

We practised putting the carrying saddles on the mules. Firstly, we placed a blanket on their backs and then positioned the saddles on top, just behind their withers. We then pushed the blankets up into the hollow in the saddles, making a gap for the air to circulate, and fixed the surcingle round the animals' bellies. At first, I wasn't sure where the girth went and on one parade had Sandy's more toward his groin than I should have done. The officer in charge of the camp, who was a captain and a dandy, did the inspection that day and, when he saw the surcingle, he said, 'If you'd got this belt a bit further back, you'd have cut its cock off!'

After about a week, I was put on a night's picket duty, looking after the mules to make sure that they came to no harm. I was to unravel them if they got tangled up and, if the rugs they wore to keep them warm slipped, I was supposed to straighten them up. It wasn't too bad because I avoided going amongst them as much as I could. But they were nervous, so when I did have to get in between them, it would disturb those lying down, who'd get up with a start and upset all the rest. It then took a while to get them settled again.

On another night's picket, the rug that was supposed to be covering Aspro was dragging on the floor, but he had a reputation for being vicious and, when I approached him, he tried to bite and kick me. Unfortunately, the captain, who was the duty officer, walked in to make his inspection and spotted the rug under the mule's feet. He wanted to know why I hadn't attended to it, so I explained that it was Aspro, hoping, but not expecting, that he'd understand. He looked at me and I awaited a dressing-down or some kind of punishment, but he then turned and walked over to the animal. I expected there'd be some commotion, but Aspro just stood there like a little lamb while his rug was being straightened. The captain turned to me and said: 'There you are. Nothing to it!' I was full of admiration.

One day, before a night picket duty, I was asked by one of the cooks if I'd wake him up at 3 a.m. because it would be nice for him to think he had another two hours to go before he had to get up to start his duties. It was bizarre, but he liked to kid himself up with that thought!

Sundays were generally rest days, although there was a duty rota because there were always some jobs to be done. Our leisure was also occasionally interrupted by a compulsory church parade, whereby a group of us would be marched to a church to listen to the service whether we wanted to or not! Other than that, we'd lie in bed or lounge about, but one day I saw a gunner going out of camp and later asked him about it. He told me that he went out as a beater with the captain, who had a pack of beagles that he used to hunt rabbits and hares. I was told that any of us could join in, but it didn't take me long to decide that I'd rather have a lie in!

One day, Sergeant Lark asked me, 'You're not married, are you, Kent?' I told him I was. He said: 'Oh, what a pity. I'd got a lovely girl for you!' I didn't think much of the incident till I got talking to another gunner, who laughed and told me the sergeant had said much the same thing to him. It seemed that Sergeant Lark had been sleeping with a one-legged girl, who was now having a baby! It appeared that he was getting panicky and trying to unload his troubles on someone else. I didn't hear any more, but I wish I'd made enquiries.

I was surprised to be given another ten days' leave, from 17 to 26 February, but I didn't complain! Fortunately, that meant I was able to go to the funeral of Grandad Wallett, who'd died on the 14th. I was very sad when I heard the news. I went home by train and the journey was a long one, with changes at Inverness, Carstairs and Crewe. I stayed with Helen and my parents and visited some of my relatives and friends, as well as attending Grandad's burial in St. Mary's churchyard, Church (now Marychurch) Road, Bucknall, on the 18th. When Big Harry saw my uniform, he told me that he'd give his right arm to be dressed like me!

Helen had been transferred from British Home Stores to carry out essential work at the British Aluminium Works Company, in Redhills Road, Milton. She was involved in making aluminium sheets for aeroplanes and the impetus for this production had come from the Battle of Britain.

When my leave ended, Helen came to Stoke Station with me. As the train was about to start, she said goodbye and then went off without turning to have a last glance at me. In those days, it was supposed to be unlucky to look back.

After I'd been back in camp for a short while, we went off on manoeuvres (or schemes, as they were called) for a number of days. They were probably what the regiment's war diary describes as 454 Battery's 'march to winter camp' on 5 March, its return on the 14th and whatever happened in between. All I ever knew about the various manoeuvres that we had while I was in the army was that they were 'Walk march' and 'Halt' and that we, the lads, were cannon fodder in between. Nobody ever told me where we were going, although details might have been on the notice board. I didn't usually digest much of what was on there because of a lack of interest, but I never heard any of the lads mention where we were going. The officers didn't confide information in us. They just told us to do the same things all the time.

On these particular manoeuvres, I was walking with my mules, which were carrying loads, and following behind some of the others. I had Susie at the front, because she was the lead animal of my pair, and Sandy tied on behind. That was my normal arrangement when we were on manoeuvres. One night, it was so dark on part of the march that I couldn't see the mule ahead of me. But I didn't want to get too close to it because, if Susie brushed against it, it risked the other mule lashing out with its hind legs. So I kept jerking her reins back. Eventually, we turned into a field and started walking uphill, but, after a while, I lost my footing and rolled about twenty yards back down. I still couldn't see a thing and it flashed through my mind that, if I tumbled among the mules, they'd kick out at me. But my luck was in and I came to a stop in a clear spot. I then had to shout for help to guide me back to my animals. When we eventually returned to base, I hadn't got a clue where we'd been or what we were supposed to have done, but I assumed the officers had sorted it all out!

From time to time, we could have a pass to go into Inverness, which was about thirteen miles away. I read a newspaper report that the people of the town spoke the best English in Britain! I got one such pass for a Saturday afternoon, but, that morning, I was told to go to a farm with another soldier and stack some hay with pitchforks, which we did. We were then getting ready to catch the train when Sergeant Lark walked in the hut and wanted to know why we hadn't obeyed his orders. We told him that we had, but he said that the farmer had complained that the hay was all over the place and we were ordered to stack it up right away. The train was soon due out, but Sergeant Lark didn't care. So I went back to the farm with the other fellow and we were surprised to find the hay scattered about the place. We came to the conclusion that the farmer's children had done the damage by jumping onto the stack and scattering it. By the time we'd straightened things up, we didn't feel like getting ready again, to catch a later train into Inverness. I've often wondered why the army was doing the farmer's job for him and whether someone was getting something out of it.

From Beauly, we could see Ben Wyvis to the north. It was a fair mountain, at 3,433 feet, and was still covered with snow even when the weather warmed up.

One morning, we were riding our mules in the village and stopped on the railway bridge. Just then, a train came into the station right below us. Steam was hissing out of the engine, which made our animals very restive and it took us all our time to keep hold of them. I prayed that the engine driver wouldn't blow the whistle and cause a mad gallop down the road, with us being dragged along. Fortunately, he turned out to be a sensible fellow.

We went on manoeuvres every so often and, when we stopped for any length of time on them, the mules were tied loosely together in groups of about six, in a star formation, with their heads facing inwards. The beauty of the system was that they'd all pull against each other and remain static. These arrangements were

called blobs and must have been a bore for the mules, forced to look into the face
of the opposite one for up to hours on end! Of course, a lot of biting went on.
However, if we were stopping for a shorter period, the forelegs of each animal
were hobbled, which prevented them from running away, but enabled them to
feed themselves.

On these schemes, we'd wear pullovers and woolly hats and had rucksacks,
which were so much more comfortable than the square canvas box army packs
we'd paraded with on occasions at Wakefield and Marske. Also, we didn't have to
keep in step, so I liked the marching style. To keep us supplied, there was another
mob, which had ponies and was a branch of the Royal Army Ordnance Corps.

After a while, I learned to get myself on my mule at the first attempt. I'd grab
the reins in my left hand and put it on Susie's withers. I'd then place my right
hand on her back and heave myself up, being careful not to push too hard in case
I went over the other side. We had one or two little fellows amongst us and it
mystified me as to how they ever got on their animal's back.

One day, we were ordered to do a three-mile run. I suppose we wore our PT
kit, which consisted of a white singlet, navy blue trunks and pumps, but we didn't
use it very often. I'd never run so far in my life before and, by the time I returned
to base, I was on my knees, but I was glad that I wasn't the last one back.

One of the gunners fell foul of the military and he was ordered to do seven
days' pack drill. That meant he had to drill on the barracks' square, with all his
equipment on his back, whilst holding a rifle, till he didn't know what he was
doing. He also had to do a spell wearing his gas mask (which made it much
harder to breathe) until he collapsed!

Another soldier told me that he'd been in a military glasshouse, where
everything had had to be done at the double, even washing, shaving and eating!
He'd had a guard behind him to rap his heels with a stick when his legs weren't
moving fast enough.

A further fellow said he'd escorted a prisoner to one of these detention centres
and had had to go inside at the double, with the prisoner, and continue at that
pace until the handing-over ceremony had been completed! When a soldier had
done one stint in the glasshouse, he didn't often go back for another.

On 5 May, we left Beauly and marched with the mules and the rest of the
regiment for six days to a practice camp at Cabrach, in Banffshire, which was in
the wild, near the Ladder Hills. The war diary shows that we were there for five
days, carrying out exercises, but I don't remember them specifically, nor the
camp, because they were just more manoeuvres in the middle of nowhere to me.

We left Cabrach on 17 May and marched for two days till we reached Ballater,
which was roughly forty miles west of Aberdeen and about eight miles
downstream from the royal residence at Balmoral Castle. We billeted in the
grounds of Monaltrie House, around half a mile from the village. The officers, of
course, lived in the large house, while the other ranks were accommodated in
huts! As usual, we had to wash and shave in cold water.

One day, one of the other mule drivers was scrubbing his animal's harness by
the River Dee when he got fed up and threw it in the water, indicating that he
wasn't going to do it any more. He was put on a charge and a trial was set up.
Sergeant Lark told me to get ready for escort duty, which meant I had to put on
my best uniform and blanco and polish my equipment and boots and be quick

about it.

When I was ready, Sergeant Lark marched us to Ballater, where we went into an office. On command, we came to a halt in front of a desk, at which sat an officer. The charge was read out and, after some discussion, a detention punishment was decreed. We then marched out to the road, where the sergeant told me to take the prisoner back to the camp. That I started to do, but, when we got to the railway station, a pal of the prisoner came up. He asked if I minded handing my charge over to him because he wished to buy the prisoner the last drink he'd be having for a while. The fellow said he'd then see that the prisoner got back to camp. It seemed reasonable to me at the time, so I said it would be alright.

So the prisoner and his mate made their way to the bar at the station and I continued on towards the camp. I hadn't gone many steps before I heard a voice from behind me shout: 'Kent! Where's the prisoner?'

I said, 'He's gone for a drink.'

Sergeant Lark's face turned all colours and he snarled at me, 'Come on!'

I followed him to the door of the bar, which he pushed open a little way. He hissed at the prisoner, 'Come on out!'

The prisoner was shocked because he was just about to take the first sip of his pint. He said: 'In a minute, Sarge. Just let me drink this.'

I thought the sergeant was going to have a fit, but he controlled himself and just said in a nasty tone, 'Come out!'

To give the prisoner his due, he didn't cause any trouble and left the bar without any further ado and back to camp we all went. The amazing thing was I didn't get into any bother and heard no more about the matter. I can now see what a daft decision I made to let him go to the bar! If he'd got drunk or deserted, I'd have been in deep trouble and no doubt been sent to the glasshouse.

I was on leave from 5 to 14 June and travelled home. Mother was in the Royal Infirmary for an operation to remove her gall bladder. Of course, I went to see her every day while I was home and wore my uniform, thinking it might make her feel proud. On one of my visits, she gave me a ten-shilling note, perhaps to pay for the bus fares. I still have it and it's of sentimental value. She was still in hospital when my leave finished, but I understood that she was going to be alright.

I returned to Ballater and one day a small circus came to the village. I didn't visit it myself, but, apparently, one of the attractions was an unridable mule! I heard that a couple of the officers had tried to master it, but were thrown off. They must have found a big difference between their usual fine mounts and that wild animal.

There were some Canadian lumberjacks in the Ballater district, who were employed to fell trees and cut them into planks for the war effort. I visited their camp once to get some timber, maybe for fire wood, and got interested in how the operation worked. Their machines grabbed logs and sliced off one side of them all the way along. The logs were then given a quarter turn and another section was sliced off and that was repeated until the logs were square. They were finally sawed down their length to make a number of planks. The machine looked crude, but was pretty effective, although there was a lot of waste.

Some of the lumberjacks went to the dances that were held in the village and apparently there were fights between them and our lads. I never attended any of those events because trouble was always expected when different Forces met, but I was told that the Canadians brandished knives.

On 12 July, I received a telegram from home, telling me that Mother had died that day. I was devastated. Her operation had been successful, but she was lying next to an open French window and got a cough, which undid her stitches and led to severe loss of blood and her death. She was only 51.

I went to the battery office and obtained ten more days' leave. When I got home, Dad was brokenhearted. He was slumped over in his chair, crying, and he didn't say much. If I'd been back for good, he might not have been so bad. I put my arm around him and said, 'She's been a good mother.'

He said, 'Yes and she's been a good wife.'

I felt awful that I couldn't help him and cursed the war to myself.

Mother's funeral was on 15 July and went off okay, though I'm ashamed to say that I remember very little of it. She was buried in Hanley Cemetery, in a plot of ground in the first-class area, near to the main entrance, and the total cost of the interment, including the minister's fee, was £13 17s. 6d. Dad went to Myatt & Leason, the stonemasons, in Edward Street (now Sturgess Street), Stoke, and ordered a gravestone.

One day, I was walking through Hanley Park with Helen, wearing my breeches, puttees and spurs, on the way to visit Mother's grave. A couple of young lads followed me, whistling the popular tune, (I Got Spurs That) Jingle, Jangle, Jingle, which both amused and irritated me.

Back at Ballater, things went on much the same as normal, with the usual chores of watering, feeding, grooming and riding the mules. On one occasion when we went out for a day's march, I had with me a small mule instead of my usual ones. I put the saddle on it, tightened up its girth and held it steady, while a couple of gunners hoisted a heavy pannier of ammunition on each side of the saddle. An officer inspected us and then we marched for an hour before having a ten-minute rest. That was standard practice, but it wasn't my idea of a break as we had to keep hold of the reins because the mules would be moving around. So we couldn't lie down. Anyhow, I noticed that the girth was loose and found I could put my arm in between the belt and the mule's belly when it was supposed to be tight. It was marvellous that the ammunition had not slipped to around the animal's stomach. It seemed that the mule had been crafty and expanded its belly when I'd tightened the girth, to make sure it wasn't tight, and then relaxed and deflated itself when we started marching! I quickly tightened the strap up again before anyone noticed.

When we took the mules to water, the same animal was so nervous that it held back, even though it was thirsty. It only plucked up courage at the last second or two when it dashed to the trough to take a quick drink.

We'd taken along a new type of tent to try out. It was round and camouflaged and had a small entrance, like a tunnel, which we had to crawl into. The idea of that was to keep the wind out and help keep heat in. The entrance was supposed to be positioned at right angles to the wind in case it snowed, to allow the snow to drift past and prevent it from getting blocked. That surprised me because I thought it would have been better on the lee side of the wind. A big advantage of the tent was that the groundsheet was an integral part of it. We'd been shown a diagram of the sleeping arrangements for about ten men, but, whenever we used those tents, we just pushed in wherever we could!

Dad wrote to me regularly and, shortly after Mother had been buried, he told me that Floss had also died. He was most upset about that too and had held her in his arms after he'd discovered her dead one morning in the lounge, bleeding behind the door. He believed she'd been trying to get to the stairs to get up to him. He buried her in the back garden. I also felt very sad about it, but there wasn't time to mope in the army.

One of the fellows in our battery was a cockney named Fred, who seemed more like a yokel than a Londoner. He had a mate in the battery nicknamed "Digger" because he was always talking about Australia. One night, when they were on sentry duty together, Digger went off guard, telling Fred he wouldn't be long. Shortly afterwards, Fred heard a noise, so he shouted out, 'Is that you, Digger, cock?'

Instead, he should have made the challenge: 'Halt! Who goes there?' The reply should have been, 'Friend,' to which Fred should have replied, 'Pass, Friend.'

Unfortunately, it was the duty officer and a voice came back saying: 'No! It's Captain Bloody Hancock and I've a good mind to stick a bayonet up your arse!'

We carried on going on schemes from time to time and the war diary says that our battery left Ballater on 10 September for 'small arms field firing practice' and that we returned on the 16th. I can't remember being involved in any of that, though!

One day, I was returning to camp, with a number of other soldiers, in the back of an army lorry. It was covered with canvas and supported by a metal frame, but had no seats in the back, so we were supposed to sit on the floor in the interest of safety. Nobody ever did that – we sat on the edge of the truck. As we were about to go through the camp's main gateway, I was gazing back and saw a man and a girl walking along the road. It struck me that the girl looked just like Helen, so I leaned forward to get a better view, but then I felt a blow in my back so hard that it was almost as if a mule had kicked me. I fell to the floor of the truck, as did the rest of the passengers. The driver had driven too close to the massive gatepost, so the backs of the soldiers on my side had hit the coping stone. He then sped into the camp, where we were treated and some of the fellows were taken to hospital. One of them was there a long while and we never saw him again.

I got off lightly, with bruising to my back. I was told to get off to bed and rest, which I did. I hadn't been there very long when a lance bombardier came in and thought I was slacking. I tried to explain what had happened, but he didn't believe me. I ignored him and stayed put anyway and I was alright the next morning. It was amazing that I'd leaned forward in the lorry just at that moment or else I could have had serious injuries.

On 24 September, Dad was sent the details of Mother's estate by the probate registry office in Chester. As he was the next of kin, he inherited all her money and property, which had been valued at £243 5s. 1d.

The war diary entry for 28 September says that our battery had an exercise from 8.30 a.m. till midday to 'practice silent registration with battery targets using ¼" maps' and the 'digging and siting of weapon pits'. As with a number of other things in the diary, I can't recall having taken part in that.

Dad had applied for the exclusive right of burial for Mother's grave (number 16364), so that it would be open for three other members of the family to be buried there in the future and would prevent any outsiders from using the ground. On 30 September, his request was granted at a cost of £9 12s.

Gambling was forbidden in the armed forces, but fellows in our battery played crown and anchor and I think that was a general thing in the army. It comprised a cloth board, with crown, anchor and other symbols on it, and three dice, containing the same signs. I never went in for betting, but the lads would put their money on whichever symbols they fancied on the board. The banker, who was running the game, would then throw the dice and anyone who'd backed the signs that came up could get two or three times his stake, but all the other lads would lose theirs. It was played in our huts, in fields and anywhere the opportunity arose. Because the board was made of cloth, if an officer came by, it was easy to whip everything out of sight!

In October, there was a big scheme called Goliath II, which we were a part of. Our Mountain Regiment had taken part in Goliath I the previous December, but I hadn't been with them then. The exercise had involved a twelve-day, 150-mile march across the Highlands from Muir of Ord (in Ross and Cromarty) to Dalwhinnie (in southern Inverness-shire) and finished with a slog at night over remote mountains around Ben Alder. I was told by one of the lads, who'd been in it, that the conditions had been terrible and they'd all got soaking wet. He said some of them had had to be carried off and taken to hospital. I was glad I hadn't been in that!

Goliath II didn't turn out to be as bad as that, but we had problems getting to the starting point of the scheme. On 10 October, we made our way to the local railway station, but had to carry a load of equipment on our backs. We couldn't possibly march with it, so it was decided to ride the mules. We had to have a lift up, but, when it was my turn, I came down with a thump on Susie's back and my rifle butt hit her spine, causing her to buck. I was thrown up in the air and landed with a crash on the road. Once more, I was lucky and escaped injury and I got on at the next attempt.

We had to entrain the mules, in cattle trucks, which was extremely time-consuming because they were very reluctant to get aboard. What a game it was! We had to heave them in, with four men pulling long straps bent in a U-shape round each animal's backside and another gunner leading the mule's head. We then tied them up for the journey, but there was no trouble getting them out at the other end because they were glad to be released.

Our destination was Aberfeldy, in Perthshire, which was only about 45 miles away as the crow flies, but by train it was well over 150 because of the impassible mountains in between the two places. So the journey took a long time, but we arrived in Aberfeldy on the same day. We then just kept marching on manoeuvres till we were told to stop when we reached Blairgowrie, over twenty miles away, nearly two weeks later! A large body of troops was involved and I think the idea was to give the generals some practice in moving thousands of soldiers about.

After one of the marches, we stopped for the night and watered and fed the mules before tying them up overnight. We didn't have any camping equipment and had to make our beds the best way we could. I found a fairly smooth piece of ground and put my two saddles about six feet apart. I strung my rainproof mac across the gap and placed my protective plastic gas cape on the ground, to lie on. The mac was roughly 6½ feet long by 2½ feet wide and fastened around the neck. It was supposed to be waterproof, but it was most unsatisfactory because it hung down unevenly at the corners and the rain would somehow get inside and drip on our trousers. It could also double up as a groundsheet. The gas cape had a hood and was designed to protect us against gas attacks, but we found other uses for it! That particular night, I had a great sleep, interrupted only when the mules' hooves got too close for comfort a time or two. When that happened, I settled back and hoped for the best. I didn't want to shout because of waking everybody up and I thought if I moved, the mules might lash out and start jumping all over the place.

At Blairgowrie, on 23 October, we had all the rigmarole of getting the mules on a train again, but this time we were taken to Edinburgh, where we moved into a new base for the whole regiment at Redford Cavalry Barracks in Colinton. The barracks had been purpose-built and was luxurious, especially in comparison with what we'd been used to. There were dormitories, proper toilets and splendid bathrooms, with hot water! The mules had plush stables that had previously housed cavalry horses. They were waterproof and gave room for the animals to move about. There was a lovely Tarmacked parade ground, which we used for drilling, and room at the back for a firing range. Beyond was open countryside, where we exercised the mules.

There, I think we saw the regimental sergeant major for the first time. He perhaps hadn't come to my attention before because the regiment had been more dispersed, whereas at Colinton we were all in the same barracks. Also, at Colinton, he could drill the troops properly because the parade ground was big. He had a screaming voice, like a woman's, and we couldn't hear him properly. Nevertheless, he was a god-like figure and I think he was more feared than anyone else because he had the ear of the lieutenant colonel of the regiment. Even the junior officers would watch their p's and q's in the sergeant major's presence. He prowled round everywhere and did the lieutenant colonel's dirty work. The lieutenant colonel wasn't one for making himself known to the troops and he must have been busy in the back room, drinking whisky and chinwagging with the sergeant major!

We worked half a day on Saturdays and sometimes, when we were off duty, I'd have a walk around the nearby streets or go to a cinema or to a pub, for a drink or two. I found Edinburgh to be a nice place. I didn't have a regular pal and so went mainly on my own. I suppose I was a loner, although I did go out a time or two with Fred, the cockney.

Dad wrote and told me about something that had happened, which was distressing him. When he was out one night, he'd left a chink of light showing out of a window. Unfortunately, it was spotted and the police broke in and turned the light out. He was summoned to go to court and he was very worried about it because he thought a big issue would be made about it. He was anxious that he'd be accused of aiding the enemy and have the humiliation of being named in the *Sentinel*.

It was perhaps around that time that I had occasion to get home urgently and I've got a feeling it was to do with Dad being ill. The only leave I could get was a 48-hour pass, which I took, even though I was warned that there wasn't much time to get home and back. When I was travelling on the train, I thought I'd better try to avoid the redcaps at Stoke Station and in Leek Road, so, to play safe, I got off at Etruria and finished the journey by bus. Helen was glad to see me and I did what I could while I was there.

However, when I started back, I was about a day late, so it looked as if I'd be in trouble when I returned to the barracks. I went back to Etruria Station because the redcaps at Stoke would be bound to look at my pass and book me as being absent without leave. When I arrived at Edinburgh, I expected Waverley Station to be alive with military police, but there weren't any to be seen, so I just strolled out and got onto a tram to Colinton. I went into the battery office to report back, but just then the battery sergeant major came in. He was a small fellow, but, fortunately, he was quite human and I got on alright with him. He looked at me and said, 'Did the MPs pick you up?' He knew, of course, that I was late and had expected me to be, with such a short pass. I told him I hadn't been spotted and he said, 'Okay.' So I got away with it!

I learned to get nearer the front of the column when we were out riding the mules, to avoid the cavalry charge at the back. We had some good-class riders, who wouldn't have been outclassed by Red Indians on their bareback ponies. I would have been better myself if Susie had had bigger withers because I wouldn't have slipped forward so much.

We went on another scheme and marched for so long that my legs turned to jelly. I felt I could no longer go on, but I was leading two mules and so couldn't stop. I looked around for help, but there was no-one spare. Then, in the distance, I could see the leaders of the expedition turn into a field to camp. That put fresh heart into me and I just about made it to the field. I don't know where it was because I only ever glanced at the orders that were posted up for each day.

I used to get blisters on my feet from all the marching and sometimes it was agony. After suffering the pain for a few schemes, I found a chiropodist in the city, offering free treatment to soldiers. She put some tape on my feet, where the blisters usually formed, and that helped a lot. Some of the lads had a quite different system of preventing the problem – they told me that they didn't wash their feet and the accumulated muck stopped blisters from forming!

Dad wrote to me on 21 November, saying that he and Helen were going to my Uncle Jack's for tea on the coming Sunday, but that he wasn't feeling too well. Then, on the 24th, Helen sent me a telegram, with the message that he'd gone into London Road Hospital (as the City General was then called). I applied for leave straight away, was granted ten days and set off the following morning.

When I got home, there was no-one in and I hadn't got a key because it would have been no use to me in Scotland. So I knocked at Halfpenny's next door and left my pack with them while I went to see Grandmother Wallett (who by then was living in a flat at 7 Tranter Road, Abbey Hulton), to see if she knew what was going on. She asked me why I was back home, but I paused before replying because I didn't want to upset her. Then I told her that Dad was in hospital and said I'd go across to the nearby St. John's Church vicarage, in Greasley Road, to ask the vicar if he'd phone the hospital for me.

In those days, there weren't many telephone booths around and I still didn't know how to use a phone properly, so it was easier to ask someone to do it for me. I wasn't the only one who was ignorant because I think it still applied to most people in the country. The vicar was very nice and contacted the hospital. After the call, he hesitated and then said, 'I'm sorry, but your father has died.' I was staggered, but I thanked him and wandered back to tell Grandmother the news. I didn't want to tell her because she'd lost her daughter (my mother) only four months previously and her husband just five months before that, so it took me a while to get the message over. I then got a bus back home, by which time Helen had returned.

She told me that, on the 23rd, she'd noticed specks of blood around the downstairs sink, but hadn't said anything. But when she got home from work the following day, our neighbours, Harold and Annie Bentley, were waiting for her in our house. They told her that Dad had had an ulcer burst, causing a loss of blood, and that he'd been taken to hospital. In those days, hospitals were very strict and the rules had to be adhered to, so she didn't know what to do. She decided to go the following day and got Leah to keep her company overnight.

However, in the middle of the night, the police knocked on the door and told her that Dad was very ill and asked if she could go there straight away. She and Leah then walked to Uncle Ted's in Etruria, woke him up, told him the news and asked him to go to the hospital with them. But he wouldn't go out right away because he insisted on making and lighting his coal fire and having a cup of tea first. That must have been the routine he went through every morning and he wouldn't alter it, even though his brother was critically ill! By the time they got to the hospital, Dad was dead, although the delay may not have made any difference. It seems that he'd bled to death in the meantime.

I didn't cry because I don't tend to show my feelings, but I hadn't got a clue what to do, although I knew I had to sort things out. So I muddled along and informed relatives and friends and wrote the necessary letters because hardly anyone was on the phone. Jim Biddulph, who was still a union representative at Taylor Tunnicliff, called and asked if workers from the factory could attend the funeral. I said they could, but I warned that there'd be no booze allowed. I might have offended the fellow, but I'd heard that some people made a party at these solemn occasions and would even gate-crash.

Aunt Pru came to see Helen and me and offered to tidy up the house for us. We accepted and she started upstairs, but came down after a while with a bundle of banknotes, which she'd found in a Wedgwood vase on the window ledge in the front bedroom. I thanked her and put them in my pocket after telling Helen. There must have been fifty pounds, a tidy sum in those days to have left lying about.

Dad's funeral was on 29 November. There were two or three undertakers' cars for relatives and close friends going from our house to Hanley Cemetery and other people marched in front of the hearse, so it was a slow procession. The soil of Mother's grave had been dug out almost to her coffin to allow Dad's remains to be placed on top. The parson said a few words and then Dad's coffin was lowered down. Afterwards, relatives and friends returned to our house for a cup of tea and a piece of currant cake. There was no liquor.

Both of my parents had gone in no time. When they were alive, I never gave it a thought that they could die. How naive I was, just thinking of myself! Nevertheless, I got on with the task of sorting out their affairs, but I ran out of time. So I went to the Rail Travel Office in Winton Square, opposite Stoke Station, where travel passes were issued to service personnel. I explained the circumstances and asked if I could have some extra time, which they granted me.

With Dad's death, Helen was left on her own and decided to go to live with Vera in Holdcroft Road. That left our house in Leek Road empty, but Helen visited it from time to time to keep an eye on things and do one or two jobs. On one occasion, when it was really cold, she lit a fire, but the inside of the boiler had frozen solid and water seeped out from underneath! She sought advice from Harold Bentley, who told her to put the fire out right away because the boiler was liable to blow up! In the event, it had to be replaced because the ice had cracked it and the job was organized by Harold, who found a plumber, even though they were in short supply.

Back at Colinton, I had to get on with the routine. One frosty morning, we took our mules for their usual exercise, but the roads were covered with sheets of ice and they were having a hard time trying to keep on their feet. On that occasion, I was riding the Wog, the biggest and daftest mule in the battery. Suddenly, he slipped and his legs went from underneath him. That left me standing on the road, with the mule's body between my legs! I had only a couple of seconds to decide what to do and opted to stay put because it was risky to try to jump clear, especially onto the ice with my hobnail boots. As it turned out, I did the right thing because the Wog got up with me astride him and he didn't slip again.

The army was saving bullets and didn't want anybody to get killed, so it was an unusual occasion when I got to fire a rifle at Colinton. We went in a field at the back of the barracks and were given one or two rounds of ammunition each, to fire at a target. The kick from the rifle wasn't as bad as expected, but I can't remember whether I hit the target.

We had some Sten guns issued to us and had some practice with them. They were very crude machine guns and were hand held. I was told they only cost a few shillings to make and they used the same ammunition as the Germans did, so, if we ran short, we could use theirs if there was any lying around! But we were only allowed a short burst of fire, about three rounds each. I had a go and it was exciting, but it only lasted a second or so.

On Christmas Day, our dinners were served by the sergeants, which was a tradition. Most of them did it in the spirit that was intended, but one or two of them resented the chore and chucked the food down in front of us in contempt! The dinner was quite good and included turkey and Christmas pudding. There wasn't any real celebration, but we didn't have to do any work, so it was like a typical Sunday.

When I was out walking one day, I passed an officer on the other side of the street, going in the opposite direction. It didn't seem as though he was going to follow the normal practice and salute, so I didn't either because a few officers didn't bother. He stopped and shouted, 'Hey, private!' He came over and gave me a lecture on saluting the queen's uniform! I listened to him and realized, from how he was addressing me, that he didn't even know the difference between a private and a gunner, the former being an infantryman and the latter serving in the artillery.

One day, I got talking to a youth who was in the pioneer corps, he said because he wasn't A1 medically. I was surprised at that as they did the labouring for the army! He was really envious of us in the Mountain Regiment, riding about on mules and having a smarter uniform than him. It was strange that our regiment had service dress because nearly all the other soldiers wore battledress. However,

I think I'd have swapped with the fellow because the mules were dangerous and very troublesome!

After a while, the regiment got posh because somebody dreamed up the idea of having a bugler. We then seemed to have a bugle call every hour of the day! I didn't understand what any of the calls stood for, except reveille, to wake us up; the one which summoned us to the cookhouse for food and the last post, which told us to get off to sleep.

On 6 March 1944, I started ten days' leave and, as usual, went back to our house in Leek Road. Helen and Leah stayed with me there while I was on furlough, as they did on all the following occasions. I was introduced to Leah's new boyfriend, Paul, a Yank, who was tall and good-looking and, of course, had a nice uniform. After I'd met him a few times, he handed me a watch that was all in bits. I looked at it and thought, 'What the hell!' I put the pieces in a cup in our china cabinet and forgot about them until after the war. Then, one day, I came across them and went to H. Pidduck & Sons Ltd., the jewellers, at 1 Market Square, Hanley, who were the top watch repairers. I asked if they could fix it up, which they did, but it took about eighteen months because of a shortage of spare parts. It turned out to be a good watch! I didn't see Paul again after that visit because he went over with the Normandy invasion force and Leah lost touch with him.

By then, aluminium was no longer needed to the same extent as before because the Germans had stopped shooting down as many of our planes and the workers at Milton and the other factories had produced so many sheets for aircraft that the Allies had complete supremacy in the air. So Helen and the other aluminium workers had made themselves redundant.

Helen was then told to go to ROF (Royal Ordnance Factory) Swynnerton to work on explosives, but she refused to do it because she so was nervous about it. She went to a doctor and said she'd make mistakes and 'drop the bombs'! The doctor gave her a note to say she was unfit to work there and so instead she was sent to GEC, in Stafford, to test aeroplane speed indicators. Unfortunately, she didn't understand what she was supposed to be doing and didn't carry out the tests properly. After her first day there, she went back to the doctor and told him that her nerves were bad and that, 'The aeroplanes won't get off the ground!'

She again got a note exempting her from the work and this time was told to report to Swinnertons (Industrial Canteens) Ltd. as a supervisor of the making of sandwiches for miners, which was being done in unoccupied buildings at my old school in Cobridge, called the Miners' Food Centre. The operation had been set up by F. Swinnerton & Son Limited, a local catering firm, in 1941. Around 55 staff were being employed there and they produced an average of 47,000 meals a week! Helen settled down in her new job and carried on working for the firm for the rest of the war and afterwards.

The manageress of the factory was Eva Jeffries, one of our neighbours, who lived at 496 Leek Road, with her husband, Vin. He'd worked for Swinnerton's since well before the First World War and was the foreman of bakers at their premises in Wood Terrace, Shelton. In his spare time, he was a conjuror and entertained children at parties and even adults with his tricks. Eva and Vin had met at work and were an unusual-looking couple because she was a big woman and he was a little fellow. Because Eva and Vin were older than us and she was

Helen's boss, we always called them Mr and Mrs Jeffries.

The war diary shows that my regiment spent most of March 1944 on schemes and, on the 8th, while I was on leave, they moved to Glendye Lodge, south of Banchory, in Kincardineshire. I can't remember travelling into the wild up there to join them, so they probably had to get by without me while I was enjoying the comforts of the barracks on my return to Colinton! Anyway, we were all back together when the regiment returned to Edinburgh on the 28th.

At the barracks, I got friendly with a lance bombardier nicknamed "Geordie", who, I think, was called that because he came from Newcastle. He was the regimental postman and also was in charge of the mules' fodder. He told me he went to a nearby village, Juniper Green, where they had Scottish dances. He invited me to go with him, which I did. We sat down in the small hall and the band started playing Scottish reels, which were pretty exciting, but I'd never danced to anything like them before. Geordie got up, joined the dancing girls and seemed to be making a good attempt at moving to the rhythms. Eventually, I was persuaded to have a go and, although I was clumsy, I kept trying. After the last dance, he told me he was going to go back with a local lady, Helen Crawford, and her daughter, Monica (who was about eighteen and pretty), to have a cup of tea at their home, at 10 Woodhall Drive. He'd become pally with them and suggested I go along with him, but I did so reluctantly because it seemed a cheek without the family's invitation.

Mrs Crawford welcomed me and said she hoped that someone would do similar for her lad, Ian, who was in an aircrew in the RAF and stationed at Stafford. She also had a daughter in the Forces. I was introduced to her husband, who was blind and didn't get in much conversation. I went with Geordie to the Crawfords' house a number of times and Mrs Crawford and Helen, my wife, started to correspond. I continued to go to the dances and, as time went on, I became more proficient at dancing the reels.

One night, Geordie and I went with the Crawfords to a theatre in the city for a show. At one point, the audience joined in with singing There'll Always Be an England, except that they substituted the word "Britain" for "England", which I suppose was correct because we were all involved in the war.

In May, I received the news, probably in a letter from Helen, that Grandmother Wallett had died on the 1st. That was a further blow because I'd been fairly close to her and I was staggered as she was yet another near relative who'd died in a short space of time. I didn't ask for leave for the funeral this time because she wasn't an immediate relative and I'd had ten days on furlough a few weeks earlier.

On 13 May, our regiment left Colinton to move to a summer camp. The regimental headquarters was transferred to Blairgowrie, in Perthshire, but our battery became based at the Spittal of Glenshee, about 18 miles to the north. It took us two days to get there.

The new place was an old shooting lodge at Dalmunzie, which had been built up to become a mansion. It was about 1½ miles up Glen Lochsie from the main road and in the hills. From it, a narrow-gauge railway track ran up the valley for 2½ miles to a hunting lodge and was used to impress visitors and transport home the deer that the laird and his mates shot in the mountains. As usual, the officers were billeted inside, in the lodge, and this time we, the men, had bell tents. We had no bathing facilities at first, but, after a few weeks, a large tent was set up and warm water was somehow pumped into it through a series of pipes. We just had to turn the taps on to get it. It was marvellous, but the poor mules were staked out in a field, which quickly became a quagmire. That coated their legs with mud and it was difficult to brush off.

Only two days after we'd got to the camp, the first scheme started and one followed another for a month. It was as though the officers couldn't wait to make up for lost time after the winter had ended.

One day, soon after we'd arrived at the Spittal of Glenshee, Geordie handed me a bulky package, which contained the deeds of my parents' house. They'd been sent by Frank Collis & Son, the solicitors, for me to sign and it seemed that I was the new owner of the property. I felt quite rich, despite the solicitors' charge of £19 12s. 3d. for sorting things out and the fact that I had to take on the mortgage, but I was sad that it had come to that. I got an officer to witness my signature and then I sent the package back.

One day, we had to strip off all our clothes to be weighed and for a short-arm inspection in the lodge. That was a routine examination of our private parts to check we hadn't got any sexual diseases from prostitutes, who were available in the towns when we went out for a night. During the inspection, someone noticed that the laird's maids, who were living there, were looking at us through a window high up in the hallway. They were having a thrill, peering at naked men, but we were quickly moved to another room!

We heard about the 6 June D-day landings in Normandy from the news. It was a big thing and couldn't be kept secret. I thought it might be the beginning of the end of the war, but I was happy to stay well away from all the action!

I was later told by Big Harry that he'd had to go down south to help build one of the two prefabricated floating Mulberry Harbours that were towed across the Channel for use in the Normandy invasion. They were like mobile piers and required hundreds of workers to build them. They were anchored on the French coast and stretched out to sea, where ships could come along and unload.

By that time, quite a lot of miners had joined the Forces and Britain was running short of coal. More miners were needed, so the government decided to recruit them from future batches of conscripts. They were called "Bevin Boys" after Ernest Bevin, the government minister in charge of the operation. My cousin, Bernard, was one of them and was sent to work in Hanley Deep Pit. He was most upset because he was looking forward to being in the Forces. He'd attained the rank of sergeant major in the army cadets and tried to get out of going down the mines, which he dreaded. I'd have felt the same. Uncle Ted later told me how Bernard had had to crawl through a hole to get to the coalface. The miners kept enlarging the hole, but the roof kept falling in. It must have been dreadful and the only good thing was that all classes of lads had to submit to it, even the sons of people with titles.

At about that time, we were told that our letters from the camp would be censored from then on. I couldn't understand the point of that because we didn't have any important information to give away and, in any case, I didn't expect the Germans would have been afraid of anything they could have read about the 3rd Mountain Regiment! This censorship put us off writing for a while because we didn't fancy having our letters read by the officer on duty. We imagined him passing around any interesting passages to his mates! So one soldier decided not to hand in one of his letters for vetting and slipped it into a letter box as we were marching along. Unfortunately for him, he was seen doing so by an officer, so he was punished and the Post Office was made to hand the letter over.

Riding mules made my behind and the inside of the top of my legs raw. Susie had a sharp, bony back and was very uncomfortable to ride, so my bottom would get in a state. I was therefore doubly glad whenever I had some leave because it enabled my raw flesh to heal up.

Because Susie hardly had any withers, I tended to slip forward, towards her neck, when we were cantering. One day, we were having an extra-long session and I felt myself sliding too far down. I tried pulling on the reins, but that made the position worse. Eventually, I finished up on Susie's neck, which must have looked comical, and she just carried on. But, finally, the weight caused her to dip her head and so I fell onto the road, in front of her and Sandy. They trampled all over me, as did the mules following on behind, but, miraculously, I wasn't hurt!

Another time, we were in the rear group of mules and the usual hold back occurred. But, when we surged forward and caught up with those ahead, I couldn't stop Susie and she careered into the animals in front. One of them lashed out with both feet either side of her, so I quickly pulled my legs back as far as I could, but one of its hooves caught my right shinbone and made a mark, which I still have. It wasn't particularly painful, but I'm sure that if my leg had been a quarter of an inch nearer, it would have been broken.

One day, we were on a scheme and came to the place where we were going to camp for the night. I started to get the saddle and ammo boxes off Susie's back, but gasped when I noticed the state of it – it was raw. Just then, along came one of our sergeants and the veterinary sergeant. When they saw Susie's sore back, they began quarrelling with each other, with the vet blaming the sergeant for her condition. Then they started fighting and I thought they were going to turn on me, but they broke it off. I never did understand why they'd got so excited because, if it was anybody's fault, it was mine, though I don't think it could have been helped. The result was that Susie was left without a saddle for a while and her back healed up.

While we were at the Spittal of Glenshee, it was a bore because there was no entertainment and not even a pub to go to as the place was so small. We were allowed to go for an occasional night out in either Perth, which was about 35 miles away, or Dundee, around 40 miles distant, and I took advantage of this whenever possible. Both seemed to be nice places. A bus was available to take us out and bring us back, but I'd often go on my own because nobody seemed to want to go anywhere. I'd have a walk around and a cup of tea at places set up for soldiers. They were run by ladies and had letters and envelopes you could write. That was very nice.

Sometimes, we were also allowed to go to Blairgowrie on a short pass for a Saturday outing. It was much smaller than Perth and Dundee and there wasn't much going on. An army truck was used for transport, driven by one of the soldiers, but I only went once because the return trip was a nightmare. An officer, who'd been out on a booze-up, turned up and said he'd drive back. He was drunk and every time we went round one of the many tight bends, I thought we were going to tip over. Most of the fellows had also had plenty to drink and were singing, so they didn't notice the dangerous ride. When we got back to base, I jumped off the truck a very relieved man.

A race over the mountains and back to camp was organized, I suppose as a diversion from the tedious routine. We each had to lead a mule and were put in groups of about six, which went off at intervals. I had Susie and just followed the fellow in front. I had no idea of the route, but right away we started climbing up an incline like the side of a house! It wasn't long before the strain started to tell on me. Sandy was immediately in front, so I grabbed his tail and he pulled me up quite a distance. Then he started breathing very heavily and I thought he was going to collapse. He turned his head and looked at me walleyed and with disgust. After that, for shame I couldn't hold his tail again.

I looked up and we seemed to be near the summit, but, when we got there, there was another peak beyond and then a further one! It was a real relief to get to the top, where the ground was fairly level for quite a distance and we made good time. We then went down the other side of the mountain, which was easier, but we had to move quickly because the mules behind us were going so fast that they were close to trampling on us. We crossed the main road just down from the Devil's Elbow and climbed another mountain on the other side. We never saw any of the other groups and I felt okay when we reached the finishing post. We were then inspected to see if anything was untidy or whether the mules were distressed! We were the third mob to finish in time, but were awarded second place because the bunch in front of us failed the inspection.

One day, from our camp, I saw what looked like a tractor going up the side of a hill. I was told that the army was experimenting with a vehicle that could pull or carry our equipment over the mountains. It had tracks, like a tank, but I never heard any more about it, even though I was hoping that it would be a success!

Another time, I was ordered to take some ammunition up to the gunners, who were practising in the mountains. I was handed the reins of the Wog, who was already loaded up, and off we went, but I started having trouble with him straight away. He just wouldn't go where I wanted him to and it was a real strain for me. Eventually, we arrived at our destination, but, suddenly, the guns exploded and he tried to run off, dragging me with him. The gunners shouted: 'Hold him! Hold him!' That I did and, after about fifty yards, I brought him to a halt. Luckily, I wasn't hurt. They then unloaded the ammo, while I wondered what would have happened had the Wog got away from me. I imagined he could have fallen down a cliff and the whole load blown up!

I was told to have a rest and someone else took the reins. The guns continued to fire and the Wog kept trying to get away. I dreaded to think what would happen if we ever got into action! After a while, I thought I'd better get back to camp before night fell because I'd become lost in the dark. I was asked if I'd like somebody to go partway with me, but, like a fool, I refused, saying I'd be alright. I soon regretted my decision because the Wog continued to muck about. I became very tired, but at last we got down to the narrow-gauge railway in the valley. I thought I'd then mount the mule and ride the last mile or so, but he wouldn't even stand still to let me do that. When I got back, I was all in, but, fortunately, I was told to go to my tent while someone else unsaddled, fed and watered the Wog.

Another time, we were lined up ready to go out on a scheme, but I'd caught a cold and lost my voice. A sergeant came to inspect us and said something to me, but I couldn't answer and just moved my lips. He thought I was mocking him and gave me a dressing down until he realized that I had laryngitis. He then ordered someone else to take the reins of my mule and told me to get into bed. I did and quickly recovered.

One day, we were all called out by the lieutenant colonel for a parade. He announced that we were now in the airborne forces and that he was having a mock-up plane made, so we could practise jumping out of it. My mind boggled at the thought of parachuting out of an aeroplane with a couple of mules, but the next day the order was cancelled and we were back to normal!

By then, the mules' field had become a morass and the mud was so bad that we had to be issued with wellingtons, to enable us to get to our animals. One of the fellows got one of his boots stuck in the mire and had to step out in his stocking foot to get it out! Things got in such a state that it was decided to let the ground dry out by allowing the mules loose to roam wherever they would. At first, they didn't realize they were free and they didn't move much, but, after a while, they got the message and galloped away. Eventually, they came back, tempted, I think, by food that was put out for them.

We encountered plenty of mud round and about, especially on one scheme, where we came to a piece of ground so boggy that the mules sank up to their bellies, particularly because of the extra weight of the gun parts they were carrying! It was a real struggle getting the animals out and we had to pull hard on the reins and hit them from behind till they made a supreme effort to force their way out.

On 6 October, we left our camp at the Spittal of Glenshee, probably because our tent accommodation wasn't suitable for winter conditions. Our battery moved to Muir of Ord, a small place about three miles north of Beauly, where we arrived on the 8th. Other parts of the regiment were quartered nearby in Dingwall and Strathpeffer. We were billeted in Nissen huts and the mules had covered accommodation. We were back in barracks, so at least we no longer had to camp in our tents.

The day after we'd arrived in Muir of Ord, I started ten days' leave and, as usual, went home to show my face to my relatives and friends. I called at Taylor Tunnicliff to see my workmates. I was walking past the lodge when a voice shouted, 'Where are you going?' I turned and saw that there was a new lodge man. I explained who I was, but he said I'd have to have the departmental foreman vouch for me. After all my years' service, I felt rather annoyed, but I suppose they'd become more security minded because of the war and couldn't take the chance of saboteurs entering the factory. Tom Reeves then came down and took me to his office, where we had a chat. I then went off to see the other fellows and girls, but I don't think they were too bothered about seeing me.

By that time, I was smoking about fifteen to twenty cigarettes a day, Woodbines, I think. Although in the Forces we seemed to be able get supplies of fags, there was a shortage in civvy street. So while I was on leave, like most everybody else, I had to go round to different shops trying to get some and almost pleading for them. Beer was also in short supply and pubs were closed half the time. When word got around that a certain pub had had a delivery, it would be packed out in no time.

I decided to have a horse ride and went to a riding school up Kerry Hill, in the back of beyond. The horses were half-starved because of the shortage of food with rationing and I could see their ribs sticking out. I paid for a ride and explained that I'd ridden mules, but I think the woman took it with a pinch of salt. She gave me some instructions because it was different sitting in a saddle. I was told to ease my behind off the saddle, by standing slightly on the stirrups, and ride with a rhythm. I took my horse around the lanes nearby, but I wasn't a very good rider.

Back at Muir of Ord, one night I saw the northern lights, which were strange. They looked like searchlights and bomb flashes and it seemed as if there was an air raid in progress.

One day, a couple of fellows were taking a wagon to Beauly to collect supplies, when the two mules pulling it bolted. They couldn't be stopped, so the driver coolly whipped them to make them go even faster, which tired them out more quickly. Fortunately, the road was reasonably straight and there was no traffic about and eventually the animals calmed down.

On another occasion, we were out exercising the mules and had dismounted for ten minutes for a smoke and to let the animals graze. We then got the order to mount and that I attempted to do, but, just at that moment, Susie put her head down to take another bite of the grass. I went straight over her neck and hit the turf with a bump, but, fortunately, I wasn't injured.

Something similar happened to Sergeant Lark. He was demonstrating to some new recruits how to mount a mule. He said, 'With this mule being tall, Sergeant Smith will give me a help up.' He then lifted up his left foot and Sergeant Smith caught hold of it and hoisted him up. Unfortunately, he heaved too hard and Sergeant Lark went right over the animal and hit the ground on the other side! He made an apologetic remark, but we all laughed – inwardly! He was cheating anyway because we ordinary soldiers had to jump on our mules no matter how big they were.

We went on a scheme down to Loch Ness, nearly twenty miles to the south. On the loch were a number of invasion barges. They looked like elongated modern skips and each accommodated perhaps ten fellows and twenty mules. We queued in a field to take our place on one of the craft and there was a commotion as we got the mules on board. There was very little room, but we had a cruise around for a while and then went back ashore. It was said that we were part of a force that was earmarked to invade Norway, but I didn't have much faith in our ability to survive if we did get involved in such a venture. However, the invasion must have been cancelled because there were no more trips on the loch.

A time or two, things went missing from my kitbag. Once, I was looking for my housewife, to sew a button on my tunic, but I couldn't find it and eventually spotted it on another soldier's shelf. Another time, one of the lads was transferred to a different unit and he left me a note, saying he'd taken one of my metal tunic collar badges so that he'd be shipshape when he checked in! Although he left me a shilling to cover the cost of a replacement, it was a nuisance and I was miffed. To prevent any further thieving from my bag, I bought and threaded a brass lock through the eyeholes at the top of it. That solved the problem, although one day I was looking for something in my kitbag and found a nest of baby mice. I can't remember what I did, but I certainly didn't eat them!

I had a letter from Helen, which told me that the fence at the front of our garden had fallen down onto the pavement. Because she was still staying with Vera, she didn't know of the incident until afterwards. When Fred Halfpenny came home that evening, he ignored it, even though it was a public hazard and he knew I was away in the Forces. Fortunately, Harold Bentley did us a good turn and nailed it back up.

The winter was really cold and we soon used up our supply ration of coke to heat our hut at the barracks. It was decided that we'd raid the coke dump in turn. When my attempt came, two of us lifted up the wire fencing that surrounded the dump and scooped some coke into a bag. I hated doing it and was all on pins until we got back safely to the hut.

When fellows went sick with some ailment and reported to the medical officer, he usually prescribed the army's number nine pill, which was a very powerful laxative and cured most ills! But, when I caught a cold and lost my voice, I had to persist in reporting it to him because he kept sending me back to duty. Finally, when we were starting on a week's scheme in snow, he ordered me to the military hospital in Dingwall, six miles to the north. The lads trudged off in the snow and I didn't envy them, but I was apprehensive about going into hospital. I gathered some of my kit together and got in a truck, which took me there. When I arrived, they told me to have a bath and then get into bed. It was lovely to be in a nice warm place and the only treatment I had to put up with was rest. There were books and magazines to read, so it was marvellous. The next day, my voice improved and I slowly got better until I was okay after a week. I was then sent back to the barracks and my usual routine.

One day, when we went to feed the mules, the biggest rat I'd ever seen ran out of the mules' food. It was the size of a small cat and must have been living well off the fodder. It ran towards the mules and they shied away from it, but one of them lashed out and caught it a glancing blow. That crippled it and one of the lads ran forward and disposed of it with a spade.

On 8 January 1945, I returned home for ten day's leave. My visit wasn't particularly eventful, but it was good to see Helen again.

Back at the barracks, we were issued with new shirts, with collars on them, and khaki ties to match, to ensure we were completely camouflaged! Before then, we'd been wearing old-fashioned shirts, without collars, of the type sported by Grandad Wallett. I wondered if the army was trying to compete with the smart dress of the Yanks, but, if so, there was still a long way to go!

Whenever the officers wanted a job doing, they'd select a group of men to form a picket. The stable picket consisted of four men and an NCO and was required to muck out the stables. The duty officer would line the group up and inspect the men, picking out the smartest one, who'd be excused from the task, but would be on stand-by in case a picket was taken ill. The selected man was called the "stick man".

On one of the picket parades, I was standing next to a fellow named Marshall, who was known as "Masher". The officer looked us over and shouted: 'Third man from my right is stick man. Stick man step forward.'

That was Masher, but nobody moved. I was second from the right and whispered from the corner of my mouth, 'It's you Masher!'

Masher whispered back, 'No, it's you "Cig",' which was what some of the men called me.

The officer was showing his impatience, so I thought I'd better do something and stepped forward a couple of paces. The officer then dismissed the parade and I dashed off, very pleased with my luck, but he shouted to me and told me that Masher was the stick man. I had no choice except to do the duty after all, but I thought it was a poor decision because Masher didn't deserve to be chosen if he couldn't even count.

In all my time in the army, I only ever saw trouble between any of the men once, which was amazing. We had a coffee-coloured fellow and he was probably a half-caste. One of the white lads insulted him and called him a "nigger". I could tell by his eyes that he was hurt inwardly, but he didn't retaliate. I felt sorry for him, but I didn't dare say anything because I didn't want to get picked on myself. The coloured fellow was well-built and, if he'd started, he'd have made mincemeat of the other youth, but he was probably worried that the white lads would have ganged up on him.

We had some air force lads posted to us. I gathered that the RAF didn't need them because there hadn't been the amount of casualties that had been expected, so they were off-loaded. It must have been a terrible shock to them, dropping down from aeroplanes to mules!

It was strange that when horses and mules were turned loose together, the latter sidled up to the former and tried to be friendly, but the horses were snobbish, being a superior breed, and moved away. In that respect, they resembled the officers who rode them!

Our veterinary staff had some mucky jobs to do on the animals. Sometimes, they had to clean the sex organs of the mules and it was surprising how much filth was removed. The mules wouldn't stand still while the job was being done, so the vets would put a wire loop on the end of the animals' nostrils. That was attached to a stick, which was twisted until the loop was tight. It kept the mules quiet, but, if they attempted to move, an extra twist on the stick would stop them. The vets would then roll up their shirt sleeves, put their hands in or around the sex organs and perform the operation.

On a scheme around that time, I had the Wog as one of my two mules, which were tied in a blob of six for the night. The lads stood by with nosebags, while the animals moved about with excitement. The order came to 'Feed up,' which stimulated the mules even more because they knew what it meant. We then moved in with a nosebag for each of our two animals, but, when I got to the rear of the Wog, he lashed out and sent me flying to the ground. Amazingly, I wasn't hurt at all, but I was going to give him a good kick in return until I thought better of it because it might have led to chaos had the Wog jumped into one or two of the other mules.

All the fiddling about with the mules seemed a waste of time, but there appeared to be no end to it. I couldn't imagine them ever going into action and standing there while the guns were going off. I couldn't make out what we were all there for, but I thought, 'If that's the way the top brass want it, that's the way it will be.' But how it was did for me because I didn't want to be in action!

Fighting the enemy sounded very glamorous, but I can't remember any of the rank and file saying, 'Get us into action.' There was only one fellow I can remember who got so fed up that he wanted to leave and he joined the airborne services. As far as I was concerned, if we hadn't had the mules, it would have been ideal!

1. MEMBERS OF THE KENT AND BRYANT FAMILIES, c. 1913:
Front row: Cyril's great-aunt, JANE BRYANT; grandmother, MARY KENT; uncle,
EDMUND ("TED") KENT; aunt, FLORRIE KENT, and grandfather, EDMUND KENT.
Back row: Third from the left, Cyril's aunt, FLORRIE BRYANT, and far right, uncle,
FRED BRYANT.

2. Cyril's grandparents, GEORGE and ANN WALLETT.

3. MEMBERS OF STAFF OF JAMES MACINTYRE & CO. LIMITED, of Waterloo Road, Burslem, c. 1913, including Cyril's father, WILL KENT (back row, second from the right), and his mother, LILY WALLETT (front row, second from the left).

4. CYRIL, 1916.

5. Cyril's parents, LILY and WILL KENT, at the back of 27 WINDERMERE STREET, COBRIDGE, where Cyril lived for most of his childhood.

6. LENNY SKERRATT, a childhood friend of Cyril, who became a Grenadier Guard, along with four of his five brothers!

7. ALBERT SHORE, CYRIL, LEVI SHORE and Cyril's cousin, SAM KENT, at Grandmother Kent's house, 344 Etruria Vale, Etruria, c. 1923. The Shores lived next door at a newsagent's, number 346.

8. COBRIDGE ALEXANDRA, with their manager, Cyril's father, far left on the back row, c. 1923.

9. COBRIDGE PICTURE HALL, on Waterloo Road, which was where Cyril first developed a taste for movies about 1924 and which is still standing.

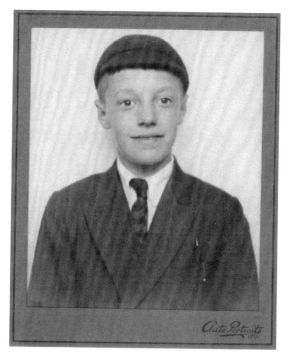

10. CYRIL, c. 1925.

11. The CAPITOL, in New Street, Hanley, one of the cinemas to which Cyril transferred his custom from Cobridge Picture Hall.

12. PICCADILLY, HANLEY, showing THE REGENT on the right, a plush new cinema, where Cyril went to see many "talkie" films.

13. THE TIPPING OF MOLTEN SLAG AT SHELTON BAR, which lit up the sky at night in the surrounding area, including Windermere Street.

14. CYRIL'S SCHOOL LEAVING CERTIFICATE, 20 December 1929.

15. Part of the factory of JOSIAH WEDGWOOD AND SONS LIMITED, Etruria, where Cyril went to work as an apprentice turner at the end of 1929. In the distance on the right is Shelton Bar.

16. One of the turning shops at TAYLOR TUNNICLIFF & CO. LTD., in Hampton Street, Eastwood, where Cyril went to work as an apprentice porcelain turner in 1931. CYRIL is third from the right and standing in the middle is the boss of the clay department, TOM REEVES.

17. Clockwise, CYRIL, his friends, BILL STREET and STAN JOHNSON, and STAN'S BROTHER, whilst camping at Rudyard in 1932.

18. HANLEY WAKES, off Regent Road, Hanley, where Cyril was a regular visitor.

19. PAT HALEY, a stylish welterweight, Cyril's favourite boxer, who fought locally on many occasions.

20. NORMAN WAINWRIGHT, an Olympic swimmer, who broke fifty British records and was sometimes still training at Hanley Baths when Cyril's swimming lessons were due to begin.

21. THE THEATRE ROYAL, in Pall Mall, Hanley, where Cyril went to see many shows and plays.

22. CYRIL'S MOTHER AT THEIR NEW HOUSE, 472 LEEK ROAD, SHELTON, c. 1935.

23. CYRIL and his dog, FLOSS, in the back garden at 472 Leek Road, Shelton, c. 1935.

24. CYRIL practising his boxing stance at CUNNINGHAM HOLIDAY CAMP, Douglas, Isle of Man, August 1936!

25. STOKE CIRCLE WHEELERS cycling club, with CYRIL, the captain, second from the left on the front row, at Chester in 1937. His former girlfriend, NORAH BURT, is on the far right of the front row.

26. RON FINAN, a close friend, and CYRIL at Quarterbridge, Douglas, Isle of Man, August 1937.

27. CYRIL and his close friend, NORMAN BANKS, at Blackpool, August 1938.

28. HELEN MIDDLETON, of 12 Rose Street, Northwood, c. 1938. She became Cyril's girlfriend and then wife.

29. Helen's father, TED MIDDLETON, who served in the army in both the First and Second World Wars!

30. Helen's elder sister, VERA POOLE, and her husband, "BIG HARRY".

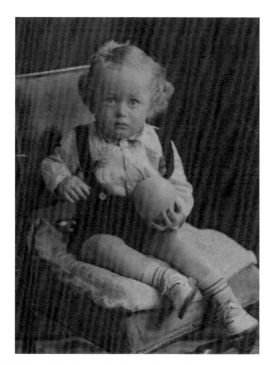

31. "YOUNG HARRY" POOLE, Helen's nephew, already showing a great interest in a ball. He later became Port Vale's second-longest-serving player.

32. CYRIL and HELEN at Morecambe, August 1939.

33. CYRIL AND HELEN AFTER THEIR WEDDING at St. Mark's Church, Shelton, on 21 June 1941.

34. CYRIL in his Home Guard uniform and NORMAN BANKS in his Boys' Brigade officer's uniform, c. 1941, in the back garden of 12 Rose Street, where Cyril and Helen were living.

35. Cyril's cousin, BERNARD KENT, who became a sergeant major in the army cadets, but was sent to work in Hanley Deep Pit as a "Bevin Boy".

NATIONAL SERVICE ACTS, 1939 TO 1941

GRADE CARD.

Roberts

Registration No. HS2 2641

Mr. Cyril Kent.

whose address on his registration card is 4 7 2 Leek Rd

Stoke on Trent

was medically examined at HANLEY

on

and placed in

GRADE* I (one)

Chairman of Board Nawh Collar

Medical Board stamp

Man's Signature C Kent

HANLEY MEDICAL BOARD (No. 2)

*The roman numeral denoting the man's Grade with number also spelt out) will be entered in RED ink by the Chairman himself, e.g., Grade I (one), Grade II (two) (a) (Vision).

N.S. 55.   [P.T.O.

36. The front of CYRIL'S NATIONAL SERVICE GRADE CARD, on which he was registered as A1 on 5 December 1941.

37. CYRIL, c. 1942.

(I) SOLDIER'S NAME and DESCRIPTION on ATTESTATION.

Army Number *1428704 2*

Surname (in capitals) ..... *KENT*

Christian Names (in full) ..... *CYRIL*

Date of Birth *14-12-1915*

Place of Birth. { Parish .....
In or near the town of .....
In the county of .....

Trade on Enlistment *TURNER - ELEC. PORCELAIN*

Nationality of Father at birth .....

Nationality of Mother at birth .....

Religious Denomination ..... *C of E*

Approved Society *PRUDENTIAL*

Membership No. *9050944*

Enlisted at ..... *WAKEFIELD* ..... On *7 SEP 1942*

For the :—
* Regular Army * Supplementary Reserve.
* Territorial Army. *D of W.* * Army Reserve Section D.
* Strike out those inapplicable.

For *D.of.W.* years with the Colours and ..... years in the Reserve.

Signature of Soldier ..... *C. Kent*

Date *17-9-1942*

38. A PAGE FROM CYRIL'S SOLDIER'S SERVICE BOOK, given to him on 17 September 1942 on being conscripted into the Territorial Army.

To my Darling Wife with Love

With Every Good Wish
for
Christmas and the New Year

From

Cyril

x x x x x x x x x x x x
x x x x x x x x x x x x

25th Medium and Heavy Training Regt., R.A.

39. THE CHRISTMAS CARD SENT BY CYRIL TO HELEN from his army camp at Marske-by-the-Sea, in Yorkshire, in December 1942.

40. CYRIL in his army service dress uniform, c. 1943.

41. THE TEN-SHILLING NOTE THAT CYRIL'S MOTHER GAVE TO HIM, the last time he saw her before she died on 12 July 1943. He kept it for sentimental reasons.

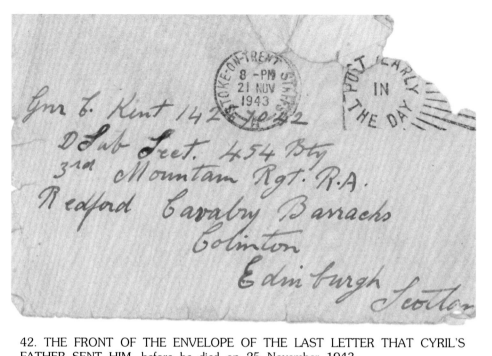

42. THE FRONT OF THE ENVELOPE OF THE LAST LETTER THAT CYRIL'S
FATHER SENT HIM, before he died on 25 November 1943.

43. 454 BATTERY of the 3rd MOUNTAIN REGIMENT of the ROYAL ARTILLERY
(including Cyril) and THEIR MULES embarking on boats in Loch Ness as a practice
exercise in the autumn of 1944.

44. CYRIL in his olive green uniform in India, c. 1945.

45. Cyril's army friend, FRED "THE COCKNEY" (left); Helen's cousin, KEN JOHNS (a sergeant in the RAF), and CYRIL posing with an Indian boy in Bombay, 1945.

46. CYRIL ON JUHU BEACH, near Bombay, 1946.

47. The quads and guns of 284 BATTERY of the 123rd FIELD REGIMENT of the ROYAL ARTILLERY in Connaught Circus at the DELHI VICTORY PARADE on 7 March 1946. Cyril was in one of the quads.

48. THE TAJ MAHAL, in Agra, which was visited by Cyril in March 1946. He climbed to the top of one of the corner towers.

49. THE GEORGIC, the troopship on which Cyril returned home from India in September 1946.

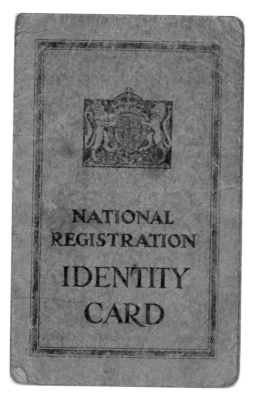

50. THE FRONT OF CYRIL'S 1946 NATIONAL REGISTRATION IDENTITY CARD.

51. FREDDIE STEELE, the centre-forward in Stoke City's fine 1946-1947 team, which Cyril and Helen regularly went to watch at the Victoria Ground. Freddie attended the same school as Cyril.

52. NEIL FRANKLIN, the centre-half in Stoke City's fine 1946-1947 team, which Cyril and Helen regularly went to watch at the Victoria Ground.

53. Helen's bother, ELIJAH MIDDLETON, and his wife, ETHEL (née Smith). They were married at St. Mary's Church, Bucknall, on 29 March 1947.

54. SID ASHER and Helen's younger sister, LEAH, after their wedding at St. George's Church, Newcastle-under-Lyme, on 24 July 1948.

55. HELEN and CYRIL at Scarborough, August 1948.

56. CYRIL on the pebble beach at Hastings, August 1949.

57. CHRISTMAS AT SWINNERTON'S FACTORY, in Raymond Street, Shelton, 1949. Helen is in the middle of the front row and was by then the assistant manageress.

58. HELEN and CYRIL at Torquay, 1950.

59. HELEN and CYRIL, with their baby, JEFF, on his christening day,
19 August 1951.

60. JEFF, HELEN and "TED", January 1952. Ted now sits next to the computer in Jeff's office!

61. Cyril's cousin, STAN PALIN, and his wife, MOLLIE. Cyril was the best man at their wedding at St. Chad's Church, Tunstall, on 6 September 1952. Stan developed a small chain of photography shops in a partnership.

62. THE FRONT PAGE OF HELEN'S 1953-1954 RATION BOOK.

63. CYRIL and JEFF at 256 Etruria Vale Road, Etruria, October 1954.

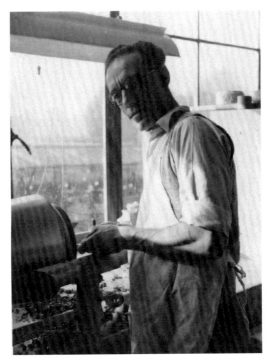

64. CYRIL WORKING AS A JASPER TURNER at Wedgwood's factory at Barlaston, c. 1956.

65. "YOUNG" HARRY POOLE, in his Port Vale strip, 1956. Cyril, Helen and Jeff watched him make his first team debut at home to Middlesbrough on 28 April and became regulars at Vale Park thereafter.

66. EVA and VIN JEFFRIES, of 311 Leek Road, who took Cyril, Helen and Jeff out in their car a number of times. Eva was the manageress at Swinnerton's and Vin was a conjuror in his spare time.

67. JACK and ROSE GREEN with their daughters, Rosie (left) and Mildred. Jack and Rose were close friends of Cyril and Helen.

68. CYRIL STANDING BEHIND THE CHINA CABINET HE MADE at his woodwork class at Milton School in 1956.

69. THE STATION ROAD POST OFFICE AND SORTING OFFICE, STOKE, where Cyril started work on 12 August 1957 when he joined the GPO.

70. ONE OF THE PACKET-SORTING FRAMES AT THE STOKE SORTING OFFICE.
Cyril used frames like this in his sorting duties as a postman.

71. CYRIL'S POST OFFICE CAP BADGE.

72. HELEN, JEFF and CYRIL in their back garden at 335 Leek Road, Shelton, May 1958.

73. CYRIL and JEFF at Prestatyn, during the building of a new sea wall and promenade, May 1959.

74. JEFF and CYRIL playing putting at Prestatyn, May 1960.

75. A POST OFFICE BARROW, of the type used by Cyril to deliver parcels in Newcastle-under-Lyme shopping centre in the autumn of 1960.

76. CYRIL sitting on the new sea wall at Prestatyn, May 1961.

77. STAN MATTHEWS showing his skills as the "Wizard of the Dribble". Cyril was one of the 35,974 spectators who watched Stan's comeback match for Stoke City at home to Huddersfield Town on 28 October 1961.

5 Indian Interlude

One day, we were issued with tropical clothing and it looked as if we were going abroad. It didn't necessarily mean that we were going to the tropics because that was the kind of thing the army did to try to confuse the enemy. Our new uniform was made of lightweight material, with khaki shorts and a pair of slacks to provide protection against mosquitoes. Soon afterwards, the news came round that we were going overseas and I was filled with trepidation because I was worried I might get killed. Then, one day, quite a lot of us discovered, from the notice board, that we were being given fourteen days' embarkation leave from 2 March 1945.

I decided to go home and, while I was there, Helen and I visited Grandmother Kent, who was in London Road Hospital and very poorly. When we arrived, my cousin, Annie, and her sister-in-law, Hilda, were already there. They had a piece of paper, which they were trying to get Grandmother to sign. I understand they were attempting to lay claim to her possessions, but Grandmother didn't know anyone and they couldn't get her to understand what to do, so they wasted their time. Grandmother died on the 5th and I suppose I went, three days later, to her funeral service at St. Matthew's Church, Etruria, and burial in Hanley Cemetery, but I can't remember anything about them. Nevertheless, she was the last of my close blood relatives to die and the fifth in just over two years! I was still only 29 and was very sad.

When I got back to Muir of Ord, there was a special notice on the board that listed a number of men who were about to be sent into action. I was concerned and looked down the list to see if I was amongst them, but I couldn't see my name, so I checked to make sure. I was very relieved. I don't think it had occurred to me before then that I might end up fighting! The lads were taking the guns with them, but I wished that they were taking the mules instead! There was quite a bit of activity and then they were gone, to give extra firepower for the successful crossing of the Rhine by Field Marshal Montgomery's army on 23 March.

I understand they gave a good account of themselves, especially in the town of Rees, on the far bank of the river. When they returned, I was told that, on one occasion, they'd manhandled a gun to the top of a house, to fire at a German position and continued to do so until the building was in danger of collapsing, with the shock of the firing. Another time, there was a strongpoint in the town that was holding up the advance, but 3rd Mountain Regiment soldiers pushed a gun into place and commenced firing, even though they were under heavy fire themselves. After a while, the Germans were silenced.

For their parts in the actions in the town, one of our officers, Captain James MacNair, was awarded the Military Cross and one of the NCOs, Sergeant Clifford White, the Military Medal. Captain MacNair had fired his gun for over 24 hours, whilst under attack himself, and killed seven Germans with his Bren gun. Sergeant White had fired his gun in the open by himself so that his men didn't have to face unnecessary danger, but he couldn't be awarded the Military Cross because he was only a sergeant. It wasn't possible for NCOs and ordinary gunners to get it. It was a class thing.

While they were away, the lads had the assistant of the quartermaster's stores along to look after them. In the assistant's absence, one of the sergeants ordered me to report to our quartermaster, to help out in the stores by humping things around and tidying up. It meant there were no mules or guard duties for me for the time being. The stores were in one of the huts and had a lot of shelves with clothing and equipment on them. So I was working under cover and didn't get wet when it was raining. It was alright for a change, but there was a snag because the sergeant expected me to steal spare shirts for him, I suppose in return for getting me this good job. I told him I couldn't do that because I was being watched all the time, which was true, and, in any case, I didn't want to steal, especially for someone else. The sergeant wasn't very pleased and kept pressing me until he got nasty and his attitude became threatening. I was wondering what the outcome would be when I was let off the hook because he had a road accident, which put him in hospital, and I never saw him again.

A number of names, including mine, appeared on the notice board to go on a short course on malaria, from 26 to 29 March, and we were given a rail ticket to Aldershot. In our train compartment on the way down, the other fellows, who were all from the London area, came up with a scheme for getting us all home before we reported to Aldershot. I was to have the group pass and meet them in London at a certain time. It seemed as if they'd done that kind of thing before and they were confident of getting away with it.

I got off the train at Crewe, leaving them to carry on, and I caught a connection to Stoke. I increasingly worried about how it would all work out and decided to give Stoke Station a miss because redcaps would be hanging around on the platform. So I got off the train at Etruria, hoping for the best because there was a possibility that the ticket collector would cause some trouble. But nothing much was said, so my first hurdle was cleared. I then got a bus to Hanley and another down to Leek Road. By chance, Helen was at our house, probably doing one or two jobs. She was delighted to see me and I was able to stay the night.

The following afternoon, I made my way back to Etruria Station, where again there were no redcaps and, once more, I was let on the platform without any trouble. I got to London before the meeting time and sat down on a bench at Euston Station, but it wasn't long before a young military policeman came along, asking questions. I showed him our pass, which satisfied him for the time being, though he kept hanging around. I wasn't too bothered, but the meeting time came and went and there was no sign of my comrades. After I'd been waiting for nearly two hours, the redcap approached me again and said that we should have been reporting to Aldershot by then and that it would be too late for us to get into the camp. He moved away a short distance, but was getting rather agitated and I think he was toying with the idea of putting me on a charge. I was getting concerned and realized I'd soon have to make a move, but then one of the fellows turned up and was presently followed by the rest of them. I was very relieved and we caught the next train to Aldershot, where we got into camp without any trouble.

While we were on the course, I listened and made notes about malaria because I thought we'd perhaps need to pass on our information to the other lads back at the barracks in case we went abroad. But, when we got back, nothing was mentioned about the course, so it was a waste of time. However, I did remember some useless information we were told, such as that it was only the females of some of the anopheles type of mosquito that could transmit malaria to people!

For the third year running, we had a race meeting with the mules, which was called a donkey derby. It was run something like horse racing and bets were taken. As usual, I didn't go along because I saw enough of the animals as it was.

On 8 May, the rumour went round that the war against Germany had ended. It was a big thing, but I can't remember anybody telling us officially. I was relieved. Our departure overseas had been delayed for some reason and so we were given another twelve days' embarkation leave, which started on 11 May. I went home and it was great to see the street lights back on at night. Young children, who'd never seen them before, must have been amazed. We were again able to leave the curtains open, without worrying about the light shining into the street. People were jubilant and the Railway Mission, on the opposite side of Leek Road (where Stoke Repertory Theatre now stands), threw a party for the kids. Helen and I went along and I took a photo of the occasion.

When I got back to Muir of Ord, I had a wonderful surprise. The mules had gone, every one of them, and I never saw them again. Also, the special force had returned from the Rhine and with them the quartermaster's assistant, so my store job had gone. Then, on 29 May, I had a cholera vaccination, so it looked certain that we'd be off soon, aboard ship to heaven knew where. I was dubious as to what was going to happen, but we were in the hands of the commanders.

We were told to complete the will form, which was in our service book. It seemed bizarre to be doing that, but it made me realize I might get killed. I filled my form in and signed it on the 30th, leaving everything to Helen. I appointed Jack Green as the executor, because I could trust him to get the job done, and got Jack Watson, a bombardier from Hastings, to sign as the witness. He had a similar build to Gary Cooper, the film star, and looked just like him. He was almost the only man I'd have followed willingly if I'd been ordered to attack because of his style. He was always confident, so I'd have been sure he'd have seen me through. I'd have been braver with him around.

Soon, we were packing our equipment up and ready for away. On 7 June, we lined up outside our huts and then made our way to the station, half-dragging our equipment because there was so much of it. We were ages getting there, despite the short distance, and it nearly crippled me. We hauled our stuff onto the train and a few townspeople saw us off. We arrived at Gourock, on the Firth of Clyde, and struggled, with our mountain of equipment, up the gangplank onto a troopship, which seemed huge. All the while, a military band played on the dock side to lift our spirits. The boat, the D. 9, was Polish and had been sailed to Britain before the Germans had got their hands on it.

When we got on deck, we were directed below and went down several flights of stairs into the bowels of the ship. The hold I landed in was packed with men and was quite warm. It had a low roof and was full of tables, with forms on both sides of them to sit on. There were no beds or bunks, but strung from the ceiling beams were lots of hammocks. The tables had already been claimed as beds, so it was a hammock for me. Word had got out that we were bound for India and the information circulated quickly amongst the men down below. I'd assumed we'd be going somewhere where the war against the Japanese hadn't finished. I wasn't thrilled about it, but I had to put up with it.

The war diary says we set out from port at 6 p.m. on the 8th. I think I was below deck when the ship's engines started and we began moving. I later watched my mates trying to get into their hammocks and what a performance it was! A lot of them grabbed their hammocks and tried to pull themselves in, but they just fell over the other side. It was marvellous no-one was hurt. I then had a go and got it right first time. I grabbed an overhead beam and hoisted myself up before lowering myself onto the hammock. Our movement through the water was nice and smooth and I soon fell off to sleep.

When I woke in the morning, I looked up and saw the deck above me moving from side to side. I couldn't make out what was happening and I began to feel unwell. I grabbed the beam above me, eased myself out of the hammock and put my feet on the deck below me. I then discovered that the ship was rolling from side to side. I realized we were in the Atlantic and that I was feeling seasick. I put my clothes on quickly and dashed up the several floors onto the open deck. I staggered to the boat rail, put my head over and was sick. I stayed there for quite a while and then slumped on the deck, with my back resting against something. I remained on deck all day and so it was a good job that it was warm. I felt so unwell that I didn't have any meals at all that day.

When the lights out order came, I dashed down below and got in my hammock. It was bliss because it kept on an even keel, however much the ship rolled, as it was suspended. I had a pretty good night's sleep, but again in the morning I had to get on deck as soon as possible, having told one of my mates that he could have my breakfast. Although I again felt unwell, I was better than on the previous day and I don't think I was sick. Again I ate nothing, but the following morning I felt much better. I'd found my sea legs and was going with the ship on its roll instead of resisting and trying to stay upright.

I had a decent breakfast of egg, bacon and sausage, although it was rather greasy. There was very little to do, excepting for, about once a day, lining up for physical jerks and boat drill, which just consisted of assembling by an appointed lifeboat so that we knew where to go in an emergency. So most of the time, we just lounged about.

On board were members of the Auxiliary Territorial Service (the women's branch of the army), the Women's Auxiliary Air Force (the Waafs) and the Women's Royal Naval Service (the Wrens). They did office work, cooking, storekeeping, postal work and things like that for the Forces. They were being transported to posts in India and places on the way.

We were banned from using the upper decks because those were reserved for the women and the officers and gentlemen! If the ship had sunk, there would probably have been no place in the lifeboats for us ordinary men because the women would have gone first. They would probably have been followed by many of the officers, to organize things, so we may well have been cannon fodder. But we were all issued with life jackets, which, we were told, would keep us afloat for a few hours until help came. We were instructed not to use them as pillows or cushions because that would spoil their buoyancy.

We were able to buy fags at a cheap rate on the ship, I suppose because we were on the high seas and so they weren't subject to tax. Also, there were showers, but the water was salty and probably taken from the sea. Ordinary soap wouldn't lather in it, so a special kind had to be used. We ate below deck around the same tables that were slept on at night, but the food was enjoyable.

We had pretty good weather on the voyage and got increasingly sunburnt from lying on deck, even though we'd been warned about the strength of the sun. We must have passed Gibraltar in the night because I didn't see it, but, once we'd reached there, we were allowed to change from our normal thick horse blanket-type uniform to our new lightweight one. In the Mediterranean, we became accompanied by what appeared to be large fish, which broke the surface and then went under the water again. I said to a pal, 'Look at those sharks,' but he told me they were either dolphins or porpoises.

There wasn't much to see as we sailed through the Mediterranean because we were in the middle of the sea. Eventually, on the morning of 18 June, we arrived at Port Said in Egypt, at the entrance to the Suez Canal. I was told that we off-loaded a gunner there because his skin was too delicate for the climate and raw with the heat. I believe he was sent back to Europe.

We then sailed through the canal and many a time I looked across the sand dunes for one of the mirages that, according to storybooks, people were supposed to see, but I never saw anything. I was struck by the narrowness of the canal and the slow speed of the ship as we went through it, but I think that was because the authorities didn't want to disturb the sand that lined the sides in case it collapsed into the water.

Late that night, we arrived at Suez, at the southern end of the canal. We stayed there overnight and, from then on, we were allowed to sleep on deck, which was great because it was cooler than being below deck, where the heat was oppressive. In the morning, another gunner was taken off the ship, this time to hospital with pneumonia.

We then sailed into the Red Sea, which was supposedly so named because its water was sometimes that colour, but it didn't look red to me. I remember lying back, on deck at night, and looking up at a mast gently moving to-and-fro past a star. Unfortunately, every morning, at six o'clock prompt, the sailors swilled the decks down, even if soldiers were lying there, so it paid to move out of the way in time!

We then sailed through the Gulf of Aden and across the Arabian Sea before arriving at Bombay on 28 June, twenty days after we'd started out. As we approached the city, I leaned on the boat rails and looked out at it. The thing that struck me the most was that it was strange to see so many coloured people moving around. I couldn't remember having ever seen anyone like that in Stoke, although I'd noticed the odd coloured person or two in Liverpool when I'd passed through on my way to the Isle of Man. I was suspicious of the Indians because I'd read in books that coloured people were villains and so I wondered if they'd all got knives in their pockets, ready to stab us! I always remained wary of them because we were one tribe and they were another and we were occupying their country.

According to the war diary, it was two days before we disembarked from the ship and we were then were transferred to India Command. Its headquarters was in New Delhi and its main job was to protect India, but I didn't really know anything about that at the time.

We didn't get to see much of Bombay, but I remember there being an imposing basalt archway, called the Gateway of India, on the waterfront. It was 85 feet high and a symbol of British power in India.

We got straight on a train to take us to Kalyan Transit Camp, about thirty miles northeast of the city. Those amongst us who were wearing glasses were warned not to put their heads out of the windows because there were loads of kids around ready to reach up and snatch them. The people were so poor that they'd try to sell anything. At each station, there were kids very close to the train, but I didn't hear of any of our lads being victimized.

We arrived at our camp, which had huts, but the monsoon was well under way by then. It seemed to rain continuously and the air was warm and humid, which made the atmosphere sticky. Our clothes stuck to us and, even though we walked about without shirts, there was a horrible damp feeling. Everything in the huts seemed damp, including our bedclothes.

Once we were there, we were paid in Indian money. The main coin was the rupee, which was worth about 1s. 6d. It was divided into sixteen annas, each of which was made up of twelve pies. These had a hole in the centre to enable them to be put on string and worn around the neck, but I didn't bother with them because they were worth next to nothing.

Also, we were given new olive green uniforms, to blend in with the jungle. That was standard for tropical countries and replaced our khaki uniforms, which had been designed to provide camouflage in clayey mud areas like Flanders. We were given shorts for the daytime and trousers for night, when mosquitoes were about. We were also each issued with a big, wide beret, in the same colour, which was a silly-looking hat!

Outside our huts, native tradesmen were allowed to operate, selling tea and fruit. There were one or two tea wallahs, with little stoves, and they brewed up all day long. Some of the lads loved this situation, whereby they lay on their charpoys and bellowed, 'Char wallah!'

An Indian would come into the hut and say, 'Yes, sahib?' He'd then be given the fellow's enamel army mug and told to fill it up, which he'd do, in return for one or two annas.

When I wanted a drink, I went to the wallahs myself because it wouldn't give them the opportunity to spit in my mug! I thought that they might do that to get their own back on us because the British were behaving as the top caste in the Indians' country. Also, some of the lads thought the Indians to be inferior and bullied them, almost treating them like slaves.

There were also one or two fruit wallahs, who sold ripe greenish bananas (amongst other things), which were nice. I also sometimes got mangos from the wallahs, which were alright, but tasted like boot polish!

There wasn't much to do while we awaited the arrival of new mules and our harnesses were packed away in wooden boxes. We got up early to drill to avoid the heat of the afternoons, when it was red hot. It was so oppressive that we wore just shorts, socks and boots on our marches, which seemed to be organized just to keep us occupied. We got drenched because, if it wasn't pouring down, we were soaking with the damp. It was horrible.

In India, we had a special airmail service as a privilege, which turned round our correspondence quite quickly. After I'd informed Helen that I was near Bombay, she asked me to look out for her cousin, Kenneth Johns, who was a sergeant in the RAF and thought to be in the city. Ken was tall, nicely spoken and an attraction to women. On one occasion, when I had a day pass, I went to try to find him and was accompanied by Fred, the cockney. We'd been told to travel second class and not to mix with the natives, who travelled third class. We made our way to the station and decided to go third class after all because it was cheaper. We got a place on the wooden benches and rubbed shoulders with the Indians, who weren't very clean and kept staring at us, but we arrived safely.

I had to decide where to look for Ken and thought it would be a good idea to ask at the Railway Travel Office, run, I think, by the redcaps. They didn't know, but directed us to an RAF centre, where we also drew a blank. I realized it was silly searching for a fellow without having an address for him, but a third enquiry pointed us to a place outside the city. We jumped on another train and arrived in a village, where I saw an Indian with ginger hair! I stared at him because he didn't seem real. There was no-one we could ask for information because most of the Indians didn't understand English and I didn't like being outnumbered by the natives, particularly away from the city. So we got the next train back to Bombay.

Fred remained very tolerant, especially considering it had been pouring down with rain all day and we'd got soaked. Fortunately, the next time of asking produced the information we required. So, finally, we found Ken in an office, where he worked. He must have been very surprised to see me, but he got time off from his superior to show us around the area. He went into his quarters and changed into a freshly-washed and ironed uniform, which made Fred and me look like tramps, with our drill, crumpled from the rain. While we were out, Ken spotted a little Indian lad and gave him an anna to have his photo taken squatting in front of us.

Ken told us that he'd come over in the Queen Elizabeth, then the largest liner in the world, which was operating as a troopship. One night, the ship had swerved violently, almost throwing the passengers out of their bunks. He thought it was trying to avoid a torpedo that had been fired at it. He also said that he really wanted to get a medal, but I didn't think he had any chance with working in an office in the middle of a city a long way from any action! Then he made a statement about the natives working in his office, which really surprised me because I'd have thought he'd have acted as though he was superior: 'These Indians are cleverer than us. They can speak two languages – their own and English.'

On 14 July, our battery and most of the regiment left Kalyan and moved to the state of Hyderabad, which was ruled by the Nizam. He was reputedly the richest man in the world. Two days later, we landed in the wild, near to Kamareddi, which was about seventy miles from Secunderabad, and were joined there by the rest of the regiment on the 21st. I don't think I ever saw Kamareddi itself, which was out of bounds for us, perhaps because the officers thought we'd cause mischief and also maybe because they didn't want us to become too friendly with the Indians.

In our camp, there were no huts for accommodation and we were put in rectangular bashas, which were made from a bamboo frame. The sides were made from grass matting, hanging from the frame, but that left a gap of about six inches from the ground. It was probably designed to let the rain run through, but it would allow all kinds of things to crawl in, though I never saw anything dangerous do so. The roof consisted of banana leaves and was virtually waterproof, whilst the floor was simply the ground beneath our feet. There were no doors, so, when we wanted to go in or out, we'd just push our way through the matting.

There were four men to a basha and our beds were bamboo-framed charpoys, strung with jute. There were two charpoys on each side, stacked in bunk fashion, and I happily had a lower one. We had mosquito nets to put around us at bedtime and I was glad of that because there were all kinds of insects flying around. In the night, there were many strange noises and, on one occasion, there was something howling in a terrifying way, which made me snuggle down in my blanket. The nights were warm, so I slept in the nude and it was good to step out naked for a shower in the monsoon rains. They were so heavy that they swilled all the soap off our bodies before we towelled down in the bashas, although not everybody participated.

Indians moved freely through the camp, though they may have been employees. They wore no shoes and I saw one of them stub his toe against a tree root sticking up out of the ground. I winced, almost feeling the pain, but the fellow said nothing, just glanced around and carried on walking. That was because the Indians were used to it. Their feet were as hard as nails. There were also Indian troops, who had their own camps. We called them "Johnnies", although I don't think I ever saw any of them.

We had no running water, but got our supply from a big hole that had been dug. An Indian was employed to scoop water out of the hole, which he did with his bullock. One end of a rope was fastened to the animal and a bucket was secured to the other. The fellow drove the bullock forward and that pulled the bucket, full of water, upwards. It emptied into a chute, which led to a tank. The animal would then be backed towards the well and the process repeated. It seemed to go on for most of the day and the bullock must have been worn out.

The water was dosed with chlorine to purify it, but it tasted horrible and contained bits of matter. The best of it was that the MO recommended that we should drink twenty pints of the stuff a day owing to the heat! I doubt if anyone ever did that, but we drank plenty of tea made from the water. On odd occasions, the MO made us parade and drink a pint of salt water each to replace that lost due to perspiration. It took some drinking and some of the fellows were sick right afterwards!

Around our camp were quite a few kite-hawks, which we nicknamed "shite hawks" because they were scavengers and a nuisance. They were large, fearless birds, with sharp eyesight, and perched on trees, watching us at meal times. Unfortunately, our dining basha was around thirty yards away from the cookhouse and we had to carry our meals, on two plates, with a mug of tea between the two. The hawks would then swoop down and try to grab two clawfuls of food off our plates! I'd step out of the cookhouse, look up at the hawks and decide whether I could get to the basha in safety. But, a few times, there was a flurry of feathers in my face and part of my meal was gone! I tried bending over my food, but even that wasn't always successful. These birds were protected by law as they were very useful in eating any rotting food or bodies lying around and so stopping disease.

Our washing was done by dhobi wallahs, who didn't have any machines to help them. They dipped our clothes in a lake nearby and bashed them on a rock, which knocked the dirt out. The clothes were then spread out and dried in the hot sun. If we wanted a clean uniform in a hurry, one of the wallahs would get it ready in about half an hour for a small fee. When they carried out this quick service, the wallahs were known as flying dhobis.

With us was Major Braithwaite, who walked very smartly and always gave us a smashing salute. He did it properly, unlike the other officers, who were sloppy and just touched their caps with their sticks.

One day, I was doing a job with another fellow and we were stripped to the waist when we saw a long green and yellow snake weaving its way through a bush. We stopped work and started poking it with sticks, but the battery sergeant major came along and told us to get on with our jobs!

Once, I accidentally kicked a stone and found a scorpion underneath, with its tail waggling! That taught me not to pick up objects from the ground until I'd moved them with one of my boots. Scorpions were quite common and I used to like teasing them by touching them with a stick and seeing them whip their tails over to try to sting it. The largest ones were longer than the width of a hand and their sting could make you ill. There was a story that a scorpion would sting itself to death if faced with impossible odds! So some of the lads experimented with one and poured petrol around it in a ring, which was set alight to see if the scorpion would commit suicide. It didn't, but instead ran round trying to get out until it burned to death. I thought it was cruel, but it was interesting.

We were issued with free sealed tins of Player's cigarettes every so often. They were tasty and a class above the Woodbines we usually smoked. I sent some of the Player's home to myself because there was a shortage of them in Britain and I thought they'd help me out when I was demobbed. Helen wasn't a heavy smoker, so I didn't think she needed any.

There wasn't a lot of drill, although there were one or two schemes around the area, where we pretended that we were facing the enemy. We camped for the night on one scheme, but, in the morning, when I was packing things up, I lifted the groundsheet and found lots of termites wriggling around on the underside of it. They were like little grubs, perhaps half an inch long, and I had to shake them off. I didn't get any on me, but they made me feel itchy.

As the summer wore on, there was still no sign of our new mules. One of the harness boxes was opened and it was discovered that the damp had got at the leather, which had become mouldy. So it was obvious that it would take us ages to get our harnesses right. Then, all of a sudden, we were told that we were going to be mechanized and I was really glad because it meant there'd be no more mules!

I hadn't seen our old artillery since we left Scotland, but one day new guns arrived, 25-pounders, each pulled by a vehicle called a quad. It was like a little tank, oblong, but with the corners sort of cut off, and made of metal. When we went out on practice, it was a lot easier because there was no longer any marching or dragging two mules behind me. I just sat in the quad and was driven around. That's all I did and it was the same for the other mule drivers! On one shoot, I stood right behind a gun when it was fired. For the very first time, I saw the shell leave the barrel and quickly disappear in the distance.

On one of our manoeuvres, there was a water tanker with us, which was driven too fast round a curve in the road. Of course, the water was thrown to one side and tipped the tanker over! Fortunately, no-one was hurt.

One day, we were paraded in front of a brigadier, who told us that he'd been pleading with the higher-ups to get us into action against the Japs. He said, 'I know you chaps are eager to get at them.' I wasn't in agreement with him because I just wanted to get home! Fortunately, shortly afterwards, on 2 September, Japan surrendered and it was a big relief when we found out, though I don't remember any great excitement.

The discipline then started to relax and we were given educational lectures in our camp to help pass the time. Also, I asked if I could learn to drive and was given the go-ahead. So I drove round in a small truck for an hour, with the usual driver giving me instructions. It was up and down, over rough ground, and I wasn't told properly what to do, so I struggled, especially with all the double-declutching required. It put me off and so I didn't have any more lessons.

As the war was over, a pub was set up in a tent and it was pretty successful. The beer was poured from the barrels, through a tap, into the lads' enamel mugs. I didn't frequent the pub myself because I didn't want to get into treating people, which was the custom then and led to a lot of drinking.

We all had leaflets issued to us, explaining how our demobilization was to be conducted, which was according to age and service. As I was 29 and had only three years' service, I had a long time to wait.

A notice went up on the board that the army was selling surplus watches fairly cheaply. There was a shortage of them at the time in Britain, so I put in for one, which came a few weeks later and turned out to be pretty reliable. Also on sale were surplus kukris and I put my name down for one of those too, but I never got one.

There was a story going around that people who were curious to see what the kukri's blade was like would have to pay for it being unsheathed, by a Gurkha nicking one of their fingers to draw blood. I suppose the idea was that the Gurkhas were committed to using their kukris once they'd drawn them from their sheaths.

In November, it started to get rather cool at night and through most of the winter we wore overcoats on guard duty. There was no fence around the camp and only one guard on at a time, so we had a roving commission. We carried a rifle and just hung around, looking for anything suspicious or anyone coming in. But it was hard to see how the camp was really being guarded!

On 1 December, our regiment was amalgamated with the 123rd Field Regiment of the Royal Artillery, whose name was used for the combined unit. Our old batteries were scrapped and I was assigned to 284 Battery in the new regiment. To help kill the time, there was a competition to design a new flag for the regiment, although I wasn't aware of the existence of an old one! The winning entry had two diagonals, one in blue and the other in red (the artillery colours), with a mule's head in the middle, but the design seemed to be clinging to the past!

One morning, I put my hand in one of my boots prior to putting it on and felt something slimy. I withdrew my hand in the quickest movement I've ever made because I thought it was a snake. I tipped my boot upside down and out came a large green frog. I was mightily relieved!

On 4 January 1946, I was put in charge of a truck and told to fetch 12 tables and 24 chairs from the camp stores for our battery. Another fellow drove the wagon carrying the furniture and I just sat in the cab with him before reporting to the battery headquarters that the table and chairs had arrived. They were signed for by Major E. S. Strickley, who was in command of the battery. I still have the receipt!

Winter was the dry season after the end of the monsoon, so we could no longer step out regularly and have a shower in the rain. Instead, we used water from the well and scooped it out of the tank with a bowl. There was a wooden trestle table nearby to put the bowl on, so that we could wash and shave, but there were no baths.

One day, I went out to wash the whole of my body, but noticed there was a woman with the bullock driver at the well. I thought she'd turn around or move away when I started getting undressed, but she didn't. I hesitated because I didn't know what to do for the best, but I decided to carry on as I'd have had to have packed up and started again later when she'd gone. I thought, 'To hell with the consequences!' She was mesmerized with seeing a naked white man and watched me the whole time. Eventually, I finished washing, dried myself and off I went.

I had a spot of leave in Bombay and travelled there on the train on my own. I stayed free at a holiday camp specially for the services and, for safety, banked my money with the officer running it. I drew it from him when I needed it and that meant that, if I was robbed, I'd only lose a limited amount. Anybody from any unit could just go in and it was surprising that there was hardly anyone else there. I lived in and my meals were provided, without any cost because the army wasn't having to pay to feed me back at Kamareddi. Also in the camp was a kind of common room, with a gramophone and some records. I put on a number of these and a song I played a few times was *Rum and Coca-Cola*, which had a catchy tune, and I still remember a line in it which went, 'Working for the Yankee dollar'.

On my first night there, I shared a bedroom with a fellow, who told me there was no need to use the mosquito net as there were none of the insects in Bombay. I did as he suggested, but all through the night there seemed to be thousands of insects buzzing around. So the next night, I rigged up my net because I didn't want to get malaria.

The camp loaned civilian clothing to the troops while we were staying there and it comprised a white shirt and a pair of white trousers, so coloured to help us keep cool. I preferred those clothes to my uniform because the military were less likely to pull me up and the Indians were campaigning for independence, so it was safer. I was able to stroll about with a hand in a trouser pocket once more and I could mix with the Indians as if I was one of them because almost all of them wore white to repel the heat. I was suntanned by then and as brown as some of the native inhabitants, but, being an Englishman, I stood out like a sore thumb. That was because of the style of my clothes and through my attitude. It gave me a superior air, which contrasted strongly with that of the natives, who were mainly downtrodden fellows, although I didn't really look down on them.

I saw several of the latest Yankee films at different cinemas and also went to different army-run canteens to pass the time. The Gurkhas were allowed to use these clubs, but the Indians were barred from mixing with us. We were told to avoid Indian drinks, apart from boiled tea, because of the risk of contamination.

In one of the canteens, I was sitting down, having char and a wad, when I saw what I thought were stuffed lizards on the wall I was looking at. Then I noticed one of them seemed to have moved a couple of inches. I thought I was seeing things and took no notice, but then the same thing happened again. So I fixed my eyes on one of them and, sure enough, it shuffled forwards two or three inches after a few seconds and then stood still. Then I realized they were real lizards! Although they were maybe a foot long, nobody seemed to be bothered about them and they didn't seem to be concerned about us, so I just accepted they were there.

Also in one of the canteens, I got talking to a fellow who'd been in action against the Japs at the backs-to-the-wall fight at Kohima, in the far northeast of India, the previous year. That was as far as the Japs reached, but if they'd broken through at that point, they'd have flooded over the plains of India. The fellow told me the order had come that there was to be no retreat and so the lads had stood their ground and a lot of them had died. He said he'd fought the enemy at the local tennis courts, which had separated the two sides. Our Forces did very well because the Japs suffered big casualties and were forced to retreat.

While I was in Bombay, I looked up Ken Johns again. He took me to the RAF's sergeants' club, which was a great place. There was a nice bar, with easy chairs around it, and we were served by waiters. There was a piano and Ken wanted me to play, but I was out of practice and had no music, so I missed the opportunity to have free drinks all night!

I went with him to the flat where he was billeted. It was in a modern block, overlooking the sea, but the toilet was strange. There was no lavatory pan, but a hole in the ground instead and two impressions in the floor to put your feet in while you crouched down!

Ken also took me to the racecourse at Mahalaxmi, which was a fabulous place. The racing was a bore to me because I didn't have a bet, having always been against gambling. So I had nothing to shout for, but Ken did place a few bets. A lot of Indians were there, putting their money on the horses, which was surprising considering the general poverty. But these people were wealthy and could well afford it. It was pretty warm and streams of sweat ran from the horses' bellies, which made it look as though they were urinating, but they must have been suffering.

Ken recommended that I have some shoes made by an Indian because he'd been well satisfied with a pair he'd acquired. They were rationed on civvy street, so I decided to try getting a pair and therefore Ken took me to the shoemaker he knew, for my feet to be measured. I had to put my stockinged feet on a piece of paper and the Indian ran a pencil around them to mark their shape. I was then told to go back a few days later for a fitting. That I did, but, when I collected the finished shoes, they were tight and hurt my feet, although they didn't cost much. The shoemaker tried to stretch them, but they were still painful. I thought they'd wear in, but they never did. When I returned to Blighty, I took them with me, but they still crippled my feet. I couldn't afford to throw them away, even though they were the worst shoes I ever had, but I was glad when I wore them out!

The Bombay bus drivers were of a very poor standard and they didn't change gear or reduce their speed when going around corners. However they avoided turning their vehicles over, I'll never know! Public transport was always overcrowded in India. I got on one bus in Bombay, which was packed to the running boards. I managed to get just my toes on the first step and both my hands on the rails inside and the bus started off with me hanging on. After a while, I felt I couldn't hold on any longer, but I didn't dare let go. Just then, the bus pulled up at a stop and I gratefully jumped onto the pavement and walked the rest of the way. I hadn't paid the fare because the conductor was trapped inside the vehicle and I suppose about fifty per cent of the passengers travelled free!

It was the same situation on the trains and people scrambled on board when they were going slowly. Again, they became so packed that people hung on the outside of them and some travelled on the roof! There were lots of deaths and serious injuries through that behaviour, but nobody bothered too much because there were plenty of unwanted people around.

In the centre of Bombay, there was a posh venue for the top people, British and Indians, called the Willingdon Sports Club. The British forces were allowed to use the swimming pool, but not the bar and lounge, and the lower-class Indians weren't allowed in at all. The pool was shaded by trees and had a lawn around it, with chairs under parasols, to give protection from the sun. There was also a diving board, but I don't think I used it because I wasn't very good on them. One day, I was in the pool and a fellow told me I'd just missed the Aga Khan, the head of the Ismaili Muslims, who was a member of the club and had gone off to play golf.

It was very enjoyable in Bombay and just like having my annual seaside holiday. One day, I went on my own to Juhu Beach to have a swim in the Indian Ocean. It was up the coast from Bombay, so I had to get a train to Santa Cruz and then a bus to Juhu. There was hardly a soul there and the beach and the palm trees were just like on a film scene, but there were no dusky maidens about! I changed into my bathing trunks and swam in the lovely warm water, keeping an eye on my clothes in case somebody tried to steal and then sell them, which would have been very embarrassing for me. I didn't go out very far because I'd also left my money on the beach and in case there were sharks about, but it was a wonderful experience. After I'd got out of the water, an Indian came over and wanted to know if I'd like my photo taken. I asked the price, which was okay, so I said 'Yes' and he took the picture.

One day, back at Kamareddi, I noticed a crowd around the notice board, so I had a look at it and discovered it had information about a victory parade to be held in Delhi on 7 March. My name was down to be involved in the procession, which was being used to show off our guns. By then, there were frequent riots as the Indians wanted independence and fought amongst themselves, so I think the idea was to display the British flag to them and really it was a last fling. We'd be driving in open trucks, with lots of Indians lining the route, so I was worried as to what might happen.

Shortly after receiving the news, I went on a day's pass with Fred to Secunderabad and we decided to try one of the Indian cinemas, which was showing a native film. Of course, we didn't understand the dialogue or the story and, after a while, Fred started sniggering. Some of the Indians looked round at us and I felt embarrassed, so I thought it was time to go. We then went for a walk along the crowded streets and came face to face with a cow wandering about. Cows were sacred animals to the Hindus and allowed to roam where they wished and eat freely off any of the food stalls.

Down another street, quite a few people were queuing for something rationed.

Hovering around were two Indian policemen, keeping order. There was no trouble that I could see, but, when the policemen saw Fred and me, they started hitting people on top of the head with their batons. I think, because we were white men, they were trying to impress us with their authority.

On 8 February, many of us travelled by train, under the command of Lieutenant Masters, to Delhi for the victory parade. Train carriages were allotted to us in groups of eight to sleep in because it was a long journey to Delhi. We slept on wooden benches, which were made a bit more comfortable by the sleeping bags we'd been given for the occasion. We were issued with Yankee K rations for our food. That was an American pack, with different amounts of various things, and it was pretty good. The problem was dividing it out because a packet of biscuits was intended for a different number of men than, for example, a tin of Spam or sausages.

The train chugged along slowly, stopping for long periods at various stations on the way. It took three days to get to Delhi and the travelling was a bore. On the stations along the way, there were plenty of tradesmen waiting to sell their wares, mainly foodstuffs, but I didn't buy anything because it didn't seem very healthy. I remember one fellow selling egg sandwiches covered in what looked like a dirty handkerchief!

When we finally arrived in Delhi, we were housed in a nearby camp with good wooden huts. The beds were comfortable and the first night I was fast asleep in no time, but, when I woke, an Indian was mucking about with my equipment! When I asked him what he was doing, he told me that he'd been appointed my bearer. I was annoyed because there wasn't much to do and I preferred to do things myself, so I didn't want a bearer. I was also angry that he'd got into the hut without me knowing about it. It didn't seem right to me because he could have got my rifle and stuck the bayonet in my guts.

All the lads had a bearer. It seemed compulsory and I paid a few annas for my bearer's services. They didn't amount to much and the bearers seemed to spend most of their time chattering to each other outside the huts.

The day after our arrival in the camp, we were set to work, gathering stones from around the neighbourhood. We had to whitewash them and I found that it was faster to dip them in the bucket rather than paint them because it was easy to wash the stain off my hands afterwards. The stones were then put around our guns and used to border paths in the camp to make everything look spic-and-span! Nobody was coming in to inspect us, so the idea was a complete waste of time.

While we were in Delhi, I saw some things that shocked me. There were people sleeping on the streets, huddled in old rags or blankets, and women swept the pavements and gutters with brushes made from bundles of twigs, which were tied together. They had to bend down to sweep up and I saw one of them, aged about 25 or 30, try to straighten up, but she had a hard job to do so!

One day, I saw my bearer in Delhi and he begged two annas off me! On another occasion, one of the Indian camp workers said to me, 'You English don't get the best out of your wives because they're old and wise and boss you about.' So he recommended that I take a young wife, about thirteen years old, even though he knew I was already married!

On the day of the victory parade, we piled into the quads that were conveying us and pulling our 25-pounders into Delhi. We had our rifles with us, but no ammo for safety reasons. In any case, the army wouldn't have wanted some maniac to start firing, the more so because there'd been riots in the city in protest at the British occupation. So I took half a house brick with me and put it at my feet, ready to defend myself if necessary. My thinking was that if missiles were thrown at me, I'd have one to hurl back, but, in the event, things were quiet.

All the soldiers I saw on the parade were riding in trucks and tanks, which was presumably designed to give a big impression to the Indians because we'd won the war. I didn't see anybody marching. I was with about three others in a truck, which towed one of our guns. Along the route was a crowd of natives sitting around, but they didn't get very excited! Shortly afterwards, I bought a photo from a shop, which showed our battery driving along the grand curved Connaught Circus.

A few days after the victory parade, the army put a truck on for any of us who wanted to go to see the Taj Mahal, but they only had about half a dozen takers! It was over a hundred miles away, in the city of Agra, but it was well worth going. We sat on wooden forms that had been put in the back of the lorry and they were pretty uncomfortable, but were a luxury compared to sitting on the floor of the truck. Just before we got to the Taj Mahal, I saw another famous building, the Red Fort, which we drove past. It was made of red sandstone and had once been the home of the Mogul emperors.

The Taj Mahal was a memorial, which had been built in the seventeenth century on the order of the emperor Shah Jahan in honour of his favourite wife, Mumtaz Mahal. Originally, the white marble structure had been inlaid with precious stones and metals and it was still a lovely sight, so I'd have liked to have seen it when it was built. We were taken to the grounds and walked along the waterway to the main building, where we had to take off our hobnail boots and leave them outside. We had a wander around in our stockinged feet and gawped at the tomb.

We then went to one of the four slender corner towers. Inside was a narrow stone staircase, with no handrail, and it was precarious to climb. It went round in a spiral and at the top it was open, with a stone floor, but no wall or rail to stop us falling off! I felt giddy when I looked down and there seemed to be a magnet trying to pull me over.

I was bitterly disappointed when I realized that the waterway wasn't repeated on the other side, where the Jumna River ran right behind. The monument was a wonderful structure, but it just flopped out at the other end.

Shortly after the trip, we entrained to Kamareddi. On our arrival back at base on 25 March, I was told that a snake had been found under my charpoy! I also discovered that Fred had been transferred to a camp at Secunderabad. He'd served longer than me and had been given a job there, which was moving him towards being demobbed.

We'd only been back for two days when an ENSA show came to give us a free live performance in the evening and I went to have a look. It was held in a tent, but, as the night wore on, it became unbearably hot and sticky. So I undid the buttons on my shirt sleeves, which I rolled up to my elbows. Even then, the atmosphere was stifling and, when the show was over, I rushed outside to get a breather. Unfortunately, I came face to face with some redcaps, who told me to stand on one side and, by the time the tent was empty, a few more fellows had joined me. It seemed we'd broken the rules by turning our sleeves up at night when mosquitoes come out from cover from the heat of the day and bite bare flesh to feed.

On 1 April, a sergeant came and told me I was on a charge. He then marched me up to the orderly room, where I was ordered to come to attention facing the commanding officer, Lieutenant Colonel Cameron, who was sitting behind a desk. He read out the charge, which was disobeying orders, and asked what I had to say about it. I explained that I'd been too hot, but he wouldn't listen and instead read the sentence out. I was to be confined to barracks for seven days, which meant that I had to parade after duty hours in my best olive green uniform and polished boots, with a very clean rifle and bayonet. I was then marched away by the sergeant. On the parades, I was joined by the other "criminals" and afterwards we had to do some drill. We were also, literally, confined to the barracks, which was no burden because there was nowhere nearby to go.

I went to visit Fred one day in Secunderabad and asked if he wanted to go for a drink, but he didn't seem to want to know. So I had a few minutes with him and then left. I was pretty disappointed and that was the last I saw of him.

There were still occasional inspections and schemes, but I don't remember any of them specifically. I suppose they were partly held to help to occupy our time because a lot of the men were waiting to be discharged and, if they'd had nothing to do, they might have got restless and caused problems. Also, secret documents with the war diary show that the army was worried about trouble with the Indians, including their troops, so the officers probably still had us training in case we had to face a new enemy.

We had an English language newspaper delivered on a regular basis. It was printed in India and was for our consumption. In one issue, I noticed a picture of Ken Johns and with it was a report that he'd won 500 rupees in a competition. That was worth about £37, which was quite a bit of money in those days.

Soon after, I had a few days' leave in Bombay and looked Ken up again. I told him I'd seen the report of his win, but straight away he asked if I'd told Helen and I admitted that I had. He wasn't very pleased because I understand that he wasn't going to mention it to his wife, Eileen. My name was mud!

While I was in Bombay, I again stayed in a leave camp, from which a truck was laid on to get us into the city. It was driven by an Indian. By then, the British weren't very popular and there were reports of riots going on. One evening, I boarded the lorry on my own, to get back to camp, and the driver took us along a street where there was a mob of Indians shouting and waving sticks. I hoped he wouldn't stop and he didn't, being, I think, even more scared than me. As we went past the mob, they banged on the canvas on the sides of the truck with their sticks to take vengeance against the army vehicle. When we were speeding away, they saw me through the lorry's open back and became even more incensed at letting me slip past. I was very relieved that we got away!

Soon after, I was put in charge of our petrol dump at Kamareddi. It comprised a fair number of one-gallon tins of petrol, surrounded by barbed wire, with a locked barbed wire gate, to which I was given the key. The petrol was stained red, so that any civilians found with that colour of fuel in their tanks were in trouble. My job was to supply the truck drivers with fuel, but it was a really haphazard affair. Nobody checked how much petrol was there when I took over and, when I felt the weight of the cans, some of them were light. I mentioned it to one of the officers and he told me that it was due to evaporation. I didn't like the situation because if someone checked and there was petrol short, I'd be in trouble. I was getting nearer to being demobbed and I was therefore concerned. Then, one of the truck drivers asked me for extra petrol, saying he could sell it to Indian taxi drivers and that he'd give me a share of the payoff. I refused because I wouldn't have done so normally, but I felt doubly strongly now home was looming more closely.

One night, someone broke into the dump and stole some cans of petrol, so I had a word with some of the drivers I saw. I told them I didn't want to report the incident because it would result in a guard being placed on the dump every night and it wasn't fair for fellows to have to do that extra duty. So I told them to play ball because I'd report any further problems. They suggested that, to cover up the loss, I should give out short rations, which I did, and nobody complained. I had nothing to measure the fuel with, so the drivers just signed for what I gave them.

Our battery had a pretty good football team and played other units and local Indian teams. I went to watch them in a game in Secunderabad against a native side. The Indians were so poor that very few of them could afford to buy a pair of football boots. So some of them played barefooted and others wrapped something, like a piece of cloth, around their insteps. The Indians were very good footballers and gave our fellows a tough game. Our chaps were rather rough and took advantage of the natives' lack of protection for their feet. Some of our tackles were so hard that they made me wince just watching!

While I was in Secunderabad, I went into a canteen, where I tried a new game, called housey-housey, which was the original name for bingo. Owing to the shortage of paper, the cards were used over and over again. To cancel the numbers, we tore up cigarette packets into little pieces and placed them on the numbers called. But it was frustrating when someone knocked the table and all the bits of cardboard came off the numbers! I didn't have any luck with the game, partly because I didn't know how to play. Also, I was hesitant to cross numbers off in case I made a mistake and shouted 'House!' to become the centre of attention, only to end up embarrassed because I'd got it wrong!

In preparation for being demobbed, I bought a tin trunk to hold a few things I'd bought for myself and some presents. One of these was a dark blue tablecloth, with a silver-threaded depiction of the Taj Mahal on it. I'd got it from a bazaar for Helen. For a small consideration, one of the gunners painted my name, number and rank on the lid of the trunk, so that it could be identified.

In Kamareddi, I had a game at right-half with the so-called non-players, that is ones who didn't appear in the battery team. The match took place on a rough pitch in fields near to the camp, I think against the non-players of another battery. I remember being in the opposing goalmouth when a cannonball centre came over and I headed it, but missed the goal.

At the beginning of August, the magic number, 40, finally came up on the notice board. That was my demob group and I was excited because it meant I was going home. On the 13th, I handed in my rifle (number GA25287A) and bayonet, the rest of my army equipment and the key to the petrol dump. I was given a Notification of Impending Release document, signed by a Captain

Dickson, which described my military conduct as 'good'. He wrote a testimonial underneath, which said I was: 'A good steady worker. A man with a cheerful disposition and a good intelligence who can always be relied upon.'

I then boarded a train bound for Deolali, which was about a hundred miles northeast of Bombay. I think I travelled on my own because I was the only one from my battery in that particular demob group. I can't remember anyone in our camp wishing me luck, so perhaps they were glad to get rid of me!

The camp at Deolali was a collection centre for service personnel being sent home and I was allocated tent 27 in line 6 for my accommodation. I was issued with an oil lamp, which provided the lighting! There weren't many duties for us to do, so I wandered around the town more or less every day and looked for something personal to buy Helen. I saw a gold-plated lady's watch on a street stall, for which the seller wanted thirty rupees. Haggling was the thing to do in India, especially in the bazaars, but I thought that was cheating, so I paid the price the Indian had asked for.

There was a saying in the army that, if a fellow was touched in the head, he'd got the "Deolali tap" or gone doolally. I understood that was because of Deolali's hot and humid climate, but it wasn't too bad when I was there. I was at the camp for a week or two and kept looking at the notice board, waiting for my name to appear. Eventually it did and, a few days later, I entrained for Bombay, along with some other lucky ones. I didn't fancy going on board a ship again, but it had to be.

When we got to Bombay, we filed aboard the troopship, Georgic, and went into the bowels of the boat. This time there were bunks for everyone and I fortunately acquired a lower one. I dumped my kitbag and tin trunk and went up on deck to have a look around at the ship. I slept well in my bunk that night and the following morning, 1 September, I went on deck to have a look at Bombay Docks after breakfast. A while later, the engines started and that gave me a funny feeling because I was leaving for home. Then the ship's foghorn sounded and we started moving away slowly. After a while, we picked up speed and I stood on the stern, watching India recede in the distance. I felt all kinds of emotions and was excited. I shouted: 'I won't ever see you again! I won't be back!' All the time, music was playing over the Tannoy and one tune I remember was Bless 'Em All, which started with the words, 'There's many a troopship just leaving Bombay, bound for old Blighty's shore.' The words were rather appropriate!

Later on, the ship began to roll about and I felt sick, like on the outward journey. I again went off my food and didn't have anything to eat for a couple of days. After then, I got my sea legs and managed to eat the greasy food that was served up.

The ship had a small swimming pool on the open top deck, in the first-class area, where the women passengers and officers were quartered. When we steamed into calmer waters, approaching the Red Sea, the other ranks were lined up and given the chance to have a dip in the pool. All we were allowed to do was dive in and then get out. And it was a very short dive at that, otherwise our heads would have hit the other end of the pool!

There wasn't much discipline imposed, but we had boat drill and some PT. There wasn't much to do and I got thinking about our home in Rose Street. I realized that Vera's friends would still be there and there'd be next to no chance of getting them out. But, as it had turned out, I'd inherited my parents' house because I was the next of kin, which was fortunate for Helen and me. However, I also wondered what it would be like at home because things change over time.

I didn't see much on the journey because I don't think we sighted any land apart from when we passed through the Suez Canal. After we'd passed Gibraltar and steamed northward, the temperature began to get cooler, so we cast off our tropical kit and changed into our thicker battledress. The sea got rougher in the Bay of Biscay and the ship seemed to be bouncing up and down quite a bit. We passed a sailing vessel that appeared to be having a hard time because it kept disappearing from view as it went through the trough of the waves. By then, I was well on my sea legs and so the rough conditions didn't affect me.

We docked at Liverpool on 20 September and went straight through customs without stopping when we disembarked. I suppose the officials knew we couldn't have much of value with us. We entrained for York, but the journey took a really long time because there'd been rain almost every day for weeks and it had been torrential that morning, so we had to take some diversions to avoid the worst of the widespread floods. When we finally arrived, we were taken to Queen Elizabeth Barracks at nearby Strensall to rest for the night. We were given three blankets each, but I still wasn't warm enough and shivered all through the night, even though it was only September.

Some of the fellows went out for a drink and one of them came back belligerent. He told the sergeant major, who was organizing things, that he'd finished with the army and wasn't obeying any more orders. The SM had him arrested and put in the guardroom for the night, but he was released the following morning.

In the morning, after breakfast, we were taken to the office to fill in some discharge paperwork. We were also given travel papers home, ration books, a warrant for money (which amounted to £60) and ten weeks' leave. That meant, to all intents and purposes, that I'd left the army because, after that time had elapsed, I just carried on as a civilian. Although I didn't know it at the time, I was in the Royal Army Reserve till 30 June 1959 and liable to be called up if another war broke out. I never saw a discharge document and, until I saw copies of my army records in November 2009, I thought I might technically still have been in the army!

We were then taken to a clothes warehouse, where we were shown a small choice of suits, shirts, shoes, raincoats and hats, so that we could be rigged out with a new civvy outfit. I picked a pinstripe suit, a trilby, a mac and, of course, a conventional shirt and pair of shoes, which were all wrapped up for me to take home. I then gathered my luggage together and left the barracks. I was glad to get away, but I still felt wary until I got home. I made my way to York Station, took a train to Manchester and then got a connection home. I was glad to see Stoke Station again. It was 21 September and I'd been in the army for four years.

I walked along Station Road and left round the corner to the bus stop in Winton Terrace (as that part of Leek Road was then named). Things looked just the same as they'd done before I'd gone to India. I hadn't been waiting long before a car stopped and the driver and his female passenger asked if I wanted a lift. I suppose they were thrilled to be of service to a returning hero! I got in the car and told them I'd just got back from India and they seemed impressed.

I got out of the car outside my house and thanked them. But before I could close the door, Nancy had rushed down the steps from next door and she threw her arms around me. She was closely followed by Leah and the last down was Helen! There was quite a commotion because I hadn't been expected. I'd let Helen know that I was returning on the Georgic, but hadn't informed her that I'd arrived in England because I'd wanted my return to be a surprise. Nancy had heard that the ship had docked and told Helen, but Helen thought she must have been mistaken because I'd have let her know.

Helen had got a decorator in, to make the house look nice for me when I got home. The job had just been finished and Helen and Leah had been cleaning up when I arrived. I dropped off my luggage and Leah then volunteered to finish things off while Helen and I stepped out to celebrate my homecoming.

6 Back To The Bottle Ovens!

At first, it seemed peculiar to be home. I was rather sad. I'd had an outdoor life for four years, which I'd got used to, and it had gone for ever. I'm glad I had that experience because it had given me a long break from the dust of the pottery industry. So it probably saved my life because I'd likely have died prematurely from silicosis. I wasn't looking forward to going back in a pot bank, but it was ingrained in me. Once a potter, you'd always be a potter.

Also, Helen and I felt like strangers because I'd been away for a long while. She'd been living with her sisters and had adapted to being with them, while I'd had different experiences and had been half a world away. I was a kind of stranger in my own home, even more so because Leah moved in with Helen and me, so I was living with two women. It didn't seem real or right, but I had to adjust and slowly Helen and I got back into the old routine.

I asked Helen if she'd got the cigarettes I'd sent from India, but she confessed that she and Leah had been smoking them and there were only one or two left! It was vexing. So I had to tour the Hanley shops on a regular basis, trying to get some spare fags because they were still in short supply. I was usually able to get British ones, but sometimes I had to settle for the horrible American fags, like Camel.

I decided to have a few weeks at home before looking for a job. Maybe I was wrong to do that, but I was used to being in the fresh air and reluctant to return to a dusty hellhole. In any case, I was on tenterhooks for ten weeks because I was still only on leave, so, if another conflict had started, I could have been told to report back again! There was an association for regular soldiers in Stoke Road and, after a while, I went to see them. I told a fellow there I was after a job in the open air and mentioned the General Post Office. As I was only a conscript, he didn't really want to know and replied that the government wanted all the demobbed men to go back to their old jobs. That put me off trying anywhere else and made me want to do the patriotic thing. Instead, I should have had a good look around because I imagine there were plenty of jobs going and years later I found out that I could have got taken on as a postman right away.

Helen was still working full time for Swinnerton's, which gave me breathing space because we had money coming in. The firm had opened a new factory in Raymond Street, Shelton, and was still involved in catering. Helen was by then the senior supervisor there and, not long after, she became the assistant manageress, so she was doing very well.

After a while, I went to Taylor Tunnicliff and asked Tom Reeves, who was still the foreman of the clay department, for my old job back. I think he was pleased to see me and said I could start up again. He told me that my starting wages would be five pounds a week and I was delighted because it sounded a lot of money. Of course, I was out of touch with reality, but it wasn't bad nevertheless. The factory was just the same as it had been before I left, but I settled in better than I thought I would regardless. I went back to my old bench and lathe, but an old colleague, Stewart Flackett, was on my left, where Dad used to be. It didn't particularly bother me because I'd got used to the idea that Dad had died. I went to work in my army uniform because I couldn't afford to be fussy.

Things were working alright with Leah living with Helen and me. Leah slept in the back bedroom and Helen and I slept in the front. We had our meals together when we were all there, but I can't remember Leah going out with Helen and me. She had her own life and her own mates and she didn't tell me much about what she was doing. She didn't get in my way and I didn't get in hers, so everything went off smoothly and I was happy enough with how things were.

Helen and I started dancing at the Majestic Ballroom again, but we only went a few times because we seemed to have grown out of it. The jitterbug, a fast, jerky dance, had become a craze, having been brought in by Yankee soldiers during the war, and we couldn't keep up with it. Men threw the girls around and it was dangerous. It was mainly done by youngsters and pushed out the usual dances that we liked.

We palled up again with Jack and Rose Green and resumed going on Saturday nights to the Coronation Club in Cobridge, which was more to our taste. One singer we really enjoyed was Ron Pye, a tall, good-looking fellow, who'd just been demobbed from the RAF. He sang *Fascination*, a song written by Fidenco Marchetti and Maurice de Féraudy, which Helen and I liked so much that we bought a copy of the sheet music for me to play it at home on my piano.

Sometimes, we'd hear a tune on the wireless that we'd like and Helen would want to listen to it again. She'd want me to get the sheet music and play it, though I wasn't bothered about doing that myself. At that time, you could buy sheet music from a number of shops because it was in fashion, but I mainly went to A. E. Green Music Stores (which later became Chatfield's Music Stores), at 2 Hope Street. I carried on getting a piece from time to time right into the 1960s until we got a record player and could then buy the popular versions of songs themselves as records. I ended up with hundreds of pieces of sheet music, some of them as collections of songs in books, and they're still under my piano stool, although I stopped playing a long time ago.

One night at the Coronation Club, Ron Pye made a mistake by announcing from the stage that people at the back of the room hadn't come to order. Unfortunately, one of the tough-looking local Drakeford brothers was sitting there with his wife and took offence because he thought Ron was referring to her. So, I was told, Drakeford waited outside after ten o'clock closing time and thumped Ron on his way home, although he wasn't seriously injured.

The winter of 1946-1947 was one of the coldest on record. One Saturday, it had been raining and the surface water quickly froze when night fell, so that the ground was like glass. Helen and I wouldn't normally have gone out in such conditions, but we'd arranged to meet Vera in Hanley. Big Harry was working in London, helping to repair the bomb damage, and so we were taking Vera for a night out to the Coronation Club. It was so slippy that Helen and I walked very gingerly along the gutter in Leek Road. We eventually reached Fenton Road and amazingly saw a bus coming from Fenton, which stopped to let us get on. It took the driver a while to get going again because the bus wheels spun round without getting a grip. Then, slowly, we started moving up the hill, with the wheels in the gutter and gripping the side of the kerb, which must have virtually worn out the tyre walls! We went down Stafford Street, where Vera got on, and then slithered into Hope Street. Passengers were getting panicky and Helen and Vera wanted to get off, but I persuaded them to stop on. We slid right down to the junction with

York Street and I thought we might crash, but, fortunately, we didn't. We were very thankful when we got off our nightmare ride at Cobridge Road!

I didn't enjoy being at the club that night because I was worrying about the return trip. We set off after closing time and I was dreading it, but a miracle had occurred while we were supping our ale! There'd been a thaw, so the ice had melted and the buses were running normally again.

The freezing weather led to a serious coal shortage and it seems as if we'd only scraped through with fuel during the war. The electricity works on Ridgway Road usually had big stocks of coal dust to keep its dynamos turning, but, by early in 1947, all that I could see left was about a lorryful. Also, as gas was produced from coal at that time, we were in a hell of a state.

On 18 January, it was announced in the newspapers that, because of the lack of coal, there'd be an immediate 50 per cent cut in supplies to all industries except for iron and steel, which were to have their allocations reduced by 25 per cent. Then, on the 27th, Taylor Tunnicliff closed our factory down for three days because of the shortage of coal to generate power.

Unfortunately, the weather got worse and, by 4 February, there were snowdrifts ten feet high after a two-day blizzard. Further snowfalls followed and the government then announced a complete cut in electricity supplies to industry, which came into effect on the 10th. That day was called "Black Monday" and most factories stopped production. It was a shock to the country and millions of workers became unemployed for a couple of weeks or so. 60,000 people were put out of work in North Staffordshire and two-thirds of them were from the pot banks. We were also laid off by Taylor Tunnicliff, for two weeks, but we got paid dole and there were great crowds of people at Hanley Employment Exchange, signing on. It was ironic that Hitler hadn't been able to stop our factories from working and I wondered who was to blame.

There was a trial reduction in street lighting and people climbed on the slag heaps, searching for bits of coal to burn to try to keep them warm. Coal supplies dropped so low that the pot banks could only just about heat their boilers to prevent their works from freezing up, but coal production gradually increased, so the government announced the return of full electricity supplies to our area from 24 February. We then went back to work, but were on short time for a week or two as things took a while to get back to normal.

The council had put bins in many places around the city as receptacles for leftover food, in a scheme which had been started by the government during the war. The food was used to feed pigs and other farm animals as their owners were unable to get many foodstuffs for them. We had one of these bins dumped between our house and Bradbury's, next door. Every now and then, someone would come along and empty the bin, but, after a while, it stank of rotting food because it was never cleaned out. If the bin was nearer to our house, when it was dark or there was nobody about, Helen or I would push it towards Bradbury's to lessen the smell. But I think the Bradburys had the same idea because sometimes the bin seemed to be nearer to us! Eventually, when the food situation improved, the bin was taken away.

On 29 March, Helen and I went to the wedding of her brother, Elijah, at St. Mary's Church, Bucknall. His bride was Ethel Smith, who came from Abbey Hulton. She was an ordinary kind of girl, but was quite shy. She knew Vera from work at Newhall Pottery and they'd become friends, which was how she'd got to meet Elijah. She seemed to fit in well with Vera, though not as much with Helen and me, but she was okay. She and Elijah later had two children, Lynn and John.

Right after the war, everybody seemed to want more entertainment and following football was a very popular choice. That season, Stoke had a really good team and almost won the First Division championship. I hadn't been a regular at the Victoria Ground before the war, but everything had been dull for a while. So Helen and I were living it up and going most weeks onto the Stoke End, which was the nearest part of the ground to us. By then, it had been extended, steepened and terraced and crush barriers had been fixed in, otherwise there'd have been chaos. There was a good atmosphere, with plenty of banter. The three players who stood out were Freddie Steele, Stan Matthews and Neil Franklin.

Steele was a really good old-type centre-forward. His strongpoint was heading, but also he could shoot with both feet.

I loved to see Matthews dribbling round the opponents, sometimes several of them at once. He was very quick, could get round the left-back most of the time and would then put the ball on Freddie's head. When Stan was transferred to Blackpool, on 10 May, with Stoke in with a chance of winning the championship, there was uproar and I didn't like it myself because I thought he *was* the team. Everything depended on their last game at Sheffield United, but Stoke lost 2-1 and finished fourth, which was a big disappointment.

Franklin looked immaculate, with his hair neatly combed and parted. He didn't look like a footballer and never seemed to get dirty, but nothing got past him. At that time, defenders rarely passed back to the goalie, but Franklin would put nice little passes back and the crowd didn't like it!

I can't remember Mother and Dad having the chimneys swept at either of our houses, but they must have done. After they'd died and I'd got back from the army, I took over getting the job done. I think it was forced on me the first time after there'd been a fall or two of soot and I suppose I got a sweep who'd advertised. After that, I usually had it done every year and was reminded about it when soot started to drop down.

On the day the sweep came, we'd move as much furniture as we could out of the front room and throw dust sheets over what was left. The sweep would cover the fireplace up with a big bag, which he'd fasten down. Then he'd get his brush head out and screw a pole into it. He'd lift up a corner of the bag and push the brush and pole up the chimney a time or two to loosen the soot and a lot of it would drop down. Then he'd add another length of pole and keep going until the brush had got to the top of the chimney. On one occasion, the sweep asked if I could go out to see if the brush had come out because he wouldn't have been able to have seen from inside. I did and it had bobbed out. The brush had bristles like spikes coming out of the side of it.

The sweep would then pull the bush down, unscrewing the poles as he went along. There'd be a pile of soot in the bottom of the fireplace. He'd carefully pull the bag down and shovel soot from the grate into a bag until it was full and then into another one and so on until the job was done. Unfortunately, while that was happening, soot would fly around and cover everything in the room. Afterwards, the sweep would brush up, but he wouldn't get all the soot up, so I'd have to finish it off myself.

One day, Leah brought a boyfriend home to meet Helen and me. His name was Sid Asher and he was a builder. He was pretty tall and had blond hair, but only one eye. He'd lost his sight in the other in an accident when he was a kid through somebody throwing a snowball at him, which contained a stone. He'd later had the eye removed. He started to call regularly to pick Leah up and take her out.

I'd heard that my Uncle Fred and Aunt Maud had gone to Cleethorpes, to live there and run a boarding house called Brookhill, at 25 Grant Street. I wrote to them and fixed up a week's stay for Helen and me for a holiday the coming August. But, before we were due to go, Leah became poorly, I think with rheumatic fever, which affected her heart, and so we cancelled our reservation. Later, Leah's health improved, so I got back in touch with Uncle Fred, but our room had gone, though he said he'd fit us in somehow.

When the potters' holidays came, Helen and I made a long, weary train journey to the resort and then Uncle Fred showed us an old hut in their back yard, which turned out to be our bedroom! We were taken aback, but Uncle Fred said we'd be alright and, surprisingly, Helen didn't complain too much, so I went along with it. The mattress was full of loose material, so we had to shake it up and settle the lumps as evenly throughout as we could. There was also a washbasin, but no mains supply, so we had to make do with a jug of water. I think the toilet was a chamber pot under the bed because we weren't able to gain access to the house during the night! Also, when Helen and I lay in bed, we could hear people going along the back entry, which was only about a yard away.

Cleethorpes wasn't much of a place. There was a pier and some sand on the beach. Of course, everything was still run down, owing to the war, and there was very little entertainment, but we made the most of things and enjoyed the holiday anyway. We walked around, did some shopping and bought an ice cream or two. Even though it was our first holiday for years, I didn't take any photos because there was a shortage of film. Also, food was still rationed, so we'd had to take our ration books with us because Aunt Maud had to present them to get our food. At the same time, she was under contract to supply meals to the prisoners in the local police station.

My cousin, Prudence, and her husband were also living in Cleethorpes. Another cousin, Annie Plimbley, and her husband, Sam, were guests at the boarding house too and they were a bit of fun, especially Sam, who was a joker. One evening, when Helen and I came in for our tea, Annie and Sam were sitting there, having just finished their meal. We waited a while for our tea to arrive, but nothing happened and Sam confessed that he thought they'd eaten our sandwiches as well as their own. Later, Uncle Fred appeared and looked embarrassed when he found out what had happened, but he brought in fresh sandwiches, even though the quantity was small.

Ken Johns returned home from India and was living at 131 Brook Street, Cobridge, with Eileen. He told us he'd been one of the last few British servicemen still in India when the natives had taken over on 15 August.

Later in the year, there was a disagreement between Helen and Leah. I still got on alright with Leah, but I think she felt uncomfortable living with us, especially as Helen was bossing her about. One Sunday, while Helen was at the evening service at Shelton Church, Sid called with a suitcase, which Leah filled with her belongings. She told me she was leaving and off they went. When Helen returned from the church, she was shocked at Leah's departure. Leah then stayed with Sid's brother, Claude, and his wife, Lilian, at 7 Seagrave Street, Newcastle, until she and Sid got married the following year.

A time or two, I went to see Leah on my bike, but Helen didn't come with me because she and Leah were still at odds and the situation between them went on for some while. Once, I was on the way back home and had reached the junction of Hartshill Road and Shelton New Road when a policeman flagged me down. He asked me, 'Where's your light?'

I had a habit of looking up the lighting-up time in the *Sentinel* if I was going to be out in the evening on my bike so that I'd be sure of getting back home in the light. That saved me from having to take a lamp with me, which had to be fitted onto a special bracket on the bike. So I knew what the time was and said: 'I don't need it. It isn't lighting-up time yet.'

The policeman was only half-convinced I was right and said, 'You can go now, but, when the time comes, get off your bike and walk the rest of the way.'

I then went off, thinking what a waste of time he was!

Once, when we visited Vera, we found she had a visitor from South Africa, who'd become Elijah's girlfriend when he was stationed there during the war with the air force. He must have got quite involved with her because she'd come all the way to Abbey Hulton after him! Elijah wasn't there, though, because he was living in Hanley with Ethel. I suppose he tried to avoid the girl, who was palmed off on Helen and me and so she came to live with us!

One day, Helen asked the girl to look after something boiling on our gas stove and then went out. When I came in, I smelled gas and saw that a knob was switched on, but there was no flame coming out of the burner. So I turned it off straight away and asked the girl what had happened. She said that, when the pan had come to the boil, she'd blown the flame out. She said they only had electricity where she lived, so she hadn't realized that the gas had to be turned off. It was a good job I came in when I did because the house might have been blown up!

After two or three weeks, the girl gave up trying to get Elijah and went to live in London, much to our relief. Vera kept in touch with her for a while and the last we heard was that she'd got a new boyfriend there. I gathered that she didn't dare tell her parents that she'd made a mistake coming to England.

Jack Green told me that his father had been accused of murder. Mr Green was employed as a fireman at Myott's Pottery. His job involved firing kilns by shovelling coal on, but it was skilled work because he had to get the temperature right. He judged that by hanging pottery rings inside and, every so often, taking one out to measure its contraction.

In 1925, a man (John Porter) had been found dead at Myott's and Jack's father was accused of killing him. Mr Green was interviewed by Chief Inspector Gillian of Scotland Yard, who said he'd got a gun in his pocket, which he'd give to Mr Green so that he could shoot himself. Apparently, he said to Jack's father, something along the lines of: 'You know you've done it. Why don't you shoot yourself?' It appears that he wanted Mr Green to have the gun, which would have made him seem guilty.

Later, it was discovered that Jack's father was innocent and another man,

Henry Adams, was convicted of manslaughter at Stafford Assizes in 1926. At the trial, Mr Green was a witness and complained to the judge about his treatment. The judge reprimanded the inspector, who was later put on the retired list. He went to see Mr Green at his home to apologize and gave young Jack half-a-crown. Mr Green was livid, snatched the coin out of his son's hand, threw it into the street and ordered the detective out of his house.

In 1948, Australia had a manpower shortage and wanted plenty of British people to go to live there. I rather fancied a change from Stoke and the pot bank, but I thought it might be too hot in Australia and so was more attracted to New Zealand, where it was cooler and English newcomers were also being welcomed. I was still unsettled and overseas seemed to be more glamorous, although I had no idea what job I might do. I mentioned it to Helen, but she didn't want to leave her relatives and, I think, was afraid of taking a chance. So it remained business as usual.

It was in the *Sentinel* that Tommy Lawton, the England centre-forward, was going to be playing for Notts County in Hanley against Vale on 28 February, so I decided to go to have a look at him. Vale's ground wasn't very big, so the match was all ticket. I went on the Bryan Street side and a crowd of 18,147 packed in. Lawton was a good old-fashioned goalscorer and it was a thrill seeing him in the flesh because I'd read so much about him. He showed his class and there was a big difference between him and all the other players. Ronnie Allen and Bill McGarry played for Vale, but they didn't stand out to me. Notts won 2-1 and Lawton scored one of the goals, with a daisy cutter.

I started borrowing books to read from Hanley Library, in Pall Mall, around that time. They were free on loan, so I joined the library and took advantage of what they had to offer. One of my favourite authors was Rider Haggard, who wrote exciting stories set in Africa, involving British officials and native chiefs. I read a number of his books, including *King Solomon's Mines*, *Allan Quatermain* and *She* and they included all kinds of adventures, disasters and wars.

About that time, the setts which covered Leek Road were ripped out and Tarmac was put down in their place. It had been a real bone shaker to ride on them on a bike! I mentioned to one of the workmen that it would have been a lot cheaper and easier just to have covered the stones up with a layer of Tarmac, but he disagreed and said the stones had to be taken out because they weren't level.

One early morning, when it was still dark and Helen and I were asleep in bed, there was a knock at the door. I was worried in case it was the police and somebody in the family had died, but, when I opened up, there was a fellow there, who said, 'It's work time!'

I didn't understand what he was talking about and asked him, 'What do you want?'

He then realized he'd made a mistake and was aghast and said: 'I'm sorry. I'm at the wrong house!'

He should have been at Ted Brennan's, number 460. Ted was a train driver and the procedure was that railway staff due in for the early morning shift had someone to knock them up! I wondered how the fellow could have made such a mistake, but I took it in my stride and went back to bed!

Ted always seemed to have his black driver's hat and blue overalls on, even when he wasn't at work. I think he fancied his chances!

During the war, I'd lost touch with Ron Finan. He must have been conscripted and he later told me that he'd gone into the recce corps. After the war, he was living at 9 Rushton Grove, Cobridge, with his family and one day he called round. It was good to see him again. His regiment, like mine, had been in the 52nd (Lowland) Division and he gave me a spare map he'd got of the division's route of march from Normandy, through Holland and Belgium, to Bremen, in Germany. The map also showed the division's main actions against the Germans from its landing in September 1944 till the end of the war. Ron and I had a good talk, but I can't remember ever seeing him again and he later moved to the Walsall area after marrying Eileen Danks, a woman from around there.

Helen and I decided to have a coal bunker built by our back fence because there was no longer much space in the hut to fit our coal supplies. Also, the coal dust was dirtying our gardening tools. I paid Big Harry £1 10s. to do the job for us, with my help. The materials cost £2 5s. and we had the bunker built of brick to about waist height, with a wooden lid, covered with felting, on top. The drawback was that we then had to go out to the back of our garden to get our coal, which could be hard in the winter, but we got a bucketful in at a time.

Leah and Sid got married at St. George's Church in Queen Street, Newcastle, on 24 July. Helen was one of the matrons of honour, having, I think, hinted that she should be. The other was Ethel. I went along, of course, and took a few photographs of the occasion.

Helen and I saw an advert for accommodation at Scarborough, so we booked up to go for our annual August holiday. We took a night train from Stoke and must have slept in our seats on the way. There was no sleeping accommodation and no breakfast was provided then. We got to our destination early in the morning and then had to wander around until our boarding house was open! Everywhere was filthy and the beach was littered with rubbish, but corporation workers set to the task and cleaned everything up when they began their morning shift.

Eventually, we got into our digs, which were near to or on the sea front, and deposited our luggage. Unfortunately, they were in the basement of a hotel, which wasn't ideal. Also, the landlady seemed to be very shortsighted and sometimes bumped into someone or something as she brought in our food, not noticing the obstacle. On one occasion, when she served up custard, she had some on the end of her nose! That was because she had to look closely at things she was cooking to see how they were doing. Another time, we had salad as part of a meal and found that the lettuce had been badly washed and was still covered with soil! We didn't have the heart to complain because she was doing her best to please. We never ate the meals, but put them in bags and threw them away when we got outside. Then we had to buy something outside to eat, from shops and cafés, so as not to go hungry.

While we were seeing the sights, we met a couple we knew, Bill and Hilda Johnson, and their son, Kenneth, who lived at 60 Fenton Road. We went around with them quite a bit and Bill and I hired a camera each because we didn't have one with us. Ken pestered his parents for a Biro pen, which was the latest fashion, and they eventually got him one. His eyes glistened when he looked at it! I was quite taken with it myself because, unlike with a fountain pen, there was little chance of its ink leaking onto your clothes when carrying it around.

One day, we went to the marina to see an open-air show. Across from where we sat was a stretch of water and beyond was a stage. A fellow dressed in a dinner suit came on and, with a beautiful voice, started singing opera. He'd only been performing about a minute, to the total silence of the audience, when a couple of men grabbed him and threw him in the water! The audience was stunned and I was shocked to think that anyone in his right mind could do such a thing. It was quite a while before I realized that it was all part of the show.

After the National Health Service had been set up that summer, I took advantage of the free dental checkups and treatment and went to see Arnold Wain, a dentist, who operated at 3 Campbell Road, Stoke. Apparently, he was unqualified, but practised the profession for almost forty years! He made a chart of my mouth, noting all the missing teeth, fillings and whatever else needed to be recorded. He then congratulated me on the cleanliness of my mouth. I was surprised at his comment because all I'd done was to brush my teeth before turning up. However, he explained that quite a number of people didn't have the courtesy to clean their mouths before they saw him! I was well satisfied with my visit and became a regular customer. I continued to go for checkups and they were every six months.

Occasionally, Helen and I used to visit Uncle Ted and Aunt Florrie at their home in Etruria Vale Road. By then, Sam had married and left and Annie had gone off in a huff after an argument with Uncle Ted over a married man she'd been going out with. But Bernard was still there, with his wife Dorothy (née Egginton), whom he'd married on 10 August 1946. Uncle Ted was interesting to talk to and he was like a father figure to Helen and me. Sometimes, we'd have a drink with him and Aunt Florrie at The Bird In Hand, down the road in the dip.

Uncle Ted had a copy of Hitler's book, *Mein Kampf*, and one day I borrowed it because I thought it would be interesting. I was expecting it to have been more of an adventure story than it was, but I found it very heavy and bogged down with politics. So I only read a bit here and there before I packed it in and I eventually gave it back to Uncle Ted.

Out of the blue, Uncle Bram called and he was still a "gentleman of the road", roaming the country! We gave him something to eat and he then asked to use our brushes and polish to clean his boots. As an old soldier, it was important to him to keep his boots shiny. He still looked tidy and again showed me how to arm wrestle, just as he'd done when I was a boy! After a while, it seemed he was settling in for the night and Helen kept asking me, 'How long is he going to be before he goes?' She was worried in case she was embarrassed by the neighbours wanting to know who he was. Eventually, Bram decided to move on and I think that was the last time I ever saw him, but I was later told that he'd gone to live at St. Augustine's Home for old folks, at the top of Cobridge Road, run by the Little Sisters of the Poor. Apparently, he was roped into carrying people out when they died, for them to be taken to the mortuary.

Joan Ratcliffe was a big, fat girl, who worked in the same turning shop as me at Taylor Tunnicliff, cutting extra features in some of our finished articles. She lived at 83 Fenton Road, in the house right next to Leek Road. One day, I was working away at my bench and lathe at work when she came over to talk to me about something. After a few moments, she seemed to go into a trance and her eyes turned slowly up to the ceiling. I thought she was going to fall on the spinning lathe, which would have been very dangerous, and maybe it was that which had hypnotized her. Anyhow, I switched off my lathe and grabbed her. I shouted the others in the shop, who came over, and an ambulance was called, which took her to hospital. She wasn't there very long and was back at work in a few days, none the worse for the experience.

Jack Green came to visit us one day and I took him into the kitchen, where we still had our old portable electric fire, with its flickering coal effect. I switched it on, but Jack was aghast and asked me to turn it off, saying it would cost a lot of money. I informed him that a unit of power only came to a third of a penny. I don't think he had a meter for power and he told me his lighting cost several pence a unit, so I could see why he thought that burning a fire would cost a fortune.

About that time, I left Taylor Tunnicliff because I was still unsettled and wanted to go somewhere different. Also, I was fed up with the conditions in the factory. I went to work at Mintons Ltd., in London Road, Stoke, as a china turner. The job was no better, but Mintons was cleaner and healthier because there was less clay scrap from making cups and bowls than electrical porcelain. Also, unlike at Taylor Tunnicliff, I had a window to look out of, onto the street and across to the library and baths on the other side. Mintons was a famous name and it made me feel better to work there. I used to ride my bike to get there because it was quite a lot further than Taylor Tunnicliff. The factory has now been demolished and replaced by Sainsbury's supermarket.

I soon noticed that some of the people walking along London Road would stop and watch me and other turners working. Sometimes, I would turn big rings (to fit inside thrown and turned bowls, to keep them in shape) and, on odd occasions, as the lathe spun round at high speed, the clay mass would disintegrate and bang on the window frame. I was afraid that one day a lump of clay would smash the glass and injure someone watching me. So I had the maintenance man place a wire partition in front of the window when I turned large items.

Watching football was still very popular and I queued with thousands of others for tickets for Stoke's fifth round cup tie with Hull City on 12 February 1949. There didn't seem to be any movement for a long while and it looked like I'd be queuing for hours, so I came away. It was a pity because the ex-England inside-forward, Raich Carter, was playing for Hull and I'd have liked to have seen him.

On 15 March, clothes rationing ended, but it didn't really affect me all that much because I'd got enough clothes to be going on with. Rationing was being reduced anyway and some people didn't use their coupons any more as things gradually returned to normal. Even with the coupons, some people couldn't afford to buy the clothes they wanted.

By then, Swinnerton's were producing around 140,000 packed meals a week for 23 mines and 350 other firms and Helen had her work cut out in helping to organize it all. They were delivering the meals as far away as Wolverhampton and it seemed as if their success was due to the lack of industrial canteens at that time and many workers being unable to afford hot food, even when it was available.

About that time, a new factory started to be built on spare ground on the opposite side of the road from us. It was for a government-owned company called Remploy Ltd., which provided work for disabled people. It was up and running by the following year and operated as a light engineering works.

Around that time, we finally bought a new lawnmower of our own and it was combined with a roller. That was a lot better than the shared one and the separate roller we'd used. Also, it saved the trouble of having to fetch the old one from whichever neighbour had got it at the time. The new mower was from Lewis's, which was then located on the shopping island bordered by Lamb Street, Stafford Street and Fountain Square. I still used it until 1998 when it became too heavy for me to lift up.

We were always busy doing some job or other in our house or garden. Our front lawn had quite a steep slope, which made it awkward to cut. We decided to take out the slope and make a garden on three levels instead. I got the job of doing it, so I levelled the ground out in each section and put some big stones into the back of the bottom two to hold up the earth above them. Then we planted aubrietia around the stones, which soon covered them, and put other plants in between. Eventually, we had a lot of spring bulbs in and, after that, Helen always said we'd got the nicest front garden along the row.

I was having some trouble with my stomach and thought I'd got ulcers. It was preying on my mind because my father had died after he'd had an ulcer burst, so I was a bit down. On 6 July, I went to see Dr MacArthur at the surgery at 108 Lichfield Street, where I'd registered as a patient on 17 October 1946 on my return from the war. Helen came with me and told him I was upset because my father had died. That wasn't true because I'd got over it years before, but it seemed that Dr MacArthur believed her. I was given two lots of medicine: Pernivit, I suppose to help my stomach settle down, and phenobarbitone, probably to help me sleep. I then went pretty regularly for the medicine for a few months until I felt better.

Lumps of the concrete steps in our back garden were coming apart, so we decided to have them replaced and got Big Harry to do the job for us in July. We had the new steps made of bricks and I helped Harry to do the job, but we paid him, of course.

We noticed an advert in the *Sentinel* for accommodation in Eastbourne. It read that everything was excellent and that the proprietors, who were from Stoke, knew how to look after people from the Potteries. It seemed ideal for us, so we booked a room for the potters' holiday week. On our arrival in Eastbourne, we found the boarding house to be a nice building and, in years gone by, it would have been home to a middle-class family. When the door opened to our knock, we saw a couple of dubious-looking characters standing there. The woman looked rather crummy and the man had a black patch over an eye, which made him look like a pirate! We realized we couldn't turn back and would just have to make the best of things.

Also in the house as guests were another Stoke couple and the wife's father, John Bradbury, who kept a newsagent's at 85 Broad Street, Hanley. The husband, Len, had a car, which was most unusual as the motor industry hadn't got back into its stride after the war. He'd driven all the way to Eastbourne, which must have been a hazardous journey because there were no motorways, the roads were in a poor state of repair and many of the signs that had been taken down during the war hadn't been replaced.

Our bedroom was on the ground floor and the first night Helen and I were in bed, we heard the voices of a man and a woman, who sounded like the landlord and landlady, having an argument just outside the room. This developed into shouting and scuffling. Helen was frightened and I was alarmed, so I got out of bed and jammed a chair under the door knob to stop the door from being opened. The man shouted that he was going to jump off Beachy Head, then a door slammed and things became quieter.

In the morning, at breakfast, we asked the people from Stoke if they'd heard anything in the night, but they hadn't because their bedrooms were high up in the building. The landlord and landlady said nothing about it either and there were no newspaper reports of a suicide from the cliffs of Beachy Head, so we never found out what had happened.

We later walked up to Beachy Head from the town to have a look at the cliffs. We got fairly near to the cliff edge and looked down at the lighthouse way below. It was quite an experience and the edge seemed to draw people to it. I was afraid to get any closer than I was in case I got vertigo. There was nothing to hang on to and, if you tripped up, you'd have been over the edge.

There were lawns by the sea front, where we sat enjoying the sun by the Wish Tower, a round Martello, which had been used by the Royal Artillery in the war as a defensive point. It had only been derequisitioned two years before.

Close by, on Grand Parade, was a great semi-circular bandstand, with stone pillars and a stainless steel spire on the roof. The bandstand had a main seating area and balconies in front of it and to the sides, with room for 3,500 people. There was a band on when we were there, so we went along and enjoyed listening to the music.

We also went on a bus trip to Hastings, which was just over fifteen miles away. Unfortunately, it only had a pebble beach, but we sat on it and Helen had a paddle in the sea. While we were there, we went to 133 Parker Road to look up Jack Watson, who'd been in my regiment in the war and witnessed my will, but he was out at work, so we didn't get to see him.

The holiday was pretty decent, even though the people running the boarding house put us off because of how they looked and behaved. We said we'd never go in it again if we returned to Eastbourne.

We used to have decorators in to do most of our painting and wallpapering and that was expensive. So, on 13 August, to cut the cost, we bought a brand new set of ladders for £6 18s. 6d. from Stafford Equipment, at 101 Stafford Street, Hanley. The outside of our house was painted in an imitation oak graining style and needed varnishing to help preserve it and make it shiny again. So, with the ladders, I could now varnish the upstairs as well as the downstairs myself. We had the ladders delivered, but, about ten minutes after they arrived, Norma Harris, of number 478, asked if her father, Stan, could borrow them! I was staggered and couldn't believe the audacity of the man, who hadn't even come himself to ask. I told Norma that I wasn't lending the equipment out and I can't remember anyone else ever asking.

At first, I was wary of getting right to the top of the ladders and looking down, especially when I was varnishing under the eaves. After a bit of practice, though, I got used to it and from then on varnished the outside of the house every year or two. I also decorated inside the house when it needed doing and I had the time.

Our back garden path was made of small pebbles and I didn't like it because it seemed hard work crunching up and down on them. So, in August, I decided to replace them with concrete and did the job myself. I used a trowel to mix cement, sand, some of the pebbles and water on a wooden board and laid the concrete down in fairly small sections, each about five feet in length. I was quite pleased with the results, but, when Sid Asher visited us, he eyed my work up and said: 'That's no good. It won't last.' But it's still there today, in almost as good a condition as when I laid it!

Around then, I saw a five- or six-year course advertised in the *Sentinel* about the manufacture of pottery for management or would-be managers. It was in the Department of Ceramics at North Staffordshire Technical College (which is now part of Staffordshire University), in nearby Victoria Road, Shelton. I didn't really want to do any bossing because I wasn't made for ordering people around, but I just fancied the course, so I applied to the college and got in. I started to study Preliminary Pottery in a night class that autumn on the first year of the course, but I didn't enjoy it much because there was too much detail in it and it was time away from pleasure, although I persisted because it was a challenge.

On 11 October, there was a write-up in the *Sentinel* about a 300-page *North Staffordshire Plan*, which had been published that same day. The plan proposed that Hanley should become a 'regional centre' and that a new road should be built through the city to link it to a 'motor road' running between Lancashire and Birmingham. At the time, the ideas seemed rather fantastic, but now Hanley is called the "city centre" and Stoke-on-Trent and Newcastle are linked to the M 6 by the "D" road.

At work, a turner, named Bill, told me about his boyhood in the Potteries. His family was so poor that he only wore his boots to go to school in, to save on wear and tear. When he got home, his mother made him take them off, so he had to go out to play in his bare feet! He also told me that one night, when he'd grown up, he got out of bed and went to what he thought was the toilet, but actually urinated in the wardrobe! He said his wife wasn't amused.

Dead rabbits were commonly sold at market stalls, but the council's Health Committee was worried about the animals contaminating other foods there. It was reported in the *Sentinel* on 24 November that the committee had recommended that rabbits should be skinned at the back of the stalls to prevent such a problem from happening. The report all seemed pretty matter-of-fact, but I can't imagine what people nowadays would think about seeing rabbits being skinned behind market stalls!

Although the BBC had started showing television programmes in 1936, they were only transmitted to people living within 25 miles of the broadcasting station in London. In 1949, a new transmitter was built in Sutton Coldfield, in Warwickshire, so that the programmes could be seen in the area around Birmingham and that included Stoke-on-Trent. The new transmitter officially started up on 17 December and, before it did, there were a lot of adverts in the *Sentinel* by shops trying to get people to buy TV sets. Television was called 'the miracle of the modern age' and sets were being sold from about £50 to £175. My cousin, Bernard, got one more or less straight away. One day, I called in at Uncle Ted's and Bernard took me into the front room to show me his set. It was a new gadget to me and I wasn't very impressed with it, especially at the price he'd had to pay for it. There was a play on and it was a bore, so the experience didn't get me interested in buying a set.

One day at work, I was talking to an old handler, named Tom I think, when he had a fit. He sat upright on his chair and went stiff, so I called for help from the workers near me. I undid his shirt collar and he came back to normal after a few minutes. He was a Stoke supporter and went on the Boothen End. He was only a small fellow and it was difficult for him to see the game when there were big crowds. So he took a block of wood to stand on and wrapped it in brown paper to convey it to the match!

Around that time, there were ideas about building robots, with artificial sight, hearing, touch and smell, to replace the ordinary soldiers in future wars. It was pie in the sky at the time, but robots are becoming involved in conflicts now. Guided unmanned planes have been used in Afghanistan, but the land still has to be taken by men.

In February 1950, our union at work, the National Society of Pottery Workers, put in a claim for a second week's annual holiday with pay, but, of course, it was turned down by the bosses through their British Pottery Manufacturers' Federation. So the claim then had to go to arbitration. I didn't get too excited about it because I couldn't imagine us doubling our summer holidays just like that.

Uncle Ted supported the Labour Party and read the *Daily Herald*, which backed it. He wrote letters to the *Sentinel* about politics from time to time and had one printed on 3 March. In it, he criticized earlier Tory correspondents for their 'jubilant tone' because Labour had just won the 23 February general election, even though the Conservatives had made a big comeback from the 1945 election and run them close.

Our union's holiday claim was considered by an industrial court in Stoke Town Hall on 18 and 19 April, but was rejected. It didn't bother me too much because a week's annual holiday was the normal practice, so I was used to it.

There was a sensation on 8 May when Neil Franklin and Stoke's versatile forward, George Mountford, secretly flew to Colombia, to play for Santa Fe in Bogotá. It was a big shock because it was unheard of footballers going to play in foreign countries. There was a maximum wage for players in England and Franklin and Mountford were offered small fortunes to sign for the South American club. The trouble was that the Colombian football association wasn't recognized by FIFA and so both players were suspended from playing in the English Football League.

Although Mountford stuck it out in Bogotá, Franklin didn't settle and came home after four weeks, but he never played for Stoke again and remained suspended till 31 January the following year. It was a pity it didn't work out for him. He was the key man at Stoke at the time and I thought it would upset the team having him out, but they did better without him!

Our hut was squeezed in between the border fence with Halfpenny's and our back garden steps and it was very awkward getting past it. I decided to transfer it to the back of our garden and so I took it to pieces. First, I took the roof off and then took the ends and sides apart. There were nails sticking out from all over it, so I had to be careful not to rip myself open on them. I had to carry all the sections of the hut up the steps and along the garden path, which was very difficult because the pieces were almost as wide as my outstretched arms, so I couldn't see where I was going! It was crazy and I should have got some help, but

I didn't ask Helen to assist me because I thought that, as a woman, she wouldn't have wanted to have got involved in doing something like that. Then, somehow, I managed to put all the pieces of the hut back together again and fitted it next to the coal bunker. It took me a day or two to do the whole job.

At the end of my pottery course, around June, I took a written exam and had to revise for it from my numerous class notes. When I was told I'd passed, I was surprised, but very pleased, and it meant I could enrol on the next year of the course, on Ordinary Pottery.

England were playing in the World Cup for the first time and I was expecting them to fly through to the final and win it. However, on 29 June, there was a big shock because they were beaten 1-0 by the U.S.A. The Americans weren't regarded as a footballing nation and their team was held in low esteem by everyone, so I was disgusted that England had lost. It didn't get any better, though, because they were also defeated by Spain, by 1-0 on 3 July, and so went out of the competition straight away. It was a big shock to everybody.

In August, Helen and I had our annual holiday in Torquay, to try somewhere different. We went with Aunt Sally and Uncle Bill, who were going to the same destination, and so we booked into the same boarding house, West Brook. We went by train from Stoke, as usual. The journey was a long one and we travelled through the night. We were in a compartment which held eight people and it was full, so it was too uncomfortable to doze off, but we could go to the toilet, which was off the corridor that ran along the length of our coach. When we finally got to Torquay, we were shattered and had to kill time before our digs opened and we could drop off our luggage.

Torquay was pleasant and there were palm trees growing. It was posher than Blackpool, but there wasn't as much entertainment. Of course, we sat on deck chairs on the sands and Helen and I had a paddle in the sea. Also, we all had a game of putting.

We visited nearby Cockington Forge, which comprised several upright wooden poles and a thatched roof and was very picturesque. It had been used for shoeing horses, though I thought that the thatch would have been a fire hazard. By that time, it was no longer in use and was there to attract sightseers. Like many other people had done, Helen wrote her name and address on a piece of paper and pinned it up on one of the upright beams.

Another day, we walked to Babbacombe, from where there were lovely views down to the quay, Oddicombe Beach and Petit Tor Point, a headland, beyond. There was a cliff railway down to the beach, but I can't remember making use of it.

We also went to Kents Cavern, which was the name of a number of different connected ancient caves in Torquay itself. It was quite a tourist attraction. Inside there were a concrete path and electric lights, which made it easy to get round, but it was strange because the lighting made the ancient caves look modern.

One day, we had a trip by boat across Tor Bay to Brixham, which had a fishing harbour. We also went to Paignton, but it was second-rate and a bit rough.

Back home, we continued to support Stoke and went to see most of their home games. Some of the players had been with the club for years, like Dennis Herod, a good, athletic goalkeeper; John McCue, a tough, but dirty full-back; Frank Mountford, a half-back, who was on the ground a lot of the time and always covered with mud, and Roy Brown, a centre-forward, who terrified the opposing defences because he was like lightning. He was a coloured player, which was very unusual at the time, but I can't remember anybody shouting at him. I also remember Frank Bowyer, who was a skilful inside-forward, and Harry Oscroft, a terrier-type left-winger.

Around that time, Elijah and Ethel moved into 55 Mill Hill Crescent, which was one of the new council houses that had been built in Little Chell. The crescent surrounded a circular green, so there was some nice vegetation to look at, and the houses had gardens.

Helen and I went to Blackpool to see the illuminations, probably in October. It was cold and everybody had their overcoats on, even during the day, but the weather was worth putting up with to see the lights, which were very nice.

The Korean War had been going on since June and was building up into a big struggle, in which we were backing the Americans against the Chinese. Although I supposed I was on the reserve list, I wasn't very worried at first because I thought there'd be plenty of younger men called up before me. But, by late November, the war was going badly and the American president, Harry Truman, said that he was thinking of using the atom bomb. Oh dear! I could see a nuclear war coming and Britain being dragged into it. Fortunately, the Americans managed to push the Chinese back, so no atom bombs were dropped and the war ended in 1953 with the situation the same as it had been before all the trouble had started!

In December (1950), over three million cards and letters were sent in the Christmas post in the Stoke-on-Trent district, which was a record. The numbers of Christmas cards sent increased a lot in the years after the war. I didn't send any before I got married and afterwards I left it up to Helen to do them.

On 28 December, the order for setting up the Peak District National Park was signed. I suppose I was aware of it, but I don't think I thought it was of much importance. But today, I think it's very important for people to be able to go into the countryside. Without that right, we wouldn't be able to get out there and see what's ours. We'd be held in the streets, like a prison, more or less how it was back then before the national parks were set up. Over the years, I've had a lot of pleasure going out to the Peak District with my family. It's a beautiful area.

One day, Helen told me she thought she was having a baby. It was a shock because I realized, if it was true, that things would become a great deal different in our lives. We didn't really decide to have a child, but we hadn't been using any contraceptives. I think I only ever used one once, so we'd been taking a chance, as we knew at the back of our minds. Helen then went to see Dr MacArthur and he confirmed her suspicions. I don't think she was particularly pleased and it wouldn't have bothered me if I'd not had any children.

As neither of us had our parents any longer, there was no-one handy we could consult for advice about having a baby, so we were struggling to know what to do. At that time, it was accepted that women should have their babies at home, but we didn't have anyone who would have been willing to help because it would have meant them having to take time off work. Therefore, Helen asked Dr MacArthur if it was possible for the birth to be in hospital and so, in January 1951, she was sent to see a specialist, Mr L. M. Edwards. He examined her and reported that everything was progressing normally, but that, because of her age, he'd arrange for her to have the baby in the Infirmary.

It was in the *Sentinel* on 6 February that the Americans were testing a really destructive nuclear weapon they'd developed, the hydrogen bomb. It was supposed to be hundreds of times more powerful than the atom bomb that had destroyed Nagasaki in Japan in 1945. I thought it was horrible. It was another threat to us, the general public. I thought it might lead to disaster and we'd all be wiped out.

On 12 February, our union at work again put in for a second week's summer holiday with pay and this time it was agreed to by the employers, along with a 7½ per cent basic wage increase. I thought the deal was very good and another week off work was very welcome. I don't think Helen and I would have had the money to have gone on holiday for a fortnight, but, as it turned out, with the baby on the way, we weren't able to go at all.

It was announced in the *Sentinel* on 7 March that Vincent Riley had died from extensive burns. He'd been found lying unconscious and burning at the top of a flue in Sneyd Brickworks, in Nile Street, where I suppose he'd gone to sleep for the night. I never met him, but he'd been in prison 246 times and been quite a character, according to the reports. He'd even had a book written about him, by Fred Glen, called *The Story of a Meth-Elated Spirit*! Life would be dull without people who are different, like Riley, and the stories that are told about them.

At Mintons, Bill, the turner, had a disagreement with Reuben, our foreman. Bill later retired, but he wouldn't let the matter drop. So when Reuben finished work and was waiting in the bus queue in Hill Street to go home, Bill would stand on the opposite side of the road and harangue him until the bus pulled out. I gathered that Reuben was most embarrassed by Bill's ranting and raving, but it carried on like that for a while!

I didn't particularly like Reuben myself and got fed up with working at Mintons. One of the night class students was a manager at A. G. Hackney & Co. Ltd., at Fairfield Pottery in Robson Street, Hanley, and he told me they'd got a vacancy for a turner there. So I applied and got the job. They made different types of electrical porcelain, including the bars for electric fires, but it was a scruffy place, so I soon got fed up there too. My last week's wages at Mintons, paid on 6 April, were £7 7s. 3d., with 8s. deducted for tax, and my first week's at Hackney's, on the 13th, were £6 11s. 7d., with 6s. tax.

Our foreman, Bill Windsor, was a fitter by trade, who'd maintained machines on the factory. That seemed funny because foremen were usually workers promoted from within their trade because they were experts in that line. But the principles of cutting metal to repair machines and cutting clay were the same, so he'd have understood the basic techniques.

On 15 May, it was in the *Sentinel* that George Mountford was back from Bogotá, having honoured his contract to his club there. He wanted to rejoin Stoke, but the FA suspended him till 3 September. Stoke decided to take him back, even though it meant him missing the first five matches of the season, but he wasn't as good a player as Neil Franklin and wasn't as important to the team.

In June or thereabouts, I took the Ordinary Pottery written exam at the end of my college course. Like in the first year, I had books full of notes that I had to revise from and again I surprised myself by passing, which meant that I could go on to the third year in the autumn and study Advanced Pottery and Advanced Chemistry.

By then, I was thinking more about what would happen when Helen had our baby. It was all new to me, but I realized it would bring big changes and we'd have to stay in to look after the baby instead of being able to go out. I suppose I was nervous because anything could go wrong, but I assumed Helen would be alright. I had flashes in my mind of how things might be, but then I'd carry on with whatever I was doing. Of course, Helen was looking pregnant by then, but I was just waiting to see how things turned out.

7 Father In The Fifties

Helen continued to work at Swinnerton's until our baby was due to be born. A week afterwards, on the night of 27-28 July 1951, she started to have pains at regular intervals, so I needed to get in touch with the hospital. In the middle of the night, I went to the phone box along the road, outside All Saints Church, Joiner's Square, and rang the Infirmary. I gave them the details, but they didn't know anything about the arrangements the specialist had made. They told me to bring Helen along anyway, but there was no mention of an ambulance. There were no buses at that time, so I phoned for a taxi and it all seemed hectic, but that was due to our inexperience.

I dropped Helen off at the hospital, where the staff took charge and pushed me off pretty quickly. I suppose that was due to the late hour because I might have woken the other patients. I then returned home to get an hour or two's sleep before going to work in the morning. After a while, I went to the works' office and asked if I could phone the hospital. One of the office girls connected me up and, when I put the receiver to my ear, I could hear babies crying and screaming in the background. I asked how Mrs Kent and the baby were and I was told they were fine and that I could visit them after tea time. That was because visits were only allowed at set times in those days. I was told the baby was a boy and I was pleased about it, as was Helen, because that was our preference.

After I'd finished work and had my tea, I made my way to the maternity ward. A nurse greeted me and in each arm she had a baby. When I told her my name, she said: 'Here's your baby. Can you tell which one it is?'

I looked and saw a big baby, with thick, dark hair, and a smaller one, with thinner and lighter hair. I pointed to the one with the dark hair and said, 'That's mine.'

The nurse laughed and said: 'No! It's the other one!'

She took me to Helen and brought Baby Kent with her. Helen told me that was the very first time she'd set eyes on him. She'd been worried all day that the reason he'd not been brought to her was that there was something badly wrong with him. There must have been an oversight because Baby Kent was okay.

The birth had been supervised by Mr Edwards and Baby Kent had been born normally, although Helen had to have stitches afterwards because she'd suffered a second-degree tear during the delivery. I can't remember her telling me that giving birth had been painful, but she told Baby Kent a time or two when he grew up!

The babies were kept in a separate room from their mothers except at certain times, such as when they were being breast fed and at visiting time. Helen and the baby stayed in the hospital for a few days and I went to see them in the evenings when he was in a cot by Helen's bed. She said that the babies cried quite a bit, especially in the night, and that she'd been told by a nurse that Baby Kent was the main culprit. Another nurse said that he had a lovely olive skin and I thought that too.

I registered Baby Kent's birth on 3 August and then the day after got him an identity card. Even though it was years since the war had ended, everybody still had to have one, even babies! Obviously I had to sign it on his behalf and he was given the number MOUH 189. He was supposed to apply for another card within seven days after his sixteenth birthday, but the registration law was scrapped in 1952.

On 5 August, Helen and Baby Kent were allowed to come home, so I got a taxi, which brought us back. Helen and I were rank amateurs when it came to dealing with a very young child. We were rather clumsy and awkward, even though Helen had some experience, having looked after Young Harry and bathed him when his parents had had nights out. But, as an only child, I didn't have a clue and, because our parents were dead, we were on our own.

We'd decided before the birth to call our baby Jeffrey John William. We gave him the names John and William after his grandfathers Middleton and Kent and Jeffrey was his own name, which we (and most especially Helen) liked the sound of. But it was a short while before we got round to using his name because he was something of a novelty, as well as a huge possession, that we'd suddenly come into.

When we got home, we put Jeff in a cot in the lounge, in a recess by the fire, and took off his outer clothes. We then waited for the next move! When he cried, we responded, but most of the time we didn't know what he wanted. His cries could be for milk, for more clothes or fewer clothes, because of a soiled nappy or just through cussedness. We'd try different things to try to find the solution, but we got it wrong a lot of the time. There were quiet times when he was asleep and we tried not to make a sound in case we woke him up. However, unlike in the hospital, I don't think he cried a lot at night, so we slept quite well overall.

We didn't go on holiday that summer, owing to our new arrival and because Helen wasn't working and bringing in a wage. We decided to have Jeff christened, I suppose because it was the custom, and did so at Shelton Church on 19 August. His godfathers were Jack Green and Sid Asher and his godmother was Vera. As far as I know, they were supposed to see that Jeff had a Christian upbringing. It was a nice day and he was wrapped in a shawl. The ceremony went off okay and then we walked through Hanley Park with our guests to have a little celebration at our house. When we got back, Helen complained that she was tired because she'd carried Jeff nearly all the way home. If I'd realized she was getting tired, I would, of course, have given her a hand.

Like practically all children at that time, Jeff had a dummy to keep him quiet. One day, when he was crying, Helen couldn't find it and searched everywhere for it. Eventually, she found it on one of his thumbs, so she quickly pulled it off and put it in his mouth!

Changing Jeff's nappies was a bore and I didn't envy Helen having to wash them, but Jeff loved to be free of them, when he'd kick his legs about. He also liked his bath time and would splash in his zinc-coated tin bath in front of the fire. But Helen was reluctant to breast feed him, perhaps because of embarrassment, so he was partly bottle fed.

With working full time and having to help Helen with Jeff, it was difficult to concentrate on my college studies, which were getting harder. The elementary formulae in the chemistry we were taught were okay to understand, but then they got more complicated and it took me a while to get the hang of them.

I wasn't getting much chance to play my piano, but still did on the odd occasion. I had it tuned every year or two by a neighbour, Alfred Jenn, who lived at number 510. He worked for J. C. Sherwin & Sons, the piano sellers at 21 Market Square, Hanley, and never wore socks, so inside his shoes were his bare feet!

On 30 November, I made the final mortgage payment, of £5 6s. 3d., to Halifax Building Society and so the house was at last ours. We were very pleased because it took a load off our minds! At that time, most people were still renting, so to own our own house outright was a big thing.

Christmas was pretty quiet because Jeff wasn't old enough to know what it was all about, so he didn't have many presents. However, Vera bought him a teddy bear and I took a photo of Jeff and Helen with it. Soon after he'd had it, I took its eyes out because they were known to be dangerous. Children had accidents with them and they were only fixed in with a pin. When Jeff outgrew the bear, we still kept "Ted" and he remained in my possession until recently, but now sits next to the computer in Jeff's office!

In January 1952, I got my cousin, Stan, to take a series of photos of Jeff, which turned out very well. Stan had become a partner in a photography business, Miller & Palin, and they had a shop at 72 Earle Street, Crewe. They did very well because people wanted to buy practically anything after years of shortages and photography became increasingly popular, so they ended up with a number of other shops, including one at 3 Vale Street, Stoke.

Stan told me that, when he'd been conscripted into the air force after the war and sent to Germany, he'd noticed that the Germans had a shortage of all kinds of goods. They were paying very good money and exchanging valuables for such things as coffee and cigarettes. Later, when he was on leave in Britain, he thought he'd cash in on the shortages and bought a large quantity of coffee at inflated prices because supplies weren't plentiful here either. On his first pass out after he'd returned to Germany, he took his coffee onto the streets in the town and awaited the arrival of the black marketeers. Poor Stan! While he'd been on leave, the Germans had received big supplies of coffee and the bottom had dropped out of the market, so he had a job to get rid of the merchandise for what he'd paid for it!

About that time, we had notification from the corporation that our house number was to be changed from 472 to 335. It was part of their street rationalization, mainly for the benefit of postmen and their customers. Because the city consisted of six towns that had grown up independently, there was a lot of duplication of street names. For example, there were thirteen High Streets within the city boundaries, but people would put 'High Street, Stoke-on-Trent' on their letters and it caused confusion. So the council got rid of all the High Streets, except the one in Tunstall, and renamed them.

Up till then, the road from Stoke to Milton had had a number of names as it went along: Winton Terrace, Leek Road (the section where we lived), Abbey Road, Trent Terrace and then Leek Road again. Through the reorganization, all the other names were scrapped, so that Leek Road then ran all the way from Station Road to Milton, making it the longest road in the city. The houses had been numbered in the direction of Stoke, but they reversed as a result of the change.

We bought a posh new perambulator from a shop in Hanley. The pram was high off the ground, with large wheels, which meant that we didn't have to bend down too far to pick Jeff up. Helen took him out in it quite a lot, especially around Hanley Park, to give him some fresh air, and she neglected the housework somewhat. At home, she also often had him in his pram outside the front and back of our house.

Helen had to leave Jeff in his pram on his own from time to time because she had jobs to do. One day, she noticed that part of the edge of the cover of the pram was damaged and wondered how it could have happened. Eventually, she concluded that Jeff had been chewing it! His milk teeth were coming through and he must have decided to see what the material tasted like. There wasn't much Helen could do about Jeff gnawing it because she couldn't be with him all the time, but we wondered if we'd later be able to sell on the pram if he kept at it. Anyway, he grew out of the habit and we did sell the pram with no problem when the time came.

I often used to take Jeff out in his pram to give Helen a break. Once, I bought an ice cream and let Jeff have a lick to see if he liked it. He wanted more, so I let him have another lick. I didn't tell Helen about it because she'd have thought that cold ice cream would be bad for a baby. But, soon after, Helen said that a woman had mentioned to her that Jeff liked his ice cream. Helen had told her that he'd never had any, but the woman had said she'd seen me giving him some and so I was told off!

Another time, I took Jeff to Cobridge, to show him off to Jack Green, but, on the way back, Jeff began to cry bitterly and I couldn't console him. At the bottom of Waterloo Road, a couple were standing in the doorway of a house and asked if I'd like to go in to check his nappy. So I did and took it off to see if there was a pin sticking into him, but I could find nothing wrong. I then fastened him up, thanked the couple and continued on my way. Gradually, he quietened down, but he was still catching his breath when we got home. Helen was very concerned, but we never found out what had caused him to cry so much.

The Post Office were having a depot built across the road from us. My old pal, Norman Banks, worked on its construction as a steel bender. He and a mate bent back the ends of long, thick steel bars, which were used to reinforce concrete and made it very strong. They put the bars in a kind of elementary vice and levered them round with hooks. It took two fellows to do it. These concrete piles were then hammered into the earth by a big pile-driver, which shook our house every time it struck! Later, the bricklayers started to work and among them was Sid Asher. Helen invited him to have his midday meal, which she cooked for him, in our house each day.

The foreman of the construction team came over one day and told Helen to watch that Jeff didn't overturn his pram because he was rocking it so much in front of our bay window, where she'd put him. Apparently, workmen had seen the pram jerking around and were so concerned that they'd told the foreman about it. Jeff was okay, but Helen did have a look at him more often after that.

One day, when Jeff was around nine months old, he was babbling away in his cot in the lounge and came out with a little word, 'Dadad'. It was the first word he'd spoken and Helen and I both heard it. We were delighted, but I think she was a bit jealous that Jeff had used my name before hers. In spite of that, she went round telling everybody that he'd started speaking and then we were listening all the time to see what other words he came out with.

I used to go to work on my bike and sometimes Helen would bring Jeff in his pram to meet me outside the factory. On one of these occasions, we started to walk through Hanley Park, but an attendant stopped me. He said I couldn't wheel a bike through the park and told me to retrace my steps. I protested that I wasn't riding it, but it was no use. He was adamant, so we turned back and had to go all the way round the park!

One day, I saw an advert in the *Sentinel* for the position of foreman of the clay department at Electric & Ordnance Accessories Co. Ltd., in Broad Street. I thought I'd see if I could land the job and so wrote a letter to the firm. Some time later, I had a reply asking me to call to see the managing director. At the interview, I stated my qualifications and the fellow listened, but he wasn't impressed with me because I later received a letter saying the position had been filled. Now, I'm pleased that I failed because, if I'd done extra years in the pottery dust, it would have increased my chances of getting silicosis.

I was still attending the pottery course night classes and asked the manager of Hackney's if there was any chance of me getting a foreman's job on the strength of it. I didn't get much of a reply, but one of the foremen, who was in my class, recommended another pupil for a staff job with the firm and he got it. I felt a little hurt, but, looking back, I'm glad it happened that way because eventually I left the industry and I might not have done if I'd got promoted.

By then, Jeff had an enclosed high chair, which he was put in for his meals and for safety, when we needed to leave him for a short period. He was secured with a harness. One day, Helen gave him his food on a dish, with a spoon, but then had to go into the kitchen. When she came back, he'd tipped all the food over his head and some of it had gone on his clothes! She had to clean it all up, while Jeff was enjoying the situation! Another time, she left him in his chair and went upstairs to the toilet. While she was there, she heard a bump and a cry and dashed downstairs, without having had the time to adjust her clothing, to find him lying on the floor squawking, having somehow fallen out of his chair.

Again at the beginning of the summer, it was exam time for me. I'd struggled to get the hang of the mathematics side of the course and needed a little more time in the exam to work out the calculations required, so I wasn't very confident about how I'd done.

In June, I noticed that Wedgwood's, who'd moved to a new factory in Barlaston, were advertising for turners, so I had half a day off work to go there on the train from Stoke. I alighted at Wedgwood Halt (where the platforms were wooden), walked to the factory and asked to see the boss of the earthenware department. He came along and, lo and behold, it was Harry Longshaw, who'd been the foreman when I'd been there previously as a lad! I don't know whether this was a help to me or not because Harry was a straight-faced fellow, so I didn't know what he was thinking. I said I was interested in coming to work there and he asked how much I was getting at Hackney's. I told him and he offered me more money. I realized that I'd have to pay travelling expenses out of my wages to get there, but I worked out that I'd still be better off. So I decided there and then to take the job, even though it would mean me being out of the house for longer. Before I left, I went to have a word with Uncle Ted, who was still working as the head handler in the department.

When I returned home, I wrote out my resignation from Hackney's, giving the required month's notice, and handed it in. My last week's wages there, paid on 18 July, were £7 11s. 7d. and I received £8 19s. 5d. on the 25th from my first week at Wedgwood's. They had the most modern pottery factory, which was cleaner and lighter than any of the others. Everything was new and it had modern conditions. It was definitely the best place I'd worked, though the travelling was a bind. In the earthenware department, where I was working, the ware was off-white and a lot of the shapes were similar to the famous blue jasper ware.

Fred Halfpenny, next door, was still throwing at Wedgwood's and was in the same department as me, so we went to work together. We walked along Leek Road to Stoke Station and, when the train came in, we got in a compartment with a regular crowd. I enjoyed the walk from Wedgwood Halt to the factory through the countryside and back again after work. Then we got a train home.

In the turning shop, we still made our own tools from sheet metal, on a special bench between us, which had a grindstone and files for sharpening the tools. We were also supplied with a "square tool" that was made of very hard metal and lasted longer. It was very versatile for shaping the clay, especially for use on straight surfaces, but it couldn't be filed and had to be sent away when it needed sharpening.

As an employee, I was allowed to purchase seconds during the meal break, after I'd applied for and been given a "ware pass". But, unfortunately, as the buzzer sounded, there'd be a rush towards the seconds' department and I was on the slow side. So, by the time I got there, the best items on offer had been snapped up, but most times I'd get something that Helen and I required. Of course, relatives and friends heard about this and so I was expected to supply the goods. It was a bore because I was losing about half my work break, applying for a pass in my piecework time, paying for the articles with my own money and then having to carry the ware home! The boxes were quite heavy with the pottery in, awkward to carry and could easily come apart when it rained. When I got the pottery home, it was also expected that I should deliver it, which meant another walk or bus ride. I don't think my efforts were appreciated by most people. I never made a profit, although I was always given the money that I'd paid to buy the items.

Leah sometimes came to see Jeff and would take him out in his pram or pushchair. At the end of one trip, he came back without his floppy hat, which Helen always put on him to protect his head and eyes from the sun. Leah said she'd lost it, but Helen swore that Leah had thrown it away because she'd never liked it!

I received the results of my third lot of pottery exams, but, unfortunately, this year I'd failed. So I decided not to go to any more classes, even though I could have repeated the year and retaken my exams. Also, it wouldn't have been fair to Helen because she needed to have a break from Jeff, while I'd been having to spend a lot of time at home studying for my classes.

On 6 September, my cousin, Stan, got married to Mollie Reid, who'd originally come from Birtley, in Durham. Their wedding was at St. Chad's Church, in King William Street, Tunstall. I was Stan's best man because his brother, Aubrey, was living and working in the London area and wasn't available. In the event, Aubrey turned up and I offered to let him take my place, but he refused my proposal. The reception was held at the Sneyd Arms Hotel, in Tower Square, Tunstall, and I stood up and read out the telegrams and cards. Helen wasn't with me because she was looking after Jeff.

Stan had his partner, Jack Miller, take the official photos, as he was a professional photographer. Some time afterwards, Stan showed me these and asked for my honest opinion about the quality of them because he thought they were poor. I was shocked and would have been ashamed had I taken them, so Jack should have had his backside kicked for getting such atrocious results, as a professional, at his partner's wedding! But I didn't want to hurt Stan's feelings and so lied and said the photos weren't too bad.

About that time, Helen and I became very worried about Jeff because we couldn't get him to eat anything. It went on for a few days, I think, so we sent for a doctor, who came down. He didn't seem too concerned and said, 'When he gets hungry, he'll start eating again,' but he told us to make sure that Jeff had drinks. The problem continued for another day or two and then he started eating again. We were very pleased because it had been really worrying.

On 21 October, I paid our 1 October to 31 March half-year General Rate bill of £5 2s. 11d. to Stoke-on-Trent Corporation. I've still got the bill and it shows that the account remained in my father's name. I've also got the payment receipt and it says that the money was received from my dad! It carried on like that for years because it didn't matter, but eventually I got the account changed to my name.

I heard that the corporation was collecting old air-raid shelters, to melt down for reuse, because there was a shortage of metal. So I decided to get rid of ours and dug it up and unscrewed it ready for collection. It was taken away on a lorry. We could have kept it and used it as a store place, as some of the shelters still are today. Maybe they are collectors' items now!

Around the same time, my army uniform finally wore out. I'd kept it for working in because clothes were in short supply after the war. I hadn't wanted to buy something new just to go to work in, so it had come in useful. I also threw my glengarry cap away because I didn't wear it, so it was in the way.

Stoke were struggling against relegation from the First Division and so the directors decided to try to pep up the team by re-signing Stan Matthews from Blackpool. They made an offer of around £11,500 on 15 December and it was big news. Stan was 37 by then, so I wondered if he'd be very effective. It became believed that Blackpool wanted £20,000, so the offer was turned down. As it happened, my doubts about Stan were proved wrong because he really turned on the style at the end of the season in what became known as the "Matthews Final" when Blackpool beat Bolton Wanderers 4-3 to win the FA Cup on 2 May 1953, three days after Stoke had been relegated to the Second Division.

My Christmas pay on 24 December 1952 was £8 19s. 5d., with 3s. deducted for tax. I received £7 1s. 6d. in my next pay, on 2 January 1953, along with a 2s. tax rebate.

There was still food rationing, although it was gradually coming to an end. I've still got Helen's 1953-1954 ration book from the Ministry of Food, with the serial number BR 786717. W. H. Nagington, who was still at 34 Fenton Road, was listed as our supplier of meat and bacon and we were supposed to get our rations of eggs, fats, cheese and sugar from J. H. & M. Bowyer, at Beech Dairy, 43 Tintern Street, who delivered our milk. We took up only our meat and bacon rations because we were able to find enough of the other foods nearer to home.

Then, on 4 July 1954, all food rationing ended and so we were free again to buy whatever we could afford.

After Young Harry had left school, he'd worked in the lodge at Geo. L. Ashworth & Bros. Ltd, of Broad Street, for a short while and then Sid Asher had got him a job with G. & J. Seddon Ltd, of 55 Duke Street, Fenton, helping with the tiling of bathrooms and floors. In addition, Harry was doing very well in local football as a right-half and had played for Carmountside Youth Club, Milton Youth Club and the National Association of Boys' Clubs. He'd had a trial at Stoke, but, apparently, they weren't too keen on him, so, in February 1953, he signed for Port Vale as an amateur. I would have thought Vera and Big Harry would have boasted about that, but they didn't. They kept pretty quiet and I didn't hear much about it.

Fred Halfpenny was still in the news and usually gave a demonstration when an important person visited Wedgwood's factory. There were lots of visitors, who were brought around by official guides, one of whom had only one hand. I believe he'd lost his other in the First World War and Wedgwood's had found him that job. I had a lot of people watch me perform with my lathe. It was embarrassing at first, but I got used to it. One famous visitor who went past was King Hussein of Jordan and it was a change to see someone different.

Some time and motion men came and watched all the turners working, including me. They made notes while they observed our methods and, as a result of that, the management put forward a new piecework arrangement to us. After discussion, we accepted it and didn't do too badly out of it.

It was about then that Helen decided it was time for Jeff to be toilet trained. He was still wearing nappies, but we tried him on a pot. One of us would put him on it every couple of hours or so in the hope that he'd use it, but the rest of the time we kept a nappy on him. Most of the time we put him on the pot, he didn't want to do anything and would start struggling, but we'd hold him there for a while because we didn't know that. When he did want to do something, he'd go running up a corner of the lounge, laughing, and do it there if we didn't catch him in time. He didn't want to go on the pot and rebelled and thought he'd got us on the run! Then we had to clean the mess up and we told him off, but it was a learning process that he gradually got used to and so we were successful with him after a while.

About that time at Wedgwood's, I was asked if I'd like to go into the jasper department, which was supposed to be superior to the earthenware one and had snob value. I said I would because it would give me more prestige, though there was no more pay. I gathered up my tools and equipment and took them to my new bench and lathe, which were better placed because they faced a window and I could see a bit of green outside.

Jeff's teddy bear was becoming knocked about and one of his legs came loose, so Helen got a needle and thread to sew it back on again. Jeff saw her doing it and broke out crying because he thought the sharp needle would hurt Ted. We had a real job consoling Jeff.

Jeff was still too young for us to go on holiday that summer and, in August, Helen decided to have all her teeth extracted. They seemed to be alright, but she resented people remarking about them being prominent. She went to G. Martin, the dentist, at 1 Howard Place, Shelton, and Leah and I went along with her for company and comfort. I regret to write that I didn't go into the waiting room with her because I was more squeamish than now. While I waited outside rather cowardly, with Leah and Jeff, my old girlfriend, Norah Burt, came past. I had a word with her, while inside the building Helen was having a rough time. It seems that the dentist was in a bit of a panic because she wasn't regaining consciousness, so he and his helpers had to work hard to get her back to herself. We'd been waiting a long time, unaware of what was happening, and I should have gone in to find out why there was a delay. Finally, Helen weakly came out of the door, looking dreadful, and told us about the experience she'd had. She was really in no state to walk home and it would have been in order to have got a taxi, but, in those days, we didn't think of such things. So walk back she did, but she was happy with her new false teeth when she had them.

I started to go to a woodwork night class, perhaps because I thought I'd try doing something different and see if I could make some useful things. The class was held at Milton County Secondary School, on Leek Road, and I travelled there by bus. These vehicles didn't have electrically-operated doors then and they were usually left open because hardly anyone bothered to close them, so the buses were bitterly cold in the winter! Amongst the first things I made were a board and easel for Jeff, as a Christmas present. It was like a toy for him to draw on with chalk, but was also to show him what school would be like.

When Jeff got too big for his cot, we got him a full-sized bed, which we put in the back bedroom. One night, we heard a bump and then a cry. We rushed into the room wondering what we'd find. He'd fallen out of bed onto the floor, he was crying and there was a lump on his head. Eventually, he calmed down and went to sleep. The next day, we took him to see Dr Kerr, at the Lichfield Street surgery. He told us he thought Jeff would be alright, but, just to make sure, he advised us to take him to the Infirmary, where the doctors also gave him a clean bill of health. That same night, we pushed his bed against a wall and put a chair on the other side, as a temporary measure, to stop him falling out again. Soon after, at the woodwork class, I made a couple of contraptions, which were like railings, to fix on the sides of his bed.

Also at the class, I made some square wooden blocks for Jeff to play with and I painted them different colours. He liked building them up, pulling them down and throwing them around.

Helen and I thought Jeff might be frightened if he woke up in the middle of the night in pitch-black, so I put a dim light in his bedroom to reassure him. As time passed, he didn't need to have it any longer and so eventually we went back to using a normal light bulb.

On 25 November, England lost 6-3 to Hungary at Wembley and it was a shock. We'd never been beaten at home by a foreign team before and Stan Matthews and Billy Wright were playing, so, of course, like nearly everybody else, I'd expected us to win. We found out that Hungary were a very good side, with new ideas, but, even if people had heard about them, their ability was pooh-poohed because we'd invented football and were supposed to be better than the Europeans. Although some newspapers called it "The Match of the Century", afterwards we felt ashamed of the England team.

Just before Christmas, Helen took Jeff to Lewis's to see Santa Claus because Jeff was by then old enough to understand such things. He had his photo taken with him, but Jeff looked overwhelmed, although it wasn't surprising because it must have been frightening to have sat on the knee of a strange man dressed in red, with a long, white beard!

On Christmas Day, I went up to Jeff's bedroom and, when he woke, I shouted: 'Come on! Santa's been!' He scuffled out of bed and rushed downstairs, to find his Christmas presents laid out in front of the coal fire in the lounge. Helen was waiting there for him and his eyes lit up, not knowing which gift to open first. I'd set the board and easel up for him and chalked on it, 'A MERRY XMAS,' for him to see when he came into the room. We mainly left him to it to use his imagination with chalk on the board, but I can't remember him using it much.

Uncle Ted hadn't been well for a while and died at his home on 20 January 1954. His funeral was at Carmountside Crematorium, at 11.40 a.m. on the 23rd. That morning, I went to work as usual, intending to break off and catch a train to Etruria, to get to his house for the start of the proceedings. While I was at my bench, Mr Lawton, the clay manager of the earthenware and jasper departments, who was a gentleman, came over and asked how I was getting to the funeral. I told him my plan, but he said that the firm were sending one or more of their cars for any workers who wished to go, so I accepted the offer. Only one other employee travelled with me, Albert Deaville, who was a handler and had worked with Uncle Ted for a good many years. Wedgwood's had a reputation for looking after the welfare of their workers and I never came across another firm that gave such a service. They were years in advance of the other pottery firms.

In 1954, Eva Jeffries became the Grand Master of the North Staffordshire branch of the Independent Order of Oddfellows (Manchester Unity), which was one of the largest friendly societies in the world. Vin had held the same position previously, which was for one year and involved chairing the meetings. Eva gave Helen and me a copy of the photograph she had taken, wearing the big double chain of office round her neck.

We were pretty friendly with Eva and Vin and I gave them four of ten table mats I made, keeping the other six for our use. I then decided to construct a deck chair and got the canvas for it from Lewis's, made to measure because my model was bigger than the standard size sold. Over the years, we wore the canvas out, but were unable to replace it because by then only the standard size had become available. Vera was impressed with our new deck chair, so I made her one too on request.

Helen didn't want me to make anything for the house because she thought Jeff would only muck it up, so I had to ask around to get orders. Whenever I made an article for a person, I only charged for the cost of the materials. Leah said she'd like a bedside cabinet. It took me months to make, but I did get expert tuition from Mr Hughes, the woodwork teacher. The finished article was quite good and I think Leah was pleased with it.

Next, Harold and Annie Bentley gave me a commission to make a unit to take a few books and odds and ends. Mr Hughes got me some Japanese oak for this and once more I made it under his guidance. Again, the finished article was pleasing to behold, but it was very heavy because it was made from solid timber and the conductor and driver weren't very happy when I carried it onto the bus to bring it home.

I then constructed a coffee table for Vera, which was circular and had four flat legs. The top and lower shelf were each made up, I think, of three planks of wood, which were glued edge to edge. It was a work of art how Mr Hughes planed the edges of the wood so that they fitted exactly together to make the table top. He then boiled some glue, which he stuck on, and held the planks together with a couple of cramps. It was all allowed to set until my next class when I unscrewed the cramps. The result was amazing – the three pieces of wood were as solid as if they'd been one piece! The unit was roughly square, so I was told to draw a circle on the wood the same size as I required the table top to be. I then sawed off the surplus wood, leaving a rough circle. Next, I screwed a metal plate onto the centre of the wood and fixed it all onto an electric-driven wood-turning lathe. This was switched on and the table top whizzed round at speed. Mr Hughes showed me how to hold the turning tool firmly on the rest. It was dangerous, but, by holding the tool steady, I was able to shave off the wood until the table top was a nearly perfect circle. I then turned the other part to form the circular lower shelf and fixed both round pieces on a framework. After that, the whole lot had to be sandpapered to a smooth finish and stained to the required colour. Finally, the whole thing was French-polished, which produced a lovely varnished effect. All of that took a lot of time to do.

On 12 April, I paid our October to March six-monthly water rate bill of nineteen shillings to Staffordshire Potteries Water Board, in Albion Street. I've still got the bill and, like with the council rates, it shows that the account was still in Dad's name because I hadn't bothered altering that one either. The water board likewise believed that I was Mr W. H. Kent because they gave me a receipt in my father's name!

It was about then that Jeff got hold of a bottle of ink from the sideboard and drank it! Of course, Helen was very worried about it and rushed him along to see Grahame Jeffries, Vin and Eva's son, who was a policeman and still living at home. I suppose Helen thought he might have some medical knowledge through his job. Grahame assured her that Jeff would be alright and told her to keep giving him drinks of milk to flush the ink out of his body. So that's what Helen did and Jeff was okay.

About June, Jeff was given a small tricycle, which he loved, and we allowed him to ride along the pavement to Mawson Grove and back on his own, but he wasn't allowed out of sight. Helen watched him like a hawk to make sure he didn't turn into the road or get into any danger.

One day around that time, Nancy and Fred Cadman were going to Trentham Gardens with other members of their family and asked if they could take Jeff with them, as company for their young nephew, Keith Bennison. At first, Helen was rather apprehensive because Jeff hadn't been away from us at all before, except briefly, but she consented. While he was away, she was worrying about him, but I think he enjoyed himself.

Keith played with Jeff whenever he was brought to visit Nancy and Fred. Jeff had an imitation steering wheel, which he'd been given as a gift, and he loved playing with it. But Jeff had to let Keith play with the wheel and make do himself with an old tin lid, to keep Keith in a good mood when he came round!

About that time, Jeff was given a white tin horse, with grey spots, on wheels, which he sat on and pushed himself along. We got him a pretend jockey's cap to try to make it seem he was having a real horse ride, but I don't think he was interested in the toy for long because it didn't go very fast!

Leah and Sid had moved to 5 Trent Road (now called Acacia Grove), Knutton, and had a daughter, whom they'd named after Helen. Sometimes, we went to visit them. It was quite an adventure to get there because we had to walk to Stoke, catch a bus to Newcastle from there and then get another bus to Knutton.

On 22 September, there was a write-up in the *Sentinel* saying that experiments were taking place with artificial fog to see if it could be dispersed by spraying it with chemicals. The idea was supposed to be to find a way of getting rid of smogs, which could be very dense at times and even killed people, especially in the Great Smog in London in December 1952 when at least 4,000 had died. The experiments seemed rather fantastic to me, but stories were often blown up by newspapers, so I didn't know how true they really were. Of course, we still had peasoupers in Stoke from time to time, but the worst of the problem was solved by the 1956 Clean Air Act, which reduced the amount of dark smoke that was produced. As a result, the coal-fired bottle ovens started to disappear from the pottery factories and cleaner fuels were increasingly used to fire the kilns.

At that time, the Dunlop Rubber Company had a factory in London Road, Stoke, which had previously been Mintons' earthenware works. They made a model whale (which was supposed to have been 75-feet long and weighing twelve tons) from wood, rubber, asbestos and plaster for a new film, *Moby Dick*. On 29 October, there was a report that it had broken away from the boat that was towing it while it was being filmed in a rough sea off Strumble Head, near Fishguard, in Pembrokeshire, and it had been lost! Because of the danger to shipping, a warning was radioed, but the next day it was reported that the "whale" still hadn't been found. I can't remember hearing any more about it, but there was a model whale in the film, which came out in 1956 and starred Gregory Peck. I remember seeing it, at the pictures I think, but I can't recall how good it was.

At night, I used to take Jeff to bed because he preferred me, instead of Helen, to do it. I'd put him in bed and make sure he was comfortable, but most of the time he'd be wide awake and not ready to go to sleep. After I'd said goodnight to him, he'd often shout down sooner or later: 'Dad! Dad!' I'd go to the door at the bottom of the stairs and ask what he wanted. He'd say, 'Come tell me a story!' So I'd go up and read him one from a book or make one up, but he'd keep wanting more stories, so, after a while, I'd run out of ideas. Then I'd get into his bed and lie down beside him to try to settle him down, but on occasions I'd nod off myself!

After a while, Helen would come up, browned-off with being on her own. She'd nudge me and say: 'Come on! You're not stopping there all night, surely?' I'd have to wake myself up and, by then, it would be time for me to go to bed! Eventually, it all stopped because, when Jeff got older, he didn't want me there any more.

Helen took Jeff to see some clowns, who came to Lewis's, and the *Sentinel* took several photos of them with Jeff and a few other kids. We thought he may have been afraid of these funny men, one or two of whom were dwarfs, but he seemed happy enough, as the photos show.

There were still plenty of slums in Stoke-on-Trent at that time and the council was busy getting them knocked down and replacing them with new houses. It was announced that they'd built 2,502 modern homes during the year, the most that had ever been put up in that time. The chairman of the Housing Committee, Harold Clowes, said that there'd be a 'major attack' on the slums in the city the next year and the council was aiming to get rid of all of them by 1963. I suppose the old houses were habitable, but they looked bad from the outside because they were smoke-blackened. They were wearing out and the new ones were clean and had everything working. They had gardens and, I suppose, better facilities.

In January 1955, Stoke were involved in the longest FA Cup tie ever played in the competition proper, against Bury. The tie went to four replays and I wondered when it was going to end, but Tim Coleman scored the deciding goal for Stoke in the last minute of extra time in the fifth game, after they'd played for 9 hours 22 minutes in total! I don't think that I went to any of the games because Jeff was still quite young and I was helping Helen out with him.

One morning, going to work, I noticed something flash across my sight. I flicked my eyes from side to side and saw it was a spot, but I couldn't fix it in one place because it just drifted away. I was worried and went to see a doctor as soon as I could. He referred me to an optician, so I went to B. Newbold Ltd., at 27 Glebe Street, Stoke, one of four different practices which were then operating along that short road! An optician examined me and said the spot was a floater and not harmful, but that I needed glasses for close-up work and reading. I was relieved, although the spot was a nuisance and I didn't like the idea of having glasses because of vanity. I thought it was showing I was deteriorating, but I did wear them when needed from then on.

Jeff still bathed in his tin bath in front of the lounge fire, protected by a fireguard. We had no heating in the bathroom and Helen was afraid of him catching a cold if he had his bath there. Of course, we weren't the only ones in that situation because I knew no-one then who had any bathroom heating.

Helen had been complaining about a burning pain that she was having from time to time in her right groin and went to see Dr MacArthur about it. He couldn't find the cause of the problem and sent her to see Mr Edwards at the City General Hospital. He examined her in April, but also couldn't find anything wrong and told her that it wasn't something serious.

About Whit, we had a bus trip to Bagnall, to see what was up there, and found there was some countryside to look at. We had an enjoyable walk around and I took photos of Jeff looking very happy and excited watching some cows grazing. It was unusual to go out to such places and I rarely, if ever, heard anybody talking about having gone to the countryside. It was thought to be low key and that the seaside was superior, with many more facilities.

We also had a trip by train to Rudyard, which I knew from having camped nearby. The place was pretty popular then and had a small fairground and trips on boats. We went to the lake and had a walk through the fields, so that was another visit into the wild and I took a photo of Jeff getting over a stile for the first time!

With Wedgwood's factory being in the country, most of the workers used to travel there by train, from all over North Staffordshire. A national rail strike started on 29 May and all the regular trains stopped running, so Wedgwood's organized buses to get the workers to the factory. I got on one of them in Stoke. The strike ended on 14 June and things then went back to normal.

On 13 July, Ruth Ellis, a mother of two, was hanged at Holloway Prison in

London for murdering David Blakely, whom she'd been living with. She was the last woman to be executed in Britain. Hanging women didn't seem to be right because the idea was for men to protect women and give way to them, although that really shouldn't have stopped them facing the same penalties.

The short fence between our back yard and Bradbury's was very old and had gone rotten, so we decided to pull it down and share the cost of building a new wall of concrete blocks. I wanted to gain experience in laying them, so I suggested doing the job myself and the Bradburys agreed. In July, I went to Wain Bros, at 774 Leek Road, and ordered some concrete blocks, cement and sand, which they delivered. I had a spirit level, a trowel and the will. It took me two or three days to do the job, but I managed it and I was very pleased with the result. The wall is still standing!

As a present, Jeff was given a toy car, which he got in and pedalled around. It had a steering wheel and he had some fun in it, even though it was on the big side for our small back yard. The car was a replica of the real thing, with a big bonnet, and he kept it for quite a few years.

During the Wakes holiday in August, we travelled to Rhyl by train, I think for the day, to give Jeff a taste of the seaside. Except when I'd visited Rhyl as a lad with my parents, none of us had been to Wales before and it wasn't too far, so we thought we'd give it a try. The weather was okay and Jeff loved playing on the sands. I think it was on this trip that he went paddling in the sea and fell in the water. All his clothes were soaking wet, so we took them off and let them blow in the wind. They didn't dry quickly enough, so we went to a café and Helen asked the staff if they'd do some drying for us, which they kindly did. They hung his outer clothes on an oven, so the problem was more or less solved.

I was still varnishing our outside paintwork every year or two, to try to keep it in good condition and make sure it looked nice, and I did the job this particular year. I then creosoted our front fence, to help preserve it. That was a job I did every so often when it seemed that it needed doing.

We still had the lounge floor covered with linoleum, but with a square of carpet on top in the centre of the room. Lino also remained the covering in our bedrooms, with a small piece of carpet by the sides of the beds. That was to make the floor feel warmer to our feet when we got in and out of bed because we didn't wear slippers then. The carpet also made us seem a bit posher! I can't remember anyone at that time having a fitted carpet.

In the first week of November, we were given a day off from work, with no pay, of course, apparently because of a lack of orders. That was worrying and I was concerned that we were heading for a slump. Then, the following month, I became forty and that was a shock!

Helen had been having backache for a while when she was sitting down and went to see Dr Kerr about it on 20 December. He couldn't find anything wrong with her, but sent her to have an X-ray the following day at the Mass Radiography Centre, in Hartshill Road, which was next to The Limes Maternity Hospital. Nothing unusual was discovered through the X-ray, so she was sent to see a specialist, Mr A. Kennard Mitting, at his consulting room at 31 Quarry Avenue, Hartshill, on 18 January 1956. He found her to be in good general health and decided that she was suffering from a mild strain at most. He ordered her a support belt, but she mustn't have used it for long because I can't remember it and I think her back settled down again pretty quickly.

I can remember hearing *Rock Around the Clock*, by Bill Haley and His Comets, and it was a number one hit at the end of 1955 and the beginning of 1956. It had quite a swing to it, which I liked, and Haley was moderately dressed, so that was acceptable as well. Then Elvis Presley became successful and he changed music a lot. He wasn't nice and smooth like Bing Crosby; his music was quick tempo and seemed out to me at first, but it was okay when I got used to it. Some of his songs were catchy and you could sing along to them or tap your feet, so I accepted him as part of the growing-up stage for teenagers.

Rock and roll was something new, but it was crazy and I wondered what would happen with it. My generation had more or less copied the adults of the time, as normal, but, in the mid-1950s, teenagers were being led by the pop stars and started doing all kinds of unusual things. Some of them became teddy boys and dressed peculiarly. They had quite a lot of publicity and I read in the newspapers that they were behaving differently to older people, but it didn't bother me a lot. I can only remember seeing a teddy boy once, in Hanley, and he was an oddly-dressed teenager. But, like rock and roll, the fashion was just one of those things that came along and then disappeared.

One day, Helen found some droppings and we concluded we had a mouse in the house. We were concerned in case it ran over Jeff's face in the night and, of course, we didn't like the idea that it might run over us too! We decided it must be caught, but ruled out traps in case they proved messy. So I bought a sticky substance in a tube and spread it on some paper, which I placed under our bed. Nothing happened for a few nights, but then one morning we saw the little blighter stuck on the paper by its legs. I dispatched it, although I can't remember how, and I've never seen any more in the house since.

I began to do more DIY and, in March and April 1956, I nailed board panels onto most of the doors in our house and replaced our old-fashioned door knobs with modern handles. I then painted the doors cream, which made them seem much brighter than they had in the brown imitation grain stain that we'd had previously, although that had been more successful in hiding the dirt! Finally, I boxed in, with wood and hardboard, two lots of exposed piping and painted that cream too.

On Saturday 28 April, Young Harry was given a run out at right-half in Port Vale's first team at home to Middlesbrough. We all went on the bus to see him and stood on the Hamil End, probably because it was the first part of the ground we came to. I don't think I'd been to Vale Park before and we didn't know our way around. Vale won 3-2 and Harry did okay, although I suppose Jeff thought it was all wonderful. I think that was the first time I'd ever seen Harry play. We went frequently after that because he became a regular in the team. He was a good player, but perhaps wasn't aggressive enough and I never gave it a thought that he'd end up playing 498 competitive first-team games for Vale! I was still a Stoke supporter and went to Vale mainly because Helen and Jeff wanted to see Harry play. So, for quite a while, we went to Vale one week and Stoke the next, like many people did then.

Harry was given a number of free tickets to the matches by Vale and he gave them to Vera and Big Harry to dish out. We sometimes got some, but there weren't always enough for the whole family. Elijah and Uncle Bill also used to go regularly and I once remember Helen complaining that Uncle Bill had got a ticket when we hadn't.

Eva and Vin Jeffries acquired a car, a black Ford Popular. Vin had driven many years previously, before driving tests were introduced, and had held a driving licence, but had let it lapse. When he applied for a new one, he was told he was still entitled to drive without having a test. But, by then, he was very rusty and Swinnerton's got one of their drivers to give him some lessons.

By about Whit, he felt confident enough to ask us if we'd like to go for a ride. We got to Newcastle, went down Brook Lane and stopped at a junction, to turn right into Friarswood Road. But then we started rolling backwards and there was a bump! Vin had hit the car behind. Eva asked him for a ten-shilling note, got out of the car and took command of the situation. She marched to the other car, thrust the note into the hand of the driver and said, 'That should take care of the damage!' Vin then drove off before the other fellow could say anything. We carried on towards Shrewsbury, but, just past the crossroads at Ternhill, the car broke down. We were there many a while before help came, I think from a garage. While we waited, we were supplied with refreshments by the occupants of the cottage where we'd ground to a halt and we had our photos taken there!

Another time, Vin gave us a run out to Rudyard. We parked up by the hotel, so we could have a wander round, and there came across Reuben, my old foreman from Mintons. I said hello, but he didn't seem very pleased to see me and hardly spoke!

I wasn't very thrilled with Vin's driving because it was erratic and he got too close when he was passing cars coming from the opposite direction, so I made excuses and avoided going out with him whenever I could. What made it worse was that Eva often panicked and screamed at him, which upset him and made him nervous, but Helen and Jeff continued to have an occasional ride with them.

In May, the management at Wedgwood's told us workers in the earthenware department that we were to work four days a week because of a lack of orders. That was worrying and I wondered whether there'd be sackings if things got worse. There was no redundancy pay then, so it was possible that I'd be without wages. We'd already booked up a summer holiday, for a week in Prestatyn, in North Wales, because we thought Jeff was by then old enough to appreciate it, and we decided to carry on with it.

I decided to buy a new camera because the blue box one I had had become old-fashioned. I decided to go to Stan's shop in Vale Street to give him some business. He wasn't there, but his assistant showed me a number of models and I settled for another box camera, a Kodak Duaflex. It was black, with a chrome stripe each side of the viewfinder and looked better. It took a square picture, as against the oblong one of my old camera. It also had a different type of viewfinder, which you looked down into, but the end result seemed no better, though I've still got it!

Around that time, the Halfpennys moved to 13a Boughey Road. The new owner of number 337, Joseph Hammond, was an awkward customer, not only with Helen and me, but also with Jeff. He was a bighead and one day, when his grid was overflowing, he just tipped the muck in our grid without asking. I saw him doing it and had a word with him. He said: 'Your manhole's on my land!' But it had been there before he arrived and since the houses had been built!

I put some sand on our back yard and Jeff used it to make roads for his toy cars. He played there for hours with them. Sometimes, his friends, Keith Bennison and Stephen Cooke, a little lad from 7 Egerton Street, joined him and helped to push the matchbox-size vehicles about.

On Saturday 4 August, we walked to Stoke Station to get a train to Prestatyn for our holiday and I carried our luggage, which was a strain. We'd decided to go to Prestatyn because it was quieter than Rhyl and there was plenty of sand for Jeff to play on. On the first day of the Wakes holiday each year, Stoke Station was very busy, with big queues forming, and a lot of extra trains were put on to take people to their destinations. Most of the holiday-makers went to the Blackpool area or the North Wales coast and would be asking the porters all kinds of questions about the trains and their destinations. We already had our tickets, but the queue was right onto Station Road. Just before our train came in, we were let onto our platform. The train pulled in slowly and there was near chaos, as men grabbed the handles of the coaches and tried to get their families and suitcases aboard.

On the journey, we made a mental note of each station as we went through it and Jeff was very interested. After we'd arrived at Prestatyn, we made our way to Clevedon, 2 Seven Sisters Road, the house where we were staying, which was just over the main road to Rhyl. We stayed "apartments" and paid for the use of our bedroom and the cooking of our food, which we brought in. It was cheaper than going full board and it wasn't much trouble to get our food.

When we'd dumped our luggage, we went down to the beach with a bucket and spade. There was hardly anyone there and so we had a huge amount of sand to ourselves, although it was cool and there was some rain. There was no promenade on the sea front then, just a track.

Near the main crossroads was a cycle hire place and Jeff had a go on their tricycles every day. Sometimes, the man in charge would let him have a free ride, which Jeff also had on occasions when the fellow was missing!

About a mile along the front was Ffrith Beach, behind which there were some entertainments. We spent quite some time there and Jeff particularly liked the miniature electric railway, on which ran imitation engines and cars that he went on. Also, I took him on a rowing boat on the small lake, although Helen didn't like it because she was afraid we'd fall in and drown. We had a few rounds of miniature golf and Jeff had a number of rides on the donkeys on the beach, wearing a cowboy hat we'd bought him, which he wore most of the time on the holiday. Of course, he liked the big, fluffy, pink candyfloss, which was made of sugar and processed by a machine.

One day, we were walking along the main road to Ffrith when Jeff complained about itching. Helen had a look at him and found he'd got a rash all over his body, so we took him to see a doctor. He said that the rash had been caused by insect bites and gave him something for it, which did the trick. Jeff had been fiddling about in bushes with caterpillars, so I suppose they must have caused the problem.

Another day, we walked up the hill at the back of the town, which had a lovely view to the sea, and came across an old comrade from the 3rd Mountain Regiment, I think named George. He was in a wheelchair after having had an accident. He'd worked on the railways and had been standing in for a mate when he was struck by an engine. We arranged to meet him and his wife later on, but they didn't turn up.

On spare ground, we found some rather broken-down vehicles, which had been used in a parade, for comic effect. They weren't laid out for tourists. They were stored there and had slogans painted all over them. One read: '$1,000 FOR THE JAMES BOYS, FRANK & JESSIE . . . . . DEAD OR ALIVE.' I took a photo of Jeff peeping round a corner of the vehicle, with his toy gun and, of course, wearing his cowboy hat. I also photographed Helen and Jeff sitting in another of the cars, daubed with the catch phrases: 'CROCKY'S CROK', 'WELLS FARGO' and 'US MAIL'. But then a fellow, perhaps the owner, came along and told them to get out of the car in case they damaged it. The car was a wreck already, but, when we protested, he was adamant and so they got out.

We didn't get round to doing any paddling because the weather was too cool. In fact, we got fed up with it being wet and having to wear our raincoats, so we travelled home a day earlier than we should have done.

We were still on short time at work and there didn't seem to be any end to it. I was worried about redundancy because I was one of the last in and therefore one of the first out, I thought. I heard that one of the turners, Harry Lewis, was leaving. I asked him where he was going and he told me that he'd got a job as a postman. I was interested and asked him for details. He said I'd have to visit the dole office in Cannon Street to get a form, which had to be filled in and returned to the people there. But he told me he'd had to wait months before he'd finally got the job. When I got home that night, I discussed what I'd heard with Helen and she didn't object to me changing jobs, so, at the earliest opportunity, I went to the dole, got the form, filled it in and returned it.

At the beginning of September, Jeff started going to school. Helen took him to Cauldon County Infants' School, in Cauldon Road, the first day and left him to the mercies of the teachers. She was very upset when she left because she and Jeff had hardly ever been parted before, but, of course, she didn't let him see her worried face. She collected him at dinner time and took him home for a meal before returning him to the school for his afternoon classes.

Jeff's first teacher, Miss Tunstall, was nice, according to Helen, but she thought the head teacher, Miss Hancock, wasn't so nice. One time, while standing at assembly, Jeff went pale and Miss Hancock told Helen she should take him to the doctor as there was something wrong with him. Helen was worried to death, but Dr MacArthur looked him over and said he was a normal healthy lad. Helen questioned Jeff and it came out that he was frightened of Miss Hancock. The next day, Helen went to see her and told her what the doctor had said and that, if she stopped staring at Jeff, he'd be alright. There was no more trouble over the matter after that.

One night, there was an advertisement in the *Sentinel* from Taylor Tunnicliff, requiring electrical porcelain turners. I decided to apply, so I had time off work, without pay, of course, and went along to the factory. When I arrived there, I found they had a personnel officer, which was a new idea then. It was a woman and her office was in the old tea-making room. She told me that there was a new boss of the clay department, Louis Page, who, in the past, had been in the progress department, which spurred on the orders through the various manufacturing shops. Anyway, I got the job.

The next day, I gave Wedgwood's a month's notice and Mr Lawton came to ask why I was leaving. I told him it was because I feared redundancies. He said there weren't going to be any and I could go back when the orders improved. I was sorry to be leaving because it was the best firm I'd worked for and I wasn't looking forward to going to Taylor's.

When I walked into my old turning shop on my first morning, my heart sank! Even though I'd worked there before, for a good many years, what I saw shocked me. I was looking at a dirty pig hole, with clay dust lying everywhere. I felt like doing an about-turn and going back home, but I had to earn a living to keep my wife and youngster, so I went back to my old bench and did my best to settle down. Stewart Flackett was still there, in the same place he'd been when I'd left to go to Mintons, so at least it was nice to have a friendly face next to me.

My first week's wages, paid on 5 October, were £9 9s. 5d., compared with my final week's pay of £10 3s. 10d. from Wedgwood's, on 28 September. That meant I was getting less from my new job than I had been from my old one with a day off! But it wasn't all bad news because I didn't have to get up so early to catch a train, I didn't have to pay travelling costs and I could go home for dinner. Taylor's, however, was a depressing place to work.

About that time, we couldn't get Jeff to eat much, so, to encourage him, we sometimes invited his friend, Stephen Cooke, to dinner. Stephen was a good eater and soon ate the cooked meals that Helen put in front of him, but Jeff didn't seem too impressed. Also, Helen and I had to peel tinned peas before Jeff would eat them! Eventually, nature took its course and he got hungry, so it all came right.

One day, I took Jeff for a walk in Hanley Park. When we were by the lake, in the Avenue Road area, he dashed off into some bushes behind the shelter that was there. I didn't want to let him out of my sight in case he fell in the water, so I rushed after him, but tore my best, expensive, long gabardine coat on something. I was in trouble with Helen when I got back because I didn't have another decent coat to put on. So we took it to a woman in Hanley, I think at Vera Dry Cleaners, at 9 Stafford Lane, who did invisible darning. She charged a pound an inch and measured the tear as just over that, but she did the repair for that sum. I continued to wear the coat for many years and only finally threw it away when the fashion changed and shorter coats became the ones to have.

When the Suez Crisis broke out at the end of October, I hoped it wouldn't go too far because I didn't know if I was in the reserve, so I was worried I might have to go back in the army. The crisis came about because Gamal Abdel Nasser, the president of Egypt, nationalized the Suez Canal as it was on their land. We were partners with the French and said no to that because it would affect our ships passing through the canal to and from the Far East. We started threatening the Egyptians, but they wouldn't give up, so, on 29 October, we dropped paratroopers and landed commandos to try to take control of the canal. The Egyptians fought back and then the Yanks told us to get out or else they'd make us suffer. So we and the French pulled out and I was happy with that because I might have been sent there myself if we'd got bogged down.

In my woodwork class, I was working on a china cabinet for Vera when a *Sentinel* photographer came along and took a picture of me and some of my classmates with it. It was supposed to be to advertise the facilities through the paper. When I finished the cabinet, Big Harry and Young Harry helped me to carry it all the way to their house in Holdcroft Road because we didn't know anyone who could have transported it for us!

Helen and I decided to have our bathroom walls tiled because they'd be more resistant to damp and it would save us from decorating them. We got W. H. Condliffe, of 19 Camp Road, Smallthorne, to do the job in December and Helen chose the tiles, which were mainly yellow, with some green strips. Mr Condliffe did a very nice job at a cost of £26 8s. 10d.

Helen was still going to Shelton Church on Sunday evenings, but one night, when she was on the way, a man exposed himself to her in Ridgway Road, just at the top of Mawson Grove. She was frightened and knocked on the front door of a house. The fellow had gone by then, but the owners came out and walked her back home anyway. She stopped going to the church after that and instead transferred to the nearby Railway Mission.

Jeff's main Christmas present was an electric train set. I bought two engines, some coaches and trucks and track to make a loop, a spur and two sidings. One of the locomotives was a main-line engine, which we named Jack, and the other, Sam, was a shunter. I made a board to fit it all on, along with a station, a signal box, a footbridge, a tunnel and a level crossing. The trouble was that the layout took up such a lot of room in the lounge that we could hardly move around and the chairs had to be away from the open fire, so that, when we sat down, we were half-frozen. Also, when it wasn't in use, I had to lean it against a wall. We kept it for about seven years, but Jeff wasn't all that bothered about it and there was a limit to what we could do with it. So we sold it to a neighbour, Nate Copeland, of number 358, for one of his nephews.

On 9 January 1957, Anthony Eden, who'd led us into the Suez mess, resigned as the prime minister and was replaced the next day by Harold Macmillan. It didn't mean much to me, but, six months later, Macmillan said most of the people had 'never had it so good'. I don't think the people were doing too well and, as a potter, I wasn't living in luxury!

In February, Jack Green gave Jeff a cocker spaniel pup, from a litter his bitch had had. The pup was a thoroughbred, with a certificate to prove it. She was a lovely dog and we called her Judy. We'd have liked a male, like most people in those days, but Jack was able to get more money when he sold them. Jeff used to tease Judy and was a bit cruel to her, doing some things like lifting her up by a leg, but she didn't bite. He did it because he liked her and didn't realize it was bad to do that. I told him off, but the idea didn't seem to register.

Judy proved to be a nuisance because she liked to rip things up and chew them. The last straw came after a few months when, in the night, she ripped to pieces the leatherette covering on an armchair. We decided to get rid of her and got put in touch with Mary Stonier, who lived at 575 Leek Road, opposite All Saints Church, and was willing to take her. I told Jeff that Judy had got to go because she was doing damage and he was being peevish with her, but he wasn't too upset at losing his pup. Mary kept Judy for a good many years, I suppose until the dog died, but she also had trouble with Judy ripping things up.

Unfortunately, Leah developed rheumatic fever, which caused serious heart trouble, so that an operation was essential. But she and Sid had got involved with the Jehovah's Witnesses, who had a taboo about the spilling of blood. So Leah and Sid were opposed to surgery, but were eventually persuaded to go against their religious convictions. Leah then had the operation at the City General. It was successful, but her lungs couldn't stand the strain and she died on 26 March. It was a shock because I'd expected her to get through alright. Helen was devastated. She and Leah were pretty close.

While out walking with Jeff one day in Leek Road, we came across a man selling pin-on flags for charity. I bought one for Jeff, who thought it was a great idea, and pinned it on him. A little further along the road, he noticed the flag was missing and it really upset him, so I took him back to buy another one. When the seller heard the story of the missing flag, he gave Jeff a free one, much to his delight!

I'd still not heard anything from the Post Office regarding my job application, so I went to the dole office and they told me they'd forwarded my details. A few more weeks went by and then I received a letter from the Post Office, asking me to go for a medical. I think it was held in a building in Winton Square, opposite Stoke Station. A doctor examined me and said he'd send his conclusions to the Post Office. Later, I got another letter from them, asking me to go for an aptitude test in the rear of South Wolfe Street Post Office, in Stoke, on 23 May.

I went along, looking tidy, but there were three other fellows there, who were dressed up like business executives! We were given books filled with diagrams, of shapes and similar things, and an answer sheet. We had to choose the correct diagram from a group of about four for each answer. We worked for about an hour and then handed in our answer sheets. They were checked while we waited and then an official called my name and told me to wait on one side. I was disappointed, thinking I'd failed, but he told the other three fellows that he was sorry, but they hadn't passed the test. I was pleased I'd got through, but it seemed incredible that three out of four hadn't passed! I was then told that the Post Office would get in touch with me.

That year, Helen decided to change the colour of the paintwork on the outside of our house and chose black and white. I was the fellow to do the job. It took quite a long while because I had to do a bit at a time to fit it in around work.

I was still attending my woodwork class, but, when the term ended, I told Mr Hughes and one or two workmates that I might be unable to continue in the autumn because I'd be working shifts if I'd started on the post by then. I was sad about that because it was nice to be able to make things.

I got a letter from the Post Office, asking me to start work as a temporary postman on 5 August. That was when I'd be on my potters' holidays, so I wrote and asked if I could begin the week after and they said that was okay. I then gave Taylor Tunnicliff a month's notice that I was quitting.

I'd heard that smoking was prohibited whilst at work in the Post Office, so I thought that this was a good opportunity to try to give up the habit. I was getting through fifteen to twenty fags (Woodbines, I think) a day. That was quite expensive, especially as the wages of a postman were less than those of a turner. So one day, a week or two before I began my new job, I stopped smoking, but I didn't tell anyone, not even Helen, what I was doing. I thought I'd see how things turned out and, if I failed, no-one would be the wiser. I got through the first day alright and managed the second one too. There was a certain amount of craving for the weed, but I resisted it.

On the third day, Helen noticed that I wasn't smoking and asked if I'd given up. I couldn't be confident I had, so I just told her that I'd abstained for three days. Helen was still smoking, so I suppose she had something to ponder. I kept up the good work and never smoked another cigarette. I felt better for it. I used to cough quite a bit, even in the middle of the night, but the coughing eased off and stopped altogether after perhaps a month or two.

On 2 August, at the end of my last week with Taylor Tunnicliff, I collected my final wages, £11 1s. 11d., and I was very pleased when I left, but I had some doubt as to whether I'd done the right thing. The following day, Helen, Jeff and I went on holiday to Prestatyn for a week. Having been the previous year, we knew the ropes, so most of the time was again spent there and at Ffrith, with Jeff playing on the sands and going on rides.

One day, while we were there, we visited Rhyl and watched a Punch and Judy show. It was alright until Punch started hitting Judy with his club, but then Jeff got really upset. He must have thought it was real. We tried to explain to him what was happening, but he couldn't understand, so we took him away and he settled down after a minute or two.

While I was on holiday, I wondered how my life would change by going on the Post Office. It was a big change and I was a bit nervous. It would be a different way of life with different hours and I didn't know how I'd get on with the rest of the fellows. I wasn't sure I'd made the right decision and I had my wife and child to think about. But having been in the army, in the open air, had made me unsettled and, as it turned out, I never regretted having left the pottery industry.

8 Pounding The Pavements

At 9 a.m. on Monday 12 August 1957, I reported to the counter of the Station Road Post Office, to start my new job. The sorting of mail in and out of Stoke-on-Trent was done in the same building, adjoining the railway track. I was directed to a room behind the counter, where there were two other budding postmen, Jeff Trigg and Frank Pepper. After a while, a young assistant inspector came to us and gave us some forms to study and sign. One of them concerned the Official Secrets Acts, to which we'd be bound for the rest of our lives. It said that we weren't supposed to give any information out about the Post Office without permission, otherwise we'd face prosecution. Of course, if we hadn't signed, there would have been no job. Another form was to do with national insurance and sick pay and I was amazed to discover that I'd become a civil servant, even though I was only a lowly postman!

Afterwards, we were handed over to a postman, who instructed us on a few jobs we were to do. He then took us to the main office, to a big bench called a facing table. By the side of it were a number of sacks of mail. We were told to empty them onto the table and to turn them inside out, which made sure that no items of mail remained in them. They were then folded up, ready to be used again.

The letters were divided into four separate piles, consisting of fully-paid items of ordinary mail and printed papers (for example, newspapers, bills and greeting cards), which were charged at a cheaper rate. The fully-paid items usually went out first delivery and the printed papers on the second (except at Christmas when the mail was delivered as it came in). Both types were divided into small and large items. Other things, such as packets, extra-large letters and thick letters, were put on a moving belt, which took them to another table, where a postman cancelled the stamps with a rubber hand stamp. While he was doing that, he pulled out items without a stamp and those insufficiently paid for.

The letters had to be faced, which meant the stamps all had to face the same way, so that they could be pushed through a machine which cancelled them. I thought everybody in the world knew that postage stamps were supposed to be affixed on the top right of letters. Yet, on occasions, I found stamps attached on the other corners, in the centre and even on the back! Such items were put out to be dealt with individually. This facing job was a bore, but we could talk while we did it. Later, some postmen came and started sorting the cancelled letters from the main sorting tables into pigeonholes. At about 5 p.m., we were allowed to go home. By that time, there was a big build-up of postmen, who'd come to work at a very busy period of the day, when most of the collections had arrived. So that was the main sorting period and there was a mad rush trying to get stuff for outside areas on the mail trains.

The three of us continued to concentrate on facing for most of the rest of the week, but it was surprising to see how many jobs there were to be done from the collection of the mail to the final delivery. We also had a try at letter sorting, under the tuition of the postman looking after us. A letter-sorting frame or fitting consisted of 48 pigeonholes and there were large numbers of these frames, back to back in a very big room.

On primary sorting, those towns which had a lot of mail from Stoke-on-Trent (such as Birmingham, Manchester and Crewe) had a pigeonhole to themselves in each frame. The mail for these towns was then sent straight off to them. Whole areas, like Scotland, Wales, the Midlands, the Southeast and overseas, also had a pigeonhole each in every frame, as did the six different areas of North Staffordshire. These were Stoke, Rural, Hanley, Longton, Burslem (which also delivered to Tunstall) and Newcastle. The mail for the last four was then sent to their main depots for further sorting. The Hanley pigeonholes included mail for Milton, Abbey Hulton, Bucknall and Bentilee and the Stoke one incorporated that for Fenton.

Then came secondary sorting. Postmen would take the contents of the pigeonholes for the areas outside North Staffordshire and sort them back into the 48 holes of the frames, now relabelled for the purpose and representing the different towns and districts of each area. Their mail would then be sent to those places for further sorting. The same thing happened with the North Staffordshire Rural mail, which was then dispatched to towns like Leek, Cheadle and Kidsgrove and many villages with their own post offices, such as Froghall.

The Stoke mail was secondary sorted into forty or so different "walks" or delivery areas. Again, the pigeonholes were used and a few of them in each frame were utilized for big firms, like Michelin, which had more mail than some towns! The mail for each of these walks then had to be further sorted into streets, house numbers and large companies and that was done by the individual postmen carrying out the actual deliveries.

At the office, there were also a bag officer, who supplied the sacks and sent the empty ones for cleaning; a printer, who printed destination address labels (which were tied onto the bags with string and a lead seal); an assistant to the inspector, who made out the weekly duties; a man who mended the bikes, used for deliveries in rural areas, and a fellow who sorted out coins from the telephone booths. It was a very complex business.

On the Friday, I collected my first week's wages, which were paid in cash, like those at the pot banks. My pay was £7 15s. (less £1 8s. tax), which was over £3 down from the last wages I'd received from Taylor Tunnicliff. However, the Post Office calculated the postmen's pay due from working Friday to Thursday each week, so I'd done a short week and my Friday pay was put into my next wages.

The same day, the next week's duties came up on the notice board. I was down for the number seventeen (Bucknall New Road) walk in Hanley, along with another fellow, Frank Machin, who'd be giving me tuition. I was told to look in the duty book, where the details of this were printed. It was essential to check the book from time to time because it stated what you were supposed to do, the hours of attendance and the office you should go to. I saw that I'd be starting work at the unearthly time of 5.30 a.m. at the Regent Road office, in Hanley.

On the Sunday night, I went to bed about 9 p.m. because I wanted to get up at 4.30 a.m. to have a wash, a shave and some breakfast. It was a bind to get up, but I managed it and made my way to the office. I didn't meet a soul on the way! I reported to an inspector and was told to sign in on a sheet. That was different to the pot banks, where I'd clocked in. I was told to sort my letters out from number eight fitting. I was surprised because I'd thought postmen just picked up a bag full of letters and went out and delivered them. I hadn't realized that I had to sort them first!

The sorting table in front of the fitting's pigeonholes was piled high with hundreds of letters, small on one side and big on the other. I stood there, wondering how to start, when Frank came along and introduced himself. All around, there was a hive of activity because there was a deadline to be met. The postmen had to catch a van at about 7 a.m. to take them to the start of the delivery.

On each pigeonhole were written the name of a street and the numbers of its houses (or part of the numbers if it was a long road) or the name of a factory or a large shop. The small letters had to be sorted first to prevent the big ones from hiding the names on the pigeonholes. Frank picked up a handful and started sorting them at a steady pace. I followed suit, but had trouble in trying to find the correct pigeonhole for the first one! After a while, Frank told me where to put the letter. I kept struggling along, but managed to get a few letters in their holes. Frank waded through and sorted them all up, with only a little help from me. This process was called "throwing out" the mail.

I thought that was the job done, but he then told me to go and get the packets, which were in one of the bags hooked on a packet-sorting frame. These frames stood the other way up from the letter ones and had bigger holes to fit hanging bags. I unhooked our walk bag and dragged it to Frank, who emptied it onto the sorting table. We sorted these packets up and then we were ready to "pick up". That meant putting the letters in the correct order so they could be delivered from the top of a bundle as the postman walked along. Bulky packets couldn't be included in a bundle of letters, so these were placed loose in the carrying pouch, the bag with mail, which was carried over the shoulder. To remind the postman that he had a packet for a certain address, he'd turn the preceding letter upside down or back to front.

Frank sat down at the sorting table and started to pick up. He gave me some letters for a street and told me to put the numbers small to big, or big to small, depending on which side of the road we'd be walking. We'd also cross the numbers, either side of a street, if we'd be walking down it one way and not coming back up.

Each of the 48 pigeonholes had to be gone through like that and then the mail tied up in manageable bundles with string and put in a pouch, so that the first bundles to be delivered were on top. There was so much mail that day that we had to have a second pouch. We then "bagged off", which meant that we'd completed putting our mail into the delivery pouches. We put on our jackets, grabbed a pouch each and got in the back of a van, which was to take us to Hanley. There were several other postmen in the van with us. Some of them stood up and others sat on the dirty floor. It was just like a cattle truck.

It was just before 7 a.m. when the van set off. It was really dangerous because the drivers swerved round the corners, so that the vans nearly went over, and I always sat down whenever I could. We were taken to the head office in Tontine Street, where everybody got out. Frank and I made our way to Goodson Street, which at that time ran right through to Huntbach Street. Frank gave me the first pouch we were delivering from because the idea was for me to get the feel of things, so he instructed me and I did the deliveries. I tried the pouch in the right-hand position even though I was left-handed. That meant I put the pouch on my left shoulder, held the letters in my left hand and pushed them in the letter boxes with my right hand. That method was awkward for me, but I persevered and mastered it.

My first letter was to the Woodman pub on the corner with Old Hall Street. Next to the pub was the Capitol cinema, which was later demolished. I delivered to two or three streets and then we came to Bucknall New Road. With Frank's guidance, I did the delivery there and then down Bucknall Road. We turned right into Leek Road and I did one or two properties by the corner. We then turned round, crossed Bucknall Road and I did Leek Road as far as Cromer Road, which was next. We went up to the canal bridge, then turned back and did Royden Avenue before continuing along Leek Road to the railway bridge in Abbey Hulton.

Then, about ten, we caught a bus to Hanley and walked back down to the office in Regent Road. At that time, we had to pay our own bus fares and then claim them back. Frank told me that the walk we'd just completed was an easy one and I thought he was kidding, but I found out later that he was right! We deposited our "dead letters" in a box. These were undeliverable, with incomplete or wrong addresses, and, if possible, were returned to the senders by the "dead letter man", who only seemed to do that one job and cleared the box every day.

Frank and I then went to have a half-hour meal break. There was no canteen, so I took sandwiches. The water for our tea was boiled by Sam, the cleaner, in huge kettles. If there was a rush of postmen, the kettles would soon empty and the next lot of men would have to wait ages for the water to boil again. In the meanwhile, their break time was running out.

There were about four cubicles in the toilet and one of them was reserved for the inspector in charge! He also had a separate place to have his meals, so there was some class distinction then.

After our break, we went back to the sorting table, where Frank told me to grab the mail that had been sorted into our second delivery walk and start throwing it out. The trouble was that this walk was number thirteen (Hope Street) and therefore different from that of the first delivery. So I was again very slow in getting letters into their pigeonholes. Frank joined me and then I got the packets from the bag and went to see if there were any registered or surcharged items for us in the "registered locker". Surcharged items were letters without stamps or with insufficient postage and they were charged at double the usual price. We had to sign for the registered mail and fork out the money for the surcharged items from our own pockets and get it back off the customers!

Usually, there were fewer letters on the second delivery, but more packets because most of the shops and factories weren't open to receive them on the first delivery. At that time, practically all football coupons were posted to home addresses. These had to be done on the second deliveries because they weren't all that important, but they had to be completed by Wednesday each week to give people time to fill them in and post them back. That involved us in a lot of work and we were allowed to book overtime if we exceeded our normal hours.

At about 10.30, when we'd thrown out, picked up and bagged off, we caught the van to the head office again and then walked along to Hope Street, where I commenced our delivery under Frank's supervision. I then delivered to Vale Place and moved on to Waterloo Road and the Portland Street area. There, I was on familiar ground, having lived in the vicinity for many years. We then came to Mulgrave Street, Derwent Street, where I'd been born, and Windermere Street, where I'd lived for many years, and it felt strange to be back there. I did the streets on the other side of Waterloo Road up to our limit at Cobridge traffic lights, the other side of which was in the Burslem delivery area. After I'd delivered all our mail, we got a bus to Hanley and then walked back to the office, where we signed off. We could finish for the day whenever we'd completed our job and that was usually about one o'clock, but this first day it was obviously later.

I had three days' tuition from Frank on those two walks and the second half of the week (including the Saturday morning) I was tutored on two other walks: number five (Lichfield Street) and number ten (Tontine Street). The starting time was the same and I reported to number five fitting, where there was a young postman, Dai Lewis, waiting to give me tuition. He knew a lot more about the job than I did, yet he was getting less pay for teaching me how to do it! Postmen then received yearly increments up to the age of 35, but not beyond. I was 41 and I started off at one increment less than the maximum.

Dai was quick at his job and he soon got our walk bundled and bagged off. We caught a van to the corner of Regent Road and Lichfield Street. Under Dai's supervision, I delivered up the latter to the top and then back down again until we reached Derby Street. We continued down Lichfield Street, doing both sides, until we got to the junction with Leek Road. There we turned left and covered the whole of Eastwood and Joiner's Square, including the council houses, called the "Free State" because they were supposedly mainly inhabited by Irish people. We then crossed Lichfield Street and I delivered along Leek Road as far as the terraced houses before Remploy. I finished off by doing Warrington Road and Egerton Street and we then walked back to the office for our meal break and to do our second delivery sorting.

Our second walk covered part of the centre of Hanley. There was a lot of mail, so we had two pouches and carried one each. We got a van to the head office and I delivered along Tontine Street. Next came Upper Market Square and Market Square and then Lamb Street, which included the classy department store of M. Huntbach & Co. Ltd., located where Primark is now. Huntbach's had a lot of mail, as did Lewis's. Then I delivered to the nice little shops in Lewis's Arcade (as the old City Arcade had become named). Unfortunately, it was later demolished to make way for a new Lewis's store. After that, we walked up Hillchurch Street and did some of the roads off, including St. John Street.

We did the same walks on the following two days, but, on the Saturday, it was hard going delivering in the centre of Hanley because there were crowds of people doing their weekend shopping, so we had to push our way through. The finishing time was about two, so, when I was going to a football match, I had to get a move on. For all my efforts that week, I was paid £9 6s. plus 1s. tax rebate.

The following week, I was down to deliver walks seventeen and thirteen on my own and I was apprehensive about it. On the Monday morning, I was very slow in sorting my mail and found it wasn't straightforward. Some of the mail wasn't for my walk, but had been put in as a guess by postmen doing secondary sorting, who hadn't been sure where it belonged. Dealing with that wasn't a problem for experienced postmen because they'd usually know where to reallocate it, but I was running around in circles, trying to find out which walk the letters were for.

Also, some of my letters didn't have a house number on them and others didn't even have a street marked, so I had to chase round to try to find someone who knew. All that took time and some of the postmen got irritated if I bothered them too much.

If nobody could identify the delivery address of a letter, you could "kill it off" by writing 'Not known' on it, initialling it and placing it in the "dead box". The same applied when people no longer lived at an address and 'Gone away' would be written on it. Then there was mail that had to be redirected to some other address. If you tried to take these mis-sorts back to the sorting frames, the inspectors didn't like it because they expected you to take it to the postman concerned.

Even though somebody gave me a hand, the van had gone by the time I'd picked up. When I'd finally bagged off, I was alone in the office, so had to walk to Hanley to start my delivery. I did it slowly, not wanting to make mistakes, and naturally was late getting back for my break, so I was only able to squeeze in ten minutes. Even then, by the time I got to my walk fitting, the other fellows were nearly ready to go out on their second deliveries!

When I'd sorted up and bagged off for my second delivery, I had to walk to Hope Street and then made steady progress. I was again late back in the office, but I wasn't bothered as long as I kept my job. My performance slowly improved during the week and I was pleased to be visiting Windermere Street again.

The following week, I did walks five and ten and, when I came along Leek Road, Helen was at home looking out for me and waved through the window. The next week, I was on parcel duty at the Station Road office from about 2 p.m. till around 10, on the "afternoon" shift.

That became my regular rotation: two weeks of "days" (from approximately 5.30 a.m. to about 1 p.m.) in Hanley and a week of "afternoons" in Stoke. There were also "nights", which had shorter hours and therefore had fellows queuing up to do them, but I only did them once or twice because I didn't fancy them. Also, Helen didn't want to be left on her own.

The Station Road parcel office was situated next to the letter office and had metal sorting frames, about three feet high, laid on the floor. From every compartment in each frame, parcel bags large enough to hold a man were suspended by four hooks. Just outside the door was a bay, which could, at a push, accommodate three vans. They kept backing into the bay, with the help of the traffic officer, and postmen drivers emptied their collected letters and parcels, ready for sorting. The parcels were put in large wicker baskets on four wheels and pushed into the office. There, a postman higher grade (an experienced and better-paid fellow) threw the local parcels onto a pile, to be further sorted. He sorted the ones going out of the area into the different bags, according to their destinations. Several of us tied up the bags when they were full, added labels with their destinations on and dragged them along the floor to an assembly room, where a postman named Jimmy Green lifted them onto a large flat truck. When it was full, he and one or two other postmen wheeled it onto the station platform, ready for loading onto passing trains.

From about the middle of September, I had to work one Sunday in about every four, from 5.15 p.m. to 7.45. This duty, number eighteen, was compulsory, but it helped to boost my wages because it was paid at time and a half and amounted to 14s. 10d. I went in after the last collection of the day, with one or two other postmen, to help sort out the mail ready for the next morning.

About that time, I started to take Jeff short runs on buses and trains at weekends and he became keen on the Loop Line, which ran through the northern pottery towns. He also liked the main line, which went through Harecastle Tunnel and it seemed to take a good while to get to the other end of it. At that time, there were two stations in Kidsgrove and, when we got to the Central station, we'd walk over to the Liverpool Road one and catch a Loop Line train back. By then, Jeff could understand the railway maps and timetables and was very interested in them.

In September and October, there was an epidemic of Asian flu and the *Sentinel* reported that people were going down like flies. A quarter of all the postmen in Stoke-on-Trent were absent by 27 September and there was concern about the mail getting through. The paper said that the staff left were working all hours to keep it flowing. I thought that was strange because I was only working normal hours! I mentioned the situation to Arthur Williams, a postman, who lived at 281 Leek Road, and he asked: 'Why? Do you want some overtime?' I said I did, so he went to an inspector, who fixed me up with some extra work. It seemed that I'd been overlooked, perhaps because I was inexperienced.

On 30 October, my temporary period with the Post Office ended and I was appointed as a permanent postman, on probation till 21 September the following year. My starting pay was £9 18s. and I was informed that confirmation of my appointment would depend on satisfactory reports regarding my health, conduct, ability and efficiency.

I received my uniform from the Post Office stores around that time. Before then, I'd worn my ordinary clothes to work, but with a red and blue armband to indicate that I was from the GPO. My uniform was navy blue, with red edges to the jacket and a red stripe down the outside of the trousers. I was also supplied with a khaki lightweight summer jacket, an overcoat, a long raincoat and leggings. In addition, I was given a navy blue cap, with a red stripe round it, and that had to be worn at all times outside the office, even on sweltering summer days. I was rather pleased with the uniform and, when I took it home, Jeff thought it was wonderful and insisted on trying it on. It was huge on him, so he looked ridiculous and I often wished I'd had some film in my camera then!

Later, I was supplied with two pairs of navy blue denim overall jackets and trousers, for use in the parcel office. I was also given an electric lamp, run by battery, for use in delivering on dark mornings. It had a hook at the back, with which to fix it onto my uniform when I used it. I was issued with a cap badge by Arthur Cubley, an assistant inspector, who lived at 25 Warrington Road and whose style of bossing involved standing around, with his hands in his pockets, watching us work! My badge was an old one, with the number 262, and unfortunately was tatty. The last number wasn't the original and the badge didn't even have a fastening to fix it to my hat, so I had to tie it on with a piece of string! I protested about it, but I never did get a fastening for the badge.

At one time, the Post Office had been run like a military establishment. The postmen were lined up and inspected before each daily shift and it was woe betide the fellow who hadn't polished his boots or brushed his uniform! Even when I started, we were expected to wear black boots and a black tie. If a postman was too poor to buy them, a loan would be arranged.

I was told that government offices didn't have to pay surcharges on mail. They had their own paid envelopes, with 'OHMS' stamped on, and, even if there was no stamp on them, the delivery was free. One day, when I was delivering on the Tontine Street walk, I went to the locker to get my registered and surcharged items. There, a young, cocky P.H.G. (postman higher grade) handed me a letter for the local office of the Ministry of Pensions and National Insurance, at 18 Upper Market Square (where Halifax now is), surcharged at the usual double rate. I told the P.H.G. that they didn't pay surcharges, but he said that the letter contained a birthday card to one of the staff and so it didn't qualify for free postage. I handed over the 5d. to cover it, but, when I got to the MPNI office, a clerk told me they didn't pay money for mail. I then wrote on the letter, 'Refused,' initialled it, returned it to the P.H.G. and got my 5d. back.

A few days later, I received a letter from one of the inspectors, asking me to explain what had happened. This letter of complaint was known as a "skin". I put my reply in writing and handed it to Jim Gardner, an assistant inspector I was friendly with, who lived at 142 Cauldon Road. He looked at it and said, 'Leave it to me!' I'd only done as instructed and I believe he gave the P.H.G. a rocket for surcharging the letter.

From how he described it, Jim had been in Libya in the war. He told me he'd been ordered to take a quantity of furniture to a distant unit, which he did after a long and gruelling journey in the heat and dust in a truck. On arrival, he reported to the office and was told to dump his load. When he did, somebody put a match to it and it all went up in a blaze because they didn't want it!

Skins were recorded against guilty postmen and I suppose, if there were too many of them, it would result in the sack, although I never knew anybody that it happened to. I only got about three skins during the whole time I was in the service, even though I made a few misdeliveries, which weren't complained about.

Helen brought Jeff along a few times to watch me working when I was loading mail onto trains at Stoke Station, which I did as part of my duties. The bags were stacked on open, flat trucks. I usually caught hold of the bags by the neck and slung them into the railway carriages, but heavy ones had to be lifted on. It could be hard work, but it only lasted a short while because the trains would soon go out. Helen asked the ticket collectors if she and Jeff could go on the platform for free to watch me, so she didn't pay for platform tickets!

As it got near to Christmas, the mail became heavier and full of cards, as the public responded to the Post Office's appeal to 'Post early for Christmas'. But the bosses told us that the mail was normal and no overtime could be booked. Then "Christmas pressure", the ten-day period immediately before Christmas Day, was upon us and I was put on nights. Helen didn't like that and barricaded the doors with furniture after I'd gone out! I was on a twelve-hour shift, sorting and getting my walk ready, and at last that included overtime. The regular postmen didn't do any delivering at that time because our experience was needed in the sorting. All the delivering was done by temporaries. I was put on sorting a Sneyd Green walk, which I didn't know, but I muddled through.

I did my shifts at the Victoria Hall, in Hanley, which was hired by the Post Office to help sort out the huge amount of mail that came in. Hundreds of temporary people were employed throughout the Stoke-on-Trent delivery area, including students, the unemployed and housewives. Most of them soon got into the swing of things, but some of them were a waste of time and I think the Post Office employed anyone, regardless of whether they could walk or work! Each postman was given two or three temporary people and the walk was divided between them.

There was Edith Baddeley, a short, fat woman, from 255 Lichfield Street, who did part of that walk. She was given a big bag, full of mail, which needed two postmen to lift onto her shoulder! She got around, even though it was very slowly.

Some of the temporary staff were put on sorting, which led to a lot of mis-sorts, as a result of which letters made unnecessary journeys round the district and indeed around the country. By Christmas Day, however, most of the mail had found the correct letter box. Toward the end of the pressure period, the head postmaster brought the city dignitaries in to have a look at the workers and to have photographs taken by the *Sentinel*.

Some people thought we got a lot of tips at Christmas, but I know I didn't. Even though I delivered in the centre of Hanley, the only tip I got was 2s. 6d. from A. Lindner, the little jeweller's at 6 Tontine Square. I did hear some postmen boasting how much in tips they'd received in that same area. They were drivers, who delivered parcels and actually went into the shops because the parcels were too big for their letter boxes.

We worked Christmas Eve and through the night to Christmas morning. There was only one delivery on Christmas Day, which I got bagged off, and I waited for my lads to come in. Of course, most of the temporary people would have been out celebrating Christmas Eve and some were in no state to turn out. I realized that, if one of my temporaries didn't turn up, I'd have to take the part-walk out myself, further to spoil my Christmas Day. One of my lads came in on time, so I fixed him up and got him off. It was agony waiting for the other, but eventually he came in and I was so pleased, I could almost have kissed him! I quickly got him moving and went to the inspector in charge, to get him to initial my overtime docket. Then I was on my way, but, when I got home, I was too late to see Jeff opening his Christmas presents!

One of the gifts that Helen and I had bought him was a magnetic football game, which was popular then. It had a plastic green-coloured pitch on legs and two teams of three small plastic men, each with a magnet underneath him. One of the teams was in red and the other was in blue. Each player held a plastic rod, with a magnet at the end, under the pitch and used it to move his men and knock the ball around. There was a small white goal at each end and the edges of the pitch were raised so that the ball didn't easily roll off. The rules were more or less the same as in football. Jeff played the game quite a bit for a few years with his friends and me, but, unlike them, I let him win most of the time.

I was very tired after working at least twelve hours every night and fed up having had my Christmas Day ruined, but I made the best of it. We then had Boxing Day off – a big deal! The Post Office top brass reckoned that the public wouldn't stand for the lack of letters for more than one day!

When we started back, the mail was pretty light and we spent most of our time clearing up the Christmas remnants. There were quite a number of cards with insufficient addresses, especially where the senders hadn't been able to remember them properly, but had put something down in the hope that the Post Office would sort it out! Of course, we tried our best, but there were limits to what we could achieve. Most items couldn't be returned because very few of the senders had put their own addresses on the envelopes. So we were busy killing them off and there was one postman, Don "Kill 'Em Off" Rogers, who seemed to delight in doing that!

On New Year's Eve, we had a mini-rush of cards, which we dealt with and took out on New Year's Day, 1958, when it was work as usual. So we had to be careful with our celebrations. I was paid on the 3rd and picked up £22 9s. 4d. (almost twice as much as the previous week), less £2 8s. tax, so the Christmas overtime had come in handy.

One day in January, when I was at work, a motorcycle and sidecar crashed into our front wooden fence and knocked some of it down. Helen must have heard the noise and went down to see what had happened. In the sidecar was a woman passenger, who was shaken. Helen asked if she was alright and made her and the rider a cup of tea before getting their address off them, which was in Tavistock Place, in Basford. The rider said he'd see to things and get the fence repaired. We hadn't experienced anything like it before and didn't really know how to proceed. After a while, I went to see them to find out what was being done. I was told that things were in hand and that their insurance company had been informed. Eventually, W. H. Wain, a builder from 201 Cauldon Road, came and did the repair and I got the impression that he was expecting a good reward from the insurance for doing the job.

In February, there was heavy snow, which was blown into drifts by the wind, and Jeff made good use of it, building a snowman in Hanley Park with Glenys Chell, of 32 Cotesheath Street, Joiner's Square, one of his friends from school. We went to the frozen park lake as well and I photographed him throwing snowballs with two of his friends. We also went out in the back garden to play in the snow. Fred Cadman joined in and threw snowballs at Jeff for a bit of fun. The *Sentinel* reported that it was the worst snow since 1947 and villages in the Staffordshire Moorlands were cut off by drifts up to twelve feet deep!

A few months after I'd joined the Post Office, one of the postmen, Clive Dunn, mentioned to me that he'd got some Penny Black stamps. That attracted my interest because the Penny Black was the first adhesive postage stamp issued in Britain, in 1840, and was known worldwide. People think it's the rarest stamp in the world, but it isn't because millions of them were made and many have survived because they were fixed to letters, not envelopes. Clive was a dealer in second-hand stamps from all over the world and was pretty well up on them. He also had a beard, which was unusual for a postman.

He brought some Penny Blacks for me to look at and they were marvellous. I thought it would be nice to have one, so I picked the one in the best condition, which only cost me about a pound. Clive sold stamps to other postmen as well and he kept coming to us when he had interesting ones. He knew the history behind them and I started buying ones I fancied and those he told me were rare. At first, I put the stamps in a box because I didn't have many, but I carried on buying them from him from time to time, so it became a hobby.

Very few postmen owned cars at that time and the chief inspector at the Station Road sorting office always came to work on his bicycle because he didn't own a car. The only car that was parked in front of the Regent Road office belonged to Clarence Rowe, an inspector. A bit later, a postman, Ernie Minshull, who did a lot of overtime, bought himself a car. That led to him doing even more overtime because, when he got a message at home to come out, he could be at the office in a short time! He was the first ordinary postman in Stoke-on-Trent to make the £1,000 a year bracket and that was a big sum in those days.

I received a telegram one day and Helen and I wondered what had happened. People only seemed to get one of those when something awful had occurred, such as a death. But all it was this time was a request to turn out for overtime. It was almost like an order, so off I went and the extra money helped us. During the early part of my service, I received a number of similar telegrams, but later on, as postmen acquired telephones, it was easier to give them a ring to do the extra work.

Every so often, when we were working at Station Road, we'd be called to form an audience to listen to the head postmaster giving a farewell speech to one of the staff who was retiring. A *Sentinel* photographer was sometimes there and I was once at the back of a group photo which they published. It was of the retirement of Harry Webber, a P.H.G., who had a waxed moustache. He later shot himself dead with a revolver.

Being one of the junior postmen, I had to choose my annual holidays from what was left after the senior men had picked theirs. Most of them chose the Wakes holiday as a lot of the wives were potters. My two weeks that year were at the end of April and the beginning of May. The second week, we went to Prestatyn and Jeff had to miss out on his schooling. We stayed at a boarding house, as usual, which was okay. The weather was cold, so we wore our overcoats and Jeff had a Balaclava on one day, but we made the best of it.

The same month, we had a trip to Mow Cop, travelling on the train from Stoke to Mow Cop & Scholar Green Station. We then walked all the way up the steep road to the village at the top and had a look at the "castle", which had been built as a ruin in 1754. There was a fine view from there right across Cheshire, which we admired.

About that time, Helen and I bought Jeff a tortoise, which he named Terry after the pop singer, Terry Dene. We let the tortoise roam free on the lawn and he was interesting to watch. He was pretty active during the summer and sometimes wandered into our neighbours' gardens, but we kept an eye on him most of the time and he didn't go far away.

In June, Helen and I had our bunker made into a coal house to store more coal. It was cheaper to buy in the summer, so we could make a good saving by getting it then in bulk. Big Harry built the brickwork up, put a plastic roof on and fitted a wooden door. I did the labouring for him and, of course, we paid him for his work. We then stacked our coal up in there higher than my head!

Jeff was interested in football and we used to go into Hanley Park to play together. We'd go in the bottom goalmouth of the pitch nearest the electricity works and kick a ball about, but we also played in the "Dingle" and "Horse Ring" on the other side of the canal. Jeff liked to be the scorer, so I'd often be in goal!

In August, we had a decorator, W. J. Fox, of 144 Ashford Street, Shelton, in to do our stairs, landing, bedrooms and bathroom, which cost £49 5s. My wages at that time were £10 13s. a week. Mr Fox was assisted by our neighbour, Derek

Bentley, and we let them eat their meals at our table. While they did so, they read their newspapers. Jeff was mesmerized by that and, at his next meal, he wanted to read his comics. We had a job convincing him that that was wrong and never really succeeded!

I painted our hut and was watched by Jeff, who was fascinated. He was longing to have a go himself, but Helen and I tried to put him off because we thought he'd get paint all over himself and his clothes. Then Helen hit on the idea of giving him a brush and an old paint tin, with water in it, and let him "paint" the hut. That worked because he seemed to be more or less satisfied as the wet surface looked like gloss paint!

In September, Jeff moved from the infants' school into the junior school, which was next door to it. Helen and I called it the "Big School" and I accepted the move for what it was, Jeff growing up a bit and progressing with having a good education.

On 26 September, I was informed that I'd successfully completed my probationary period on the Post Office. As a result, my appointment as a permanent postman was confirmed.

While I was playing with Jeff, an idea came into my head that I'd catch a bird for him. I propped a clothes basket up with a stick, to which I tied a long piece of string, and I placed some bread underneath the basket. When several birds went after the bread, I pulled the string and the basket fell over the poor things. I put my hand underneath and pulled out a sparrow, which I showed to Jeff. He was thrilled, but I felt rather guilty, so I let all the birds go.

In the autumn, Terry stopped eating and moving about, so I had to get him ready for hibernation. I'd read somewhere what to do, so I made a wooden box, lined it with straw, put him in and covered him with more straw. I put a lid on and covered the box with wire netting to stop rats from eating him while he was asleep. I then put the box in the hut for the winter. It was said that some people kept their tortoises awake all winter, but that would have meant letting him wander around a room for about six months, which seemed cruel.

About that time, I was made a leave reserve, which happened to more or less every postman once he'd got enough experience. It meant that I could be put on any job that was vacant owing to holidays and sickness. It also meant that I was thrown into the deep end every week because I didn't have set walks. Also, I could be sent to any office in the Stoke-on-Trent delivery area and maybe to any in the country in an emergency! That had happened to George Humphries, whom I got to know at the Station Road parcel office. He told me he'd once been sent to Coventry because there was a shortage of postmen there as many men worked in the motor industry, which was well paid. In a way, the appointment was a compliment to me because it meant the bosses thought I'd got the experience to do it, but it was for their convenience. New postmen were starting and so I moved up, but I had no more money.

As Christmas approached, we became busier with the mail and I was sent to St. Mary's Church Hall, in Werrington Road, Bucknall, which the Post Office had hired for the period. That became the office for deliveries in Milton, Abbey Hulton, Bucknall, Bentilee and Ubberley. Jim Gardner was in charge and working there was pretty comfortable because he was friendly to everybody and felt more like a mate than a boss. Also, it was away from the head office and the big guns weren't around.

Jeff was doing well at junior school and, at the end of his first term, brought home a report. He'd finished fourth out of forty pupils and the teacher, A. M. Birch, had written, 'Jeffrey is a good worker.' Helen and I were very pleased.

On Christmas morning, I got my temporaries away on their deliveries, had my overtime docket signed by Jim and then walked home. Jeff was busy playing with his new presents and I helped him out. We'd bought him one of the new Vale black and amber strips to play football in. He was very keen on Vale and, at the time, they were near the top of the Fourth Division, which had been set up that season. We'd also got him a metal globe of the world, which he found very interesting. It was his sort of thing because he'd become interested in geography and history. The day was pretty quiet. There were just the three of us.

Unfortunately, on part of Boxing Day, I was on security duty at the Station Road office. Jeff and Helen were disappointed, but nothing could be done about it because it was part of the job. The idea was to see that everything was in order and nothing was stolen. A P.H.G. was on with me and we spent most of the time talking and wandering around. There was nothing to do and it was boring.

I started taking Jeff to the pictures, but, the first time we went, he didn't realize that the seats were automatic tip-ups, so he sat on the upturned edge! That was okay because it enabled him to see over the heads of the people in front. If there was a good cowboy or action film on, we usually went to have a look at it. Sometimes, we went at tea time and took sandwiches to eat and crisps to crunch as quietly as possible. We went on these excursions for years and both found them very enjoyable.

The very first film we went to see was *Escort West*, which was on at the Gaumont (as The Regent had been renamed), in Hanley, from 5-10 January 1959. It starred Victor Mature and was a Western about a journey full of action through the lands of hostile Indians. I don't remember it, but Jeff was mesmerized by it and it stuck in his memory, probably because it was the first time he'd ever been to the pictures.

Some time later at work, I was sent to Longton for a week or two as part of my duties as a leave reserve. I was given a lift there by the van that took the Longton mail to the office. While I was delivering mail, people would ask for directions to certain streets and look in disbelief when I told them I was a stranger and didn't know! A walk I remember doing there was Longton Hall Road, down to the junction with Blurton Road. When I'd finished my day's deliveries, and those I did at other places I was later sent to as a leave reserve, I'd get a bus back.

At our Stoke office was Joe Pankhurst, an assistant inspector. He claimed he was the son of Emmeline Pankhurst, the famous suffragette, who'd campaigned in the early part of the century, but the records show that she never had a son named Joseph.

I was told a story about Arthur Cubley and George Preston, another assistant inspector. They were big Vale supporters and, apparently, when they were working on Saturday afternoons, they'd borrow a van and go to watch the match!

George's brother, Colin, who was a P.H.G., had played the piano regularly in a band at the Majestic Ballroom before the war. I remembered having seen him then and he must have been pretty good to have got the job in the band.

There was also Bill Pierpoint, who, I was told, had been a seaman on ships taking supplies to the USSR on the North Sea run during the war. His nerves were shattered because of the German bombers trying to get them and he was all on the go. He was a driver and didn't do much sorting, so, on the occasions he did, he'd push in next to me so he could ask me questions because I knew the walks better than he did.

It was around that time that Helen and I had our first washing machine. Until then, she'd washed our clothes in a galvanized tub before squeezing most of the water out of them with a hand mangle and finally putting them on the washing line in the back garden to dry. Our new machine was really a boiler, with a hand-operated agitator. This was inside the lid, which was fastened down, and was operated by turning a handle. It shook the clothes up and moved them about in the water, which was run into the machine from our hot water tap through a hose. Sometimes, Helen had to boil a kettle or two to help it along because our hot water tank wasn't all that efficient. Also, she still had to use the hand mangle for drying the clothes.

When the winter of 1959 seemed to have ended, I went to the hut to see if Terry was still alive, but alas he was quite dead. Perhaps he'd frozen to death or maybe woken up too early and died through lack of water or food. But there was nothing to do except bury him in the back garden.

Skiffle was popular at that time. It was quite primitive and members of groups strummed washboards, but I was open-minded about it and listened to what was being played before I decided whether I liked it or not. Lonnie Donegan had a popular Skiffle group and had a big hit in the spring with *Does Your Chewing Gum Lose its Flavour (on the Bedpost Overnight)*, but the words seemed common somehow. Then, in 1960, he got to number one with *My Old Man's a Dustman*, which was alright, but it wasn't a classic!

When the weather had warmed up in the spring, I went to a pet shop and got Jeff a new tortoise, which he called Marty after the pop singer, Marty Wilde, whom he liked. We gave the tortoise the run of the back garden, but, of course, he used to wander off. At first, he wasn't too difficult to find, but one day Marty caused a panic because he couldn't be found in our garden or those either side of us. It looked as if he'd gone forever, but then Helen started searching the field behind us, which was covered in thick grass. I thought that would be a waste of time and that we'd be better to buy another tortoise. Then a minor miracle happened because Helen came upon the absconder manfully trying to crawl up a steep slope in what must have appeared like a jungle to him. She quickly brought Marty back home and I constructed a wooden enclosure, two plank widths high, to put him in. But it didn't stop Marty getting away, although I couldn't understand how until I saw it happening. He wedged himself between two upright pieces of wood (which held the twin planks together), stood on his hind legs and forced himself up and over the top of the enclosure!

Vale were still doing very well in the Fourth Division. Young Harry was a regular in the team and had played most of the matches in the forward line. On 27 April, they were at home to Millwall in their last match of the season and needed to win to make sure they'd be the first ever champions. Harry was the centre-forward that night and scored one of the goals in a 5-2 win as they finished in style.

We again went to Prestatyn in May for a week for our summer holidays because we thought it was a nice place for Jeff to go. It had nice sands and was away from most amusements, so it stopped him from spending money and helped us along. Also, perhaps we became afraid of going anywhere else in case it was bad. We stayed bed and breakfast, as usual.

There was a big building operation going on in constructing a new sea wall and promenade from Prestatyn, through Ffrith, to link up with the Rhyl sea wall. There had only been sand dunes to walk along previously and that was still the case except for a small completed section of the promenade. It was 1962 before the whole thing was finished. There were also new buildings being put up and it looked as if Prestatyn was becoming commercialized, which we weren't very keen on.

One day, Jeff had a ride, with other children, on a mechanical elephant, probably at Ffrith. It was powered by a petrol engine and ran on wheels, but looked just like the real thing!

At work, I was sent to Stockton Brook to deliver mail and got a lift from the van that took it there. The postmen's nickname for the village was "Stocking Foot" and the office was on the main road, next to the station buildings. It was a small hut and, even though it was summer, it was so cold in there first thing in the morning that I shivered. When the van pulled up, I helped to unload the bags of mail and stack it on the fittings, ready to be sorted into the different walks. I couldn't help much in doing that because the area was strange to me.

I was told which walk to do, so I gathered my mail and took it to my walk fitting, but I hadn't got a clue where to start. A lot of the letters just had a name, or the name of a farm, and 'Stockton Brook' written on them. Fortunately, another postman came along and threw out the walk. He explained to me where to start, which was most important, where to go and what to look out for.

I began delivering outside the office on Leek Road and went along to the sign at the boundary with Endon before returning, on the other side of the road, to the crossroads by the office. By then, it was warming up. I turned right up Moss Hill and delivered to the area around there, but, by the time I'd finished my walk, I was sweating. These rural walks usually only had one delivery of letters a day, though I remember going around again with parcels. The experience was okay and the surroundings were pleasant, but I wouldn't have liked a walk which just did farms and out-of-the-way places because the postmen sometimes had to go across fields. I was told stories of them getting lost, especially in the dark and the fog, and getting into some difficult situations.

On 30 June, Helen and I had an immersion heater put in our hot water tank by the M.E.B. (Midlands Electricity Board). It was something of an innovation and was much better than stoking up the coal fire for most of the day to get the water warm enough for a bath. The job, including the plumbing, wiring and lagging, cost us £13.

On 24 July, Jeff brought home his school report. This time, he was seventh in the class. His teacher, J. C. W. Bailey, had written: 'In the main, excellent work. On occasions he tends to be a little careless. This is probably because the work is so well within his compass.' Helen and I were again very pleased.

I was watching Marty in our garden one day and he seemed to be digging in the soil. He dug out a hole and then laid some eggs in it. So he was a she! I covered the eggs up with soil because she hadn't made a proper job of it and I kept my eye on the spot for a few weeks, but no young emerged. I suppose the conditions were by no means ideal.

From time to time, I took Jeff to visit my cousin, Bernard, who was still living at 256 Etruria Vale Road, with Aunt Florrie. By then, Bernard and Dorothy had two children, Pam and Paul, and a rather nasty mongrel dog, named Rex. I was always edgy when I was near it in case it bit me. Sometimes, they shut it in the next room while we were there, but then someone would open the door and it would come in. On one occasion around this time, as we sat there talking, Jeff suddenly became upset. He wasn't crying, but there was a tear in his eye and I saw blood coming from his fingers. The dog had bitten him! Bernard dressed the wound and said I ought to take Jeff to hospital to have an injection. I decided against it because Jeff would have dreaded the idea and Helen would have been wondering where we were if we weren't back home at a certain time.

The steps at the front of our house were made of concrete and were by then tilting to one side. One or two neighbours said it was due to mining subsidence and that was worrying if it was true because it meant the house could be subsiding. We went to the National Coal Board Area Office, at 72 Leek Road, to see what they thought about it. They sent an official to have a look, which he did, and then he went into the field behind us to see if there were any telltale signs. He came back and said there was no mining subsidence because there was no tunnelling underneath our property. We were rather suspicious about that because Berry Hill Collieries were still working nearby, on the far side of Victoria Road.

There was nothing much we could do except to have the steps dug up and new ones (made of red bricks) put in their place. Joe Davies, a builder from 384 Leek Road, did the job in October, but the height of the new steps was different from that of the old ones, so he had to replace the path at the front of the house as well. He removed it and then redistributed the earth beneath so that concrete flags could be laid on a slight slope to fit against the top of the steps.

We also asked Joe to construct a wall and a gate at the side of our house to replace the old wooden partition, which was rotting. That meant sawing the partition in two and leaving next door's section up, but Joe warned us that this might collapse.

Mr Hammond had constructed a lean-to on the side of his house, made from odd bits of wood and flattened tin cans, and had attached it to the partition! Helen and I decided to take a chance, so we gave the go-ahead to the builder, but held our breath when he sawed through the partition. Our luck was in because Hammond's half held. The total cost of Joe's work was £35.

When the cold weather came, Marty became drowsy and had to be put away for hibernation. I packed her up in the wooden box, which I made nice and snug, and put it in the hut for the winter. I hoped for better luck this time.

Young Harry became famous for his swerving free kicks. He'd watched the Brazilians doing them and then he had a go at goal with one in a league match at Queen's Park Rangers on 28 November. The ball went in the net and the *Sentinel* said the goal was 'fantastic'. Harry later told Jeff that the QPR goalkeeper, Mike Pinner, had thought the ball had gone out for a goal kick and went to get it before he realized what had happened. Harry scored a few more goals from swerving free kicks and, on 26 August 1961, the *Sentinel* discussed them and asked, 'How does he do it?'

My Christmas duty for the Post Office that year was at Booth Street Drill Hall, in Stoke, which had been hired, but this time I was working on parcels during the day time. We had quite a lot of temporaries with us and the few postmen who were there were, in effect, little bosses. The students soon picked up the sorting idea, but some temporaries were a waste of time. The Post Office still seemed to hire anyone who cared to apply for a job or be sent by the Employment Exchange. There was a big, fat fellow, who did very little and mostly leaned on the skips holding the parcels. He was busy talking to me while I was trying to get around him to pick up parcels to sort. It was frustrating, but I felt sorry for him because he couldn't get his breath and I think he was ill. That would have been the only bit of work he could get.

There was another fellow, who could only manage an odd day or two before he was off sick. He'd turn up on paydays, with his Indian wife and a couple of kids, to claim his bit of money. He looked like a regular soldier and I think he must have been in the army in India in peace time. In those days, there was no going home on leave from such places. You could be stuck there for years till your regiment was ordered back to Blighty. I suppose the soldiers got frustrated with no or very few white girls about and so some got married to coloured ones. I felt very sorry for this fellow and his very patient wife, who was perhaps used to hard times.

I was put on security duty over the Christmas period again and it seemed very unfair to have been given it for the second year running. I should have complained, but I asked one of the postmen if he wanted the duty. To my amazement, he accepted it, saying that his Christmas was already spoiled because he'd got to work on Christmas morning and that he might as well be at the office. I couldn't believe my luck, but I went to the duty officer right away and had the other fellow's name put down instead of mine. The Post Office didn't mind that kind of thing, as long as the duty was covered.

I think it was that Christmas that Bernard asked me if I'd like to bring Helen and Jeff to tea on Christmas Day. I accepted and we walked all the way to his house in Etruria. Pretty soon, he was showing us his wine cellar, which was a converted pantry. He'd installed some wine racks and filled them with bottles of all kinds of different wines. He knew all the names and backgrounds of them. I thought we were going to have a good time, but Bernard kept talking and elaborating on wine and other things he was interested in. We had something to eat at tea time and a cup of tea. There was more talking and eventually a drink of wine was produced. I thought to myself, 'This is the first of many,' but it proved to be the last! Later, we were offered another cup of tea! I wondered why he'd accumulated all that wine because Christmas seemed the perfect time to drink it. On the way back, the rain was pouring down and we got soaked. I thought how we could have stopped in our own home in the dry and had a really good time instead of having a lecture on the merits of different wines!

I'd been doing overtime as usual on the Christmas mail and, on 1 January 1960, I was paid £23 19s. 10d., of which £2 7s. was deducted in tax. Although we still worked normally on New Year's Day, the amount of mail obviously dropped off, as did the overtime, and, on 8 January, I was only paid £12 2s. 7d., which was a more normal amount.

Vale had been having a good run in the F.A. Cup, with Young Harry playing at centre-forward. On 20 February, they met Aston Villa, the Second Division leaders, at home in the fifth round and Harry travelled to the game on a bus, with the supporters, as he did regularly in those days. There was so much interest that 49,768 spectators turned up, which broke the ground attendance record, but most of them were disappointed because Vale lost 2-1 after taking the lead from a penalty awarded when Harry had been fouled in the area.

George Humphries told me that one day a car had been parked in the driveway of a house he was delivering to and he'd had difficulty getting past it. He was so vexed that, on his return to the road, he deliberately dug his pouch buckle into the side of the car and pulled it along, causing a deep scratch. He was a fool because, if someone had seen him and reported him, he'd have had the sack.

There was mild weather in March, so I decided to have a look at Marty and took Jeff up to the hut with me. As I unwound the wire netting, I felt excited, wondering what I'd find. When the box was opened, I detected a movement, which meant that Marty had made it through the winter. Jeff was excited too and we brought Marty into the house, where it was warmer. She slowly came to life and, eventually, when the weather improved, we put her outside.

One day, an assistant inspector at the Regent Road office told us that he'd had an order from the head office that caps need no longer be worn. That concession proved to be very popular because sweat would be rolling down our faces on a hot day. Previously, not wearing a cap could have resulted in a fine, although I can't remember ever seeing anybody without one. Standards began to slide and some of the fellows eventually turned up looking really scruffy.

Jack Green had packed in his job in the pottery industry and gone to live in Blackpool with his family. I don't think he had a job to go to, but he loved the town. He'd been renting his house in Douglas Street, but he got a mortgage on a property in Blackpool – 7 Elizabeth Street, near to North Station. He got a job as a bus conductor, but it didn't last very long and he then went to work at Windscale nuclear power station, in Cumberland.

We went to visit him and his family for a day at Easter. It was good to see him again and we all went down to the beach, where we sat on deck chairs, even though it wasn't particularly warm.

Helen, Jeff and I went to Prestatyn again for our holidays in May because I was still a junior postman with little choice of dates. When we arrived there, we looked around for accommodation. Helen went to one house to enquire and was shown round. She was well satisfied and was about to accept when the landlady mentioned that her young son had polio! That scared Helen, who thought Jeff might catch it and so she quickly made an excuse and came away. We soon found somewhere else.

It must have been fairly warm on the holiday because none of our photos show us wearing coats and Jeff and I put on our swimming trunks and went in the sea. He had a life buoy around him, but he didn't go too far in the water, just up to his knees. He hadn't learned to swim and I suppose he was afraid of the depth of the water. He loved playing in the sand, so that meant Helen and I could sit around and take it easy.

One day, we all had a game of putting and we also tried our hand at bowls.

We went on the bowling green off Highbury Avenue and I showed Jeff how the game was played. He soon got the idea of it and in no time at all had the right style of bowling down to a T.

We had one or two walks in the countryside outside Prestatyn. On one of them, we came across a white horse in a field. I showed Jeff how to feed it, with my hand held open and flat.

On another walk, we came to a restaurant and Helen fancied some chicken sandwiches. I went and got some, at rather a stiff cost, and came out with them on a silver tray. Helen was startled and asked how much I'd paid. When I told her, she asked if the silver tray was included in the price!

Also, we had a trip to Rhuddlan Castle, which was by the River Clwyd and inland from Rhyl. It was made of stone and was quite impressive, with crumbling curved towers, but we had to pay to go in, even though it was a ruin.

On 25 May, I paid the M.E.B.'s bill of £3 7s. 7d. for what they called their second supply period of the year. The charge consisted of the tariff for 443 units of electricity used and 5s. for the cooker which we hired from them. I've still got the bill and it shows that their headquarters was at 234 Victoria Road and their service centre in Albion Square. They had three district offices in Stoke-on-Trent and a branch in all of the six towns except Fenton. The nearest office to us was in The Parkway, at the top end of Hanley Park.

At work, I got the Leek Road, Shelton, walk that included my home, but I couldn't call in for very long. It was just a quick hello and I was off on my travels again. I was wary and Helen didn't want me to stay in case someone reported me to the bosses. The very first day, our neighbour, Reg Parrish, of number 331, asked me for his football coupon. I told him I hadn't got it and he became a bit shirty, saying that he always had it delivered on a Monday. I said that I was allowed three days to deliver my coupons and, though that didn't satisfy him, he didn't get it till the Wednesday.

Jeff was following football keenly and he thought Burnley were the best team. They'd just won the First Division championship, so Helen and I decided to get him a Burnley football strip (consisting of a claret and blue shirt and socks and white shorts) for his birthday. We couldn't get one locally, so we decided to write to the town itself to see if we could get one from there. I put a letter together, asking if one was available, and addressed the envelope to 'the nearest Sport Shop in Burnley'! We soon had a reply, with a strip and a badge, which had been sent without us having paid any money, and it was very nice of the shop to have taken a risk and trusted us to pay. As luck would have it, the strip fitted Jeff and I sent the payment immediately. He was thrilled to have a strip similar to that which the top team played in. Burnley were a good side then and they had plenty of talented youngsters coming up.

Unfortunately, Vin Jeffries had died on 2 March. Afterwards, Eva had driving lessons and passed her test, although I gathered, from how she described it, that it was a miracle. She then took us all to Southport for a day trip, but expected me to help her find our way there. I hadn't known about that till we were on the way and we didn't have a map, though she had some kind of a route written down. Somehow or other, we muddled through and managed to get to our destination and back and we had a nice day.

About that time, Mr and Mrs Hammond moved and I was particularly glad to see the back of him. In their place came a young couple, Brian and Joan Cotton. Brian was very friendly and Joan was pleasant, but seemed to be bossy with him. Brian's parents lived at 277 Leek Road, in a house named Royce. His father, Ralph, was the chauffeur for the Lord Mayor of Stoke-on-Trent, whom he drove round in a Rolls-Royce.

Brian had Mr Hammond's ramshackle lean-to taken down and replaced it with a brick structure. While it was being built, Helen noticed that the workmen were adding guttering to it, overhanging our side. When I pointed it out to them, they said I'd be able to use it when I had a lean-to built! I told them I didn't know what I was going to do with my space and so I didn't want the guttering hanging in it. They then took it down and arranged it on top of the brickwork.

Jeff had been bought a football rattle for his birthday by Young Harry, so that he could make a noise when he went to watch Vale and Stoke. It was made of wood and had a handle, with cogs, which, when rotated, struck thin blades and made quite a loud clacking noise. The idea was to create noise and atmosphere and spur the team on. Rattles were all the rage at that time and Jeff took his to the matches regularly. He was always itching to let go on it. One Saturday, we were near to the wall at the front of the Stoke End, watching Stoke play, and he spun his rattle round. Unfortunately, he was so excited that he didn't watch what he was doing and hit a lad on top of the head with it! The lad wasn't hurt and I don't think there was any fuss, but I had to say to Jeff, 'Stop that now!'

I was sent to the Newcastle office in Ironmarket for a week or two to deliver mail and was given a lift there by one of their inspectors, Ken Shemilt, who lived at 144 Cauldon Road and was rather superior. One of my walks was in the Chesterton area, adjoining Dragon Square, and it included part of Crackley Bank. It was like Bentilee, only worse! It was a rough place. One or two of the road signs had been taken away, probably by vandals, so I didn't know where I was!

On my first day there, it was raining and near to freezing point. It was cold enough for me to have worn an overcoat, but that would have been no use in the rain, so I wore my macintosh and leggings. I didn't wear gloves because they'd have soon been soaked and I had to keep my hands free to hold and deliver my letters. After a few minutes, my hands were stiff with cold and I couldn't hold or bend my fingers, so I had to stop, put the bundle of letters in the pouch and rub my fingers vigorously to get some life into them. Also, it was dark and I was having to use my lamp for illumination. Then I came to a street with no name on it. I asked a passer-by what it was called, but he didn't know. So I took a chance and delivered my next letters there and found out later that I'd done the correct thing. I was very relieved when I finished the walk and went back to the office!

One day, on one of my Newcastle walks, I was in the middle of a housing estate and wanted to use a toilet. I didn't know what to do. I knocked on a door and a woman answered. I asked if I could use her toilet, but she just said, 'No!' I didn't blame her for not letting a stranger into her house and I struggled on until I eventually found somewhere to relieve myself.

One of my duties at Newcastle was delivering parcels around the shopping centre. I took them in a wicker barrow, with two big wheels and two handles. It also had two legs to take the weight and stop it running away when it was put down. It looked heavy, but the weight wasn't too bad at all. I felt embarrassed pushing it around, but I suppose it was a good way to have got rid of the parcels.

I'd continued since my army days to have a regular check on my teeth and, when necessary, to have fillings put in them. Finally, my dentist, Mr E. B. Massey (who'd replaced Arnold Wain), told me I could no longer have that done because the teeth that I had left were by then comprised mainly of fillings, so I'd have to have them out. I went along with that and decided to have them done under cocaine because I didn't fancy gas. I was to have about four teeth pulled each visit and went for my first session after an early shift. The dentist injected my mouth with anaesthetic and it went numb. Then he pulled out my first four teeth, but I went to work the following morning feeling pretty decent.

My next visit was about a week later, but my mouth didn't stop bleeding afterwards. It was still doing so at 4.30 a.m., so I decided to phone the Newcastle office and let them know I wasn't turning in. I went to the public phone outside Hanley Park and opposite Boughey Road and told Walter Holmes, the assistant inspector in charge, to help him to get someone to do my duty. I went to the dentist later on and he gave me some medicine to staunch the blood. That proved to be effective and I went to work the following morning.

The rest of the extractions were okay and then I had to wait some months for my mouth to heal up before I could be fitted with false teeth. During that time, I could only eat soft stuff, like bread and soup. Getting used to my new teeth was an experience because they didn't seem to fit properly and I had to go back and have them adjusted. But I did get used to them.

After Jeff had finished school on 16 November, I took him to the pictures in Hanley. He wanted to see *Hannibal*, which was on at the Capitol, but, when we looked at the stills of the film on the board outside, I thought it would be too frightening for him. I suggested we should go to see something else, but he wasn't to be put off and so *Hannibal* it was. It told the story of the general from Carthage who marched his army, with elephants, over the Alps to attack the Romans in 218 B.C. and the lead actor again was Victor Mature, whom Jeff must have liked as a kind of rugged hero. The film had scenes of soldiers falling off the mountains and Hannibal having his eye put out with a red-hot poker, but Jeff must have liked it because he wrote in his school diary that it had been 'super'!

The same week, Helen and I bought him a Joe Davis billiards table, with two cues and a set of three balls. I gave it to him on 20 November and he was very pleased. The table didn't have legs, so it had to be rested on top of the dining table, which I had to carry into the lounge from the kitchen. I showed him how to play the game and he was pretty keen. We played each other a number of times, but there wasn't a lot of room in our lounge to use the cues properly and we kept knocking the furniture. When we weren't using the table, I propped it up against a wall, so it was in the way a bit.

There were points for potting and going in off the other balls and a player could also score by cannoning into them. Joe Davis was a famous player and long-standing world champion and he and the other top players could knock up loads of points by getting the balls all together and just keep touching them to get cannons. It must have been a real bore watching them do that!

At Christmas, Jeff had a set of snooker balls, so that he could play a different game on his billiards table. Of course, there were a lot more balls than in billiards and they were in eight different colours, so snooker was more interesting. I suppose that's why it became so popular when colour television arrived. Jeff didn't bother with billiards much any more, but, for a while, he had his friends round quite often to play snooker.

We postmen were issued with a nice, new Post Office badge, which this time was fixed on our lapels. It was golden and shaped like a barrel on its side. I think the reason for the new badge was that most of us now went out on delivery without our caps, which had our numbers on. It used to be common for members of the public to take a postman's number, if they thought we were doing anything wrong or looked scruffy, and report the offender to our bosses. I suppose there'd been a number of complaints that postmen couldn't be identified because they weren't wearing their caps. So I was given three numbered badges: for my jacket, raincoat and overcoat. When I retired, I had to hand them back, but I've still got my original badge.

From time to time, I'd hear some of the lads at work talking about the Post Office football team and saying how they'd done in their last match. My ears pricked up and I thought to myself, 'I'll go along and have a look at them some time,' so I did. I knew most of the players by sight and some of them to talk to. The team was called Postal Sports Club and played in the Half-Holiday League on Thursday afternoons against Fire Services, Clover Dairies, P.M.T., various police sides and other local works' teams. Thursday was the early day for shops closing in Stoke-on-Trent, which is why the league started up.

I think the first time I saw them play was at a pitch off Trentmill Road, Eastwood, and it was very interesting watching because the team were pretty good and the players were very enthusiastic.

Jeff started getting interested in the team as well, probably because they were my works' side, and he'd join me at the matches when he could after he'd finished school for the day. Eventually, he became keener than me and carried on supporting them for a few years.

I was sent to work in Cheadle for two or three weeks and went along with Harry Lewis. We reported to the Station Road office, in Stoke, about 4 to 4.30 a.m. and helped to load our van with mail for the town. The driver was Fred Thorpe, the brother of Eva, whom I'd known at the Co-op Club in the thirties, and I'd not been to Cheadle since cycling there then. On the way there, we dropped off the mail for Tean because it had its own sorting and delivery office then.

On arrival, we unloaded the van and stacked the mail in the office, which was on the main street and quite small. The mail had to be sorted into the different walks and I was allocated a town walk to deliver, which took me down High Street, from the office. I then went onto Queen Street and took in the streets on either side. It was pretty cushy because the properties were mainly terraced and right next to one another. Harry did a different walk and, after we'd finished, we got a bus to Longton, where we had to change to get back to Stoke. At the end of each week, of course, we claimed our expenses.

On Easter Monday 1961, Helen, Jeff and I went on a day trip to Prestatyn. While we were there, Prestatyn Town football team were playing a friendly match against Lindley Athletic, a side from London. Because Jeff was so interested in football, we ended up going to watch the game and he noted in his school diary a 4-3 win for the home team.

One day, on my walk at Cheadle, I came across a hedgehog lying on a garden path and I was in two minds whether to put it in my pouch and take it home for Jeff. Then I thought about the fleas they were supposed to be infested with and also I realized it might belong to someone, so Jeff didn't get a hedgehog.

On another occasion, an Alsatian grabbed hold of one of my forearms and I was frightened. The owner was standing nearby, so I complained to him, but all he said was: 'He won't hurt you. He's got no teeth!' The dog eventually let go and I carried on unhurt. I decided not to make a complaint about it because I wasn't going to be in Cheadle for long.

I took Jeff to see *The Magnificent Seven*, a new cowboy film, at the Gaumont, Hanley, on 22 April. It was pretty good, even though it was far-fetched because just seven gunmen rescued a Mexican village from a small army of bandits, so that the goodies beat the baddies as usual! It starred Yul Brynner and Steve McQueen and the music was quite rousing. Jeff was mesmerized by the action and wrote in his school diary that it was the best film he'd seen.

On 13 May, we went to Prestatyn for a week for our holidays again and enjoyed it. Jeff and I played football on Prestatyn Town's pitch, did some paddling in the sea and had a game of crazy golf. Jeff had a donkey ride on the beach and built a sandcastle, as usual, but, by then, it had become a more elaborate affair, with a moat and an outer wall. We also had day trips from Prestatyn to a number of places, which Jeff really enjoyed.

One of the visits was to Chester Zoo on the 15th. Jeff was fascinated by the animals there, especially the lions, tigers, rhino and pygmy hippopotamus. The day after, we went to Gwrych Castle, near to Abergele, which was actually a nineteenth century mansion built to look like a castle. The following day we were off again, to Llandudno, and, while we were there, we went on the Great Orme Railway, which ran to the top of the hill from the town.

I was continuing to collect stamps and started knocking on people's doors when I was delivering letters, asking them if I could have the stamps from the envelopes if I thought they were interesting or unusual. The customers would usually open their envelopes there and then and give me the stamps and I can't remember anybody ever refusing. I got a lot more stamps that way than buying them from Clive Dunn and they were free!

Eventually, I'd got so many stamps that I decided to put them in albums, which I made up myself with loose-leaf sheets in files. That arrangement meant that, when I got new stamps in, I could keep them in order fairly easily. To start with, I had one album for British stamps and another for overseas ones and I spent quite a lot of time stamp collecting.

Jeff was curious and always experimenting and finding out about things, which I suppose was good. After a while, I didn't take much notice of what he was doing unless it was something unusual because I thought he was okay. We used to have a lot of caterpillars in our garden and Jeff started collecting them. One day, he put them in a big tin and kept them. I don't know what he expected to do with them, but he put the lid on and so they couldn't get out. He punched holes in the lid for them to breathe and put in some vegetation for them to eat, but he hadn't got any knowledge of how to look after insects. So, although he was doing what he thought was right, it was an impossible task. A few days later, there was a stench from the tin in the garden, so I had a look inside and saw all this rotting flesh! Obviously, I put the whole lot in the bin.

On 21 July, Jeff came home with his school report. He'd finished second in his class (2A) out of 39 pupils and scored 627 marks out of 700 in his tests, which were in maths and English, so Helen and I were very pleased with him. His teacher, Harry Whalley, who lived at 54 Avenue Road and was very strict, had written that Jeff had made 'excellent progress'.

There was a special showing of a cowboy and Indian film, *The Charge At Feather River*, 'in life-like 3-dimension,' at the Essoldo cinema in Albion Square, opposite Hanley Town Hall, between 30 July and 5 August. Jeff and I went to see it and were given a pair of special spectacles to view it with. The spectacles made things appear in three dimensions. For instance, when the Indians fired their arrows, they seemed to come straight at us and we instinctively ducked!

In August, we made a trip to Blackpool to see Jack Green and his family and took in the sights while we were there. That may well have been the last time I saw him, but I've still got a photo I took of him and our families that day.

It was about that time that Helen and I first had a television and the pictures were, of course, in black and white. We were pretty late in getting one compared with most people, but we were resistant to new ideas and thought watching it would be a bad habit. Also, I thought it might distract Jeff from his homework, but he wanted one and had been going round regularly to Bradbury's, for a year or two, to watch theirs. I wasn't particularly bothered about having a TV, but Helen thought it would be good for Jeff and save the neighbours talking about us having to send him next door because we hadn't got one! Next door rented their set from Radio Rentals and we followed suit because they repaired it free if anything went wrong.

I started watching the TV myself and soon got to have some favourite programmes, like the cowboy shows and *Coronation Street*, which was first broadcast later in the year. I also watched *What's My Line?* regularly. That was a guessing game, with a panel of celebrities, who questioned the contestants to try to find out their occupations. Once, the job was a saggar maker's bottom knocker and I don't think the panel got that one right! The show was presented by Eamonn Andrews and I saw Gilbert Harding on it as a guest a number of times. He was a real character and came up with funny, sarcastic remarks.

Jeff's school had a football team. It was usually made up of lads from his new class (1A), which was for the children in the last year at the school. Of course, Helen and I wanted him to be in the team, which was organized by Mr Whalley. So she told Jeff to mention that Harry Poole was his cousin. Helen thought that by making it known that Jeff was related to such a famous player, Mr Whalley would be sure to pick Jeff for the team! So he did as Helen had told him, but Mr Whalley said, 'So what, Jeffrey?' Jeff did get in the team, but it was no thanks to Young Harry!

One day, I was delivering mail off Bucknall New Road and decided to knock at 87 Ludlow Street, the house of Stewart Flackett, my old colleague at Taylor Tunnicliff. It took him an age to answer the door and he had to stop halfway to get his breath. He said: 'I'm sorry to have been so long. It's my silicosis.' The state he was in made me realize that I might have got the same disease if the army and the Post Office hadn't saved me from the pottery dust. I had a chat with Stewart, but I then lost touch with him and he died the next year.

Stan Matthews returned to Stoke on 18 October. He was 46 and was signed for around £3,000 from Blackpool, who no longer wanted him. But he was world famous and I remember the excitement the news caused in the Potteries. Stoke weren't doing too well at the time in the Second Division and people were hoping Stan would turn them around, which he did. His signing was a masterstroke.

His first match was at home against Huddersfield Town on 28 October and I think Helen's Uncle Alf, who was originally from Stoke, came down from Mirfield to see it. I went to the game and I think Helen was with me. So probably was Jeff. The crowd was over 35,000 and Stoke hadn't had so many supporters in for quite a while. There was a buzz of excitement as the crowd waited for Stan to come out of the tunnel and then a roar went up when he appeared. I don't remember anything about the match itself, but Stoke won 3-0 and the next season got promoted to the First Division as champions.

On 18 November, Helen and I got a letter from Rose Green, saying that she and Jack were in a fix because they had no money to pay the mortgage for the next two months. She asked if we could lend them £20 and promised to pay us back. She said Jack was very worried, but that she hadn't told him about writing to us. Helen and I discussed the matter and decided to send the money right away. Jack wrote to us on the 21st and said he was shocked, but very grateful to have received it. They paid us back the following year.

Jack wasn't able to enjoy being in Blackpool for long because he died of cancer in 1963, but he'd had the foresight to take life assurance out so that the mortgage was paid off and Rose then owned their house. I thought he'd got the cancer from working at Windscale, but Rose said he'd had it before then. We lost touch with her after a while.

Jeff had been a pupil of the Railway Mission Sunday School for a number of years. He was still going most Sunday mornings and afternoons, as the gold stars in his attendance card for this year, 1961, show. I remember the assistant secretary, Jim Bentley, quite well and he was tall and a bit superior. His wife, Beryl, was also very involved with the mission and her mother, May Bromley, was the superintendant. They all lived at 42 Avenue Road. Helen did a bit of cleaning for the mission from time to time and I helped by swelling the audience on odd occasions if there was something special on.

There was also Joe Parton, who seemed to be the leader of the mission and later became the superintendant. He lived at 4 Keary Street, Stoke, with his wife, Gladys, and daughter, Jean. In August 1952, they'd all been on holiday to Lynmouth in Devon. While they were out on the 15th, there was a terrible rainstorm and Jean got cut off, but found her way to shelter in a partly-collapsed building. The rain continued to pour down and the rivers running into the town rose dramatically, carrying huge boulders along. The mass of water swept away buildings, cars and people. Jean watched the flood getting higher and higher, expecting her shelter to be swept away. Then the rain eased off and the level of the water started to go down. After a good many hours, she was able to get away and go in search of her parents, whom she found to be safe. That was their involvement in the famous Lynmouth Flood Disaster.

My wages hadn't gone up a lot and, on 15 December 1961, I was paid £16 0s. 3d. for the week, with £1 2s. deducted for tax. The week after, my pay went up to £25 5s. 6d. because of the Christmas mail overtime and it was £28 16s. 4d. on the 29th for the same reason. The only trouble was that the tax I had to pay increased as well and was £4 5s. on the 29th.

That year, for the first time on the Post Office, I didn't have to work on Christmas Day. The union had been pushing for an end to Christmas Day deliveries and the change was progress. At first, the holiday was on a trial basis, but it became permanent in 1965. It was very nice to have the whole day off and to be with Jeff while he opened his presents.

Ben-Hur was the latest blockbuster at the pictures. It started a six-week season at the Capitol on 14 January 1962 and I went with Jeff to see it. The story was set in the Roman Empire at the time of Jesus. It got a record eleven Oscars and the thing I remember about it was the chariot race. It was crazy, with crashes and riders getting killed as they raced round a spectacular arena in front of a big crowd. Charlton Heston was the leading actor, but he didn't stand out to me, though Jeff must have been excited by it all because he wanted the souvenir programme, which I bought him.

Vale were doing well in the F.A. Cup and had reached the fourth round, in which they played Second Division Sunderland on 27 January. Young Harry was at right-half and nearly 50,000 spectators turned up to see Vale stop the famous goalscorer, Brian Clough, from having a single shot and hold out for a goalless draw. Harry moved to inside-left for the replay four days later and scored Vale's second goal in a historic 3-1 win. In the next round, on 17 February, they lost 1-0 at First Division Fulham, but claimed that they'd been robbed through poor refereeing decisions.

In February, Helen and I received a leaflet from the corporation, giving us information about the eleven-plus exam that Jeff would soon be taking, to decide whether or not he could go to grammar school in the autumn. The leaflet also listed the various possible options on offer. We discussed them with Jeff and selected Hanley High School, which had a good reputation, as our first choice.

One morning, when Helen went into Jeff's room, she looked through the window and saw something white running about in the field behind us. She realized that it was a rabbit and told Jeff, who was still in bed. He soon jumped out to have a look and got his clothes on! Helen procured a cardboard box and she and Jeff dashed around to the field. They located the young animal and, after a bit of a chase, captured it. Jeff wanted to keep it, but Helen told him it must belong to someone near to. They made inquiries, but no-one claimed ownership, so Jeff acquired a new pet.

When I got home from work, Jeff excitedly informed me about what had happened. The box holding Bobby, as Jeff decided to call the animal, was only small and it was getting filled with excrement. It was surprising how often the rabbit needed to defecate! I had to build a hutch for our new pet, which I did with some pieces of wood and wire netting. It had two compartments. One was fronted with wire netting, through which we could see Bobby, and the other was enclosed, where our rabbit could get away from the public gaze. I placed the hutch in front of our garden hut, on bricks to keep it above the ground and dry. After a few days, I noticed a cat standing in front of the hutch looking at Bobby, who was terrified. I ran out of the house and shooed the cat away, but I realized the situation would occur again. So I fixed four wooden legs onto the hutch. Each was about two feet long and they did the trick.

We used straw for Bobby's bedding and got the first lot from a pet shop, but it was dear. So I thought about trying a packing department in a pot bank because straw was the traditional material used to protect pottery in transit. I walked to the factory of George Howson & Sons Ltd., a firm making sanitary ware, in Clifford Street, Hanley, and asked a worker there if they had any spare straw. He said they had, but asked whether I wanted the treated or untreated kind. Treated straw complied with international regulations about vermin by killing the bugs in it. I told him it was for my son's rabbit, so he recommended untreated straw and gave me a big bag full free. I continued to get it free from them for a long time!

We occasionally had the rabbit loose for some exercise. At first, I thought of letting it run about on the lawn, but the risk of it escaping through one of the hedges was too great. Instead, we blocked off the steps up to the back garden and let it exercise on the concrete yard.

Marty didn't come out of hibernation alive in the spring, after we'd brought her into the land of the living twice before. We buried her in the back garden and had a bit of a ceremony. I can't remember whether Jeff was upset about it, but he was bound to have been.

I was arranging the stamps in my collection in date order, but it became increasingly complicated to do so as I got more and more stamps in and the sequences got out of hand, which was frustrating. Despite that, collecting stamps continued to be one of my main interests for many years.

Helen had been working part time as a night supervisor at Swinnerton's Stafford Street café for quite some while and had also become a part-time supervisor at their Raymond Street factory. One day, Frank Swinnerton, the firm's managing director, knocked on our door and asked her if she'd work full time for them to manage their catering and production of Kia-Ora (a kind of orange squash drink) operations. Eva Jeffries had reached retirement age and the company was looking to replace her. Helen said she'd go full time if Jeff passed his eleven-plus, which he was about to take, and was out all day at grammar school. It was then left at that and depended on how Jeff got on.

About that time, we had a letter from the M.E.B., saying that they were discontinuing the hire of cookers and so the one we were using became our property. We'd had it a good many years and it had done us good service.

It was about then that I got a regular round at work. When somebody left or got promoted, it left a vacancy, which would be posted on the notice board and anyone who was interested could put his name down for it. The vacancy would be advertised as regular duties in a section, for example, four walks (consisting of a first and second delivery one week and different ones the next) and an afternoon or night shift (done in the third week), all of which would be done in rotation by three postmen. The vacancy would be left there for a while and then withdrawn. The most senior postman to put his name on the list usually got the job, but the actual decision was taken by Walter Holmes, who was known as "The Fixer", I suppose because he made the choice.

A vacancy came up for number seventeen walk (Bucknall New Road), number thirteen (Hope Street), number five (Lichfield Street), number ten (Tontine Street) and an afternoon shift in the parcel office. I put my name down on the notice board as being interested because they were the walks I'd done until I became a leave reserve, so I was quite familiar with them. Eventually, Walter decided I'd got the job and I was pretty pleased because it was a regular thing and meant I could settle down into a routine. Also, Helen would know in advance when I'd be doing what and so we could plan things more.

I stuck with those walks until I retired because I was happy with them. The only times there were any changes were odd occasions when I did a swap to help somebody out and when I was asked to leave my parcel office duties to do a walk because of postmen being off sick.

By then, I was at around the halfway stage of my life and I was pretty settled. Helen and I were coping. I had a steady job and was looking forward to Jeff doing well in his education because there was every prospect that he would. My family life was okay and we all got on alright.

I was more or less settled at the Post Office and I was happy enough being a postman, but there's nothing perfect and all jobs have their snags. My wages weren't very good and it wasn't very pleasant getting cold and soaking wet at times, but it was a steady job. I was more or less my own boss and it was pretty clean work. I liked being outside, so I preferred delivering to sorting. I'd never been very ambitious and how things were suited me fairly well. I wasn't bothered about promotion because that would have meant all indoor work.

I didn't think much about the future. As long as things carried on the way they were, it was alright. I was pretty happy as I was.